Enterprise Series:
Downsizing to NetWare

Michael Day

Contributing Authors:
Scott Ivey
Larry Morris
Scott Orr
Karanjit Siyan
Roger White

NEW RIDERS
PUBLISHING

New Riders Publishing, Carmel, Indiana

Enterprise Series: Downsizing to NetWare

By Michael Day

Published by:
New Riders Publishing
11711 N. College Ave., Suite 140
Carmel, IN 46032 USA

Printed in the United States of America 1 2 3 4 5 6 7 8 9 0

Library of Congress Cataloging information in Publication Data.

Enterprise Series: Downsizing to NetWare/Michael Day

    p.   cm.

   Includes index.

   ISBN 1-56205-071-0 : $39.95

   1. Operating Systems (Computer) 2. NetWare (Computer file)
I. Day, Michael, 1961-

   QA76.76.063E49   1992   92-35626

   005.7'1369—dc20

Publisher

David P. Ewing

Associate Publisher

Tim Huddleston

Acquisitions Editor

John Pont

Acquisitions Assistant

Geneil Breeze

Managing Editor

Cheri Robinson

Product Director

Drew Heywood

Developmental Editor

Nancy E. Sixsmith

Production Editor

Rob Lawson

Editors

Margaret Berson
Gail Burlakoff
Alice Martina Smith
Rob Tidrow
Becky Whitney

Technical Editors

Jim McCarter
Scott Orr
Drew Parker

Editorial Secretary

Karen Opal

Book Design and Production

William Hartman
Hartman Publishing

Proofreader

Nancy E. Sixsmith

Indexer

Sharon Hilgenberg

About the Authors

Michael Day is a documentation engineer for the NetWare 386 development program at Novell, Inc. At Novell, he contributes as a programmer and technical writer, specializing in network operating systems and network programming. Day has written books on NetWare workstation troubleshooting, LAN Manager troubleshooting, and has published more than 150 magazine articles on the subject of networking. He is the former chief technical editor for *LAN Times* magazine.

Scott Ivey is an advanced network administrator and Certified NetWare Engineer (CNE). He is co-author of *Troubleshooting NetWare for the 286*. In addition to writing and publishing, Ivey has served as Test Lab Manager for *LAN Times* and as an MIS professional for a number of years.

Larry Morris is a freelance writer based in Salt Lake City. Formerly Technology Editor with *LAN Times* magazine, he specializes in NetWare and Novell-compatible networking products. Morris has written for clients such as Novell, U.S. West, and Blue Lance Software. He has also published articles in several general-interest magazines as well as a novel. (Morris can be contacted, via MCI Mail, as LMORRIS.)

Karanjit Siyan is president of Siyan Consulting Services, Inc. He has authored two courses for Learning Group International on Novell networks and TCP/TP networks, and he teaches advanced technology courses in the U.S., Canada, and Europe. Siyan has published articles in *Dr. Dobbs' Journal, The C Users' Journal*, and *Databased Advisor*. He is a CNE and has been involved with installing, configuring, and designing Novell-based networks since 1985. Before becoming a consultant, Siyan was a senior member of the technical staff at ROLM Corporation.

Roger White has evolved from an MIT chemical engineering graduate into a computer industry commentator and businessperson, with an MBA from the University of Phoenix. In 1977, he opened the first Computerland retail store in Utah, and he joined Novell in 1981 when it launched the NetWare local area network system. White has developed a broad insight into the dynamics of the personal computer industry and follows companies that produce NetWare-compatible products. He has a particular interest in workstation-user interaction and in adapting personal-computer technologies to information-age challenges.

Acknowledgments

New Riders Publishing expresses sincere thanks to the following individuals for their contributions:

Drew Heywood, for developing and nurturing the project.

Rob Lawson, for managing the project through its beginning challenges, and Nancy Sixsmith, for steering it through production.

Margaret Berson, Gail Burlakoff, Alice Martina Smith, Rob Tidrow and Becky Whitney, for their cheerful demeanors and for their accurate and timely editing.

David Knispel, Jim McCarter, Scott Orr, and Drew Parker, for their thorough technical review of the manuscript.

Karen Opal and Geneil Breeze, for acquisitions and editorial help wherever needed.

Jerry Ellis, for cheerfully helping to avert crises.

Bill Hartman, as always, for his excellent layout and creating figures with his artistic skills.

Trademark Acknowledgments

New Riders Publishing has made every attempt to supply trademark information about company names, products, and services mentioned in this book. Trademarks indicated below were derived from various sources. New Riders Publishing cannot attest to the accuracy of this information.

Apple, Apple II, AppleTalk, and Macintosh are registered trademarks of Apple Computer, Inc.

ARCnet is a registered trademark of Datapoint Corporation.

AT&T is a registered trademark of AT&T.

Cray is a registered trademark of Cray Research, Inc.

dBASE is a registered trademark of Ashton-Tate Corporation.

DEC is a registered trademark of Digital Equipment Corporation.

HP, Hewlett-Packard, and OpenView are registered trademarks of Hewlett-Packard Co.

IBM, IBM AT, IBM PC, OS/2, PS/2, System Network Architecture (SNA), and Token Ring are registered trademarks; and NetBIOS, NetView, and Structured Query Language are trademarks of International Business Machines Corporation.

Informix is a registered trademark of Informix Software, Inc.

Intel is a registered trademark of Intel Corporation.

Lotus and 1-2-3 are registered trademarks of Lotus Development Corporation.

Microsoft, Excel, FoxPro, LAN Manager, MS-DOS, QuickBASIC, Windows, Word, X Windows, and XENIX are registered trademarks of Microsoft Corporation.

Motorola is a registered trademark of Motorola, Inc.

Novell, NetWare, and Native NetWare are registered trademarks of Novell, Inc.

Oracle is a registered trademark of Oracle Corporation.

Paradox and Turbo Assembler are registered trademarks of Borland/Ansa Software.

Sun and Sun Microsystems are registered trademarks of Sun Microsystems, Inc.

UNIX is a registered trademark of UNIX System Laboratories, Inc.

VINES is a registered trademark of Banyan Systems, Inc.

Xerox and Ethernet are registered trademarks of Xerox Corporation.

Trademarks of other products mentioned in this book are held by the companies producing them.

Warning and Disclaimer

This book is designed to provide information about the NetWare computer program. Every effort has been made to make this book as complete and as accurate as possible, but no warranty or fitness is implied.

The information is provided on an "as is" basis. The author and New Riders Publishing shall have neither liability nor responsibility to any person or entity with respect to any loss or damages arising from the information contained in this book or from the use of the disks or programs that may accompany it.

Contents at a Glance

Table of Contents

Part Two: NetWare 386 and Large-Scale Processing

Part Three: NetWare 386 and "Super-Server" Hardware

Part Four: Developing "Downsized" Software for NetWare 386

Part Five: Downsizing Tools

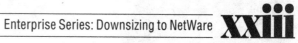

Introduction

Computer technology has changed the world, and it continues to do so. At the same time, computer technology itself is changing: computers are becoming at once smaller and more powerful. As computers change, new models for data processing systems have emerged. Perhaps the most significant change in the world of data processing is the emergence of the networked computer system, which consists of microcomputers connected over a local area network (LAN).

Downsizing is the process of moving data processing (DP) applications from a large host computer to a networked computer system. Networked computer systems offer massive reductions in the costs associated with data processing, relative to older, host-based computer systems. Organizations all over the world are downsizing their data-processing systems in order to realize lower costs. The trend toward downsizing appears to have reached a "critical mass," and the move toward network computer systems now has too much momentum to ignore.

NetWare is the premier downsizing platform on the market today. NetWare was designed with needs of "downsizers" in mind: it has both the horsepower and the integrity you require to process your organization's data. NetWare is a mature and stable platform, one which has been improved incrementally over the last 10 years.

NetWare's environment is much different from a traditional host environment, however. NetWare is a specialized operating system, designed to control computer networks. NetWare provides a platform that is more modern, more efficient, and more flexible than that of traditional host systems .

As you contemplate downsizing your data processing applications to NetWare v3.11, you probably have many questions. How effective is NetWare's security? What does NetWare do to ensure the integrity of my organization's data? How much data can I store on a NetWare system? How much horsepower does NetWare really have? How tolerant is NetWare of hardware faults? How can I ensure that my hardware is reliable? Can I port my data processing applications to NetWare?

Downsizing to NetWare v3.11 answers your questions about NetWare, and it also provides you with information you can use to get the most out of NetWare v3.11. It provides you with suggestions and tips to make your downsizing project run more smoothly. Using this book, you can not only downsize your data processing system, but you can improve it in the process.

Who Should Read this Book?

If you are planning to downsize your data processing system, or if you have already decided to do so, you need concise, thorough, technical information about networking, distributed processing, and NetWare that is written from your point of view.

Most books about networking, NetWare, and distributed processing assume you already know and are familiar with PCs and microcomputer technology; they assume that you already have lots of

PCs to connect to each other over a network. Most books also contain little or no information that is relevent to your situation, which is that of moving a working data processing environment from a large host-based computer system to a networked computer system.

Downsizing to NetWare v3.11 is written from your point of view. It assumes that you are downsizing, rather than "upsizing." It answers your specific downsizing questions and has information that is useful for executives, technicians, and programmers who are currently or who will be involved in downsizing efforts.

How this Book is Organized

Downsizing to NetWare v3.11 is divided into five parts. Part One provides theoretical information regarding the economic benefits of downsizing, client-server computing, and new directions in data processing software. Part Two addresses NetWare v3.11's qualifications as a downsizing platform. Part Three provides specific information about networking hardware, configuring computers for NetWare v3.11, and establishing security measures. Part Four provides information about the NetWare v3.11 software-development environment, porting applications to NetWare v3.11, and developing client-server software. The final section, Part Five, provides a survey of downsizing tools—products you can purchase to aid your downsizing effort.

Part One: The Challenge of Downsizing

Chapter 1, "The Economic Imperative of Downsizing," tracks the evolution of computer technology and explains why microcomputers and LAN technology offer sharply reduced computing costs.

Chapter 2, "The Breakthrough in Distributed Processing," explains why client-server computing is the software equivalent of the semiconductor. Client-server computing offers distinct advantages and disadvantages, which are discussed in detail.

Chapter 3, "Traditional Data Processing Applications," reviews the traditional data processing model and discusses issues raised by the application of client-server technology to traditional data processing applications.

Part Two: NetWare 386 and Large-Scale Processing

Chapter 4, "The Architecture of NetWare v3.11," discusses the design and mechanics of the NetWare operating system.

Chapter 5, "NetWare's v3.11's Suitability for Downsizing," reviews the features and characteristics of NetWare v3.11 that were designed specifically to perform large-scale data processing.

Part Three: NetWare 386 and "Super-Server" Hardware

Chapter 6, "Server Configuration," outlines the choices you must make when purchasing server hardware for NetWare. Although NetWare runs on a wide range of PC hardware, this chapter makes specific recommendations regarding server hardware for NetWare.

Chapter 7, "Network Input/Output (I/O)," reviews the options you have when choosing network media, adapters, and protocols.

Chapter 8, "Customizing the NetWare Installation for Large-Scale DP," provides the specialized information necessary to configure NetWare v3.11 when downsizing.

Chapter 9, "Customizing NetWare for Large-Scale Data Processing" outlines tuning procedures which can help you gain performance from your NetWare system.

Chapter 10, "NetWare Security," discusses making NetWare a very secure environment and provides the "inside story" of NetWare v3.11's security system.

Part Four: Developing "Downsized Software for NetWare 386

Chapter 11, "The NetWare Development Environment" provides an overview of NetWare software development, and discusses how to write, compile, link, and load server-based software for NetWare.

Chapter 12, "Thread Control," explains the importance of NetWare's multithreaded execution and demonstrates how to start, stop, and control execution threads in NetWare.

Chapter 13, "Interprocess Communication," provides advanced programming techniques for controlling multithreaded server-based applications.

Chapter 14, "Working with the NetWare File System," demonstrates the most powerful features of the NetWare v3.11 file system.

Chapter 15, "IPX Message-Passing Architecture," provides a full-fledged client-server record manager that uses IPX, NetWare's native communications protocol.

Chapter 16, "NLM Reliability," discusses specific techniques you can use to ensure that your server-based NetWare applications are reliable and robust.

Part Five: Downsizing Tools

Chapter 17, "NetWare-to-Host Communications," presents a survey of products that enable NetWare-to-host communications.

Chapter 18, "Btrieve," discusses Btrieve, which is NetWare v3.11's built-in database management system.

Chapter 19, "Choosing a Commercial DBMS for NetWare v3.11," presents an overview of commercial DBMS products for NetWare, and provides criteria for selecting such products.

Chapter 20, "Application Toolkits," discusses commercial code libraries that provide the foundation for industrial-strength data processing applications.

Chapter 21, "Nondistributed Record Managers," discusses DOS-based database products and how to get them to work well with NetWare.

New Riders' Enterprise Series

Downsizing to NetWare 3.11 is a volume in the Enterprise Series by New Riders Publishing. This series addresses the problems encountered by organizations attempting to integrate diverse computing platforms to achieve a cohesive data-processing strategy. (A companion in the Enterprise Series to this volume is *Downsizing to UNIX.*)

Also currently available is *LAN Connectivity*, which considers enterprise computing at the lowest level. First, it examines network cabling standards, protocols, and hardware devices that are most commonly found in enterprise networks. In addition, this volume explains how the three most popular network operating systems— Novell NetWare, Microsoft LAN Manager, and Banyan VINES—

solve various network-connectivity problems. Finally, a chapter on network management explains the technologies for making enterprise networks reliable and easy to manage.

LAN operating systems and LAN applications are among the topics that will be examined in future volumes.

Other Networking Titles From New Riders Publishing

New Riders Publishing offers an expanding line of books about Novell NetWare. These books are addressed at various levels of user requirements and experience. The following titles appear in the New Riders catalog:

Novell NetWare in the Fast Lane is both an introduction to NetWare and a task-oriented guide to managing a NetWare network. New administrators will find that this book enables them to set up a NetWare server properly, with a minimum of fuss. Experienced administrators will find that the task-oriented approach makes this an effective reference guide to NetWare management procedures.

Inside Novell NetWare, Special Edition is New Riders' general-purpose tutorial and reference for Novell NetWare. It is an excellent first book for new systems administrators, but it covers the subject in sufficient depth that it is sure to find a permanent place among your NetWare documents. The Special Edition has been updated to reflect new products. It also includes a bonus disk that is filled with useful network applications and utilities.

Maximizing Novell NetWare is a tutorial and reference for intermediate and advanced managers of NetWare LANs. This comprehensive volume introduces you to the inner workings of NetWare, including NetWare protocols, support for Macintosh and UNIX workstations, and local and wide area networking. *Maximizing Novell NetWare* describes advanced techniques for managing NetWare servers and LANs.

NetWare: The Professional Reference is a detailed reference for the most prominent LAN operating system. If your NetWare LAN has grown and your other NetWare books cannot keep up, or if you find yourself looking for comprehensive information presented clearly, this book is what you need to get your network back under control.

Conventions Used in this Book

As you work through this book, you will notice special typeface conventions that show you at a glance what actions to take.

- ❖ On-screen messages, such as listings, appear in this `special typeface`.

- ❖ Information you type appears in this **bold typeface**.

- ❖ All variable elements appear in this *italic typeface*.

This book also uses four special margin icons, which help you to identify certain parts of the text:

A **note** presents brief, additional information relating to the current topic. A note can also be used as a reminder or to clarify a point.

A **tip** is an added insight for your benefit.

A **warning** serves as a caution. It points to the careful use of a procedure or to an event that may cause the loss of data or work.

 A **see also** reference refers you to other parts of the book in which the topic appears.

Part One: The Challenge of Downsizing

The Economic Imperative of Downsizing

The Breakthrough in Distributed Processing

Traditional Data Processing Applications

Topics covered in this chapter:

Decreasing Costs of Technology

Manufacturing the Microcomputer Age

Downsizing Effects on Free-Market Competition

Understanding Historic Barriers to Downsizing

Chapter 1

The Economic Imperative of Downsizing

What is meant by downsizing? Although downsizing is a frequently used and broadly defined word, within the pages of this book, *downsizing* refers to one simple idea: moving data-processing applications from large mainframe or minicomputer hosts to microcomputers running NetWare 386.

Downsizing entails the transfer of data and programs from a single large-host computer to a series of microcomputers that are connected by a network. Downsizing involves not only the transfer of data and programs but also a redesign of the methods that MIS personnel use to manage and maintain those data and programs.

Downsizing, however, is more than transferring data, porting applications, and retooling management and maintenance procedures to a new platform. It also involves a difficult conceptual leap from the centralized paradigm to the distributed paradigm.

The *centralized paradigm* is one in which all data-processing resources—including CPU, storage, data, and programs—are located at a single point (or concentrated among a small number of key resources). The *distributed paradigm* is one in which those same data-processing resources are located among a number of physically disparate points. In fact, the location of data-processing resources in the distributed paradigm is dynamic—it can and will change frequently and sometimes unpredictably.

Downsizing, then, involves not only a new technology, but also a new mindset. Many of the questions raised by the concept of downsizing are not yet answered. Perhaps you will encounter as-yet-unmet challenges in your quest to downsize your data-processing resources.

This book does not attempt to answer all the questions raised by downsizing. Rather, it provides you with a solid foundation on which to base your downsizing efforts. It makes you familiar with NetWare 386—today's premier downsizing platform—and manages your expectations of what downsizing can mean to you and your organization.

This book helps you meet the challenge of understanding the distributed paradigm. After reading this book, you will know enough about downsizing to NetWare 386 to ask the appropriate questions when the time comes to make your move to a networked computer system. And that time will surely come. How can that be said? The answer is simple economics.

Decreasing Costs of Technology

Perhaps the only constant in the field of data processing is the decreasing cost of computing resources. Certainly your own experience, not to mention history itself, tells you that this constant is practically a law of nature. No one today can foresee the time when computing resources will not become less expensive. In fact, the price of computing resources continues to decrease as you read this. Today you can buy a $20,000 computer that 15 years ago might have cost one million dollars. Memory, storage, communications gear, and all types of computing paraphernalia are available today for practically nothing, in relative terms.

Today's new and inexpensive computer hardware works differently from yesterday's hardware, however. The difference between today's inexpensive hardware and yesterday's expensive equipment can be summed up in one word: *microcomputer.*

Manufacturing the Microcomputer Age

The Digital Equipment Corporation (DEC) VAX was one of the first commercial computer systems to feature a single-board central processing unit (CPU). Before the introduction of the VAX (and for some time after), most computer systems featured multiboard CPUs. Silicon-manufacturing techniques advanced exponentially, however, and led to the development of the microprocessor in the 1970s. (A *microprocessor* is CPU that is contained in a single chip.)

To understand the microcomputer, an analogy between the VAX and the Apple computer is useful. The VAX was one of the most commercially successful computer products; it defined a new class of computers called *minicomputers.* The VAX, having a single-board CPU, used advanced manufacturing techniques to make computing power more affordable and scaled-down than that available with mainframe computers. Minicomputers brought computing power to an entirely new group of medium-sized businesses that had been too small to buy a computer system.

The Apple computer was the first commercially successful micro-computer, and it defined a new class of personal computers. The Apple computer was made possible by the invention of the micro-processor, or single-chip CPU, which itself was made possible by stunning advances in silicon-manufacturing techniques. Like the VAX, the Apple computer made computing power affordable to a new group of businesses—in this case, small businesses—that pre-viously were priced out of the computer market.

Here the analogy ends, however. Minicomputers represent a downscaling of traditional mainframe technology; microcomputers represent an entirely new concept of the way computers are used. Minicomputers—like mainframes—are multiuser host systems, which are used to drive scores of dumb terminals. Users of a mini-computer share a central CPU and memory, just as users of a main-frame do.

Microcomputers, on the other hand, are revolutionary because each machine is a self-contained, single-user computer. No more dumb terminals. Users of microcomputers have their own CPU and memory. Because of the way microcomputers are designed and used, the operating systems written for them are entirely dif-ferent from minicomputer and mainframe operating systems. Mi-crocomputer operating systems are single-user, single-tasking control programs. Moreover, they are extremely sparse, doing little more than providing an Application Programming Interface (API) to the microcomputer's hardware.

Since the creation of the Apple computer, manufacturing tech-niques have continued their stunning advances. Today's micro-computers are as powerful as yesterday's VAXes and mainframes. And today's microcomputers are unbelievably inexpensive. Be-cause of these cost advantages, many larger businesses have incor-porated them by the thousands into their data-processing (DP) systems.

The microcomputer created a new type of software, too. Shrink-wrapped productivity software, available for hundreds (rather than thousands) of dollars, have become mass-market products. Microcomputer software is increasingly sophisticated and flexible, available off the shelf, and can be installed by the user. You can purchase a surprisingly powerful database management system, word processor, spreadsheet package, and communications package for well under a thousand dollars.

 Productivity software is designed to make individiuals more productive, rather than to replace them or to automate business functions.

Downsizing Effects on Free-Market Competition

The cost advantages of the microcomputer—in terms of both hardware and software—have led to the ironic situation in which even the largest businesses are implementing microcomputers. The situation is ironic because, originally, the microcomputer was thought to be for only the smallest businesses. Yet, even with their power, today's microcomputers are much different from yesterday's mini-computers and mainframes. Microcomputers are still single-user systems, which means that they do not work easily within the DP host-processing environment.

The desire to place business information systems on microcomputers (a use that the original designers of microcomputers did not foresee) has led to yet another new technology: the local area network (LAN). Early LANs were also the result of developers needing to standardize while taking advantage of cheap, DOS-based hardware and software.

Networking is not the same as data communications. Networking entails cooperative processing among multiple intelligent microcomputers. Networking is the key to taking advantage of the low-cost microcomputer because it makes possible the implementation of world-class information systems on microcomputers. All of this means that downsizing is an economic imperative.

The Darwinian law of competition and market forces ensures that the organizations that operate at a lower cost survive; those that do not match the economic gains of their competitors do not survive. Organizations that adapt to changing circumstances continue to grow; those that fail to adapt become extinct.

 Although downsizing is not easy, it *is* possible. Downsizing saves money because it is the only way organizations can truly realize the decreased cost of computing resources. If your organization can downsize more successfully (and faster) than the "other guys," you will realize the sweet fruits of the economic laws of competition and market forces. If someone is going to win, it might as well be you.

Understanding Historic Barriers to Downsizing

Regardless of the economic benefits, downsizing is not possible unless certain conditions exist. First, you must have available microcomputer hardware that offers reliability and performance sufficient for the data-processing applications that are being downsized. Second, the microcomputer operating systems must offer the capabilities required by the data-processing applications to be downsized.

Until recently, downsizing has not occurred on a significant scale because microcomputer hardware and operating systems were incapable of providing the resources required by data-processing applications. Typically, these applications need the following hardware capabilities:

❖ 32-bit CPU register space

❖ 32-bit CPU memory address mode, allowing up to 4G of addressable memory

❖ 32-bit memory bus bandwidth

❖ 32-bit I/O bus bandwidth

❖ Fast operating speeds (16MHz or higher)

❖ Fast and large magnetic media (1G and higher)

❖ Hardware-based error checking, such as CRC on data and memory bus (or the equivalent)

In addition to hardware requirements, data-processing applications typically require robust and advanced operating systems that include the following elements:

❖ Multitasking execution

❖ Multiuser operation

❖ Multiuser file system

❖ Large-capacity file system (several gigabytes or larger)

❖ Fast file system

❖ Fault-tolerant file system, including transaction control, file and record locking, and redundant indexes

Microcomputer Limitations

Historic barriers to downsizing have involved a lack of reliability and performance in microcomputer hardware, a lack of appropriate microcomputer operating systems, or both. For example, the eight-bit Apple computer of the late 1970s and the 16-bit IBM PC of the early 1980s did not come close to addressing the reliability and performance requirements of data-processing applications. Furthermore, CP/M (the Apple II operating system) and PC-DOS simply reflected the architecture of the hardware on which they ran, and therefore did not provide the capabilities required by data-processing applications.

Until the mid-1980s, microcomputer hardware was characterized by the following capabilities:

❖ 8-bit or 16-bit CPU register space

❖ 8-bit or 16-bit CPU memory-addressing modes, allowing a total addressable memory space of 1M or less

❖ 8-bit or 16-bit memory bus bandwidth

❖ 8-bit or 16-bit I/O bus bandwidth

❖ Slow operating speeds (8MHz or slower)

❖ Lack of fast and large magnetic media

❖ Lack of hardware-based error checking and fault tolerance

Until the mid-1980s, microcomputer operating systems reflected the shortcomings of the microcomputers themselves. They had the following characteristics:

❖ Single-tasking

❖ Single user

❖ Small file system (30M or less)

❖ Single-user file system

❖ Simple file system

❖ Small memory space

Hardware barriers to downsizing began to fall in the mid-1980s with the introduction of the Intel 80386 and Motorola 68020 microprocessors. Today, microcomputer hardware enjoys the following characteristics:

* ❖ 32-bit CPU register space
* ❖ 32-bit CPU memory-addressing mode, allowing a total addressable memory space of 4G (or greater, with segmented memory models)
* ❖ 32-bit memory bus bandwidth
* ❖ 32-bit I/O bus bandwidth
* ❖ Fast operating speeds (up to 50MHz)
* ❖ Fast and large magnetic media
* ❖ Emergence of hardware-based error checking and fault tolerance

Obviously, today's microcomputer hardware is sufficient to fulfill the requirements of traditional DP applications.

The Operating-System Barrier

Despite the striking advances in microcomputer hardware, a perception remains that microcomputer operating systems are still not up to the task of running world-class data-processing applications. DOS remains the dominant microcomputer operating system, and DOS is inadequate for data-processing applications.

The failure of OS/2 to dislodge DOS is based on many factors, not all of which are related to the technical capabilities of OS/2. The OS/2 file system remains inadequate for data-processing applications, mostly because of its internal limits on file-system size and concurrent file handles and locks.

Two microcomputer operating systems have emerged and proven capable of running data-processing applications. One is UNIX System V Release 3.2, which is a version of UNIX that was adapted specifically for the 386 microprocessor. On larger computers, UNIX has only reluctantly been accepted as a data-processing operating system, because of its experimental and academic history. Although UNIX has well-documented shortcomings, especially in the security and file-system areas, it is a good operating system for data-processing applications. Much headway has been made by organizations using UNIX as an operating system when downsizing data-processing applications.

The second operating system suitable for downsized data-processing applications is NetWare, introduced in the following section.

NetWare and the Operating-System Barrier

The second microcomputer operating system capable of running data-processing applications is NetWare 3.11. Among the characteristics of NetWare that make it a viable operating system for downsizing data-processing applications are its prodigious file system, its 32-bit architecture, and its multitasking execution.

NetWare has garnered a reputation as a high-performance operating system. This reputation has been enhanced recently by companies such as Oracle, Informix, and SyBase, which have ported their database-management engines to NetWare. All three of these companies report that their engines perform better on NetWare than on many larger and much more expensive computer systems. NetWare also has many internal-design features that are constructed specifically for data-processing applications, especially in the file-system area.

Many systems analysts and IS personnel still do not know what to think about NetWare as a platform for data-processing applications, however. (This hesitation is because the architecture of NetWare is so different from that of traditional operating systems.)

The key to understanding NetWare is to realize that it was designed to run traditional data-processing applications in a nontraditional way. NetWare was designed from the ground up to run in a *distributed* (rather than centralized) environment. Many of the services provided by NetWare are optimized for distributed processing, including its multitasking architecture, its inter-process communications architecture, and its file system.

As an operating system, NetWare was designed to work just as well with other instances of itself (that is, with other machines running NetWare), as with its own local operating environment. Understanding NetWare's design philosophy is an important prelude to understanding how powerful it is and why it can run data-processing applications less expensively, faster, and more effectively than any other operating system, including mainframe and minicomputer operating systems.

Remaining Barriers

No technological barriers to downsizing remain. A mental barrier remains, however, grounded in the differences between microcomputers and larger computers. A large mainframe or minicomputer system runs data-processing applications on a centralized host CPU. Users gain access to the application using dumb terminals, which serve as input/output stations. On the other hand, a large network of microcomputers has no dumb terminals; each station on the network is a full-fledged computer. Each station on the network can store, retrieve, and process data independently of other stations. To build a large system using microcomputers, you must coax them into working together to process data cooperatively. Because no single point exists at which an IS professional can control data and processing, however, all types of problems emerge.

The fact is, you cannot force a network of intelligent microcomputers to behave like a large, centralized host computer. Instead, you must develop data-processing applications by using a different model: the *client-server model*.

 Chapter 2 explains the client-server processing model in more detail.

As you see in this book, the client-server model in general—and NetWare in particular—offers many advantages that make NetWare a platform that is superior to the centralized host model. These advantages are not without a price, however. To implement a world-class data-processing application on NetWare, you must master the following tools:

❖ Client-server development tools

❖ Client-server data-communications tools

❖ Distributed network-management tools

In addition, you must learn to deal with the uncertainties of a distributed environment with thousands of individual microcomputers instead of one centralized host. These uncertainties offer challenges that are both intellectual and practical. They also provide unique opportunities for improvement on the old centralized model. The remainder of this book explains these opportunities and points out the pitfalls associated with them.

Summary

Businesses rely heavily on computers for generating, managing, storing, and retrieving all types of information. Applications that businesses use to manage and process data traditionally have been designed for (and run on) large mainframe and minicomputers.

Downsizing is the process of moving data-processing applications from large computers and onto microcomputers. Within the context of this book, *downsizing* refers specifically to moving data-processing applications to NetWare 386.

In the past decade, the microcomputer has become a prominent business tool. Advances in manufacturing techniques and microcomputer design have made the microcomputer the most cost-effective type of computer available.

Until recently, however, the microcomputer has been incapable of running world-class data-processing applications because it lacked the capacity required by DP applications. The microcomputer operating systems also proved incapable of running such software. Today, however, microcomputers are powerful enough to run data-processing applications and microcomputer operating systems have improved to the point at which downsizing is a viable option. Traditional data-processing applications are difficult to implement on microcomputers in the traditional manner, however. The key to downsizing involves understanding distributed processing and the client-server computing model.

NetWare v3.11 is an excellent platform for downsizing. It is important to understand that NetWare is designed to operate in a client-server environment. Therefore, NetWare is quite different from traditional computer operating systems; it requires a nontraditional approach when downsizing data-processing applications to it. The purpose of this book is to point out the correct approach to downsizing, to explain the advantages NetWare offers over traditional operating systems, and to point out potential trouble areas you may encounter when downsizing.

The next chapter discusses the breakthrough in technology that makes microcomputers—and particularly microcomputers running NetWare v3.11—an excellent choice for downsizing DP applications.

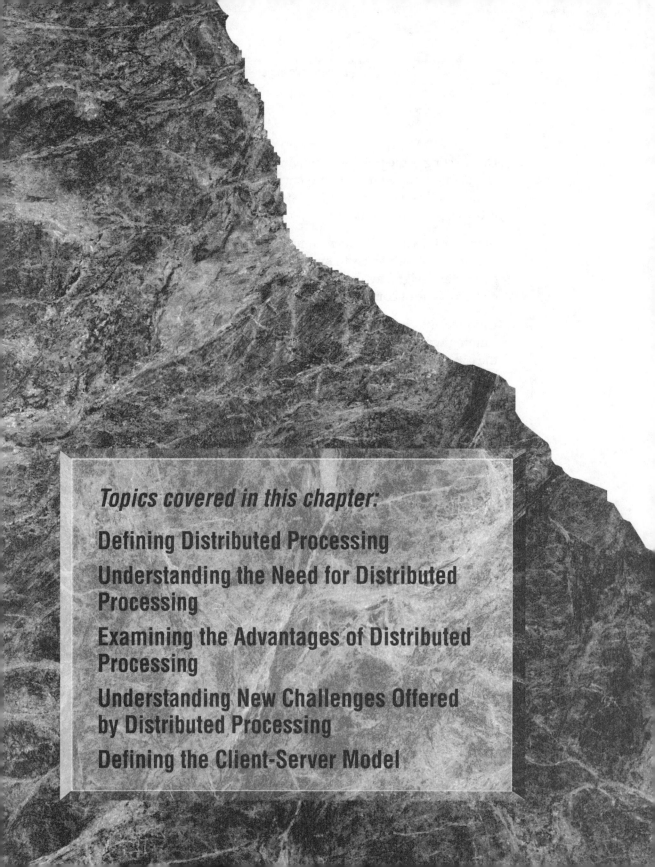

Chapter 2

The Breakthrough in Distributed Processing

Chapter 1 explained the advancement of the microcomputer, which is now as powerful as yesterday's mainframe computers. The microcomputer is much different from the mainframe, however. Two technological breakthroughs combined to produce today's fast and powerful microcomputer: the invention of the semiconductor transistor and the creation of the integrated circuit. Together, these inventions made it possible to manufacture microcomputer hardware as powerful as the old mainframe computer (for a price of two-tenths of one percent of that computer.)

This chapter introduces you to distributed processing, which is a software invention that is as significant to the future of data processing as the inventions of the transistor and integrated circuit were to the development of the microcomputer.

Defining Distributed Processing

Merging the power of networked computers is both the goal and definition of *distributed processing*. In its elemental form, distributed processing entails the division of an application among two or more computers. Distributed processing is inverse in many ways to *multiprogramming*, in which a single CPU executes multiple programs.

 Distributed processing has the potential to be a much more powerful tool than multiprogramming because it exploits multiple processors of memory spaces, protocol stacks, code libraries, storage media, and whatever else is loaded on or attached to one or more computers. Multiprogramming, on the other hand, is an attempt to squeeze every last bit of computer power out of a single CPU.

To understand why distributed processing is an advancement over the centralized host model, the next section looks at the conditions that led to the centralized host model in the first place.

Assumptions of the Centralized Model

During the 1950s and 1960s, when the centralized model became the standard for business data processing, CPU and memory were prohibitively expensive, data storage was slow and expensive, and software was prohibitively expensive.

These conditions made it imperative to design data-processing applications to make the most of expensive computer resources. As a result, the centralized model evolved.

With the centralized model, all computing resources were located at a central host computer, multiprogramming techniques enabled concurrent users to run programs from dumb terminals, and all data was stored at a central location.

Figure 2.1 shows an example of the centralized model, in which all computing power is located in or controlled by the central host computer.

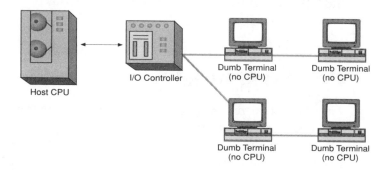

Figure 2.1:
The centralized model.

As a result of the constraints that led to the centralized model, and because of the difficulty of developing software with the tools of the day, software had minimum use of computer core memory and sparse design and program logic.

Although the centralized model was necessary, given the limitations of the technology under which it was developed, it was not always the best model for data-processing applications. For example, the centralized model created several following problems, which IS organizations are still coping with today. These problems include access to centralized corporate data through a single point, the need to create software for specific processing tasks, and performance bottlenecks (because all computing resources are centralized).

On the other hand, the centralized model continues to offer benefits, including the capability of managing large databases from a single point. The consolidation of all corporate data into a single host system makes it easier to eliminate redundant data, to police access to data, and to back up data. These benefits of the centralized model are, in fact, shortcomings of the distributed-processing model—the solutions you read about later in this book.

Assumptions of the Distributed-Processing Model

The distributed-processing model (see fig. 2.2) assumes more modern conditions than those assumed by the centralized model and places microcomputer resources where they are used most productively. As a result, the distributed model is a more modern assessment of the ideal data-processing configuration. Among the assumptions made by this model are the following:

❖ Computing resources are relatively inexpensive

❖ Data storage is readily available and inexpensive

❖ Human resources are prohibitively expensive

❖ Software, while not inexpensive, is readily available

The first assumption deserves qualification. Specifically, *microcomputer resources* are relatively cheap—mainframe and minicomputer resources are still relatively expensive. This difference in cost stems from the basic design differences between microcomputers and their larger ancestors.

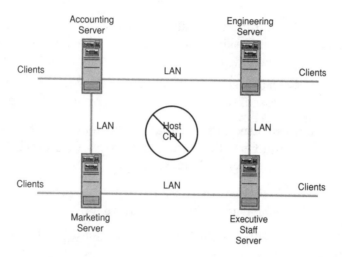

Figure 2.2:

The distributed-processing model.

The third assumption, that human resources are prohibitively expensive, was not directly addressed by the centralized model. One of the purposes of the computer was (and still is) to free humans from performing repetitive and mundane tasks. The centralized model was developed at a time when computer resources were far more expensive than human resources, however. Today, the opposite is true. The focus of the distributed-processing model is to make human beings more productive. (You learn how the distributed-processing model accomplishes this task later in this chapter.)

The assumptions of the distributed-processing model lead to configurations with the following characteristics:

❖ Computing resources are located where they are used and exist throughout the organization

❖ Multiprogramming techniques are not used; rather, multitasking and multithreaded techniques are used when they increase the performance of software

❖ Data is stored where it is generated, where it is processed, where it is consumed, or at all three points

Software used in a distributed-information system also reflects the assumptions of the distributed-processing model. Such software has the following characteristics:

❖ Core memory is used freely to aid performance and to enable user-friendly software interfaces

❖ Program logic is increasingly sophisticated to serve the needs of the user

❖ Software is easy to use and to customize

❖ High-level programming languages increase programmer productivity

❖ Fourth-generation programming languages (4GLs) enable the user to accomplish simple programming tasks

When applied properly, the distributed-processing model increases the productivity of the entire organization by allowing better and more effective communications, by increasing access to existing data, by introducing more methods of obtaining data, and by placing computer resources throughout the organization, especially where they are used most productively.

The centralized model was designed to limit access to computing resources and data. Conversely, the distributed-processing model is designed to provide easy access to computing resources and data. Of course, there are some strings attached. Although the cost of computing resources is no longer an issue, valid reasons exist to limit access to data. Likewise, valid reasons exist to control the collection of new data. These reasons have nothing to do with the technology itself, however—they have to do with the nature of the data in question.

Understanding the Need for Distributed Processing

Without the microcomputer, the need for distributed processing and local area network (LAN) technology is questionable. Certainly, the commercial success of these two complementary technologies would not be assured. The centralized model meant many users and one computer; the distributed-processing model means many users and many computers (at least one computer, in fact, for each user).

LAN technology enables stand-alone computers to exchange data as self-contained, intelligent computers. LANs were actually developed to enable microcomputers to share expensive peripherals. For example, one of the first LANs was developed in the late 1970s at the Xerox Palo Alto Research Center (PARC) to allow experimental microcomputers to share an experimental laser printer.

LANs are different from traditional data-communications technology because a LAN connects a series of intelligent computers over a data pathway. Traditional data-communications technology, on the other hand, provides a host computer with a series of input/output stations (dumb terminals). All communications between a host computer and input/output stations are controlled by the host computer (directly or indirectly). LANs are not controlled by any one computer—each computer can transmit or receive data over the LAN at any moment. Thus, LAN technology is more complicated and powerful than traditional data-communications technology.

When organizations began to implement microcomputer technology (mostly because of cost advantages), the need for a communications medium was made evident rather quickly. Each microcomputer accumulated its own data, ran its own programs, and performed its own processing, independently of other microcomputers in use by the organization.

 An organization, by definition, cannot function effectively without communications between its different components. Because microcomputers soon became very important to organizations, the need for communications between microcomputers became critical.

Early LAN technology enabled microcomputers to exchange data, which was an important first step toward effective communications within an organization. Most early LANs, however, were installed to enable microcomputers to share mass-storage devices and high-capacity laser printers.

The capability of microcomputers to share data over a LAN introduced the further possibility of distributed processing (the harnessing of multiple microcomputers to execute single tasks concurrently). The theoretical presumption of distributed processing is that combining many low-cost microcomputers and having them work together is much cheaper than obtaining a single, large host computer.

Distributed processing continues to present challenges to engineers and systems analysts because the microcomputer was not designed to perform distributed processing. Moreover, much traditional computer theory assumed a centralized model. Consequently, most of the tools used by engineers and analysts today were developed with the centralized model in mind.

Distributed processing remains a leading-edge discipline. One aspect of NetWare that makes it especially appropriate for downsizing is that NetWare was designed to perform distributed processing. Many of the chapters in this book focus on the specific features of NetWare that make it ideally suited for distributed processing.

Examining the Advantages of Distributed Processing

The advantages of distributed processing can be summed up by the following points:

* Scalability
* Modularity
* Exploiting underused hardware
* Leveraging repeated tasks
* Redundancy
* Flexibility

Each of these points is explained in the following sections.

Scalability

Scalability is a real advantage of distributed-processing technology. *Scalability* is the capability to add users to a network, one at a time, while also increasing the capacity of the network.

Although networks have scalability, mainframes and minicomputers do not have this capability. When you add another user to a mainframe, you typically hang a terminal on the system and increase the load on the mainframe's CPU (you do not actually increase the computing power of the system, its storage capacity, or its memory). With a network, each additional workstation brings to the system more processing power, memory, and so on.

Without distributed processing, however, scalability is theoretical. Consider the way the typical e-mail program makes a network scalable. Most e-mail programs for networks are divided into a server element and a client element. The *server* element routes mail and stores messages in a central database; the *client* element opens messages, deletes messages, creates messages, and so on. The client element runs on a workstation; the server element runs on the network server.

When you add an additional user to the network, you also add another workstation. That additional workstation provides the incremental processing capacity that is necessary to run the new client element. You still need only one server element because you added an additional client without making any significant addition to the server's load.

On a mainframe system, both the client element and the server element run on the host system. When you add another user to the system, you hang on another terminal, but you do not make a corresponding addition to the system's processing capacity.

Modularity

Modularity, which is the capability of breaking functions down into modules, is another advantage of distributed processing. Continuing with the previous e-mail example, if you divide the mail application into a front end and back end, you now can mix-and-match front ends. Perhaps some of the workstations on the network are DOS machines, some are UNIX, and some are Macintosh. If you have DOS-specific front ends, UNIX-specific fronts ends, and Macintosh-specific front ends for the e-mail application, modularity enables all three types of clients to gain access to the mail-delivery services of the same back end.

Tip

Scalability and modularity are both readily accessible to software developers. It is a relatively simple thing to divide an application into a front end and a back end. The easiest thing to do is isolate an application's user interface and make that the front end; make everything else the application's back end.

Most of today's distributed applications are simple front-end, back-end applications. Many of these were ported to PCs and networks from host environments. You do not need to do any radical redesign of the average stand-alone application to port it to a distributed environment.

The next two advantages of distributed processing—exploiting underused hardware and leveraging of often-repeated tasks—are more difficult to achieve. To gain these advantages, the software developer must design the application from the ground up to run in a distributed environment. Further, the developer must distribute the application more finely than for a simple front-end, back-end architecture. Rather than dividing the application into two pieces—the user interface and everything else—the developer must divide the application into routines and subroutines. Then the decision must be made about the best place on the network in which to run each piece of the application.

Exploiting Underused Hardware

The hallmark of the microcomputer is that it spends up to 95 percent of its computing cycles doing nothing (waiting for I/O). When the user is ready to initiate a processing task, the microcomputer performs that task. When the user is thinking, taking a break, reading a book, or doing something else, the microcomputer executes empty loops.

The empty loops executed by microcomputers represent latent computing power that is available for other uses, and the trick is getting to that latent power. Distributed processing enables the harnessing of the latent computing power of many microcomputers connected over a network.

The distribution of an application's processing load among multiple machines frequently leads the application designer to make a decision to place all the heavy work on the most powerful machine. Sometimes, however, the most powerful machine is not necessarily the least-used machine. For example, the most underused machine on the network may be a humble IBM PC AT.

Consider a front-end, back-end database management system. The database engine (the back end) runs on the server; the user interface (the front end) runs on the workstation. The back end does the heavy work—storing and filtering data, processing queries, building indexes, and so on. The front end displays data and accepts input. When you request a record from the database, your workstation runs through idle cycles while waiting for the back end to process the request and deliver the data.

There may be 10, 50, 100, 500, or more clients running front ends to the database's single back end. Each client front end runs through idle cycles waiting for the database back end to process its request. Given this scenario, it is not hard to infer where on the network the excess processing capacity lies.

 To take advantage of idle processing capacity on a network, distributed applications should be designed to sense and use idle capacity in a dynamic fashion. Needless to say, developing this type of distributed application is considerably more complicated than developing a simple front-end, back-end application.

Leverage of Often-Repeated Tasks

In a network environment, the capability to *leverage* often-repeated tasks can lead to great gains in performance. For example, both NetWare and LAN Manager (with HPFS) servers perform large-scale file caching. When network clients use common files, server-based caching provides leverage because a file is cached only once by the server to make it available to every client. For example, a server with 100 clients, each of which is using a common database file, must cache that file only once. If caching were performed by the clients, each client would have to cache the file, resulting in the file being cached 100 times—once for each client.

In fact, the best example of a distributed application that leverages repeated tasks is a file server. In simple terms, a file server, in tandem with workstation/client software, provide a distributed file system. In other words, the file system you use from your network workstation is divided between your workstation and the file server.

Of course, *file server* is a somewhat obsolete term. Today's network operating systems can be all kinds of servers—database servers, communications servers, multimedia servers, mail servers, and so on. Each of these server applications presents its own possibilities for leveraging.

Redundancy

Closely related to the advantage of scalability is the advantage of redundancy. *Redundancy* provides protection against downtime because of hardware failure: LAN technology provides multiple, redundant data routes between any two networked computers, which means that you can suffer a LAN hardware failure and still enjoy communications over a LAN (see fig. 2.3).

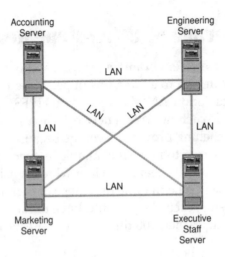

Figure 2.3:
Redundant data routes.

To implement redundant LANs, you must have bridges and routers present on the network. *Bridges* enable communication across two or more different LAN segments; *routers* act as traffic controllers, ensuring that data arrives at its correct destination. NetWare has bridging and routing modules built into its operating system at the lowest level. NetWare was designed to take advantage of redundant LAN configurations to provide robust network communications.

In addition to LAN redundancy, a network always has redundant microcomputer hardware. On a multiserver network, the failure of a single server never brings the entire network down. Remaining servers and workstations continue operating as before. Likewise, the failure of a workstation never brings a server or another workstation down.

NetWare also features *disk duplexing,* which enables a single server to have redundant hard drives and drive controllers. This means that a drive failure on a NetWare server need not bring the server down. The server continues operating, even while the technician replaces the failed drive.

Flexibility

Flexibility gives you many options regarding hardware and software when building a NetWare installation. NetWare accepts multiple client operating systems, including DOS, Windows, OS/2, UNIX, and Macintosh. NetWare also accepts multiple transport protocols, including IPX/SPX, IP, OSI, and AppleTalk. NetWare also supports the UNIX Network File System (NFS), and can act as an NFS server.

When creating a distributed system using NetWare, you can match hardware and software to the job at hand without regard to previously installed systems. If, for example, your engineering department requests UNIX workstations, you can install them without worrying whether they will work with the present installed base of hardware and software. NetWare can accommodate them. The distributed-processing model enables you to compartmentalize different types of hardware and operating systems, thus masking their differences from the system at large while still enabling them to communicate and cooperate with other systems on the network.

A flexible network enables you to invest in the computer resources that make the most sense. You can place powerful microcomputers in the hands of those workers who need the greatest computing power, and provide less powerful microcomputers for those workers who do not need as much power. Because users have their own computers, you can match computing resources to user needs.

Understanding New Challenges Offered by Distributed Processing

Each of the advantages of distributed processing discussed in the preceding sections has one thing in common: it helps you reduce the cost of computing. The distributed-processing model also introduces new challenges to the IS professional, however, including the following:

* Data duplication
* Network management
* Security
* Configuration management

Each of these challenges is described in the following sections.

Data Duplication

Simply stated, *data duplication* occurs when there is more than one instance of the same data. Data duplication is never a problem (sometimes it is a benefit) unless it is unintentional or unmanaged. Under the old centralized model, data duplication was not such a vexing problem because all data was processed at a central point.

The distributed-processing model diminishes the problem of data duplication, in comparison to the situation in which many microcomputers exist as stand-alone, non-networked stations. Data duplication is still a serious problem in a distributed-processing model, however.

Data duplication happens because data can originate at any station on a network, data can be altered at any station on a network, and data can be stored at any station on a network.

The key to solving the data-duplication problem in a distributed-processing environment is to implement data-processing applications that address the problem and take steps to avoid it.

Network Management

Managing a network is actually not much different than managing a centralized host computer. Network management involves managing many computers (often thousands), each of which can suffer problems similar to those suffered by a host computer. To further complicate the situation, each microcomputer on a network can be different from all other microcomputers. In addition, managing a network means managing LAN hardware, bridges, routers, hubs, repeaters, and all the hardware components that make up a LAN.

Unfortunately, tools for managing networks have not evolved to the extent of networking technology in general. Thus, network management remains a difficult, although not insurmountable, problem of distributed processing.

Security

The problem of security management in a distributed-processing environment is not necessarily serious. Tools and methods exist to help implement a secure network. IS professionals frequently become overwhelmed by the complexity of a distributed-processing environment (relative to a centralized environment), however, and allow security to drop to the bottom of their list of priorities. Although this means that security management can be more difficult on a network than it should be, there are things you can do, especially with NetWare, to make security a manageable problem.

Although security should not be a barrier to implementing even the most critical or sensitive applications on a network, you may need extra planning and work to implement a sufficiently secure environment.

Configuration Management

The downside of scalability and flexibility—key advantages of the distributed-processing environment—is that configuration management is difficult and complex. Virtually any hardware/software combination is possible in a distributed environment, so enforcement of standard configurations is left to the manager rather than being a by-product of the installed base of systems.

The greatest amount of work involved in the configuration management of a distributed-processing environment is in tracking the configuration of the installed base of microcomputers. Fortunately, tools exist to track the current configuration of the network and the computers that are installed on it. The greatest challenges involve deciding how strictly to enforce standard configurations and where to place the responsibility of implementing standards.

Hopefully, you can reach a solution that enables individuals to choose the most effective hardware for their tasks while providing some standards for the system's configuration as a whole.

Defining the Client-Server Model

The client-server model is nothing more than a high-level, intellectual formalization of distributed processing. Under the client-server model, one program acts as a server (it provides services to other programs). *Services* can be defined as hardware or software resources. Clients use the services provided by the server to accomplish various tasks. Typically, one server program enables multiple concurrent clients to make use of the resources it offers.

Together, a client program and a server program combine to form a *distributed application* (an application that is divided among more than one CPU).

Technically, a client program and a server program can run on the same CPU, although this arrangement dilutes the benefits of the client-server model.

You can view client-server computing as the computer equivalent of the economic principles of specialization and division of labor. Under specialization, individual organizations specialize in one or several areas and compete by being expert in those areas. Under division of labor, large composite efforts are divided among firms specializing on one or another discipline.

For example, Firm A specializes in manufacturing, Firm B specializes in advertising, and Firm C specializes in accounting. Firm D, a producer of brand-name products, contracts with Firm A to manufacture a new product, with Firm B to publicize a new product, and with Firm C to determine the profitability of the new product. Firms A, B, and C are expert at what they do; better, in fact, than Firm D. The result is a composite effort, organized and initiated by Firm D, but carried out by several firms specializing in different areas. Other factors come into play, such as economies-of-scale, agility, and experience in specific disciplines.

Client-server computing is very similar to these economic concepts. A computing task is divided among several software modules, with each module specializing in one or more aspects of the task at hand. A specific module's specialization may result from the hardware it is running on, the operating system running it, the module itself, or a combination of all three.

Client-server computing requires that all technologies described in this book are "downsizing technologies," including microcomputers, LANs, and distributed processing. It is within the context of the client-server model that the advantages of NetWare can be realized most fully. NetWare, in fact, is nothing more than a collection of services that client modules can use. The most obvious service made available by NetWare is file service, but NetWare offers many additional powerful services to network clients.

Summary

Distributed processing means getting multiple computers to work together, cooperatively, on a single task. Distributed processing is more powerful than multiprogramming, in which a single computer works on many tasks concurrently. Distributed processing enables you to take full advantage of all resources offered by multiple computers.

Distributed processing is made possible by developments in networking technology, but it is made economical by the emergence of the microcomputer. Distributed processing is the only way to harness fully the power of a LAN.

The client-server model is a formalization of distributed processing, in which one computer acts as a resource server and other computers act as resource clients.

 Resources can be defined broadly to include any type of computer resource, such as storage, data, processing power, and so on.

Distributed processing is a more modern model on which to build an IS facility. Distributed processing offers important benefits, such as redundancy, scalability, flexibility, and leverage.

Distributed processing has caused problems in the areas of data duplication, configuration management, and network management. These challenges are not insurmountable and do not negate the many benefits of distributed processing, however.

The next chapter takes a look at traditional data-processing applications, the evolution of tools to assist in processing data, and the way NetWare v3.11 can boost productivity even further.

Topics covered in this chapter:

Evolving Database-Management Technology

Implementing Different Data Models

Exploring Traditional Data-Processing Applications

Applying the Client-Server Model

Chapter 3

Traditional
Data Processing
Applications

This chapter discusses the evolution of data-processing (DP) applications, from their inception in the early days of mainframe technology to the newest client-server data-processing engines.

 A *data-processing application* manages the acquisition, control, manipulation, and reporting of information used to run an organization.

Many terms and concepts are introduced in this chapter. The conceptual material helps you make connections between traditional DP concepts and more modern concepts which, in turn, enable you to grasp the importance of specific features of the NetWare v3.11 operating system.

49

As computer technology advances, organizations broaden the types of information that computers manage. The current digital revolution has introduced new types of computer data, including images, sounds, and complex data types that consist of many different forms of information.

Consequently, the working definition of a data-processing application has a broader scope today than it did in the early days. This chapter discusses the broadening scope of DP applications, describes today's prominent types of applications in use today, and deals with some leading-edge DP applications.

Evolving Database-Management Technology

Database-management technology consists of the methods, designs, and devices that DP applications use to do their jobs of storing data, sorting data, retrieving data, and processing data. Database-management technology has long been a mainstream discipline of computer science because it poses some interesting problems for software engineers. Most of these problems pertain to obtaining good performance while working within the limits of hardware and operating-system resources.

 Research in database-management technology has benefitted by the fact that most of the money spent on computer systems is spent to implement DP applications.

Batch-Oriented Data-Processing Applications

In the early days of the mainframe computer, large host machines processed corporate accounting data. This occurred for two reasons. First, accounting data tends to be the most voluminous type of data produced by a large corporation (and can be the most critical data). Second, accounting systems (whether manual systems or computer-based systems) are designed for batch-mode processing. The accounting cycle is a static system of steps, beginning with a transaction and continuing through the posting of that transaction to two or more accounts. At regular intervals, all accounts are "closed" and their sums are transferred to various reports, including balance sheets, income statements, statements of changes in cash position (cash-flow statements), and others.

Early DP applications were mostly batch-oriented accounting packages. Individual transactions were recorded on punch cards and technicians ran posting programs that read the transactions and posted them to the database. To "close the books" on a reporting period, technicians ran closing programs against the transactions contained in the database. To generate reports, technicians ran reporting programs against the closed-out accounts contained in the database.

The database for these early DP applications consisted primarily of flat files, stored on sequential media (usually tape). The batch-oriented mode of these applications enabled the database manager to process individual data records (*transactions*) sequentially as they existed in the database, rather than in some other (perhaps sorted) order. (To sort, technicians ran a sorting program against the database, which created a new sorted version of the database.)

Because these batch-oriented DP applications had no real-time requirements (they worked with transactions that occurred earlier), performance was defined in terms of optimizing access to the sequential storage media, rather than in terms of optimizing access to specific transactions.

Individual records in these early databases were defined by rigid file structures. Each record typically contained information that applications could use to determine the length of that record and the lengths of each field within that record. This information enabled "streaming access" to transactions recorded in the database and also provided the running program (be it a posting, closing, or reporting program) with the information it required to interpret the transaction. Although individual transactions provided an index into their own information, there was no index that provided information regarding keys or the locations of the transactions themselves.

The Advent of Indexing

As the use of computers expanded among large corporations, methods for storing and accessing database information became more sophisticated. One of the first advancements was the use of an *index file*, which provides information about specific records within the database. For example, an index file in an accounting system can contain the account number and offset of each transaction within the primary database file. In this example, the account number is *indexed* (it is contained in the index file); it is the *key* of each transaction. A posting program can accumulate posting totals for an individual account by reading the index file to obtain only those transactions with that specific account number. The posting program reads the entire database file sequentially, but it can obtain specific transaction offsets for that account by reading the index file.

To be effective, indexed databases require storage media that can be accessed randomly, rather than sequentially. The media must be able to seek a specific offset within a file and read data from that offset, seek another offset, and so on. This approach to accessing media is markedly different from accessing sequential media such as tape, which must be read sequentially from beginning to end. The emergence of the disk-drive subsystem provides the random-access capabilities required by indexed database-management systems.

The use of a separate index file lead to further advances in DP applications. For example, by including file names in transaction indexes, you easily can divide a database into multiple files. (This was possible without indexes, but not nearly as easy to manage.)

For example, an index file can contain the account number (key), the file name, and the offset within that file for each transaction. The inclusion of the data file name in the index enables the application to proceed without prior knowledge of where (in which file) the data record is located. Division into multiple files makes the entire application more efficient and easier to maintain.

Indexed Sorting

Because indexed databases enable DP applications to access specific records randomly (not in sequential order), it is possible to "sort" entire databases without creating a new sorted file. Instead, DP applications can sort a database by changing the order of index records in the index file. In an indexed database, access to specific records is gained by reading the offset of that record in that record's index. To sort an entire database, the DP application can create a sorted index file. Then the DP application obtains database records in sorted order by gaining access to those records through the sorted index file.

 Indexed sorting represents a major gain in efficiency and performance for DP applications because index files are much smaller than the database they describe. (*Index files* contain information about database records, and not the more lengthy data itself.)

Relations among Record Types

Indexed databases made practical the establishment of relations among different record types. For example, suppose that designers of an accounting application want to link a transaction record to information about that transaction's customer, and this customer information is stored in a database file that is separate from the transaction information. By including in the index of the transaction-database file the name of the file containing customer records and the offset of the customer record for the current transaction, the DP application can form a relation between a specific transaction and the customer who initiated it.

It is easier, however, to establish a one-to-many relation between a customer record and each transaction initiated by that customer. For example, suppose that customer records are maintained in a file called CUST; transaction records are maintained in a file called TRANS. Each customer can have multiple transactions stored in the TRANS file. An index for a customer record can include an entry for each transaction "belonging" to that customer, as in the following:

```
Customer Index
customer record:
      file:       CUST
      offset:     0x00003000
transactions:
      file:       TRANS
      offset:     0x01fa0000
      file:       TRANS
      offset:     0x0003b000
      file:       TRANS
      offset:     0x0005b100
```

Alternatively, designers of the DP application can store the transaction information within the customer record itself instead of within the customer index. Using this approach, the customer record serves, among other things, as an index into the transaction database.

The one-to-many relation described in this example lays the foundation for the hierarchical database-management model, the first (and still most widely used) model for large-scale DP applications. Indexing and random-access storage media are the two technologies that make practical the one-to-many relation, as described here.

The Data Dictionary

As DP applications became more complex, simple indexing methods began to force complicated logic within database-management modules. As a result, the *data dictionary* was developed, which is another file (or series of files) that describes the structure, relationships, indexes, and data files of a complex database. The data dictionary is not an index, nor is it a data file. Rather, it is a map of the database as a whole. A database can encompass many different files and file structures, and the data dictionary is a centralized storehouse of all the data necessary to manage such a complex database.

Controlling Transactions and Concurrency

The emergence of the data dictionary lead to discussions of transaction control and concurrency. *Transaction control* preserves the integrity of the database in the face of errors writing data to a data file. In particular, transaction control ensures that partial records are never written to a database: either the entire record is written successfully or no part of the record is written to the database (the record remains in its unmodified state, as if the failed attempt to update the record were never made).

The hypothetical accounting DP application used in the preceding sections of this chapter provides a good example of the need for transaction control. In a double-entry accounting system, all transactions must "balance." That is, a credit to sales must be joined by an equal debit to accounts receivable, and a credit to cost-of-goods sold must be joined by an equal debit to inventory. Transaction control ensures that either all debits and credits making up a transaction are applied to the database, or none of them are. This control maintains the balance of the accounting database (the sum of all debits equals the sum of all credits), even when errors writing to the database occur.

Transaction control is critical when a database spans multiple data files, as most do. Record updates must consist of multiple individual write operations (any of which has the potential for failure); write operations also may be targeted toward many different data files. A single transaction, then, can depend on many successful writes to many different data files.

Transaction control is a necessary component of a DP application because it ensures that the entire record update is completed successfully or not at all. If a transaction fails, the DP application can retry the transaction without worrying about the point among the many discrete write operations at which the transaction previously failed.

 Ideally, transaction control is provided by the host operating system rather than by the DP application itself. An operating system-level implementation of transaction control provides a global scope; an application-level implementation does nothing to prevent other applications from interrupting transactions by gaining access to the files involved in a current transaction.

Concurrency Control

By the time that indexing, the data dictionary, and transaction control were integrated into mainstream DP applications, another issue also became important: *concurrency* control. As DP applications moved from batch-processing to multiprogramming, it became possible (even likely) that multiple users would require access to database records at the same time. This raised many possible conflicts between users wishing to gain access to or update records concurrently (*race condition*). For example, if two users attempt to update a record at the same time, what is the result? Clearly, the DP application should not allow such a situation to occur.

The solution to concurrency problems brought on by multiprogramming involves locking the database or portions of the database when a user is processing data. A *file lock* locks an entire file; a *record lock* locks a specific portion of a file. Most DP applications make use of two types of file and record locks: an *exclusive lock* prevents other users from reading or writing to the locked file or record; a *share lock* prevents other users from writing to the locked file or record, but it does not prevent them from reading that file or record.

DP applications should run on operating systems that provide file and record locking as an integral component of their file systems. This makes concurrency control more robust and more difficult (if not impossible) for other applications to bypass.

Most DP applications, however, implement some logic for concurrency control, independently of the host operating system. For example, a DP application should be able to report on the locking activity of its users and inform them when they open a record that is locked by another user.

Synopsis of Data-Processing Application Development

The traditional DP application has not evolved significantly (with one exception) since the emergence of random-access media and multiprogramming. Random-access media made possible sophisticated indexing techniques that used the random-access capabilities of storage media to speed up and streamline many basic database operations. Indexing led to the data dictionary, which made practical multifile databases with intricate relations among files and records.

As the use of indexing and the data dictionary became prominent, DP applications branched out into more and more business disciplines, including inventory control, point-of-sale, and payroll. The emergence of multifile databases led to transaction control, which preserves the integrity of the database by ensuring that multirecord or multifile updates are executed completely or not at all. A failed multirecord or multifile update can be retried by the DP application, without regard to the specific point of failure within the complex update.

Multiprogramming enabled DP applications to emerge from batch-oriented operation to real-time operation. Transactions could be entered directly into the database rather than on punch cards that were run at a later time. Multiprogramming led to multiuser database-management systems, which enabled multiple users to enter, retrieve, and process transactions concurrently. *Concurrency control* refers to methods used by the DP application to prevent corruption of the database as the result of concurrent access to it by two or more users. Concurrency control is accomplished through file and record locks, which can be implemented by the DP application itself or by the host operating system.

The one exception in the evolution of the traditional DP application is the client-server DP application. Downsizing to NetWare v3.11 is possible (and practical) because of the client-server model. In this book, you read about the specific features of NetWare that make it amenable to client-server DP applications.

 As you read in Chapter 2, the client-server model is one that divides the duties of a particular application among two or more computers.

Understanding Database-Management System Architecture

A *database-management system* (DBMS) is a collection of program modules that manage and process a database. All traditional DP applications use an industrial-strength DBMS. The typical DBMS consists of several distinct programs that work together to manage a database. In addition, most DBMSs provide techniques by which programmers can customize the operation of the DBMS.

A DP application represents a specific, systematized use of a DBMS. The subject of the DBMS's activities is the *database*, which is a collection of files that constitute the corporate data managed and processed by the DP application (and, at a lower level, by the DBMS). Given these assumptions, a basic DBMS architecture can be constructed that applies to both traditional and modern scenarios.

The basic DBMS architecture consists of the following three components:

Physical database

Logical schema

Conceptual schema

Each of these three components is described in the following sections.

The Physical Database

The *physical database* consists of the storage media and the methods that the DBMS uses to store and retrieve data from that media. It includes the organization of raw (uninterpreted) data on that media, including storage-allocation units such as sectors and clusters. The physical database also includes routines for writing data to and reading data from the media, as well as routines for both sequential and random access to the media.

The physical database also includes the structure of the files of which the database consists. It includes the reservation of storage-allocation units for database data, and the implementation of a directory that the DBMS can use to gain access to files or to specific portions of files (records).

Concurrency control and transaction control are both part of the physical database, although these two elements of the DBMS have implications for both the logical and conceptual schema of the system.

Many DBMSs implement the physical database entirely; others make use of host operating-system services to implement the physical database, such as file structures, directory structures, low-level input/output routines, and operating system device drivers. If a DBMS implements the physical database itself, it usually constructs some type of logical file or record system that resides at the same level as the host operating system's file system.

A DBMS also can implement part of the physical database itself while making use of the host operating system for the parts not implemented by the DBMS. For example, the DBMS can use the host operating system's file and directory structures and device access while implementing its own concurrency and transaction control.

The Logical Schema

The *logical schema* consists of record formats that include field and key definitions; indexes (including relations between records, fields, and keys); the data dictionary; searching and sorting algorithms and query formats; user security and auditing; and more. Most of the work done by modules in the logical schema involves translating user input or queries into requests for reading and writing allocation units from or to the physical storage media.

The logical schema of a DBMS also includes constraints on the types and formats of data that can be stored in records and record fields. Remember that the physical database is largely responsible for storing and retrieving raw (uninterpreted) data to and from the physical media. The logical schema is responsible for ensuring that such data is coherent and valid before committing it to the lower-level physical database modules.

For example, a DBMS may require that a particular key field be unique within a database. The logical schema must implement checking routines to ensure the uniqueness of each record's key field before committing the record containing that field to the physical database. By definition, the checking routine must interpret record data to do its job. Hence, it is valid to say that the logical schema must interpret record data; the physical database does not.

Valid data types for specific record fields within a database are also defined within the logical database. Traditional DBMSs typically allowed numeric data (such as integers, real numbers, and Boolean) and character data. Modern DBMSs also allow graphical and audio data, including uninterpreted data (large binary objects).

It may seem contradictory that a record field is uninterpreted at the logical schema level. Remember, however, that such fields are explicitly defined as uninterpreted. Moreover, records still must consist of one or more interpreted fields for the logical schema to exist. Otherwise, normal DBMS operations are impossible.

When engineers create a DP application by using a DBMS, most of their work involves defining and creating the logical schema. The DBMS provides rough tools that engineers use to construct a set of rules, data types, data sets, constraints (such as requiring unique record keys), and logical functions. These rules, types, sets, constraints, and functions combine to form a full-fledged DP application.

 One element of a good downsizing platform is the availability of suitable DBMSs ("engines" that provide engineers with a robust set of tools they can use to create full-fledged DP applications). Much of the second half of this book details the tools available for downsizing to NetWare v3.11.

The Conceptual Schema

The *conceptual schema* consists of the way that the information contained in the database is made available to users, including methods available to the user for gaining access to database records, the logical framework with which data is presented to the user, and methods available to the user for manipulating the data and introducing new data to the database.

The conceptual schema also includes data-entry programs, reporting programs, and data-access languages. There is no reason for a single database (or DP application) to support only one conceptual schema. Indeed, most DBMSs that are capable of supporting mainstream DP applications allow several conceptual schemas for a single database.

A conceptual schema must interpret a user's actions and translate them into a set of instructions that make sense to the logical schema. The logical schema, in turn, resolves instructions that it receives from the conceptual schema into machine language executed by the computer (most frequently by way of operating system calls).

The conceptual schema enables a user to perform data-processing tasks without requiring the user to have knowledge of data file names; index file names; record formats; index formats; relations among records and fields and files; and so on. Likewise, the logical schema enables the DBMS to do its job without worrying about the format instruction of the host computer's processor, and so on.

Just as the layering of the conceptual schema above the logical schema enables a database to support more than one conceptual schema, the layering of the logical schema above the physical database enables a particular DBMS to support different host computers and operating systems. Companies such as Oracle and Informix exist today, specifically because they use a layered approach to run their DBMSs on many different types of host computers and operating systems.

Table 3.1 lists the components of the physical database, the components of the logical schema of a DBMS, and the components of the conceptual schema of a DBMS.

Implementing Different Data Models

Within the constraints of the basic DBMS architecture (which were defined in the preceding sections), a DBMS can implement different data models. A *data model* defines the types of relations that can be formed among records, fields, and files; it also defines the conditions for establishing such relations.

Table 3.1

Components of the Physical Database

DBMS Element	Components Handled by that Element
Physical database	File system
	Read and write routines
	File and record locking
	Transaction control
	Media-device drivers
Logical Schema	User accounts
	User auditing
	User security
	Field data types
	Record format
	Index format
	Data dictionary
	Searching and sorting routines
	Relations among files and records
	Application Programming Interface (API)
Conceptual schema	User interface
	Data-entry program
	Reporting program
	Interactive data-access language
	Fourth-generation programming language (4GL)

Several kinds of data models exist: the hierarchical data model, the network data model, and the relational data model. Each of these three basic models is described in the following sections.

The Hierarchical Data Model

The oldest (and still one of the most widely used) data models for DP applications is the *hierarchical data model*. The hierarchical model establishes a hierarchy of records by linking higher-level record fields to lower-level records. For example, the root-level (highest) record in a hierarchical database may be a customer account. One field in the root customer record may be linked to a child record showing the customer's latest purchase. One field in the customer's latest purchase record may be linked to a record containing data about a specific product that the customer purchased. The hierarchical data model shown in figure 3.1 establishes one-to-many relationships among fields and records in a top-down fashion. A field can have many child records, but a child record can have only one parent field.

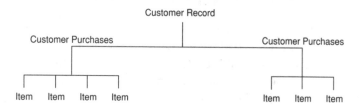

Figure 3.1:
A hierarchical data model.

The hierarchical data model forms many multilevel, one-to-many relations among fields and records. All relations are in the form of parent and child, however. A strictly enforced hierarchical data model enables parents to have many children, but children can have one parent only. Most hierarchical DBMSs (and DP applications based on them), however, allow the establishment of *soft* relations, which technically break the hierarchical model.

The hierarchical model is ideal for DP applications with very strictly defined and static conceptual schemas. Accounting packages are one example, as are Computer-Aided Manufacturing (CAM) or Materials Requirement Planning (MRP) applications. (The rigidity of the hierarchical data model makes it less suitable for more general-purpose applications that have several primary functions, however.)

 From the computer scientist's point of view, the best thing about the hierarchical data model is that finding a specific record (even in a large database) is almost always a fast operation. Hierarchical data models perform very well, which is why many OS file systems are based on this model.

The Network Data Model

The *network data model* enables many-to-many relations among fields and records. Although it may sound like anything is legal in the network data model, this is not true. The logical schema of the database establishes constraints on the types of relations that can be formed. (For example, the logical schema may dictate that relations can be formed only among fields of like or compatible data types.)

Actually, the network data model is based on the hierarchical data model. That is, most hard relations used for primary searching and sorting routines are hierarchical in nature; soft relations are used in second-phase searching and sorting. This provides the DBMS with performance advantages while also allowing flexibility in forming relations among fields and records.

You can view the network data model as a fleshy body built on a hierarchical skeleton. The network data model is more suitable for mainstream DP applications than is the hierarchical data model, which is why most DBMSs created in the last few years are based on the network data model.

The Relational Data Model

The *relational data model*, originally developed at IBM, is a highly-touted, little-understood phenomenon of computer science. To be a purely relational DBMS, a system must adhere to 12 "laws" that form the logically intriguing, impractical world in which the DBMS resides. Technicalities aside, the hallmark of the relational data model is that relations among fields and records can be established in an ad-hoc manner, according to the data-processing task of the moment.

In the relational data model, databases are defined in terms of *tables*, or matrixes, that consist of rows and columns. A *row* corresponds to a record in the database; a *column* corresponds to a field in a record. Multiple tables can be joined by establishing relations among them, based on rows or columns.

Virtual tables can be constructed by combining rows and columns from many tables; virtual tables can be further related to other tables, virtual and real. Such virtual tables are commonly referred to as *views*, or composite databases. During the process of constructing virtual tables, the DBMS (acting on instructions from the conceptual schema) can filter out rows or columns meeting a filter criteria, or can calculate virtual rows and columns by applying operators to the source values.

Although the physical database and logical schema of a relational model DBMS can be implemented in many different ways, the conceptual schema of a relational DBMS must support the ad-hoc joining and creation of tables and virtual tables. Furthermore, the conceptual schema must support the filtering and processing of virtual tables. These characteristics place requirements on the physical database and logical schema that surpass the analogous requirements imposed by the hierarchical and network data models.

A relational model DBMS must allow the joining of tables that have different row and column formats. In other words, dissimilar tables—which may have different numbers of columns or columns of differing data types (or both)—must be joinable by the DBMS. This requires the DBMS to implement special data types (such as the *NULL data type*, which means the value is "unknown") to fill in empty (non-matching) columns or columns that may not be compatible with corresponding columns in other joined tables.

 As a result of these requirements, relational data models never perform as well as hierarchical or network data models. Certainly, there are many techniques that the DBMS can use to improve the performance of a relational model, but the ad-hoc nature of this model requires most of the indexing to be performed at run time by the host computer's CPU, thus slowing performance significantly.

The relational data model persists (and even thrives) despite its performance disadvantages because of the enormous benefits of ad-hoc indexing, filtering, and joining of tables. It is possible (and even simple) to use an existing relational model database for future applications, the design and purpose of which is not known at the time the physical database and logical schema are constructed. Because of the possibilities of ad-hoc processing algorithms, construction of a conceptual schema for a relational model database can be much easier than for other types of database models. Most relational model DBMSs feature extremely flexible and powerful query languages, such as the Structured Query Language (SQL), to leverage the ad-hoc processing of the relational data model.

Using SQL (and other similar data-access languages), application designers can construct user interfaces, querying programs, and reporting programs without running into the barriers associated with the logical schema. This is not true for network data model and hierarchical data model DBMSs, which limit the types of things application designers can do at the conceptual level and impose more logical constraints on the processing of data.

Exploring Traditional Data-Processing Applications

Most traditional types of DP applications have long histories (in terms of the evolution of the computer, which is really not a very long time) and are basically the same at the logical schema and physical database levels. These traditional types of applications include the following:

- ❖ Accounting
- ❖ Materials Requirement Planning (MRP)
- ❖ Banking
- ❖ Point-of-sale
- ❖ Inventory management

These traditional types of applications represent the core activities of most large businesses. *Accounting applications* provide a wealth of financial, sales, and other information that executives use to perform all types of management functions, including finance, growth planning, and cost control.

MRP applications control the manufacturing process, including ordering and stocking of raw materials, scheduling production, and calculating the cost of manufactured goods.

Banking applications are used by banks and other financial institutions to process financial transactions, transfer funds, calculate interest, and amortize loans.

Point-of-sale applications record sales transactions, including cost of goods sold, price of goods, payment for goods, and store inventory.

Inventory-management applications track the level of inventory and record shipments received, shipments made, the value of inventory, and orders for new inventory.

All traditional types of DP applications perform related functions. In the largest, most vertically configured, and most computerized enterprises, these different types of DP applications are often consolidated into one "super application" that leverages the related tasks of individual applications.

The one thing that all traditional types of DP applications have in common is that they perform a lot of small transactions. For example, an inventory-management application records shipments of goods and received goods. A particular transaction, such as the receipt of a shipment, is small—probably less than a 200-byte record written to the physical database.

What makes these traditional applications so stressful to hardware and operating systems is the volume of transactions, not the nature of the transactions themselves. Depending on the scope of the application, it is not uncommon for a DP application to submit hundreds of transactions to the DBMS in a single second. Clearly, this level of activity—even though individual transactions are very small—places a prodigious burden on hardware and software.

Comparing Real-Time Performance to Volume Performance

Different types of DP applications have different performance requirements. Frequently, the differing requirements can be discussed in terms of real-time performance versus volume. *Real-time* refers to the capability of a DBMS (and also the capability of the underlying operating system and hardware) to accomplish a task (such as performing a transaction) within a fixed time period, such as a number of milliseconds. (A *millisecond* is 1/1000 of a second).

To guarantee that a task is accomplished within a given number of milliseconds, the host operating system must guarantee each task running on the computer access to the computer's CPU at regular intervals. (The length of these intervals depends on the real-time guarantees of the system in question.) To do this, the operating system must employ *preemptive multitasking* (the operating system must synchronously switch tasks). Synchronous task-switching is, by definition, preemptive because a particular task can be "switched" at any moment by the operating system.

Preemptive task-switching imposes overhead on the operating system because a task is not guaranteed to be in a specific state when it is preempted. Thus, the operating system must perform housekeeping every time it preempts a task to guarantee the integrity of the system as a whole. The alternative to preemption is a *nonpreemptive operating system,* in which the tasks themselves relinquish the CPU when they finish performing a small amount of work (a nonpreemptive operating system does not have to perform extra housekeeping when task-switching).

Because of the characteristics of preemption, a tension exists between real-time performance and volume performance. That is, a real-time system can guarantee that a transaction is processed in a given number of milliseconds. Over a period of time, however, the number of transactions performed by a preemptive system lags behind the number performed by a nonpreemptive system. Thus, an operating system must choose between obtaining the greatest number of transactions possible over a period of time versus guaranteeing that a specific transaction is processed within a number of milliseconds. (Although a nonpreemptive system produces a greater volume of transactions, there is no guarantee that any single transaction is processed within a defined time period.)

A nonpreemptive system processes the bulk of its transactions well within the parameters of a similar real-time system (for example, in a given number of milliseconds). There is always the odd transaction that takes seconds (as opposed to milliseconds) to be processed, however. In other words, the average time of processing all transactions falls within real-time constraints, but every single transaction does not.

Most DP applications do not have real-time requirements, but they have volume requirements. For example, in a point-of-sale application, it really does not matter if the sales clerk waits one second for a sale to be recorded, as long as the system keeps up with the volume of transactions being generated by every sales clerk. The types of applications that require real-time performance include factory automation, embedded-control systems, and (in some cases) stock-trading programs.

NetWare v3.11 is a nonpreemptive operating system. The designers of NetWare placed a higher priority on volume than on real-time response. NetWare does not provide immediate response—immediate response is not guaranteed, especially under high-load conditions.

As a result, NetWare is volume-oriented, which is what most traditional DP applications require. NetWare is not suitable for applications that control manufacturing machinery or that have strict real-time requirements.

Applying the Client-Server Model

Now that you have read a thorough discussion of DBMS theory in the context of DP applications, the question is "How do you apply traditional applications under the client-server model?" The most common method is to separate the DBMS at the conceptual schema level, run the back end (the physical database and logical schema) on the network server, and run the front end (the conceptual schema) on network workstations. When this is done, the back-end component is called the database *engine* or database *server*, and the front-end component is called *client software*.

Splitting the database at the conceptual schema level also has other advantages. Specifically, it is easier to support many different front ends. For example, a database engine running on NetWare v3.11 can support commands from client software running on different types of network workstations, such as PCs, UNIX stations, and Macintoshes. It also simplifies the support of different types of client software, including spreadsheets, interactive command-line utilities, and full-fledged graphical database interfaces.

Table 3.2 shows the client-server distribution of some of the DBMS components discussed in this chapter.

Table 3.2
Application of the Client-Server Model to Traditional Database Architecture

Component	Location
Physical Database	
Device drivers	Back end
Directory format	Back end
File format	Back end
Concurrency control	Back end
Transaction control	Back end
Logical Schema	
Record format	Back end and front end
Data dictionary	Back end
Indexing	Back end
User tracking	Back end and front end
User auditing	Back end and front end
Security	Back end
Data model	Back end
Searching and sorting	Back end
Conceptual Schema	
Data access language	Front end and back end
User interface	Front end

Notice that table 3.2 shows some items implemented in both the back end and the front end. If an element is implemented primarily in the back end, but must receive some cooperation or information exchange from the front end, it is designated as *back end and front end*. Conversely, if an element is implemented primarily in the front end but must receive some cooperation or information exchange from the back end, it is designated as *front end and back end*.

Summary

This chapter discussed the evolving database-management (DBMS) technology, as well as transaction control and concurrency issues.

You learned about DBMS architecture and ways to implement different data models. Traditional data-processing applications were explored and real-time performance was compared to volume performance.

Finally, you learned how to apply the client-server model.

 You read more about client-server DBMSs and DP applications in Chapters 17 through 20.

Part Two: NetWare 386 and Large-Scale Processing

The Architecture of NetWare v3.11

NetWare v3.11's Suitability for Downsizing

Topics covered in this chapter:

Configuring NetWare v3.11

Supporting NetWare Architecture

Utilizing Management Support

Managing Remotely

Routing Processes

Chapter 4

The Architecture of NetWare v3.11

Novell developed NetWare v3.11 as a successor to NetWare 2.x and has implemented a number of novel and unique features. NetWare v3.11 is a complete rewrite of NetWare for the Intel 80386 architecture. NetWare 2.x was written for the Intel 80236 (80% in C and 20% in Assembly language). Although NetWare v3.11 was also written 80% in C and 20% in Assembly language, it has greater flexibility and is more adaptable to changes. NetWare v3.11's architecture has been redesigned to overcome the resource limitations of earlier NetWare versions. This chapter examines some important elements of the NetWare v3.11 architecture.

NetWare v3.11 provides an open architecture and support for a rich variety of application program interfaces (APIs) that make it possible to provide third-party extensions and functionality to the network operating system (OS). In this open computing platform approach, application and network modules, such as additional transport protocols and database services, can be added much more easily based on a software architecture called the *NLM software bus* (see fig. 4.1).

 NLMs are discussed later in this chapter.

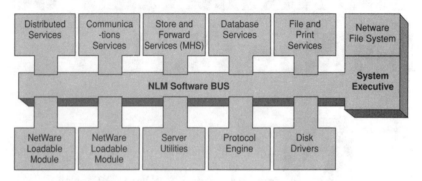

Figure 4.1:
The NLM software bus.

NetWare v3.11 and above began to provide support for multiple protocols at the server. In addition to SPX/IPX, which is the native transport protocol supported by NetWare, support was added for other protocols, such as AppleTalk Phase 2, TCP/IP, and OSI. Multiprotocol support is a key element in the NetWare v3.11 architecture. Support for AppleTalk on the server, for instance, allows integration with Macintosh machines. The Macintosh machines can run their native AppleTalk protocol and communicate with the AppleTalk stack on the NetWare v3.11 server. The Macintosh machines, therefore, can view the NetWare server as an AppleShare server.

Configuring NetWare v3.11

NetWare v3.11 represents a radical departure from earlier NetWare versions. One key difference is the dynamic manner in which NetWare v3.11 can be configured. Many important server parameters in NetWare v3.11 are not fixed during installation. They can be changed at any time without bringing down the server. Determining the number of communication buffers or the maximum number of open and indexed files is not necessary because they can be changed dynamically.

In many situations, the server can monitor its use of resources and tune itself accordingly, based on its history of parameter usage. The following list shows some elements of the NetWare v3.11 internal architecture that make it dynamically configurable. The following architectural elements are discussed in this chapter:

❖ NetWare Loadable Module (NLM)

❖ NetWare kernel

❖ Memory architecture

❖ Application services

The NetWare Loadable Module (NLM) Environment

In earlier NetWare versions, object modules selected during installation had to be "bound" together somehow. The mechanism used was *static linking*, or *generating NetWare*. In NetWare v3.11, NetWare generation is not necessary because object modules can be linked at run time or when they are loaded in memory. Linking at run time is called *dynamic linking*.

If you are familiar with OS/2 or Microsoft Windows, you probably have heard of Dynamic Link Libraries (DLLs). NetWare v3.11 NetWare Loadable Modules (NLMs), can act as DLLs. One difference is that, although OS/2 DLLs are linked at run time, NLMs are linked at load time.

NLMs can be viewed, therefore, as a group of cooperating software tasks or engines.

NLMs are activated by typing the command LOAD and then the name of the NetWare Loadable Module, such as:

```
LOAD NameOfNLM
```

NLMs supplied with NetWare are usually installed on the SYS:SYSTEM directory on the server. The one exception to this is BTRIEVE.NLM.

NLMs can be deactivated by unloading them using the UNLOAD command and the name of the NetWare Loadable Module, such as:

```
UNLOAD NameOfNLM
```

When an NLM is loaded, it occupies a certain portion of the server RAM and competes with other processes for CPU time. The amount of memory occupied by an NLM can vary, depending on the way the NLM is written. The amount of memory used can be monitored by using the MONITOR.NLM utility.

Some NLMs make system calls to allocate additional memory for the tasks they are performing. Because this requested memory can be released during execution, the amount of memory used by the NLM can vary during execution. When an NLM is unloaded, all allocated resources are returned to the NetWare OS.

NLMs can be linked, either by Novell or third-party developers, to establish a loading sequence. RSPX.NLM cannot be loaded, therefore, until REMOTE.NLM is loaded. When an NLM is loaded, it expects to have all the external interfaces it needs in memory already. If it cannot find a required external interface, an error message is reported and the NLM is not loaded. Certain NLMs, such as network card or disk drivers, can accept command-line parameters to modify the NLM's behavior. If these parameters are not specified, you are prompted for the parameter values. As an example, the WDPLUSSV NLM, a driver for Western Digital Star/ EtherCard PLUS, can be loaded in these two ways:

```
LOAD WDPLUSSV port=280 mem=D0000:200 int=3 frame=ETHERNET_802.3
```

or

```
LOAD WDPLUSSV
```

In the first example, all the parameters are specified on the command line in the parameter=value syntax. In the second example, the parameters are not specified. When WDCPLUSSV loads, it prompts the user for these parameter values.

Network card driver NLMs can be bound also to the protocol stack with which they will communicate. This protocol stack is also written in the form of an NLM. Although SPX and IPX are also NLMs, they are statically linked into NetWare, so you do not need to load them explicitly.

TCP/IP support is implemented in the form of the TCPIP.NLM. The Simple Network Management Protocol (SNMP) agent support is implemented as SNMP.NLM. In fact, any extensions to the server operating environment by third-party vendors is provided by NLMs. NLMs permeate the entire NetWare v3.11 architecture.

NLM utilities can be loaded whenever they are needed and unloaded after they are used. Other NLMs, especially drivers, should be loaded every time the server is booted. The commands to load them are stored in files with a NCF extension. The NCF files are similar to batch files under DOS, and contain commands for loading the driver NLMs. Configuration commands to establish the server operating environment, such as loading and binding of drivers, are stored in AUTOEXEC.NCF.

NLM names have an extension that is similar to a DOS extension. You can tell the nature of the NLM by examining the extension portion of its name (see table 4.1).

Table 4.1

Common Extensions Used for NLM Names

NLM Extension	Meaning
DSK	Disk driver
LAN	NIC driver
NAM	Name space modules
NLM	Management utilities Server applications

The CLIB NLM, a major programming interface for applications writers, provides access to the standard C library and many low-level functions exported by the NetWare kernel. The CLIB NLM has knowledge about the internal data structures used by NetWare v3.11 and exports this knowledge by using functions. NLMs, such as CLIB, usually export functions to other NLMs. They may also import functions from other NLMs. Other NLMs that want to gain access to the NetWare OS must do so by using functions exported by CLIB. The advantage is that, although the internal data structures of the OS might change in future releases, the function interface remains the same. This *data hiding* concept is used in well-designed programming interfaces.

Table 4.2

NLMs Supplied with NetWare v3.11

NLM Name	Description
CLIB	The standard C library function calls with extensions to include calls to the STREAMS interface and many low-level APIs.
EDIT	Used to modify or create text files with less than 8K at the server console on DOS and NetWare partitions. Particularly useful for modifying NCF batch files.
ETHERRPL	Implements Ethernet protocol stack to enable remote booting of Ethernet stations. Must be bound with Ethernet driver on server using ETHERNET_802.2 frames.
INSTALL	Major utility that performs installation functions such as server disk maintenance, loading NetWare v3.11 disks on server, server configuration, and product installation and configuration on the server.
IPXS	Implements IPX protocol for STREAMS services. Automatically binds to the TLI NLM, which must be loaded before IPXS is loaded.
MAC	Macintosh name space module. Implements support for Macintosh file names on server.
MATHLIB	Interfaces with the math coprocessor on the server. Makes use of CLIB, which must be loaded before MATHLIB is loaded.
MATHLIBC	Emulates the math coprocessor functions in software. Used on a server (Intel 80386) that does not have a math coprocessor. Makes use of CLIB, which must be loaded before MATHLIBC is loaded.
MONITOR	Major utility that performs file-server monitoring.

Table 4.2—continued

NLM Name	Description
NMAGENT	Used for registering NIC drivers and passing network-management parameters. Must be loaded before the NIC driver is loaded. If the NIC driver is not loaded, the OS tries to autoload NMAGENT.
NVINSTAL	IBM's NetView Management Agent support on the server.
PSERVER	Print server.
PCN2RPL	Used to enable remote boot for IBM PCN2 NIC.
REMOTE	Implements RMF at server.
RS232	Asynchronous communications driver. Used for remote management support.
RSPX	SPX/IPX protocol, used for RMF to send keystrokes and screen information across LAN.
SNMP	SNMP Agent support on server.
SNMPLOG	Logs SNMP trap messages.
SPXCONFG	Used to configure SPX parameters.
SPXS	Implements SPX protocol for STREAMS services. Automatically binds to the TLI NLM, which must be loaded before SPXS is loaded.
STREAMS	Implements STREAMS protocol. Must be loaded before CLIB is loaded.
TCPIP	Implements TCP/IP protocols.
TLI.NLM	Transport Layer Interface.
TCPCONFG	Used for configuring TCP/IP.
TOKENRPL	Used to enable remote boot for IBM Token Ring network boards.

Table 4.2—continued

NLM Name	Description
UPS	Implements the software link between server and Uninterruptible Power Supply (UPS) device.
VREPAIR	Volume repair utility that corrects volume problems.

Kernel Architecture

In the context of this discussion, *kernel* means a group of routines that are central to the operating system's purpose. The NetWare kernel consists of these components:

- ❖ A system executive
- ❖ A scheduler
- ❖ Native protocols, such as SPX/IPX and NCP
- ❖ A router mechanism
- ❖ Memory management: file cache, permanent pool, and memory allocation pool (alloc pool)
- ❖ A file system that can support multiple name spaces, and file and record locking
- ❖ Semaphore management
- ❖ TTS
- ❖ Hooks for multiple protocol support (TCP/IP, OSI, and so on) and multiple ODI drivers

The list shows that the NetWare kernel keeps busy doing a number of processes. The kernel can perform these processes simultaneously by using a scheduling mechanism. The NetWare *scheduler* is a group of processes in the kernel that control the execution of all other processes. It determines which task (including NLMs) should run next, but not how long a task should run. This type of scheduling mechanism is *non-preemptive*.

NetWare expects processes to be well-behaved and relinquish control of the CPU frequently so that other processes can run. The alternative to non-preemptive scheduling is *preemptive* scheduling, in which the scheduler determines how long a task should run. Preemptive scheduling is common in many desktop operating systems and operating systems that perform time sharing between user applications.

In an operating system that is based on preemptive scheduling, time is a resource that is shared by processes, but the scheduler determines how much time a process should have. Preemptive scheduling works well when fairness issues are more important than system throughput. In preemptive scheduling, a process is given a specific amount of time, and, when the time has expired, the CPU is assigned to another task, regardless of what it is already doing. Assigning the CPU to another waiting process may be more democratic and fair, but it has an adverse impact on the system throughput, especially when critical processes are interrupted.

NetWare adopts the philosophy that a process can monopolize the CPU for as long as it needs to in order to complete critical processes. Processes should be well-behaved and yield the CPU to others when they finish performing critical processes.

The nonpreemptive scheduling nature of NetWare makes its scheduler simple and fast. The decision to relinquish control of the CPU is left to the application running on the server.

Memory Architecture for NetWare v3.11

NetWare v3.11 manages its memory using a dynamic approach. A maximum of 4 gigabytes (G) of RAM is available. This limit is due to the Intel 80386 microprocessor's 32 address lines. The maximum RAM for this machine is 2^{32}. The Intel 80386 architecture can support a segmented address space—as much as 48 terabytes (T)—but NetWare v3.11 does not make use of segmented memory. Instead, it uses the *flat memory model*. NetWare v3.11 sets all segments to the same physical offset, but because a segment is 4G on the Intel 80386, it is adequate for now because no machines have been built yet with 4G of RAM.

A controversial aspect of NetWare's memory use is that all programs, the OS, and NLMs run in ring 0 of the Intel 80386 architecture. In OS/2, the Intel 80386 architecture defines four rings: rings 0 to 3 (see fig. 4.2). The OS kernel runs at ring 0, and other programs run at one of the outer rings. Programs running at ring 3, for example, can access the RAM used by programs running in ring 3, but cannot directly access RAM for programs running at rings 2, 1, or 0. Therefore, if the OS kernel is running in ring 0, a program at ring 3 has to make an inter-ring gate call to make service requests from the OS kernel.

If the program goes haywire because of a software bug, it cannot touch the OS kernel. The program can crash, but the OS kernel is unmoved. This architecture makes the system more reliable, at the expense of speed, because of the inter-ring call overhead. OS/2 is an example of an operating system that uses the ring architecture.

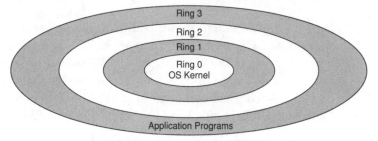

Figure 4.2:
Intel 80386 processor ring architecture.

NetWare v3.11 does not use this ring architecture. The NetWare OS, NLMs, and all programs run in ring 0. What NetWare loses in reliability by running at ring 0, it gains in simplicity and speed. Moreover, Novell has an NLM certification program to check the reliability of third-party NLMs. Developers can use tools such as those from Nu-Mega to detect badly behaved NLMs.

NetWare v3.11 does not recognize RAM automatically beyond 16M in some systems. You then must use the REGISTER MEMORY command at the console. This command has the following syntax:

```
REGISTER MEMORY  memoryStartInHex memoryLengthInHex
```

To add 4M of memory above 16M (for a total of 20M RAM), therefore, you use:

```
REGISTER MEMORY 1000000    250000
```

 This command can be added to the AUTOEXEC.NCF file for automatic registration of memory when the server is booted.

For EISA-based machines, the SET command must be used for registering memory above 16M.

NetWare v3.11 uses memory for a variety of functions. A minimum of 2M of RAM is required; at least 4M is recommended, however, to run useful NLMs.

Figure 4.3 shows memory utilization at the server. This figure shows that DOS uses RAM up to 640K. DOS is necessary to boot the server. When the NetWare v3.11 OS loads, it takes up residence in *extended memory*, which is memory above 1M. After NetWare v3.11 is loaded, DOS can be unloaded if more memory is needed for the OS. DOS is unloaded by using of the following command:

```
REMOVE DOS
```

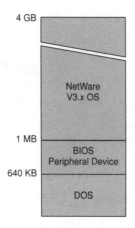

Figure 4.3:
NetWare v3.11 memory map.

With DOS unloaded, NetWare v3.11 uses the lower memory for file caching. Using the EXIT command with DOS unloaded results in a warm reboot of the server. This technique is sometimes used to reboot the server by using RMF from a remote workstation. Memory that the NetWare operating system and DOS do not use is given to three memory pools (see fig. 4.4).

NetWare v3.11 allocates as little memory as possible to the permanent and Alloc memory pools, allowing these pools to grow or shrink based on demand. Memory not allocated to these pools and the OS kernel is used for file caching.

The *file-cache buffer pool* is used to store file blocks from the most frequently used files. It uses a Least Recently Used (LRU) algorithm to manage file-block usage. Two pools, *movable* and *nonmovable*, interact with the file cache buffer pool. They obtain their memory from the file cache buffer pool and return memory to it when they finish. The movable pool is used for system tables that change size, such as FATs and hash tables. Tables and objects in the movable pool can be moved around in memory to prevent memory fragmentation.

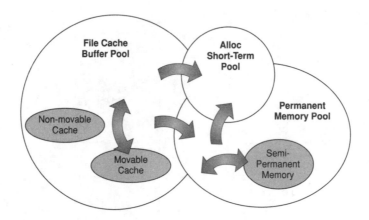

Figure 4.4:
NetWare v3.11 memory pools.

 It makes sense to allocate relatively large objects from the movable pool because this method yields the maximum payoff in reduced fragmentation if objects must be moved. Moving memory to get larger chunks of free memory sometimes is called *garbage collection*, which is a popular technique used in many operating systems such as OS/2 and Mac OS. The nonmovable pool is used for NetWare Loadable Modules.

The *permanent memory pool* is used for long-term memory needs, such as directory cache buffers and packet receive buffers. Although it is called permanent memory, it is very dynamic. A portion of the permanent pool is static, but the rest is semidynamic. Communication buffers are an example of permanent pool memory use.

When NetWare loads and initializes itself, it sets up a certain number of communication buffers. With increasing network activity,

NetWare allocates additional communication buffers to store the extra data packets. These buffers are allocated from permanent memory, but, after they are allocated, they are not released even if network activity subsides. This approach allocates enough resources to handle peak loads on the network.

The *alloc memory pool* is used to store information on the following:

- ❖ Drive mappings
- ❖ Service request buffers
- ❖ SAP tables
- ❖ Open/Lock files and semaphores
- ❖ User connection information
- ❖ NLM tables
- ❖ Queue manager tables
- ❖ Messages queued for broadcasting

The alloc memory pool is used temporarily for fulfilling short-term processing needs. During NetWare execution, data objects may need to be created dynamically and destroyed after the OS finishes using them. The following list shows some examples of this short-term use:

- ❖ SAP table entries may need to be allocated to hold SAP advertisements from new servers added to the network.
- ❖ When drive mappings are deleted, memory used for storing mapping information must be released.
- ❖ When a user logs in to the network, information must be stored for the network connection. When a user logs out, the memory used for the connection information must be released.

Memory used for the alloc pool is managed by a series of linked lists of free memory blocks. Using this linked-list approach, the OS can quickly find the memory it needs. When memory is needed, it is allocated from this free list. When the memory is released, it returns to the free memory list, where it can be reused. This approach prevents memory fragmentation.

NetWare tries to allocate memory from the alloc pool for NLMs. As memory requirements for NLMs increase, the alloc pool is depleted. To satisfy the NLM memory requirement, NetWare borrows memory from the file cache buffer pool. This memory then is not returned to the file-cache pool, even if the NLMs are unloaded.

In a worst-case scenario, many NLMs are loaded and unloaded frequently. Under these circumstances, the permanent borrowing of memory from the file cache area can deplete it severely and degrade the server performance. NetWare has control mechanisms to prevent this *memory leakage* from occurring.

 You can limit the size of the alloc pool by using the SET command. Although the default limit usually is 2M, it can be set as high as 16M or as low as 50K.

The amount of RAM needed for a server depends on the size of DOS, NetWare, and any name-space support on the server's volumes. A certain amount of RAM is necessary for server file caching, the permanent memory pool, and the alloc memory pool.

The following two sections present the rules for estimating server RAM and a simple case study that uses these rules.

Server RAM Use

The NetWare operating system kernel needs about 2M of RAM. For every DOS partition and NetWare volume at the server, the amount of megabytes of server RAM needed can be estimated by the following equation:

M(DOS) = 0.023 × volume size (M) / block size (default is 4)

For each volume with added name space, the amount of megabytes of server RAM needed can be estimated by this equation:

M(name space) = 0.032 × volume size (M) / block size (default is 4)

The remaining memory is used for file caching, permanent pool, and alloc memory.

Estimating Server RAM: A Case Study

Suppose that you have been called as a consultant for the fictitious Kali Corporation to estimate how much RAM is necessary to install a NetWare v3.11 server. You have determined the following server requirements:

❖ There are four volumes: DOS, SYS, a UNIX volume, and a Macintosh volume.

❖ The size of the volumes and the block size to be used are shown in this table:

Volume	Size	Block Size
DOS	60M	4K
SYS	120M	4K
UNIXVOL	600M	8K
MACVOL	100M	4K

You can calculate the server RAM by using the following worksheet:

NetWare v3.11 Server RAM Estimation

1. NetWare kernel RAM (2M):	2M

2. RAM for server volumes:

$M(DOS\ or\ NetWare) = 0.023 \times$ volume size (M) / block size

$M(name\ space) = 0.032 \times$ volume size (M) / block size

a. $M(DOS) = 0.023 \times 60\ / 4 = 0.345$	0.345M
b. $M(SYS) = 0.023 \times 120\ /\ 4 =$	0.69M
c. $M(UNIXVOL) = 0.032 \times 600\ /\ 8 = 2.4M$	2.4M
d. $M(MACVOL) = 0.032 \times 100\ /4 = 0.8M$	0.8M

Total RAM for server volumes	4.235M
3. Total RAM for server ([1] + [2]):	6.235M
4. Total RAM to nearestM	7.0 M
5. Actual physical RAM:	8.0M
6. RAM for file caching and other memory pools:	1.765M
([5] – [3])	

The worksheet shows that the server needs 6.235M. It used a physical size of 8M because additional RAM (1.765M) is well spent for file caching.

Application services are functions that the operating system provides to developers. These functions enable you to add different "networking" features to applications.

Application services include printing services, message services, accounting services, diagnostic services, security services, and bindery services.

Examining Multiple Transport Protocol Support

NetWare makes use of the SPX/IPX protocols derived from XNS, which are the native protocols that NetWare supports. Before examining the other protocols that NetWare v3.11 can support, you should understand the strengths and weaknesses of SPX/IPX.

The transport protocols play an important role in the performance and functionality of a network operating system such as NetWare. Fast transport protocols result in a fast OS; slow transport protocols make an OS sluggish. A transport protocol that is fast on a LAN may be slow on a WAN. In terms of functionality, if the transport protocols are obscure or not well known, interconnecting with other networks is difficult.

Native Transport Protocols in NetWare v3.11

The native transport protocols used by NetWare are IPX for layer 3 and SPX for layer 4.

In most situations, a layer 5 protocol is not necessary. If an application is written to make use of NetBIOS protocol, an optional layer 5 can be provided that implements it. The NetBIOS software emulator implements its services by making use of the SPX protocols. The transport protocols are shown in figure 4.5.

The native NetWare protocols were derived from the Xerox XNS (Xerox Network Standard) protocols. Table 4.3 shows the relationship between XNS and NetWare protocols.

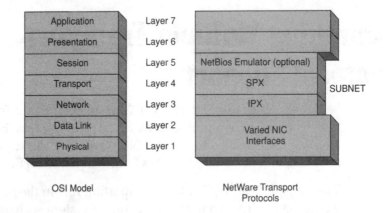

Figure 4.5:
The relationship between OSI and NetWare transport protocols.

Table 4.3
XNS and NetWare Protocols

XNS Protocol	NetWare Protocol
Internet Datagram Protocol (IDP)	Internet Packet Exchange (IPX)
Packet Exchange Protocol (PEP)	Packet Exchange Protocol (PXP)
Sequenced Packet Protocol (SPP)	Sequenced Packet Exchange (SPX)

Novell based its transport protocols on XNS because these protocols had the reputation of working efficiently in a LAN environment. XNS protocols were not designed to be used for wide area networks (WANs), which have larger time delays and lower data rates. Novell's IPX and SPX protocols suffer, therefore, from the same limitations as XNS for WANs. Novell offers a Packet Burst NLM that implements a streamlined version of its protocols for WANs to overcome some of these limitations. Packet Burst NLM enables a stream of packets to be sent without requiring an acknowledgment for each of them. A single acknowledgment can acknowledge a stream of packets that is sent. This *sliding window* technique is common for many protocols designed to run on wide-area links that have high delays and low bandwidths.

The IPX protocol provides the capability to send data across different interconnected LANs. IPX is a datagram (connectionless) service. SPX provides a virtual circuit (connections-oriented) service for applications that need it. Because SPX has a larger overhead for processing time, NetWare avoids this overhead for its internal operation.

Figure 4.6 shows an IPX packet encapsulated by an Ethernet packet. The IPX packet in turn encapsulates upper-layer protocols such as SPX and NCP. Table 4.4 summarizes the meaning of the fields in the IPX packet.

Table 4.4
IPX Packet Structure

Field	Meaning
Checksum	Optional 1's complement checksum
Length	Byte length of IPX packet
Transport Control	Used by routers as a "hop count" field
Packet Type	Identifies type of data encoded in the data portion of IPX packet
Destination Network Number	Uniquely identifies destination network from a number of interconnected networks

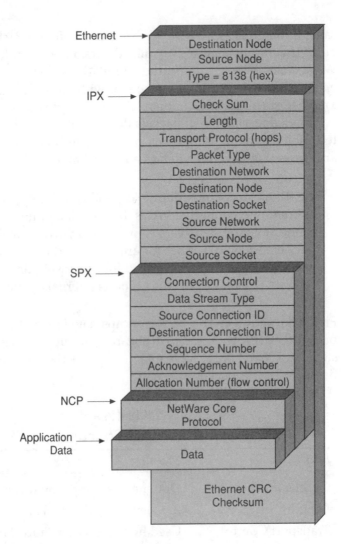

Figure 4.6:
An IPX packet.

Table 4.4—continued

Field	Meaning
Destination Node Address	Uniquely identifies the node address of the destination station
Destination Socket	Software address in destination node
Source Network Number	Uniquely identifies source network from a number of interconnected networks
Source Node Address	Uniquely identifies the node address of the sending station
Source Socket	Software address in sending node

The single most important application layer protocol that NetWare provides is NetWare Core Protocol (NCP). Without it, none of the file services offered by NetWare is possible. Many reference materials mistakenly show the NCP protocol as belonging to layer 5 or layer 6. NCP provides remote services to client nodes and rightfully belongs in layer 7 of the OSI model. Some of the misunderstanding about NCP functions may occur because Novell is reluctant to reveal details about the NCP protocol. Developers can obtain, for a large sum of money, details of the NCP protocols after they sign appropriate nondisclosure agreements.

The following list shows a few of the functions provided by NCP:

- ❖ Opens a file under different modes
- ❖ Closes operations on an open file
- ❖ Reads data blocks from an open file
- ❖ Writes data blocks to an open file
- ❖ Gets a list of directory entries
- ❖ Manipulates the server database (bindery)

❖ Connects high-level services

❖ Synchronizes operations

The NCP is used for all requests for services by the clients and for the server's response to these requests. The NCP provides its own session control and sequence control rather than relying on SPX, a transport layer protocol that provides this function. The NCP protocol running on IPX is very streamlined, therefore, by avoiding the overhead of layers 4, 5, and 6.

Figure 4.7 shows the general structure of the NCP packet. The Request Type field determines the type of NCP packet, such as Connection Request or Negotiate Buffer Size. The client assigns the Sequence Number field by starting with an initial value of 1 after the connection is established. Every request by the client is assigned a sequence number that is one higher than the preceding request. The server's NCP response contains the same sequence as the corresponding NCP request. The client then can ensure that it is receiving the correct response for its request. The client also allows the shell and the server to determine when a packet is lost.

Other Transport Protocols in NetWare v3.11

Multiple transport protocol support includes support for protocols other than SPX/IPX, such as TCP/IP, AppleTalk, LU6.2, and FTAM. Support for other transport protocols, such as DECnet transport and XNS, can be added easily later, thanks to the flexibility of the OS architecture. The transport protocols are implemented in the form of NetWare Loadable Modules.

This implementation enables the network manager to dynamically configure support for multiple protocols. The practical benefit of multiple transport protocols is that the NetWare v3.11 server can exist and operate in non-Novell environments. As you learned in

Chapter 3, interoperability exists at the transport layers, a key step in achieving interoperability in a multi vendor environment.

Other than SPX/IPX, the single most important protocol supported by NetWare is TCP/IP because of TCP/IP's emergence as the protocol of choice in a multivendor environment. Support for TCP/IP on NetWare v3.11 enables it to be integrated easily with UNIX networks and other networks that use TCP/IP as their native protocol or as an interconnectivity protocol (see fig. 4.7).

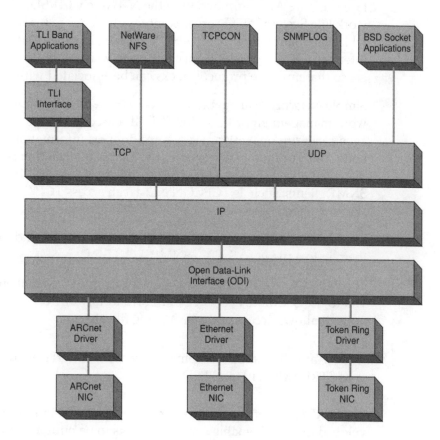

Figure 4.7:
NetWare TCP/IP architecture.

Because TCP/IP support includes IP routing, the NetWare v3.11 server can be used as an IP router in addition to being used as an IPX router. IP tunneling support exists also: the IPX packets can be encapsulated in an IP packet and routed ("tunneled") by way of an Internet transport consisting of IP routers. Two NetWare LANs can be connected, therefore, over the large distances spanned by Internet.

The BSD 4.3 socket interface and its AT&T Transport Layer Interface (TLI) are APIs supplied with the NetWare v3.11 SDK. The Network File System (NFS) server comes with NetWare for NFS, which is an implementation of SUN's NFS. The Open Datalink Interface (ODI) is a flexible mechanism to write network card drivers so that multiple protocol stacks can be associated with an NIC.

Simple Network Management Protocol (SNMP) is a popular network management protocol for TCP/IP-based networks. SNMP agents can run on NetWare servers and report information about node configuration and status. The available information is a set of managed objects called a *Management Information Base* (MIB). SNMP clients, such as TCPCON NLM, can access TCP/IP protocol stack managed objects.

The SNMPLOG NLM processes SNMP trap messages and logs them in to a file in SYS:ETC/SNMP$LOG.BIN.

The TCPLOG NLM presents a menu-driven interface that enables you to use SNMP to access TCP/IP MIB locally or from a remote node. It allows access to the SNMP log file also.

 NetWare v3.11 supports common transport interfaces such as STREAMS, TLI, and BSD sockets.

The STREAMS general-purpose transport protocol interface, developed by AT&T, enables protocol stacks to be built dynamically. The head of the STREAMS protocol is the STREAMS interface, and the tail is usually the network card driver. Between the head and the tail, any number of protocol elements can be connected as if they are part of a string or stream. These protocol elements can be the transport and network protocols, such as SPX/IPX or TCP/IP.

The Transport Layer Interface (TLI), also defined by AT&T, is functionally similar to STREAMS. Like STREAMS, TLI also provides a uniform transport interface to upper-layer protocols. Applications then can be written to a common programming interface, which makes them portable across different environments implementing the same TLI interface. TLI differs from STREAMS in the details of the mechanism and the interface to upper-layer protocols. The NetWare v3.11 TLI implementation follows the spirit of the AT&T definition, but they differ. TLI currently supports only SPX/IPX and TCP/IP.

The Berkeley System Distribution (BSD) socket interface, developed as part of BSD UNIX at the University of California at Berkeley, is a popular and simple interface to the TCP/IP protocols. Many programmers are fond of the BSD socket interface and prefer it over the more general (and more complicated) STREAMS and TLI interface.

NetWare v3.11 supports alternative frame-encapsulation techniques at the data link layer of the OSI model. This support is valuable for supporting multiple protocol stacks at the server. The key to providing different frame-encapsulation schemes is in the FRAME parameter that can be set when binding a protocol stack to a driver.

The FRAME parameter can be used for Ethernet and token ring NICs and tells the NIC driver the type of header to use for packets. This parameter controls the MAC layer encapsulation.

Many modern Ethernet NICs can generate either IEEE 802.3 encapsulation or Ethernet II (version 2.0) encapsulation. NetWare's default Ethernet encapsulation is IEEE 802.3 (see fig. 4.8). It corresponds to a FRAME value of ETHERNET_802.3.

In practical terms, the NetWare server by default can speak only to stations or other computers that can understand the IEEE 802.3 headers in the packets. Many non-Novell networks, such as UNIX-based networks or DECnet, use Ethernet II encapsulation. To communicate with these networks, NetWare provides the flexibility of changing the MAC layer encapsulation to Ethernet II (see fig. 4.9). The FRAME parameter in the LOAD NIC_DRIVER command is set to ETHERNET_II. Other values for the FRAME parameter for Ethernet are ETHERNET_802.2 and ETHERNET_SNAP.

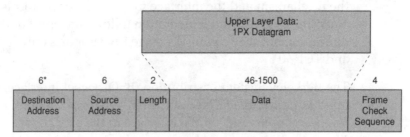

Figure 4.8:
NetWare's default FRAME encapsulation for Ethernet.

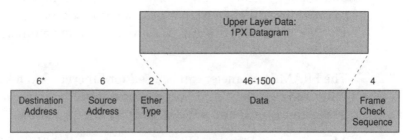

Figure 4.9:
Ethernet II FRAME encapsulation.

If ETHERNET_802.2 is used for the FRAME parameter, it implies an IEEE 802.3 MAC layer encapsulation, but, in addition, the data portion of the IEEE 802.3 frame contains a IEEE 802.2 frame (see fig. 4.10). Using LLC, multiple sessions are possible between Link Service Access Points (LSAPs). If NetWare v3.11 is being used on a network that uses IEEE 802.2, the NIC driver should be configured for using IEEE 802.2 encapsulation. If it is not, nodes that expect IEEE 802.2 encapsulation cannot communicate over the network.

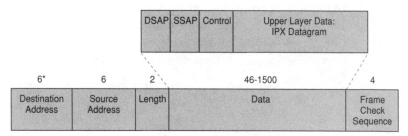

FRAME = Ethernet 802.2

Figure 4.10:
IEEE 802.2 frame encapsulation.

The "SNAP" in ETHERNET_SNAP stands for *Sub-Network Access Protocol*. SNAP, described in RFC 1042, was developed as a means to send IP datagrams and Address Resolution Protocols (ARP) used in the Internet over IEEE 802.3, IEEE 802.4 (token bus), IEEE 802.5 (token ring) and FDDI networks.

IP datagrams historically have been tied to Ethernet II frames and SNAP offers a way to transport them across non-Ethernet II networks. The SNAP mechanism is general enough, however, to be used by other protocols, such as AppleTalk Phase 2, used for Macintosh networks. Because NetWare v3.11 supports AppleTalk- and TCP/IP-based networks, it defines a FRAME value of

ETHERNET_SNAP for Ethernet and TOKEN_RING_SNAP for token-ring networks.

Figure 4.11 shows the use of SNAP. The first three bytes of IEEE 802.2 and the SNAP protocol are the same; that is, the LLC headers are the same. This statement is not surprising because SNAP was designed to use IEEE 802.2. In SNAP, a special value of AA (hex) for the Destination Service Access Point (DSAP) and Source Service Access Point (SSAP) in the LLC header means that the next five bytes (40 bits) contain a special *protocol identifier*. The first three bytes of the protocol identifier represent the Organizational Unit Identifier (OUI); as its name suggests, it is unique to an organization. Apple's OUI, for example, is 00 00 F8 (hex). The remaining two bytes contain information similar to the Ether Type field used for Ethernet.

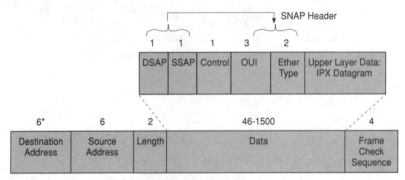

FRAME = Ethernet 802.2

Figure 4.11:
SNAP frame encapsulation for Ethernet.

The translation of an Ethernet II frame to a SNAP format is shown in figure 4.12. The OUI is assumed to be 00 00 F8. In this translation, the size of the frame grows by eight bytes, which represents the SNAP header length. If the original Ethernet II had a maximum size of 1,500 bytes for the data size, it would translate to a data frame size of 1,508. This number exceeds the maximum data frame size of 1,500 bytes for IEEE 802.3, and can potentially cause problems for IEEE 802.3 networks.

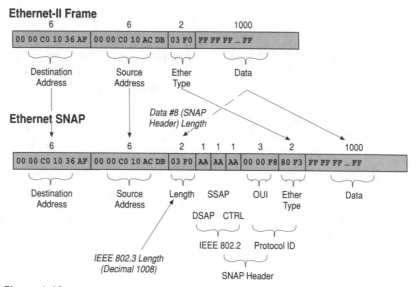

Figure 4.12:

Translation of original Ethernet II frame to ETHERNET_SNAP in NetWare v3.11.

For Token Ring networks, the possible FRAME values are TOKEN_RING and TOKEN_RING_SNAP. TOKEN_RING uses IEEE 802.2 header in its data portion, and TOKEN_RING_SNAP uses the SNAP header in the data portion of the token ring frame (see fig. 4.13).

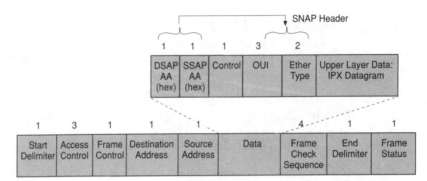

FRAME = Token Ring SNAP

Figure 4.13:
SNAP frame encapsulation for token ring.

TOKEN_RING_SNAP and ETHERNET_SNAP can be used for supporting TCP/IP applications on Token Ring protocol's frame and Ethernet, respectively. The different frame types are summarized in table 4.5.

Table 4.4
FRAME Parameter Values

FRAME	Meaning
ETHERNET_802.3	Default Ethernet encapsulation
ETHERNET_II	Ethernet II encapsulation; uses Ether Type value of 8137 (hex) for IPX packets
ETHENET_802.2	LLC encapsulation in Ethernet data
ETHERNET_SNAP	SNAP encapsulation in Ethernet data
TOKEN_RING	Default Token Ring encapsulation
IEEE 802.2	(LLC) encapsulation in Token Ring data
TOKEN_RING_SNAP	SNAP encapsulation in Token Ring data

The amount of RAM needed for a server depends on the size of DOS, NetWare, and any multiple name space partitions. A certain amount of RAM is necessary for server file caching, the permanent memory pool, and the Alloc memory pool.

Supporting Multiple Files Systems

One of the problems in achieving data-level interoperability (refer to Chapter 3) is that different client workstations use different file systems because their operating systems are different. The Macintosh OS uses two files: a data fork and a resource fork to represent a file folder. OS/2 and UNIX allow longer file names than DOS does, and the OS/2 High-Performance File System has improved performance and security over DOS.

NetWare v3.11 enables support for multiple file systems by implementing a general, or universal, file system at the server. A client's file system can be mapped to the NetWare v3.11 file system. The practical benefit is that Macintosh, UNIX, and DOS workstations can store files on the NetWare v3.11 server and can perform operations on them.

Multiple name space support is implemented by running the appropriate name space NLM at the server.

Support for the Network File System

The Network File System (NFS) is a popular server architecture on UNIX networks. It was developed by SUN Microsystems and is licensed to a large number of vendors. NFS makes possible a remote file system that can be accessed across a LAN by clients that may be running different operating systems. Because NFS traditionally has been implemented on UNIX, its servers are UNIX-based servers.

The NetWare for NFS product, available from Novell, can run as an NLM on the NetWare v3.11 server. It must be purchased separately because it is not included as part of NetWare v3.11.

Support for OSI's File Transfer Access Management (FTAM)

The ideas behind the development of File Transfer Access Management (FTAM) are similar to those for NFS. FTAM provides a virtual store at a machine that can be accessed by other FTAM clients (called *initiators*). FTAM, part of the Government Open Systems Interconnection Profile (GOSIP) 1.0 and 2.0 recommendations, is a procurement guideline for federal agencies to buy OSI-compliant products. FTAM, a layer 7 protocol, is included in the GOSIP document.

The NetWare for FTAM product, available from Novell, can run as an NLM on the NetWare v3.11 server. It must be purchased separately because it is not included as part of NetWare v3.11.

 NetWare v3.11 comes with a backup NLM utility, called SBACKUP.NLM which enables the backup of files to take place directly at the server. In previous versions of NetWare, backup-typically wereperformed at a client station across the network. If the network was down, backups could not be performed. SBACKUP enables backups to be performed even if the network is down. SBACKUP can be used to back up all possible files, including Macintosh files.

Utilizing Management Support

NetWare v3.11 comes with support for an SNMP agent that can run on the server. The SNMP NLM acts as an agent for remote clients. It has an understanding of MIB objects relating to TCP/IP and can generate trap messages, as required by the TCP/IP protocol stack. No support exists yet for a full-blown SNMP manager NLM on NetWare v3.11. Rather, an NLM called SNMPLOG can be used for logging trap events generated by SNMP agents. The SNMPLOG can be considered to be a client of the SNMP NLM agent that runs on the server.

In addition to support for SNMP, NetWare v3.11 supports IBM's NetView. This support consists of a group of NLMs that enable a token ring adapter, installed in a NetWare v3.11 server, to forward NetView alerts to a NetView host. The NetWare Management Agent for NetView NLM (NVINSTAL NLM) responds also to statistics requests from an IBM host.

A number of management NLMs, such as Frye Utilities and Monitrix, provide proprietary management capabilities. The number of management tools is likely to grow as NetWare v3.11 evolves and matures. Some of these management tools likely will come directly from Novell.

Managing Remotely

The Remote Management Facility (RMF) is a boon to many network managers. It permits server administration from a remote location, such as any workstation on the network. RMF enables users with console-level privileges to execute server console commands at remote workstations, as if they were actually using the keyboard and monitor on the server.

To support RMF, two NLMs, called the RCONSOLE.NLM and RSPX.NLM, must be run on the server. The workstation that runs the remote console must run a program called RCONSOLE.EXE. This program establishes connections with RCONSOLE.NLM running on the server using the SPX protocol. This connection allows keyboard strokes at the workstation to be sent to the server, and screen-image changes at the server to be sent to the remote workstation. The net effect of this process is that the workstation "takes over" the server console.

When RCONSOLE.NLM is run on the server, it uses the Server Advertising Protocol (SAP) to advertise its existence. Servers and routers record the SAP broadcast in an internal temporary database. When RCONSOLE is run at a workstation, it can query any server for servers that are available for remote management. The list of remote servers available for remote management are shown on a list. The user can select from this list a server to be managed remotely.

After providing the correct password, which is set when RCONSOLE.NLM is loaded on the server, the user can take over the remote server console. Any command that can be run at the server, therefore, can be run at the workstation, including the capability to run console utilities such as MONITOR, INSTALL, and VREPAIR; and the LOAD and UNLOAD commands to load and unload NLMs.

 RCONSOLE also has the capability to perform remote management using the serial port. This capability is handy when the network is down: a modem can be connected to the serial port on the server, and a user can use a modem and telephone line to dial in and perform remote management. For performing remote management over a dial-up line, the RS232.NLM must be run on the server.

Routing Processes

All NetWare servers are capable of acting as internetwork routers for the IPX protocol. Additionally, ordinary PC workstations can be configured to act as routers. Because servers perform the dual role of router and server, such configurations are called *internal routers*. If a PC workstation is set up to perform DOS and routing functions, it is a *nondedicated router* also; if it is set up to perform only routing functions, it is called a *dedicated router*. Because the routing is performed on a separate external device, these routers are called *external routers*.

Figure 4.14 shows the routing processes running on a router. This routing process is an integral part of a NetWare server. In addition to IPX routing, NetWare v3.11 servers can be set up as IP routers using TCP/IP protocol support. The routing protocol used for IP in NetWare v3.11 is RIP. (The RIP used here is different from Novell RIP.)

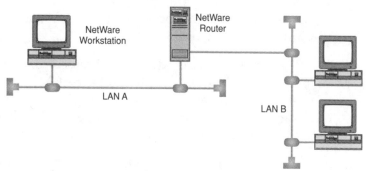

Figure 4.14:
NetWare router processes.

The MultiProtocol Router can be used to support routing of other protocols. This NLM runs on a NetWare server and performs routing for OSI, AppleTalk, NetBIOS, IPX, and TCP/IP. Used in conjunction with WAN Links, it can provide routing over wide-area links. Routers from vendors such as Cisco perform similar functionality, but at a higher performance and cost. The NetWare MultiProtocol router, on the other hand, can provide routing for small networks at a much lower cost.

In addition to routing, the MultiProtocol router provides Telnet, X-Windows, SNMP, and Point-to-Point Protocol (PPP) support. The Telnet service is particularly valuable because it enables stations running a Telnet client session to log in remotely to the router and perform basic administration functions. X Windows support enables the router to be managed by UNIX workstations running X Windows and TCP/IP protocols. The PPP capability permits point-to-point connection with other routers, such as Cisco routers, that support this protocol.

The network management station can be Novell's Network Services Manager for Windows or third-party network management stations such as SUN Microsystem's SunNet Manager, Hewlett-Packard's OpenView, or IBM's NetView 6000.

The router runs a Service Advertising Protocol (SAP) filter that can be used to limit the number of times that SAP broadcasts are performed on a wide-area link. Without this filter, the frequent SAP broadcasts made by services can consume the already limited bandwidth of many wide-area links.

Wide area links can be run with multiport serial boards, and a WANIS interface is defined that can enable third-party manufacturers to support WAN Links. WANIS extends Novell's Open Data-Link Interface (ODI) to the WAN environment.

The MultiProtocol router includes NetWare Hub Services. This monitoring and management system for hubs can run on a NetWare platform. When these hubs are installed in PC workstations, they allow the PC to be controlled by the NetWare hub services.

Summary

This chapter has described the architecture of NetWare v3.11. A key concept that provides much of the flexibility of the NetWare architecture is the NetWare Loadable Module. The concept of NLM was examined in this chapter, and many examples of NLM use were provided. The chapter examined the memory architecture of NetWare and the way memory allocation is performed, and also described the multiprotocol support in NetWare. Examples showed routing and routing principles under NetWare.

The next chapter discusses NetWare's features that are specifically targeted to downsizing.

Topics covered in this chapter:

Understanding the NetWare File-System Capacity

Understanding Transaction Tracking

Looking at Operating-System Performance Characteristics

Understanding Specialized and General Operating Systems

Chapter 5

NetWare v3.11's Suitability for Downsizing

T his chapter discusses the specific design and performance characteristics that make NetWare today's premier downsizing platform. Specifically, you read about the capacity of the NetWare file system, its performance, and the services it provides large-scale DP applications. You also read about other features of NetWare's operating system that provide it with the necessary horsepower for running large-scale DP applications. As you learned in Chapters 1 and 2, NetWare was designed from the ground up to run distributed applications; in this chapter you read about some of the implementation details regarding this revolutionary aspect of NetWare. Finally, you read about some traditional services that NetWare lacks, why NetWare lacks them, and what their absence means to your effort at downsizing.

Understanding the NetWare File-System Capacity

The heart of a good downsizing platform is its file system. The file system must have a prodigious capacity, must be robust and tolerant of faults, and must be very, very fast. In addition, a file system that runs DP applications must be multiuser. In a *multiuser file system*, files have owners, and files must be secure from access by users whom the owner does not want to view or manipulate the file. The NetWare file system is all of this. In addition, the NetWare file system offers a service usually associated with DBMSs: transaction control. The existence of services like this at the kernel level is evidence that NetWare's designers were thinking of downsizing before they wrote a line of code.

A single NetWare server can have up to 32 terabytes (T) of storage space. (A *terabyte* is 1024 gigabytes, or one million megabytes). Because of file-entry caching, however, the real limit on NetWare storage space is the amount of installed RAM, as you read in Chapter 6.

Although a terabyte server has never been installed, many current servers sport multigigabyte storage systems. The important thing to note is that the NetWare file system was designed to support multigigabyte storage systems without slowing performance. All low-level file-system routines in NetWare are optimized to perform well with super-large file systems. This is evident throughout the array of resources provided by NetWare, including concurrent file handles, file and record locks, and concurrent transactions (each of which is prodigious).

The Volume

The basic structure of a NetWare storage system is the volume. A *volume* is a logical structure, analogous to UNIX file system. NetWare servers can have up to 64 volumes, and each volume can consist of up to 32 segments. A *segment* is an area of physical storage stamped for use by NetWare. (A *stamp* consists of information, like the size of the segment and other control items, written directly to the physical media.)

Segments making up a NetWare volume reside on different physical storage devices. That is, you can create segments on up to 32 different storage devices and combine those segments into a single NetWare volume. When you do this, NetWare *stripes*, or spreads data among, the different physical devices, giving NetWare built-in split-seeking capability. On a volume consisting of four segments, each of which resides on a separate hard disk, the reading and writing of data is four times faster on the multisegment volume than on a single-segment volume.

Volumes consist of *blocks*, which are logical storage-allocation units. A block is the smallest unit the NetWare file system allocates to store a file. The user can define the block size of a NetWare volume when the volume is created. Valid sizes range from 4K to 128K, in increments of the power of 2. Blocks are analogous to DOS clusters; they provide a mechanism for NetWare's low-level file-system routines to translate a logical file offset in a read or write command into a physical disk sector. In NetWare file-system logic, blocks are mapped to a volume segment, which is in turn mapped to a physical disk; the block number and physical disk are then resolved to an actual sector or sectors on that physical disk.

Figure 5.1 presents a graphic description of the NetWare file system. In summary, the volume is the basic structure of the NetWare file system; volumes consist of blocks, which are logically related (by way of disk segments) to actual disk sectors on storage devices installed in the server machine.

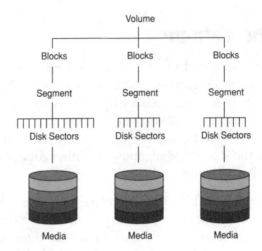

Figure 5.1:
The NetWare file system.

Extending a Volume

You can extend NetWare volumes at any time. To extend a volume, you simply add a prepared segment to it. NetWare extends its logical volume data structure so that all the physical disk sectors on the new segment are addressable through the extended volume. NetWare can do this at any time, even when the server is up and running, even when the server is being used for heavy disk I/O.

Striping Data

When a volume consists of more than one physical segment, NetWare automatically arranges files so that they are spread evenly across all segments allocated to that volume. This arrangement allows simultaneous read and write operations because the operations are done by multiple physical storage devices. This phenomenon is called *data striping*, and it allows for *split seeking*, or splitting a seek among multiple physical devices.

The File Allocation Table

The second primary data structure of the NetWare file system is the File Allocation Table (FAT). The FAT contains information about every single block within the volume. Each block within the volume exists as an element within the FAT. Moreover, the *entire* volume FAT is cached in server RAM for as long as that volume is mounted. Figure 5.2 shows a graphic representation of a FAT for a volume.

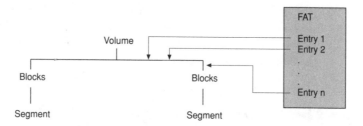

Figure 5.2:
The File Allocation Table (FAT).

NetWare files are chains of FAT entries. That is, a large file consists of a series of FAT entries linked together in sequential order. The actual file data are located on volume blocks that resolve to physical disk sectors. The FAT chain provides the information the NetWare file system needs to read or write the file to or from the correct physical disk sectors in the correct order.

Free space on a NetWare volume shows up in the FAT as unallocated entries. *Unallocated entries* represent physical disk sectors that do not contain any file data. Because the entire volume FAT is cached for as long as that volume is mounted, unallocated FAT entries are cached along with allocated ones. This enables the NetWare file system to find and allocate empty FAT entries—and their corresponding volume blocks and physical disk blocks—very quickly.

Each NetWare volume contains a redundant FAT. Only one copy of the volume FAT is cached when a volume is mounted; the uncached (mirrored) FAT is kept up-to-date by the file system. Mirrored FATs protect the integrity of the volume in the face of I/O errors or physical device malfunctions. If one copy of the volume FAT becomes corrupt, NetWare can restore the FAT by using the redundant copy. NetWare can usually restore the integrity of the FAT even if both copies are damaged—provided that they are not damaged in the same location.

The Directory Table

The third primary data structure of the NetWare volume is the Directory Table. The Directory Table contains an entry for each file located on the volume. An entry in the Directory table consists of information such as the file name, creation date and time, last access date, owner of the file, users who have access to the file, their access levels, and so on.

A key element of each Directory Table entry is a pointer to an entry in the volume FAT. The *pointer* allows the operating system to locate the first block of a given file. Once the first block is located, the operating system can read the entire file, because each entry in the FAT contains a pointer to the next block. Figure 5.3 shows the connection between a Directory Table and its associated FAT.

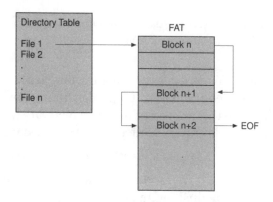

Figure 5.3:
The relationship between a Directory Table and its FAT.

  The last FAT entry in a file chain contains an end-of-file (EOF) marker, informing the operating system that it has located the last block of the file.

Directory Caching

Every time NetWare is instructed to open a file, it must search the Directory Table to find the directory entry for that file. Once NetWare locates the entry for that file, it reads the file by traversing the file's FAT chain. Although this is all pretty simple, it can take a while to search the Directory Table because a volume typically contains thousands and thousands of files (which results in a Directory Table with thousands and thousands of entries). Hence, NetWare caches the Directory Table on an as-needed basis.

The entire Directory Table is rarely cached. The first time NetWare opens a file, however, it caches that file's entry in the Directory Table in server RAM. The next time NetWare must access that file, it does not need to search the Directory Table because the entry for that file is located in RAM.

 NetWare manages cached Directory Table entries using a Least-Recently Used (LRU) algorithm. You can set an upper limit to the amount of memory NetWare uses to cache Directory Table entries with a special server-console command:

```
(SET maximum directory entries = n).
```

When NetWare reaches this upper limit, it caches additional entries by flushing the least-recently used entries from cache memory and replacing them with the new entries.

NetWare limits the number of cached Directory Table entries so that more server RAM is available for caching the files themselves. NetWare's file-caching algorithms are discussed in more detail later in this chapter.

Directory Hashing

Despite the performance gains offered by cached Directory Table entries, it still takes some time to locate a file's Directory Table entry the *first* time the file is accessed, which is where directory hashing comes into play. To hash a directory entry, the file system constructs a numeric key by processing the file's name. (*Hashing* is computer-science jargon for the method used to generate a numeric key from a string of bytes such as a file name.)

When searching for a file entry in the Directory Table, NetWare can perform an indexed search on a numeric key—an order-of-magnitude quicker than searching on the file's name. Once Netware locates the file's entry in the Directory Table, the entry is immediately cached, making subsequent searches even quicker than the first one.

It is not uncommon for NetWare volumes to have hundreds of thousands of Directory Table entries. Thanks to directory hashing, first-time search times through the Directory Table increase—an exponential curve is steeper than a logarithmic one (therefore hashing makes the search times shorter). This is the same type of performance metric achieved by tree-based (rather than table-based) file systems, such as those implemented by mainframe and minicomputers.

That's just the beginning. The real fireworks occur after the NetWare operating system locates the file's first block and begins read/write operations on that file.

File Caching

After the NetWare operating system loads, initializes itself, and mounts volumes, it allocates all remaining server RAM as file-cache buffers. *File-cache buffers* hold volume blocks which are in use (or which have been in use) as the result of file access by a network client or by a program running on the server operating system. When the operating system needs to read or write a volume block as part of some file I/O operation), the read or write occurs hundreds of times faster if it can read from or write to a cache buffer instead of the physical storage media.

 A *cache hit* is when data can be read from or written to a cache buffer, rather than to or from a physical disk sector.

The NetWare file system is so highly optimized that a read or write operation that generates a cache hit executes using only about a hundred machine instructions and occurs in microseconds. Although this is impressive, it is made more so by the sheer size of the file-cache memory on the typical NetWare server.

For example, a server with 16M of memory typically has at least 12M of that memory dedicated to file-cache buffers. This means the server can hold in cache 4,000 volume blocks. On a server with 32M of RAM, it is likely that at least 28M is devoted to caching data files.

The NetWare file-system cache algorithms use an LRU algorithm to manage the flushing and filling of file-cache buffers, just as the Directory Table caching algorithms do. This means that only the most recently used volume blocks remain in cache when the server uses all its cache buffers.

It is important to note that NetWare's allocation and use of file-cache buffers is dynamic. That is, running processes or programs can allocate memory from the file-cache system. When another process or program needs memory, the Netware operating system allocates that memory in the file-cache system for the process or program. Thus, NetWare uses all available memory for file caching, but does not prevent other processes or programs from borrowing file-cache memory for their own uses.

The size of NetWare's file-cache memory is the single greatest variable in determining how fast a NetWare server performs. When the file cache is large, the NetWare server performs very well. When the file cache is small relative to the level of file I/O on the server, performance slows significantly. The greatest thing you can do to improve the performance of a NetWare server is to give it plenty of RAM, which translates into plenty of file-cache buffers.

When file-cache memory is 80 percent or more of server memory, you can achieve a 90-percent cache-hit ratio. That is, 90 percent of all server read or write requests are filled from file-cache buffers rather than disk access. For an average server, 16M of RAM is usually sufficient to guarantee that 80 percent of all RAM is in use as file cache. On a heavily used server, the more RAM the better; 32M is usually sufficient, although some NetWare servers have 128M of RAM.

NetWare's memory-management and file-cache management algorithms do not slow down significantly when server RAM increases (even to 128M). Most NetWare resource-management algorithms impose no significant penalty for configuring a massive server in regard to the amount of disk storage and RAM. Indeed, any algorithm slowdowns resulting from huge volume sizes or numbers of cache buffers are more than compensated for by the ways that NetWare uses massive hardware configurations.

File-Cache Integrity

Some people who use DP applications may be concerned that so much file data is cached by the NetWare operating system. What if the server fails? What happens to cached data?

Application designers can force cache buffers to flush immediately after write operations, depending on the way the application opens the file. Such a design is equivalent to a write-through cache. For critical database files, a write-through cache is the best way to go. Although read operations still occur in microseconds, write operations are guaranteed to go directly to disk.

NetWare's file-cache system is different from analogous systems in other operating systems. The file-cache system is an integral part of the NetWare file system; it is built into the file system at the lowest levels and dominates most file system code. This is mentioned only to underscore how well the NetWare file system manages cached data.

In addition, three fault-tolerant features of the NetWare file system work together with the file-cache system, making it rare for an application to open a file in write-through mode. These three fault-tolerant features include disk duplexing and mirroring, hot-fix, and read-after-write verification.

Disk Duplexing and Mirroring

Disk duplexing and mirroring enable you to install redundant hard disks in a NetWare server. During normal operation, NetWare writes all data to both disks and reads data from whichever disk is available first. This arrangement makes read operations faster and slows write operations somewhat. If one disk or disk controller suffers a failure, NetWare switches to the nonfailed disk or controller exclusively until the failed disk or controller is replaced. When the failed disk or controller is replaced, NetWare re-establishes the mirror by duplicating all data on the nonfailed disk to the restored disk.

You can mirror a single partition to as many as 15 other partitions, which enables you to implement a multiple redundant storage system.

 Chapter 6 describes disk mirroring and duplexing in more detail.

Hot-Fix

Hot-fix refers to the capability of the NetWare file system to detect bad physical disk sectors and replace them "on the fly" with good sectors from a collection of reserved volume blocks. (Remember that volume blocks correspond to physical disk sectors, although not necessarily in a one-to-one relationship.) A hot-fix is similar in principle to what you do when you format a disk (formatting a disk also maps out bad sectors but destroys data in the process), except that it occurs transparently during the course of server operation. NetWare detects bad physical disk sectors when it suffers a read or write error, or when read-after-write verification fails.

Read-After-Write Verification

Read-after-write verification refers to the capability of the NetWare file system to verify that data it has just written to disk has been recorded correctly on the disk's physical media. Here's how it works: NetWare calls the disk's device driver, causing the device driver to write a buffer of data to disk. Immediately after the device driver returns to NetWare, Netware calls the device driver to read the just-written data back to a check buffer. NetWare then compares the check buffer to the original data buffer. If the two buffers match, everything continues normally. If the buffers don't match, NetWare uses hot-fix to replace the block or blocks corresponding to the bad physical media.

Read-after-write verification slows write operations somewhat, just as disk mirroring and opening a file in write-through mode do. Most hard-disk manufacturers today produce disks that perform read-after-write verification using software encoded on the disk's controller. When this is the case, NetWare senses that it does not need to perform read-after-write verification because the hardware is doing so. Hardware-based read-after-write verification does not slow write operations at all, and is obviously the best option. (Even with hardware-based read-after-write verification, NetWare knows when it must use hot-fix to replace bad blocks, although such times are far less frequent.)

 Read-after-write verification complements hot-fix very nicely. In fact, either of the two forms of file-system fault tolerance are less effective alone than they are together. The combination of disk mirroring and duplexing, hot-fix, and read-after-write verification ensure that cached data retains its integrity throughout its journey from server RAM to physical media.

Many of the traditional concerns you may have regarding file caching are not as relevant to NetWare as they are to other operating systems. However, you can always ensure that your DP applications open all their critical files in write-through mode (use the FEOpen API instead of Open). Another way to ensure write-through mode is to use the NetWare Transaction Tracking System (TTS), discussed later in this chapter.

Elevator Seeking

Elevator seeking sounds like something you do when you don't want to climb stairs. That may be, but it is also a feature of the NetWare file system that makes file I/O operations as efficient as possible.

Elevator seeking is an attack on the relatively long time it takes for a magnetic hard disk to *seek*, or to move its read/write head from one track to another. Although most hard disks on the market today can read or write at a rate of about 1K of data in a single millisecond, it takes them (on average) 16 milliseconds just to move their read/write heads into position for reading or writing data. As a result, most of the time consumed by a read or write operation is spent seeking, or moving the read/write head to the correct track.

Seek time is especially wasteful for multitasking operating systems, in which each task contends for control of the hard disk. Moreover, each task has different files open, which markedly reduces the chances that a read or write operation can be filled from contiguous locations on the hard disk's physical media.

Any mechanism that reduces the amount of seeking required to perform read/write operations provides disproportionate gains in performance. Elevator seeking attempts to do this by grouping read/write requests according to the track of the hard disk they target. Read/write operations targeted to the same track are grouped together, as are read/write operations targeted to contiguous tracks.

The *elevator* is a memory buffer in which NetWare stores the grouped read/write requests. Under normal operation, NetWare flushes file cache buffers by emptying them into the elevator. When the elevator is full, NetWare flushes the elevator by executing the read/write requests in the optimal order (the order that results in the least amount of time spent seeking). In certain conditions, however, such as for writes to a file opened in write-through mode, NetWare flushes the elevator before it is full, diluting the performance advantages of elevator seeking.

 Even with a write-through file, elevator seeking improves the performance of file I/O over what it would be normally. Under favorable circumstances, elevator seeking produces dramatic gains in performance, sometimes reducing the time required to perform reads and writes up to 90 percent.

Understanding Transaction Tracking

Because transaction control is such a vital component of a DP application, it is appropriate to discuss NetWare's built-in transaction control in some detail. The following sections provide a technical discussion of NetWare's transaction-control system. DP applications can take advantage of NetWare's transaction control system by using a very simple API.

Before you start the tutorial on transaction control, here are a couple of terms you should become familiar with:

❖ **Log file.** The transaction control file that contains original data from database files. This original data must be restored to the database file in the case of an I/O error.

- ❖ **Target file**. The database file that contains transaction records. The target file is the target of write operations. If the write fails to occur completely, the target file must be restored to its prewrite state.

- ❖ **Back-out transactions**. The process of restoring target files to their pre-error state.

The Purpose of Transaction Tracking

The NetWare 386 Transaction Tracking System (TTS) is a component of NetWare's System Fault Tolerance (SFT). TTS protects the integrity of data files by controlling if and how those files are modified. TTS also attempts to recover from system crashes and data errors by restoring affected data files to their pre-error states.

TTS works best for transaction-oriented data-management applications, in which modifications to data files must be "all or nothing" propositions. That is, either an entire transaction is added (deleted, changed, and so on) to the data file, or none of the transaction occurs. When TTS is active, NetWare uses it to modify the bindery.

 The *bindery* is a special database maintained by the operating system. It tracks sector use by objects such as users and groups, and contains other important information.

Transactions are clusters of data objects and read/write instructions grouped together by the application for a specific purpose. Every transaction consists of a beginning point and an ending point. Most transactions also have at least one data object and at least one read/write instruction.

For example, in a financial accounting application, a transaction might consist of a series of debits and credits that are balanced (all the debits added together equal all the credits added together). In such an application, the database lacks integrity if a single transaction is out of balance. There is always the possibility that the system could start a transaction but not complete it because of an unforeseen event such as a power failure. This, in turn, leads to the possibility of the database being left in an out-of-balance state. TTS is a fail-safe device to prevent this from happening.

How TTS Works

TTS is simple in theory: it notes the beginning of every transaction and records the progress of that transaction. Before TTS allows a process to write data to the transactional target file, TTS reads the existing data from the target file at the start of the impending write. After reading the existing data, TTS rewrites the data to the TTS log file. Only after the original data from the target file is recorded in the TTS log file does TTS allow a process to write data to the target file. After successfully writing data to the target file, a process can end a transaction. If the transaction progresses through its end point successfully, TTS forgets about that transaction and erases the data from the TTS log file.

If the transaction fails to progress through its end point, TTS restores the data file associated with that transaction to its pretransaction state. When possible, TTS does this immediately. In the case of a fatal error that shuts down NetWare, however, TTS restores the data file to its pretransaction state as soon as the system comes back up.

TTS is implemented in several parts of NetWare 386. First, TTS exists as code segments in NetWare's low-level file routines. Second, TTS exists as code segments in NetWare's file- and record-locking routines. TTS code is embedded throughout the NetWare file system; there is virtually no file-handling routine that doesn't interface with TTS in one way or another.

Starting TTS

TTS is always in one of the following three states:

State	Description
Uninitialized	TTS is not active and has not been initialized. This state should occur only when a server is booting.
Disabled	TTS is initialized but is not active. TTS data structures are resident in server memory but the file system ignores them when performing writes. TTS is disabled when an administrator explicitly disables it.
Active	TTS is initialized and active.

Any time NetWare mounts a volume, it first checks to see whether TTS is initialized. If TTS is not initialized, NetWare checks to see whether the newly-mounted volume is a transactional volume; if it is, NetWare initializes TTS. Because NetWare automatically mounts volume SYS on booting, and because volume SYS is always a transactional volume, NetWare always initializes TTS on booting a server.

What Activates TTS

For TTS to become active, NetWare must be able to initialize the TTS data structures and a TTS log file. The TTS log file has system and hidden flags set. When TTS tries to initialize a new log file and discovers an existing log file, it tries to rename that file and back out the transactions recorded on it. If TTS cannot initialize a new log file, or if there is not sufficient memory to initialize TTS data structures, NetWare cannot make TTS active.

Once TTS is active, it only engages a transaction for target files that are *transactional* (that is, files that have their transactional bit set). TTS supports two methods of engaging a transaction: explicit transactions and implicit transactions. *Explicit transactions* occur when an application calls the server API `TTSBeginTransaction()` and the application tries to write to one or more transactional files before calling the server API `TTSEndTransaction()`.

During explicit transactions, TTS generates a physical record lock for each transactional file that the application tries to write to. As soon as the application ends the transaction by calling `TTSEndTransaction()`, and as soon as a record of the transaction exists in the TTS log file, TTS commits the transaction to the target file or files, and releases any physical record locks generated by the transaction.

Implicit transactions occur whenever an application breaches a workstation's application threshold or causes a breach to the workstation's workstation threshold. The *workstation threshold* is the number of file or record locks that a workstation can have active before TTS begins a transaction for that connection. The *application threshold* is the number of file or record locks that a specific application running at a workstation can have active before TTS begins a transaction for that connection. Applications can set these thresholds by calling `TTSSetWorkstation-Thresholds()` or `TTSSetApplicationThresholds()`. Applications can query the operating system for current thresholds by calling `TTSGetApplicationThresholds()` or `TTSGetWorkstationThresholds()`.

As soon as either the workstation or application threshold is breached for the active connection, TTS begins an implicit transaction. Any time the active connection attempts to lock a transactional file, TTS generates a transaction. TTS does not, however, generate a physical record lock, because such a lock began the implicit transaction and thus already exists. When the application tries to release the lock on the file or record, TTS generates a call to `TTSEndTransaction()` and retains the lock on the file until the log record for that transaction is complete and the cache buffers holding the written data are flushed to the target file.

Because implicit transactions are triggered by file or record locks, TTS monitors all locking activity. Because transactions are engaged only for transactional files, all file routines check the file's transaction bit for every write operation when TTS is active. NetWare automatically sets the transaction bit for the bindery. Whenever NetWare initializes the TTS system, it creates a new TTS log file, which becomes the active log file. Only a single TTS log file can be active at a given time. The beginning of the log file contains a record of the Volume Name Table as the table existed when TTS was initialized.

 The *Volume Name Table* is a mapping of volume numbers to volume names. (The NetWare file system uses volume numbers when calling I/O procedures; it uses volume names for command processing, alerts, and error messages.) Because the state of a given volume is dynamic when NetWare 386 is running, TTS cannot assume that the Volume Name Table at transaction time is identical to the Volume Name Table at backout time.

Whenever TTS attempts to back out a transaction, it resolves the value contained in the current Volume Name Table with the name associated with the TTS log file's copy of the old Volume Name Table. Then it checks the current Volume Name Table and tries to match the old volume name to a name in the current Volume Name Table. If it can't match names, TTS assumes that the volume indicated by the TTS log file isn't on line. If the match is successful, TTS continues the backout.

TTS manages its log file much like NetWare manages cache buffers: TTS tracks which blocks within the log file are being used by a transaction. When a new transaction initializes a write to the log file by allocating blocks within the file, TTS first checks for blocks previously allocated but not currently in use. If TTS finds such a block, that block is allocated to the new transaction. TTS only allocates new blocks if there are no previously used blocks within the log file. This process keeps the TTS log file as small as possible. Additionally, managing access to the file by individual blocks (or chains of blocks) provides the most efficient record locking possible, and is critical to NetWare's performance: transactional writes must wait for TTS to create a backout record within the log file before they can return to their calling procedure.

Backing Out Old Transactions

After initializing its internal memory resources, TTS checks its volume for old backout (log) files. If any old log files exit, TTS attempts to rename them by adding a number (from 0 to 99) to the file name. Because of the DOS limitation of eight-character file names, some renamed backout files have the *T* truncated. (For example, BACKOUT9.TTS, BACKOU10.TTS, BACKOU11.TTS, and so on.) If TTS fails to rename all old backout files, it returns an error. For the rename to fail, however, 100 old backout files must be already present on the TTS volume's root directory.

 Previously-renamed backout files aren't renamed again. They do, however, count toward the limit of 100 old backout files on the TTS volume.

After identifying old backout files and renaming them when appropriate, TTS scans for old backout files. (At this point, the definition of an old backout file has changed: *old backout files* are defined as backout files with a number from 0 to 99 added to their names.) On the first scan, a backing-out function initializes a set of internal memory resources for each old backout file it identifies. The purpose of this conditional memory allocation is to ensure that the TTS system has work buffers large enough to manage the backing out of every old transaction file.

With old backout files identified and renamed, and with sufficient memory allocated for work vectors, a backing-out function enters a loop that searches for and opens old backout files. If, during this loop, TTS finds and opens a specific old backout file, it backs out all the incomplete transactions recorded in the backout file.

Recording Transactions

When NetWare initializes TTS, it allocates a linked list of transaction nodes. Each transaction node represents a potential transaction and contains fields for associating the node with a specific station and task. To begin a transaction, a station makes a call to the API `TTSBeginTransaction()`.

`TTSBeginTransaction()` scans the linked list of transaction nodes; if it finds an available node, it associates that node with the calling station and task, making the node at once unavailable and active. An active transaction node is, in essence, an active transaction. If there are no available transaction nodes, `TTSBeginTransaction()` tries to allocate memory for a new node. If the allocation is successful, the new node becomes unavailable and active.

When beginning a transaction, `TTSBeginTransaction()` always sets a bit in the transaction node to indicate that the transaction was started but not written to. The setting of this specific bit is important because it alters the behavior of the NetWare 386 logical file system, triggering some additional file-system events necessary to begin a transaction.

An active transaction node is the only thing the NetWare file system needs to process and complete a transaction. Everything else required is contained in the standard NetWare 386 logical file system.

Whenever the NetWare file system writes data to a file, it first checks the file's attributes to see whether the file is a transactional file. If the file is transactional, NetWare finds the file's transaction node by looking at the address pointed to by an element of the file control block. If the transaction node indicates that the transaction has been started but not written to, NetWare correctly infers that it is about to perform the first write of a new transaction.

After setting up to perform the write, NetWare checks the file's attribute field once again, this time to verify that it should generate backout information for the TTS log file.

If so, NetWare copies the original data from the target file and prepares to write that data to the TTS log file. NetWare then writes the original data to the TTS log file. Before writing the data to the log file, however, NetWare ensures that the write doesn't occur until the original data is logged to the backout file. As soon as the original data is logged to the backout file, NetWare continues the normal course of the write operation by writing the new data to the target file.

After NetWare performs all the writes for a transaction, it clears the `TransactionActive` bit for the transaction node. `TTSEndTransaction()`, then unlinks the transaction node from the active transaction list and links the node to another list. The second, linked list contains transaction nodes that have logged and written all their data, but are waiting to be completed.

At this point, the application that generated the transaction believes that the transaction is complete: it called `TTSEndTransaction()`, which returned successfully. Although it's true that the original data from the target file has been written successfully to the TTS log file, the transaction data currently reside in NetWare cache buffers and hasn't been committed to disk. If the server were to go down at this point, the transaction would be incomplete, and TTS would attempt to back the transaction out when the server next booted.

As soon as `TTSEndTransaction()` places a transaction node on a special list of transactions that need to be completed by the OS, NetWare wakes up a special process, the purpose of which is to officially end the transaction. This process makes one final write to the TTS log file: a record containing an end-of-transaction code.

The special process to end transactions then waits until all transaction data currently in cache is flushed to disk. Finally, this process unlinks the transaction node from the list containing logged and written transactions, and places the now-free transaction node on the appropriate list, thus recycling the transaction node.

Certain aspects of TTS are important to note: TTS guarantees that database files are not corrupted through partial writes. A transaction is not considered complete until all written data is flushed from file-cache memory and *successfully* recorded on physical media. (It is important, especially for those who are wary of file caching.)

TTS provides an alternative to opening a database file in write-through mode. Although transactional writes do not occur as quickly as nontransactional writes, they *do* occur more quickly than write-through writes.

The TTS API is easy to use, especially because it automatically performs all file and record locks necessary for multiuser database access. This is an attractive feature for those who use the NetWare API to construct DP applications.

Finally, TTS is integrated completely into the NetWare file system at the lowest levels. This ensures that TTS is robust and that there is no possible way that TTS can conflict with the NetWare logical file system (they are one and the same).

See Chapter 21 for ways to issue explicit calls from a DOS DBMS.

Understanding NetWare File-System Limits

As a downsizing platform, NetWare provides a file system with comfortable limits, even for large DP applications. The limits of the file system are as follows:

- ❖ Up to 64 volumes
- ❖ Each volume can consist of up to 32 segments
- ❖ Total volume capacity of 32T
- ❖ A single file up to 4G
- ❖ A single NetWare server may have up to 100,000 active file or record locks, listed in Novell literature as total TTS active transactions
- ❖ No hard limit on number of directories; 500,000 is not uncommon
- ❖ No hard limit on number of files

Despite the efficiency of NetWare's file system and its massive file-caching capabilities, NetWare remains a disk-bound operating system. Most hard disks on the market today have an upper limit for data throughput of about 3M per second. NetWare itself can move data around at least 300 percent faster. Ensuring good file-system performance with NetWare means taking advantage of its performance-oriented features by doing the following.:

- ❖ Always construct multisegment volumes
- ❖ Ensure that at least 80 percent of server RAM is in use as a file cache; the more RAM in the server, the better
- ❖ Install caching disk controllers (when NetWare flushes its file cache, it must flush the cache to some other

media; a cache on a drive controller is the fastest media to which NetWare can flush its file cache)

❖ Try to avoid opening files in write-through mode; use TTS instead

Looking at Operating-System Performance Characteristics

Now that you know more about the NetWare file system, you should know about the operating system itself. The following are the main performance characteristics of NetWare:

❖ 32-bit operation

❖ Flat memory model

❖ Non-preemptive multitasking

❖ Multithreaded execution

❖ Highly optimized kernel-level code

Because it runs on a 32-bit CPU (either the Intel 386 or Intel 486), NetWare executes in full 32-bit mode. (32-bit mode is technically called *protected mode* on Intel CPUs.) NetWare is unlike other operating systems that run on Intel platforms (OS/2, for example, runs in 80286 16-bit protected mode).

The following sections describe each of these operating-system characteristics in more detail.

32-Bit Execution

Running in 32-bit mode effectively halves the number of machine instructions NetWare executes for any given sequence of tasks (as compared to what it would execute in 16-bit mode). All registers are 32 bits wide, and all instructions are capable of using 32-bit operands. Although you don't need to understand the technical details, you should realize that 32-bit execution is a requirement for achieving the performance required by DP applications.

 In addition, you should know that 32-bit execution is something of a rarity in the microcomputer world. Although UNIX was the first operating system to execute on microcomputers in 32-bit mode, NetWare followed shortly thereafter. As of this writing, NetWare and UNIX are the only two mainstream microcomputer operating systems to run in pure 32-bit mode. Even OS/2 version 2.0, touted as a 32-bit operating system, contains whole chunks of code that uses 16-bit operands and instructions.

Flat Memory Model

Memory management refers to the way an operating system addresses memory and, once the memory is initialized and addressable, how an operating system controls access to it. Intel microprocessors provide two models for addressing memory: segmented and flat. Operating systems written for an Intel processor can use either segmented memory addressing or flat addressing, but not both.

Segmented memory evaluates each memory address as a segment:offset pair, the *segment* component is a marker, or segment descriptor, that designates a specific address within the machine's physical memory. The *offset* component is an address relative to the segment. The Memory Management Unit (MMU) of an Intel microprocessor resolves the segment:offset pair to a single address within the range of memory addresses available to the processor. For example, a segment:offset pair with an offset of 0 is resolved by the MMU to the same address as the segment. A segment:offset pair with an offset of 20 is resolved by the MMU to the address 20 bytes beyond the address of the segment.

In terms of addressing memory, the primary advantage of segmented memory is that it provides a larger memory space (more addresses) than the flat model does. For example, the Intel 80286 processor has 16-bit registers. With the flat memory model, a 16-bit register can address 2^{16}, or 65,536 memory addresses. By defining an address as a segment:offset pair, the 80286 processor can address 2^{24}, or 16,777,216 memory addresses. The 80286 processor uses an 8-bit segment and a 16-bit offset, which, if you add the bits, allows 24-bit memory addressing, even though the processor itself only has 16-bit registers.

The downside of segmented memory is that each segment is somewhat isolated from the other segments. Instead of one contiguous range of addresses, the 80286 has 256 separate ranges of addresses, each with 65,536 specific addresses. To gain sequential access to the entire memory space, you must proceed from segment 0, addresses 0 through 255 (0:0 to 0:65,535), shift segment selectors, and start counting over (from 1:0 to 1:65,535, 2:0 to 2:65,535, and so on). Although there is little performance penalty associated with this process (the MMU takes care of memory resolution), some programming tasks become overly complex (consider how to increment pointers across segment boundaries). Segmentation also increases the flexibility with which an operating system can dynamically allocate and free memory objects.

The *flat memory* model does not use segments per se; it sets all segment registers to the same address and views the entire address space as a contiguous range of memory addresses. A specific memory address is a single number, rather than a pair of numbers. The flat memory model makes many programming tasks simpler than for segmented memory, and increases the granularity with which the operating system can dynamically allocate and free memory objects. The downside of flat memory is that a processor can address no more than the amount of memory afforded by the width of its registers. This becomes less of a problem as the width of a processor's registers increases.

The memory model an operating system uses affects the way that operating system implements virtual memory. Virtual memory has further implications for operating-system design that are discussed in detail later in this chapter.

NetWare uses a flat memory model, which increases performance and makes application programming easier.

Nonpreemptive Multitasking

NetWare schedules threads using nonpreemptive multitasking, which enables the system as a whole to perform more efficiently, although certain tasks can occasionally be delayed for a few milliseconds.

Multithreaded Execution

NetWare allows multiple *threads*, which are instances of routines, to execute concurrently. The system then runs efficiently by keeping the processor busy executing code while some programs are waiting for resources to become available.

 Chapter 13 covers multithreaded execution in detail.

Optimized Kernel-Level Code

The NetWare kernel is a simple and elegant piece of software. It has been optimized to run as fast as possible, specifically for a networked environment.

Understanding Specialized and General Operating Systems

Two fundamental approaches to operating-system design exist: the specialized approach and the general approach. Both approaches have strengths and weaknesses.

The *specialized* operating system makes certain assumptions about its application, the hardware it runs on, and the software it runs. These assumptions form a narrow definition of the operating system's purpose. The more assumptions an operating system makes, the narrower its defined purpose. By adhering to its defined purpose, the specialized operating system can eschew many of the responsibilities that a more generalized operating system must bear. Moreover, the specialized operating system can ignore contingencies that fall outside its defined purpose.

The nature of the specialized operating system is to hone in on routines critical to its purpose; it focuses processing resources on a small number of possible states and dispatches its responsibilities with the utmost efficiency. All other things being equal, a specialized operating system has fewer routines, shorter routines, and faster-executing routines than a more general operating system. By inference, a specialized operation system has a smaller executable image and requires less data space than a more general operating system—all other things being equal.

The weakness of a specialized operating system is that, when misapplied, it is ineffective. The more specialized an operating system is, the more focused and efficient it is; by the same token, however, the more narrow its application.

The general-purpose operating system makes a minimal number of assumptions about its application, the hardware it runs on, and the software it runs. Consequently, the generalized operating system has a broadly-defined purpose. The fewer such assumptions an operating system makes, the more broadly-defined its purpose.

The nature of a *general-purpose* operating system is that it devotes its resources evenly among its many routines and does not focus its resources on one area of its responsibilities to the detriment of any of its other responsibilities. Because of its broadly defined purpose, the general-purpose operating system performs meticulous and extensive housekeeping so that it is prepared at all times for the most unlikely contingency. Housekeeping overhead makes the general-purpose operating system less efficient but more widely applicable than a specialized operating system. Conversely, a general-purpose operating system cannot be as effective or efficient for a given purpose as an appropriately applied specialized operating system.

Both approaches to operating-system design—specialized and general-purpose—are capable of rendering excellent results. The choice between the two approaches depends on many factors, but primarily on the intended use of the operating system in question.

The aspect of NetWare that influences all of its performance characteristics is that it is a specialized operating system. NetWare's focus is to provide back-end services to front-end clients over a network. As you may have inferred from the early parts of this chapter, NetWare's primary service involves its performance-oriented and robust file system. NetWare can offer an endless array of services through its capability to run NetWare Loadable Modules (NLMs).

NLMs are server-based applications that extend the NetWare operating system by providing custom services to NetWare clients. You learn more about NLMs in Chapters 11 through 16.

NetWare does not have a sophisticated console interface, nor does it have other elements of a traditional operating system (the lack of which you read about in the last part of this chapter). NetWare is singularly focused on providing services over a network.

NetWare gains its high-performance characteristics through highly-optimized kernel code. Almost 80 percent of the NetWare operating system is written in the C programming language. The remaining code is written in 32-bit assembler. The assembler-based portions of the NetWare operating system provide the core of the NetWare architecture. The assembler-based portions are the low-level routines that execute hundreds of times each second. The assembler code in NetWare is designed specifically for high-performance execution. The technical details of the way to achieve performance out of assembler code are inappropriate for this discussion; if you could take a tour through the NetWare source code, however, you would be struck by its tightness and single-minded pursuit of performance.

Some of the most highly-optimized routines in NetWare involve allocating memory, scheduling and switching threads, handling semaphores, opening and locking files, reading and writing file data, and network communication. These optimized functions execute in as few as several machine instructions to as many as several hundred machine instructions. These metrics are startling when compared to other operating systems such as UNIX, VMS, and OS/2.

NetWare is an event-driven environment. That is, NetWare is governed by external events, such as service requests from NetWare clients. Therefore, the speed at which NetWare executes is dominated by the speed of its links to the outside world and the speed of its links to secondary storage media. A slow network interface card limits the speed at which NetWare executes because the events that drive NetWare (client request packets) arrive more slowly. Similarly, a slow disk controller limits the speed with which NetWare fulfills client requests.

 It is critical, then, to configure your NetWare server with the best LAN and disk hardware you can afford. If you give NetWare good hardware to work with, it can perform much better than you probably expect it to.

The two overriding concerns that influence every aspect of NetWare's design are performance and data integrity. The high priority given to these concerns explains some of the aspects of NetWare that mystify newcomers (for example, NetWare's non-preemptive multitasking).

Examining Operating-System Elements Lacking in NetWare

NetWare lacks elements usually found in traditional operating systems, including virtual memory, memory protection, and pre-emptive scheduling of tasks. The following sections explain why NetWare eschews these elements, how their lack affects efforts to downsize, and what all of this means to you.

Virtual Memory

Virtual memory refers to the capability of an operating system to address more memory than is physically present in the computer. Virtual memory is usually created by substituting a portion of secondary storage, such as a hard disk, for RAM. Chunks of memory are written to a swap file located on secondary storage and swapped in to actual RAM when needed by an application or the operating system itself.

Most CPUs provide some type of hardware support for virtual memory. For example, OS/2 provides virtual memory using segment descriptors. Each Intel segment descriptor has a segment-present bit that, when set, indicates that the memory segment resides in RAM. When the segment-present bit isn't set, the memory segment is virtual memory and resides in the OS/2 swap file on disk. When an OS/2 application attempts to read from or write to virtual memory, the processor generates an exception and the Memory Management Unit (MMU) of the Intel CPU intervenes.

 The intervention by the MMU is complex. It entails unloading a segment from RAM, clearing that segment's segment-present bit, copying the unloaded segment descriptor from its register to the processor's Global Descriptor Table, loading the segment requested by the application into RAM, placing the segment descriptor in the appropriate register, setting that segment's segment-present bit, resolving the address, and restarting the instruction that generated the exception.

The advantage of virtual memory is that applications needing up to the total amount of addressable memory have what they need. Because the processor can execute several thousand memory-to-memory operations in the time required to make a read from disk, swapping to and from disk is much slower than using RAM. For some types of applications, swapping extracts little no performance penalty. (Such applications are CPU-bound and don't notice the slowness of disk-based virtual memory.)

For other applications, however, virtual memory presents a measurable performance penalty. These applications typically maintain large static data structures, execute repeated memory-to-memory and disk-to-memory moves, and rarely become CPU-bound. For such applications, swapping virtual memory not only represents an increased burden on the disk and memory channels, it causes the already idle CPU to idle further as it waits for swapping to complete.

A file server is the perfect example of an application that slows considerably when working with virtual memory. A file server uses extra memory to cache directory information and frequently used files. Swapping such cache memory to disk defeats the purpose of the memory. Worse is a situation in which the operating system must load a directory table from the virtual swap file to load a data file, unload the directory table to fit the data file in physical memory, swap out the data file and load the directory table to know where to write the data file to disk, and so on. Although this type of situation is extreme, it's possible for applications such as file servers that use heavy caching.

In a virtual memory system, device drivers must be prepared to work with virtual memory. For DMA and BusMaster device drivers, virtual memory presents a big problem. DMA and BusMaster devices are designed to increase performance by transferring data directly from their device to the machine's memory. When accomplished, this increases performance in two ways: first, it eliminates a memory-to-memory move by the CPU. (Traditional device drivers copy data from the device to their memory, and then copy the same data from their memory to the processor, which places the data in machine memory.) Second, DMA and BusMaster devices free the processor from controlling the device-to-memory transfer of data.

Virtual memory undermines DMA and BusMaster devices because such devices assume that all memory is real memory and not virtual memory. When a DMA or BusMaster device attempts to gain access to virtual memory, it generates an exception; the processor's MMU must intervene and perform swapping. The interruption alone prevents DMA and BusMaster from freeing the processor. In addition, the device driver must be restarted by the processor as part of the memory-management exception. This process entails much housekeeping on the part of the device driver. As a result, virtual-memory device drivers are much more complex and less efficient than they would be if the operating system didn't offer virtual memory.

Because NetWare places such a high priority on LAN and disk performance, virtual memory would place a real damper on NetWare's overall performance. The lack of virtual memory in NetWare places constraints on server-based NetWare applications; they are limited to RAM physically present in the NetWare server machine.

 Chapters 11 through 16 explain some methods you can use to override the constraints placed on applications because of NetWare's lack of virtual memory.

Preemptive Multitasking

Operating systems designed to run more than one task concurrently must provide a stable method for switching execution among tasks. Switching among tasks is not unlike calling a procedure. When calling a procedure, the caller must save some or all of its registers on the stack so that execution of the caller can resume when the called procedure completes execution. Although a *procedure* making a call must save only its return-entry point and important registers, if any, a *task* preparing to switch must save all its registers plus registers it doesn't have direct access to, such as the flags register. Depending on the operating system's method of switching among tasks, a task may have to do additional housekeeping. When the operating system returns to an inactive task, it must be able to load the saved-state information and resume executing the task at the point execution was previously stopped.

Most multitasking operating systems use either preemptive or non-preemptive switching schemes. *Preemption* is a switching scheme in which the operating system has total control over each active task. An individual task can be interrupted by the operating system at any time, at which point it must save its state and perform other housekeeping tasks. A preemptive operating system can interrupt a task because of some external event or simply to ensure that each task receives equal access to the processor.

A non-preemptive operating system doesn't interrupt a task as that task is executing; it waits until a task quits, goes to sleep, or relinquishes control before it switches to another task. All things being equal, a non-preemptive operating system makes fewer switches between tasks than a preemptive operating system, executes each switch more quickly, and incurs less total overhead. By the same token, a non-preemptive operating system cannot guarantee instant response to external events and cannot guarantee that each task receives equal access to the processor.

When switching tasks, Intel microprocessors save a task's registers and other state information to a structure called a Task State Segment (TSS). To keep track of TSSs, the processor maintains a table of TSS descriptors, much as it maintains a table of memory-segment descriptors. To switch from task A to task B, task A executes a CALL to the TSS for task B. Or more likely, something generates an interrupt and the appropriate interrupt handler CALLs the TSS for task B.

When a TSS is called, several things happen. For operating systems with segmented memory, the processor first checks that the current task is allowed to switch to the new task (unless the task switch is generated by an interrupt). The processor then checks that the TSS for the new task is present in memory. If the TSS isn't in memory, the MMU must intervene and swap memory so that the TSS is present in RAM. The processor then saves the state of the current task to that task's TSS, loads the TSS descriptor of the new task into one of its registers, and finally loads the new task's state and begins execution of the new task. Note that a task switch involves at least two memory operations, and possibly four.

Both preemptive and non-preemptive multitasking schemes have important uses. Preemption is necessary for real-time applications in which some tasks must be guaranteed immediate execution. Nonpreemptive multitasking usually results in quicker overall execution for applications that create concurrent tasks, in which each task executes the same (or similar) instructions repeatedly. The choice of preemption or nonpreemption for a particular operating system affects how that operating system shares memory among active processes. (These implications are detailed shortly.)

Most commercial multitasking operating systems, such as OS/2 (NetWare excluded), use preemptive multitasking. This discussion focuses on OS/2 and NetWare, although any preemptive operating system would be equally valid for purposes of comparison.

OS/2 uses preemptive multitasking, based on both synchronous and asynchronous interrupts. OS/2 synchronous interrupts are maskable interrupts, triggered by the system clock, and occurring at regular intervals. OS/2 asynchronous interrupts are typically generated by software or caused by a system fault. When an interrupt occurs, the processor looks at the interrupt vector to find the corresponding interrupt table. (Each type of interrupt can have its own table of specific interrupts.) Each interrupt vector has specific interrupt descriptors, or gates, that cause execution to proceed to a defined procedure, another process, or a trap.

Interrupts that cause a task switch in OS/2 execute a CALL instruction to the Task State Segment (TSS) of the OS/2 scheduler. The scheduler maintains a linked list of TSSs and simply CALLs the foremost TSS in the list. (Note that the OS/2 scheduler is independent of the OS/2 multitasking scheme, which is preemptive multitasking.) OS/2's scheduler associates a priority with each TSS, so that a critical TSS reaches the head of the list before a noncritical TSS. OS/2's scheduler has the added capability to change a task's priority dynamically if that task uses too much or too little processing time relative to other currently running tasks.

Operating systems that use a scheduler—including both OS/2 and NetWare v3.11—effectively double the number of memory operations involved with a task switch. For example, if task A simply calls the TSS of task B (assuming no virtual memory), there are two memory operations: unloading and saving the TSS for A and loading the TSS for B. A scheduler requires four operations: unloading and saving A, loading the scheduler and calling the foremost TSS on the list (assume that that TSS is B for simplicity's sake), unloading and saving the scheduler, and loading and executing B.

 Because of preemption, an OS/2 task must assume two things: it will be interrupted before it finishes execution, and it may be interrupted at any time—even before it executes a single instruction. If an OS/2 task isn't interrupted by an asynchronous event, it is guaranteed to be interrupted very soon by a synchronous interrupt.

In addition to the characteristics of preemptive multitasking described earlier in this chapter, preemption has some not-so-subtle effects on applications that require shared memory. For example, both NetWare and OS/2 maintain global variables such as file-system cache blocks and network communication buffers. In addition, OS/2 screen groups and NetWare thread groups maintain memory objects global to a screen group or thread group.

In a multitasking environment, a task that has access to shared memory must be prepared to go to sleep with the possibility that another task can write to the shared memory before the first task resumes execution. For example, a task executing a series of reads from a chain of cache blocks must account for the possibility that another task can come in and write to some of those cache blocks before the first task finishes reading them. When this is a possibility, the first task must have the means to gain exclusive access to shared memory until it finishes reading the memory.

In a preemptive environment, a task can be interrupted at any time. The only way a task can gain exclusive access to shared memory in a preemptive environment is to lock the shared memory immediately, perform the instructions that must have access to the shared memory, and then release the shared memory. By locking the shared memory, however, the task guarantees that no other task can subsequently gain access to the shared memory until the task that locked it releases it.

The OS/2 scheduler not abnormally cycles through its linked list of TSSs several times between the point at which a specific task locks shared memory and the point at which that task releases shared memory. Each cycle through the linked list of TSSs entails $2n$ task switches, in which n is the number of TSSs currently running.

In the case of OS/2, when multiple tasks need access to shared communications buffers and disk cache, preemption causes many meaningless task switches. The hypothetical OS/2 system depicted in table 5.1 shows how meaningless task switches can occur.

In this table, the hypothetical OS/2 system has 10 concurrent tasks running. Six tasks must write to a common shared-memory object (Object 1), but Task A holds a lock on the object.

For the OS/2 system depicted in table 5.1, the scheduler cycles through the tasks in the following manner: First, Task A begins a series of writes to the shared-memory object. Task A is interrupted, and Task B resumes execution. Task B executes some instructions but is interrupted, and Task C resumes execution. Task C executes some instructions but is interrupted, and Task D resumes execution. However, Task D requires access to shared-memory object 1, which was locked by Task A. Task D then puts itself to sleep until the scheduler wakes it up on the next cycle, at which point it tries again to gain access to shared-memory object 1. Tasks E, F, G, and I likewise attempt to gain access to shared-memory object 1, fail to do so, and put themselves to sleep. Tasks H and J don't require access to shared-memory object 1 and thus execute normally during their time slice.

Table 5.1:

*Effect of Preemptive Multitasking on
the Number of Task Switches*

Task	Writes to Shared-Memory Object 1?	Holds a Lock on Shared-Memory Object 1?
Task A	Yes	Yes
Task B	No	No
Task C	No	No
Task D	Yes	No
Task E	Yes	No
Task F	Yes	No
Task G	Yes	No
Task H	No	No
Task I	Yes	No
Task J	No	No

This cycle repeats for as many time slices as necessary for Task A to complete writing to shared-memory object 1 and release the lock it holds on the object. Each scheduler cycle thus executes six meaningless task switches. If Task A required three scheduler cycles to complete writing before it released the lock on object 1, the scheduler performs 18 meaningless task switches.

A nonpreemptive environment such as NetWare avoids the meaningless task switches by allowing Task A to execute until it completed writing to shared-memory object 1. Task A, in a nonpreemptive environment, is not interrupted; it is guaranteed sole access to the shared-memory object until it finishes executing or relinquishes control. As a result, Task A doesn't have to lock the shared-memory object. (The exception to this occurs when Task A needs to put itself to sleep, at which point it locks the shared-memory object.)

The disadvantage of a nonpreemptive environment for the situation depicted in table 5.1 is that Tasks B, C, H, and J wait longer before they get a chance to execute. That waiting period can be arbitrarily long, depending on how selfish the other tasks are with the processor.

 A nonpreemptive environment such as NetWare makes the assumption that each task executes quickly, puts itself to sleep quickly, or relinquishes control quickly.

For applications that require shared memory, such as OS/2, preemption entails a significant amount of overhead in the form of locks on memory and meaningless task switches. The reason OS/2 uses preemptive multitasking is simple: it can't assume that every application it runs requires the degree of shared memory that OS/2 requires. Further, it can't assume that every application it runs spawns tasks that execute quickly, put themselves to sleep quickly, or relinquish control quickly. In short, OS/2 must be prepared for many types of applications that spawn many types of tasks. For a general-purpose operating system such as OS/2, preemptive multitasking is, on the whole, the correct multitasking method. For a network server, however, nonpreemptive multitasking is more efficient.

Nonpreemptive multitasking allows NetWare to share memory on a massive scale without causing needless task switches or unnecessary locking and unlocking of shared-memory objects. Because virtually every active task on a NetWare server requires access to a common set of shared-memory objects (cache buffers, communications buffers, and cached-file systems), NetWare can initialize and allocate these objects once for the benefit of every process.

For NetWare to perform a task switch, the currently running task must finish executing (this may entail returning from a function call), put itself to sleep, or relinquish control of the processor. NetWare dispatches with the overhead of preemption by assuming that each task executes quickly, puts itself to sleep, or relinquishes control.

It's important to note that NetWare retains the functional capabilities of preemptive multitasking for situations in which preemption is appropriate. NetWare can perform real-time multitasking based on interrupts, and each active task can defer to other tasks when necessary. The NetWare C library includes a `ThreadSwitch` function that saves the state of the current process and makes a call to the NetWare scheduler. The call to `ThreadSwitch` is as follows:

```
void ThreadSwitch(void);
```

In addition to `ThreadSwitch`, the C library includes a delay function that puts a thread to sleep for a period of milliseconds. The call to delay is as follows:

```
void delay(unsigned milliseconds);
```

The NetWare C library includes two calls, `SuspendThread` and `ResumeThread`, that put a thread to sleep and wake that thread up, respectively. A thread that needs to execute immediately, for example, can use these calls to put to sleep and then wake up another thread. The calls are as follows:

```
int SuspendThread(int threadID);
int ResumeThread(int threadID);
```

To protect threads from being put to sleep when they're executing critical instructions, the C library provides the calls `EnterCritSec` and `ExitCritSec`. After calling `EnterCritSec`, a thread can be guaranteed to complete whatever it's doing without being put to sleep. (This means that the thread doesn't have to lock any shared resources.) As soon as the thread calls `ExitCritSec`, it behaves normally. These two calls are as follows:

```
int EnterCritSec(void);
int ExitCritSec(void);
```

The programmer is responsible for identifying code segments that are compute-intense, and to insert calls to `ThreadSwitch`, if necessary, so that all NetWare tasks receive sufficient opportunity to execute. By assuming the NLM programmer is competent and aware of this need, NetWare can give tasks control over their own execution. As a result, NetWare enjoys increased speed and efficiency for both task switching and memory sharing.

Memory Protection

Memory protection refers to the capability of a multitasking operating system to protect memory errors in one task from corrupting memory belonging to another task. This means that one errant application should not cause other applications to crash.

Operating systems implement memory protection in different ways, usually using CPU hardware features such as segmentation and paging. Each process running in a protected operating system owns an area of memory. Other processes cannot gain unauthorized access to memory they do not own.

On a multitasking operating system with memory protection, the operating system itself, device drivers, and other proven processes run using the same memory space. That is, they each own, in common, the same memory addresses. Code that owns common memory addresses with the operating system is said to be *trusted code*.

Trusted code has an advantage over protected code in that it can address memory without being checked by the operating system's memory-management kernel. This translates into better performance and unquestioned access to global memory areas (such as network-receive and disk-transfer buffers). Clearly, code that must execute fast should be trusted code.

A multitasking operating system, however, has no control over which programs the user decides to run as nonoperating-system processes. For this reason, applications in a protected operating system are nontrusted code. Nontrusted code cannot gain access directly to global memory areas such as network-receive buffers and disk-transfer areas; they generate a protection exception when they attempt to do so.

 The operating system usually intervenes in the case of a protection exception and makes a copy of the global memory area for the application attempting to address it. Copying memory areas takes a relatively long period of time away from other things the operating system must do.

Despite performance disadvantages of memory protection, most operating systems implement it because it is imperative that rogue applications do not corrupt operating-system memory.

NetWare does not have memory protection for a couple of reasons:

1. NetWare has more global memory areas than other operating systems. This is true because NetWare is a specialized operating system that offers network services to network clients. Applications running on NetWare (NLMs) are more similar to the operating system itself than to other user-oriented, interactive applications that run on operating systems such as VMS, UNIX, and OS/2.

2. NetWare places a higher priority on performance than it does on policing rogue applications. The NetWare philosophy places the responsibility for preventing memory corruption on the programmer, rather than on the operating system. Application development for NetWare should be considered a relatively serious affair. If the programmer does his or her job correctly, however, the application runs faster on NetWare than on any other similarly configured platform.

The disadvantage to this approach is that a rogue NLM can corrupt operating-system memory and bring down the NetWare server. Of course, memory protection does not prevent an application from corrupting *its own* memory. Sometimes a self-corrupting application can be more of a problem than an application that corrupts the operating system. For example, a DP application—even running under a protected operating system—can trash its accounts-receivable database without generating a protection exception.

Although it would be nice if NetWare implemented a flexible form of memory protection—one that allowed you to run trusted applications in operating-system memory space and nontrusted applications in a protected memory space—there are some advantages to having no memory protection whatsoever.

By default, NetWare v3.11 shares certain memory objects among NLMs and also among threads within an NLM. These objects include the command line (`argc`, `argv`), open files, open network semaphores, resource tags, and more. Each thread group shares by default the current task, current screen, current connection, `stdin`, `stdout`, `stderr`, current working directory, and more. All these memory objects, and more, are shared automatically by NetWare v3.11 and require no action on the part of the thread, thread group, NLM, or operating system. These automatically shared memory objects are called *global data objects*. Some global data objects have a scope of OS, meaning that they are global to all active NLMs; other global data objects have a scope of NLM, meaning that they are global to a specific NLM; other global data objects have a scope of thread group; still others have a scope of thread.

Because NetWare v3.11 is a specialized operating system, it can assume that, more often than not, certain items must be shared among tasks. NetWare therefore creates these items as shared-memory objects automatically, relieving each NLM, thread group, and thread from the responsibility of making shared-memory system calls. If a situation exists in which a memory object must be private, an NLM, thread group, or thread can explicitly lock the memory item and gain exclusive access to it. (That is the purpose of the `EnterCritSec()` and `ExitCritSec()` calls, by the way.)

NetWare's system of global data objects is in marked contrast to general-purpose operating systems such as UNIX and OS/2. For example, OS/2 doesn't share data objects among threads; it copies global objects such as the environment and command line to newly created thread information blocks (TIBs). Thus, each OS/2 thread gets a *copy* of the global data object, which is not the same thing as having access to the same data object. As a general-purpose operating system, OS/2 cannot assume that each thread requires shared access to specific memory objects. In the case in which OS/2 is required by running threads to share these objects, it must do so explicitly by making shared-memory calls. The result is additional overhead.

The difference in how these operating systems share global memory areas is due entirely to whether they implement memory protection or not. Shared memory can be a powerful advantage to programmers and application designers if they use it responsibly.

Summary

NetWare scores very well for having the capacity and resources needed to run DP applications. Chief among these items is the high-performance, highly optimized nature of NetWare and its prodigious file system. NetWare also places a high priority on maintaining the integrity of data stored on its volumes. NetWare provides services such as TTS and concurrency control that DP applications must sometimes provide for themselves.

On the other hand, NetWare differs from mainstream commercial operating systems. It does not have virtual memory, preemptive multitasking, or memory protection. The lack of these features did not result from oversight on the part of NetWare's designers; it resulted from logical design decisions, given NetWare's focus as a specialized operating system.

Part Three: NetWare 386 and "Super-Server" Hardware

Server Configuration

Network Input/Output (I/O)

Customizing NetWare Installation

Customizing NetWare for Large-Scale Data Processing

NetWare Security

Topics covered in this chapter:

Understanding the I/O Bus

Understanding the High-Speed Memory Bus

Using Modular Architecture

Understanding Power Subsystems

Handling Mass Storage

Chapter 6

Server Configuration

In order to be an effective NetWare server, a microcomputer must have certain components. Specifically, a server machine must have a 32-bit input/output bus with bus-mastering capability, a high-throughput (at least 60Mbps) memory bus, heavy-duty mass storage and power subsystems, and a modular architecture that uses coprocessors.

All server components are equally important, although it is possible (but not preferable) to combine certain components. (For example, IBM's PS/2 server machine integrates the I/O and memory buses under the MCA.)

NOTE The specific design of a server machine can be flexible. For example, you can place coprocessors on a server machine's memory bus, on its I/O bus, or on both.

If a server machine lacks a specific server component, however, it is an unbalanced system. An *unbalanced system* typically has too

169

much of one type of server component relative to another. For example, a machine that has a high-performance I/O bus but a weak mass-storage subsystem is an unbalanced system. An unbalanced server system may be perfectly suited for other applications, such as Computer-Aided Design, but it is not optimized for use as a server machine.

 Server machines for NetWare must have an Intel 386sx CPU or better. For your purposes, however, you should always prefer a 486 that runs at 33MHz or faster. NetWare v3.11 can sense that it is running on a 486 and, in certain critical spots, uses 486 instructions. This means that NetWare performs best on a 486 processor.

You should avoid the 386sx processor because it moves memory around in 16-bit chunks. The 386sx processor was designed by Intel to replace the old 80286 CPU in machines that were designed for the 16-bit 80286. (In other words, the 386sx is *pin-compatible* with the 80286.) Thus, the 386sx is really underpowered when it comes to running a full 32-bit operating system such as NetWare v3.11.

Understanding the I/O Bus

The most crucial work of a server machine involves moving data from one place on the network to another and then storing it. As distributed applications become more common, server machines will do more processing on behalf of clients than they currently do. Moving and storing data will always be the main processes of a server machine, however. In this sense, server machines are dissimilar to minicomputers or mainframes, which do not regularly move data around a network, and which are primarily processors of data.

Whether moving or storing, the data must pass through the server machine's I/O bus. Most of the microprocessors currently in use as servers have a 32-bit i386 processor in combination with a 16-bit ISA I/O bus. As a result, such servers can route data much faster than they can move data. That is, they can process the necessary network overhead associated with a data packet in a fraction of the time it takes them to shove the data packet onto the wire or to write the data to the storage subsystem.

As a result, most of today's PCs that are used as servers place heavy stress on their I/O bus and their processor operates at well under full capacity. As a result, ISA machines are unbalanced when used as servers (their I/O bus is overpowered by their processor).

One solution is to increase the width of the I/O bus so that it is at least as wide as the processor. Both MCA and the Extended Industry Standard Architecture (EISA) are 32-bits wide, enabling the I/O subsystems to better keep up with the processor.

To take advantage of I/O burst mode transfer capabilities, server machines use a technique called *bus mastering*. With bus mastering, a device residing on the bus takes control of the machine's resources—including the machine's processor and memory—and thus gains direct access to the data it needs. For example, a bus-mastering Ethernet card can take control of the machine's memory and send data directly from the machine's RAM to the network. A non-bus mastering Ethernet card must receive data from the machine into the card's buffer and then place the data on the wire, which involves an extra step beyond the method a bus mastering card uses.

Bus mastering offers performance benefits to server machines that go far beyond the speed and width of the underlying bus. Because bus mastering enables devices to gain control of machine resources, placing coprocessors on a bus-mastering device is a quick and efficient way to give a server machine multiprocessing capabilities.

Using a combination of a wide I/O bus, high operating speed, burst transfers, and bus mastering, server machines have the musculature to handle major communications throughput. A quick checklist of the I/O tasks that a server machine must perform on a regular basis gives you an idea of the I/O strain that network computing can place on the server. For example, not only must servers store, retrieve, receive, and send data, but they must also handle login requests, route broadcasts, and perform processing. Login requests under NetWare are particularly I/O-intensive.

Micro Channel Architecture

The MCA (Micro Channel Architecture) was developed by IBM and was used first in PS/2 models. After its introduction, other clone manufacturers developed some systems based on this bus technology. (It is still being used in many of the PS/2 models.)

The MCA technology offers the capability of 8-, 16-, and 32-bit data transfers. Its main benefits are automatic configuration; 8-, 16-, and 32-bit data transfers; and a central arbitration controller for bus-sharing devices, such as bus masters, a DMA slave, and the system microprocessor. When an MCA machine is configured, it copies device drivers (known as *. ADF files) to its non-volatile memory.

The MCA automatic-configuration utility (part of the IBM Reference Disk) enables the system to easily determine possible hardware conflicts with the system. When a new board is added or a change is made to the system, this utility uses configuration files that are usually provided from different hardware manufacturers. With these files on the Reference Disk, however, the utility recognizes any changes, refers to the reference disk for information about the changes, and displays the current configuration to the user. If the changes are correct, the user can then write the configuration to nonvolatile memory.

The micro channel bus ownership is controlled by a central arbitration control, which prioritizes up to 16 devices on the bus. The arbitrating devices can be a DMA slave, bus master, or the system microprocessor. If either a bus master device or the system microprocessor wins the arbitration, it then becomes the owner of the bus (and the controlling master). Likewise, the DMA slave can win arbitration and become the owner of the bus (and the controlling master). The advantage of central arbitration is that it allows burst-data transfers and prioritzation between devices.

EISA

The EISA (Extended Industry Standard Architecture) standard defines a 32-bit bus hardware architecture (on which many of today's 80386 and 80486 systems are based). Its features are very similar to MCA, but the EISA is more widely used by the industry.

The major benefits of EISA are the following: it is auto-configurable; it provides a full 32-bit expansion on the bus; it provides centralized bus-arbitration control for bus sharing among the CPU, DMA controller, refresh controller, and bus masters; and it is downward-compatible with existing ISA (Industry Standard Architecture) boards.

The automatic-configuration utility (usually supplied with the EISA system) uses configuration (CFG) files to resolve possible conflicts that the system may have with added system resources (system and expansion boards). When the utility is executed, it first resolves any conflicts, writes the configuration information to nonvolatile memory, and then backs up the configuration to a disk. Like micro channel systems, it makes configuring a system easier by resolving any possible conflicts.

The major benefit of an EISA system is its 32-bit bus availability, which enables a 32-bit data path from 80386 or 80486 processors. NetWare v3.11 is a 32-bit operating system that can utilize LAN cards that have been designed for this data path.

You should always use 32-bit LAN and disk controller cards to increase the performance of your server.

Like micro channel systems, bus arbitration enables the EISA systems to maximize performance by allowing devices to assert themselves onto the bus. The main advantage to the bus arbitration is that it allows fair and predictable usage of the EISA expansion bus by means of a centralized arbitration controller. The controller is responsible for controlling whether the CPU, DMA controller, refresh controller, or bus master has control of the bus. If no other device requests the use of the bus, it is given back to the controller. Some systems may be designed to let the CPU have control of the bus for extended periods of time.

The EISA system provides a multilevel rotating priority arbitration, allowing all devices asserted on the bus to process requests. In this way, the bus is fairly shared by devices.

Since the introduction of the IBM PC, the ISA bus has become a stable platform for hardware- and software-platform development. It also provided to the industry a non-proprietary bus architecture. Because of its popularity, many companies have made investments of hardware and software. To protect the investment of products that were previously purchased, the EISA standard provides downward-compatibility to eight- and 16-bit ISA products.

The EISA bus slots look similar to the ISA slots, and both types of cards are used in the slots. The difference between the EISA and ISA cards are that the EISA extends down into the slots, enabling the connectors to make contact with EISA boards. With the ISA board, however, the EISA cannot extend itself down into the bus connector.

Understanding the High-Speed Memory Bus

Like the I/O bus, the memory bus can become overloaded by the machine's processor if the memory bus is too narrow or if the memory itself is too slow. Many PC vendors recognized this years ago and separated the memory bus from the I/O bus, increasing the width of the memory bus to 32 bits and leaving the I/O bus at 16 bits.

In such a design, the processor and memory share one bus; all other expansion devices share the I/O bus. Communications between the two buses are managed by the processor, or, if the machine is a bus-mastering machine, by the actual device controlling the I/O bus.

Although many PCs today offer a separate 32-bit memory bus, the amount of RAM that you can install on the bus is many times less than optimal for a server machine. A general guideline is that a server machine should have at least 8M of 32-bit RAM (RAM with a 32-bit pathway to the processor), and more than 8M is preferable.

 Many PCs enable you to add expansion RAM by installing a memory card in the I/O bus. Although NetWare uses such RAM to speed things up, the performance gains that NetWare derives from such RAM is less than dramatic because the RAM is essentially part of the machine's I/O system.

The difference between RAM on the I/O bus and RAM on its own bus may appear to be a subtle one, but consider that a separate memory bus is doubly beneficial to an I/O-bound server machine. Placing RAM on a dedicated memory bus removes memory allocation and access operations from the I/O bus, leaving more room on the bus for true I/O operations.

It also gives the RAM a dedicated line to the processor, thereby speeding up all memory operations (memory busses are typically three times faster than their counterpart I/O busses. For example, the Compaq SYSTEMPRO has an I/O bus with a burst transfer rate of 33 Mbps; the same machine's memory bus transfers data at the rate of 100 Mbps.

Using Modular Architecture

A modular architecture is important to a server machine because it speeds up its development cycle and lowers the manufacturing cost of the machine. A *modular architecture* is one that uses off-the-shelf components—chip sets, processors, subsystems, and specifications—to build the system. The art of building server machines pertains mostly to the way the engineer puts the pieces together instead of the pieces themselves.

In terms of modularity, server machines are the opposite of mainframes, in which every part—processor, bus, memory, microcode, and subsystems—is designed from scratch. Thus, building a mainframe used to be achievable by only a handful of companies.

Building a server machine, on the other hand, does not require a vendor to design the individual parts. Instead, it involves making the existing parts work together faster and more efficiently. Most of the work involves designing a system board, tuning the machine's BIOS (usually licensed from a third party), and writing drivers for existing operating systems and devices.

Although creating the machine's memory architecture still involves a lot of work, the process of building a server machine today is dramatically simplified over the old mainframe-building process.

Moreover, introducing new iterations of a basic server machine enables a company to develop an entire range of server machines that are based on a single modular architecture. A good example of this design philosophy is the Compaq SYSTEMPRO, which enables users to run the machine with a single processor, with two processors, or mix and match i386 and i486 processors.

 The SYSTEMPRO is a high-performance microcomputer that is used for server systems.

Another machine that epitomizes modularity is the TRICORD Powerframe, which allows the same processing options as the SYSTEMPRO, but also allows an i860 chip as a coprocessor.

Because of the modularity of server machines and the general availability of standard parts, some of the emphasis has shifted from tweaking the machine's performance to manufacturing the machine inexpensively but with high quality.

Understanding Power Subsystems

A server machine must have a heavy-duty power supply, preferably having a rating of 400 watts or greater. In addition, the power supply must have enough connectors to power the greatest possible combination of drives and other devices to fit inside the server machine.

A subsystem that is not up to the task of powering a server can cause serious problems. For example, if the power supply does not put out enough wattage, the server may produce erroneous data, even though it appears to be working. Another possibility is that one or more of the disk subsystems will fail or write scrambled data without appearing to fail.

With most servers, there are usually more RAM, drives, and network cards then you usually find in a microcomputer. The important thing to remember when purchasing or converting a microcomputer to a server is to always estimate the power rating needed to handle the current hardware configuration, plus possible growth.

What power rating do you need? Only you can answer that—by adding the power-rating of your different components together. Devices (such as floppy drives, network adapters, and hard drives) located in the server each has an individual calculated power rating. After calculating the actual power ratings for each device, you can add them together to total the amount of power you need for your server.

To calculate the actual power rating, you can use the following Ohm's Law equation, in which P represents power (in watts), V represents voltage (in volts), and I represents current (in amps):

$$P = V \times I$$

This formula is not the most accurate for calculating power, however. To obtain a more accurate power rating, you need the actual power rating and then multiply it by a power factor. Because the V and I factors in the equation err on the side of safety, they should be sufficient for your needs.

For some devices, a power rating is published with either a kVA (kilovolt ampere) or a VA (volt ampere) suffix, instead of a W (watts) suffix. This represents the voltage and current multiplied without the power factor.

Most power requirements can be obtained from the manufacturers of the different components. It does not have any specific power information—you can use the Ohm's Law formula for a close calculation.

If you know that you are going to purchasing a machine to be a server, always check to make sure you have a sufficient power rating to handle added hardware.

Handling Mass Storage

Another critical subsystem for a server machine is its mass storage device. The mass storage subsystem has two components: a controller and one or more drives. Some machines dedicate each controller to one and only one drive; others use a single controller to manage multiple drives. The controller should match the bandwidth of the server machine's I/O bus. That is, you do not want to use a 16-bit controller inside a server with a 32-bit I/O bus. Although this is possible, you create an artificial bottleneck and make latent some of the machine's power.

There are currently two strategies for increasing mass-storage performance in server machines. The "brute force" strategy involves placing a large amount of RAM (anywhere from 8M to 80M) directly on the controller card to cache reads and writes to the drives. When the server writes data to the drive subsystem, the controller places the data in the controller RAM and the server continues whatever it was doing. Later, the controller flushes its RAM and writes the data to the drive.

The second approach is more sophisticated—it involves an intelligent multitasking controller and two or more drives configured as an array. Although this approach does not offer the same performance as the controller under low to medium loads, its performance does not drop off under high loads (it continues in a linear fashion).

A multitasking controller, when combined with a disk array, enables the server to read from and write to the disk subsystem concurrently, offering significant performance advantages whenever multiple processes are hitting the drive. The ideal subsystem combines the two approaches into a third "super subsystem" that features a caching multitasking controller and an array of two or more drives.

Mirroring

Mirroring is one of the most important features of a successful fault-tolerant system. The overall benefit from mirroring is to provide protection against data loss. NetWare mirroring can currently be broken down into two different categories: disk mirroring and disk duplexing.

Disk Mirroring

Disk mirroring provides fault tolerance to possible hard disk failure by writing the same information to two NetWare-partitioned hard disks. In the case of a hard disk failure, the functioning mirrored disk continues to retrieve and store data; the operating system sends a warning message that disk failure has occurred.

Disk Duplexing

Disk duplexing, or *disk-channel mirroring*, provides complete mirroring of any component (controllers and disks) that exist on the disk channel. If any component on the disk channel fails, the operating system can still retrieve and store data on the hard disk(s). During a failure on the channel, the operating system then sends a warning message of disk-channel component failure.

Another benefit of disk duplexing is a NetWare feature called *split seeks*, which provides read requests on different disk channels simultaneously. (Disk mirroring cannot do split and multiple seeks, however).

Disk Arrays

Like NetWare fault tolerance, disk-array systems were developed to prevent loss of data and to improve disk I/O performance. The most popular concept of disk arrays is known as Redundant Array of Independent Disks (RAID), which was developed by a team of researchers at the University of California at Berkeley.

 You can compare the RAID concept of fault tolerance (data striping, disk mirroring, duplexing) with the fault-tolerance features of NetWare v3.11. With relatively close fault-tolerance concepts, however, disk arrays function differently. When compared with NetWare's fault tolerance, they fall short in performance, they are more costly, and they lack hardware flexibility.

Operation of a Disk Array

To help you understand the way NetWare can be used to offer equivalent fault tolerance, greater performance, lower cost, and more flexibility, it is important to understand the way a disk array operates.

For example, RAID has six different levels: RAID 0 through RAID 5. Using several of these levels, you can do what NetWare does: data striping (spreading of blocks of data across all drives), disk mirroring, duplexing, and error recovery. To accomplish error correction, one of the disks in the array is dedicated as the *parity drive*, which functions as a checksum for all data scattered across the drives. The *checksum* is produced by adding up all of the data bytes and keeping only the least-significant two byes of the result.

For example, in a five-disk array system, you are also writing data. The information is sent to the controller and each block of information is spread across each drive in the array. The disk array controller then calculates the parity byte by adding the data bits from each drive. The job of the parity byte is to ensure that if one of the data drives fail, the data stored on the fail drive can be recovered.

NetWare gains its performance by being hardware-independent, (having its fault-tolerance features closely knitted to the operating system). It also does not have to maintain the task of a parity drive.

Some critics of NetWare think that NetWare's software-based fault tolerance can increase the use of the server's processor. This is not true, NetWare uses data structures to maintain its fault tolerance, freeing-up the server's processor. In contrast with disk arrays, NetWare is not required to maintain parity-data information when reading or writing.

Because NetWare's fault tolerance is software-based, it makes it flexible enough to use SCSI, Enhanced Small Device Interface (ESDI), or Integrated Drive Electronics (IDE) drives and controllers. For instance, you can buy cached disk controllers (which increase the performance of I/O on the disk) and drives from different manufacturers. Hardware-based disk arrays usually require you to have drives and controllers that are specific to your disk-array system.

Disk arrays can be an excellent solution for other operating systems, such as UNIX. Disk arrays work with NetWare, but you already have the features built into the operating system. NetWare's fault tolerance also has greater performance, and it is hardware-independent.

SCSI

Small Computer System Interface (SCSI) is a set of hardware and software guidelines used for connecting peripheral devices (hard disks) and the associated controllers to a microprocessor. SCSI is important to NetWare (even though other drive interfaces are supported) because SCSI provides speed and expandability.

In order for SCSI devices to communicate with the microprocessors, there needs to be an interface, which is referred to as a Host Bus Adapter (HBA). The HBA is designed to relieve the server's processor from data storage and retrieval tasks, thus providing increased performance.

For example, a SCSI driver can inform a disk that the disk should prepare for I/O (a wake-up-call). During the period that the disk is preparing for I/O, the SCSI driver continues to send messages to other SCSI disks or it performs disk I/O. When the disk is ready to receive or send data, the disk sends a ready message to the SCSI driver, and then the I/O request is performed.

Aside from the performance benefit of SCSI, it is also easy to expand by adding more devices. A disk channel is made up of the HBA, all attached peripheral devices, and their controllers. A NetWare v3.11 server can support up to four HBAs (with the possibility of up to 16 drives on each HBA). The HBA design enables drives to exist internally and externally.

If the server system continues to grow, you can daisy-chain together multiple subsystems on the disk channel.

SCSI is an excellent way to provide expandibility, flexibility and performance for any NetWare v3.11 server.

Summary

The worst place for you to save money when downsizing to NetWare v3.11 is at the server. In other words, you can save money by purchasing clone workstations, but you should never purchase a clone server. Your server machines must be as reliable as possible. You should only consider machines from major-brand vendors, and you should only consider machines that have been certified for use with NetWare v3.11. Do not skimp on anything when it comes to purchasing a server machine.

A good server machine for NetWare v3.11 has a fast 386 or 486 CPU (33 MHz or quicker). In addition, it should have a fast (100

MBps) memory bus, a 32-bit I/O bus, a heavy-duty power supply, and a top-of-the-line drive subsystem. It is also good practice to purchase modularly constructed server machines. You should be able to upgrade part of a server machine, such as the CPU or cache, without purchasing an entirely new machine.

 It is also good practice to purchase a service contract for your server machine.

Disk arrays are typically large, fast, and powerful. They do not add any capabilities to NetWare, however. Unless you have a compelling reason to purchase one (such as an excellent relationship with the vendor), you should not require your server to be configured with a disk array.

SCSI drive subsystems are always the preferred configuration for NetWare server machines. NetWare v3.11 works well with other types of drive subsystems, but it works best with SCSI.

Chapter 7

Network I/O

etwork Input/Output (I/O) determines the overall performance of a file server. Network I/O is a measure of how rapidly data can be transferred between a server and a workstation. Because the server acts as a repository of data files on a remote file system, it is important to understand the factors that affect the server.

Understanding Server-LAN Configuration

Many factors in a server configuration have a direct impact on network I/O. A few of the more important factors are the following:

- ❖ Network interface cards (NIC)
- ❖ Network drivers
- ❖ Protocols
- ❖ Network operating system
- ❖ Bus speeds at the server

These elements can interact to either improve or decrease network performance. The discussion that follows addresses some of these issues.

Understanding Network Adapters

Network adapters provide the physical connection between a node (workstation or server) on a LAN to the LAN cable. These devices have names such as the following:

Network adapter unit/board/cards

Network controllers

Network interface card (NIC)

Network cards

Network adapters

Intelligent network interface card (INIC)

These names refer to the network electronics that fit inside a node on a LAN and implement layers 2 and 1 of the OSI model.

A functional description of a network adapter is shown in figure 7.1.

A number of modules on the network adapter perform specialized processing, as follows:

❖ Transmit/receive module

❖ Encode/decode module

❖ MAC layer processing

❖ Frame buffers

❖ Host-bus interface

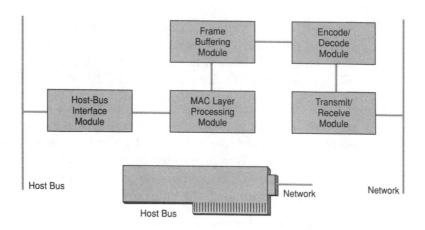

Figure 7.1:
Block diagram of a network adapter.

The following discussion explains the way that these modules interact with each other. This interaction is important to understand so that you can avoid potential network I/O bottlenecks with a network adapter.

The *transmit/receive* module contains the interface electronics to drive the signal over the network media and receive the signal from the network. As signals propagate through the network media, they are reduced in strength. The transmitting station must send the signal with sufficient power to be understood by the farthest node that needs to hear the signal.

Before a signal is transmitted, it may be encoded to put clock information as part of the data stream. The clocking information is necessary for the receiving station to keep its clock synchronized to the transmitter clock. When a signal is received by a station, it needs to decode the signal, that is, to recover the data bits. The *encode/decode* module performs these functions.

A variety of encoding techniques are used by different LANs. Ethernet and IEEE 802.3 use Manchester Encoding, IEEE 802.5 uses Differential Manchester Encoding, and FDDI uses a combination of NRZI (Non Return to Zero Inverted) and 4B/5B encoding.

When a frame is to be transmitted to the network or has been just received from the network, it is kept in a special area of memory on the adapter card for processing. In many network adapters, this frame-buffer area is implemented by RAM chips on the network adapter. The amount of memory reserved for frame buffering can vary from a few kilobytes to a megabyte.

Many network adapters implement in firmware (intelligent buffer-management algorithms). Some use scatter algorithms that can keep the header separate from the data portion of the frame. These algorithms eliminate the need for moving headers and data into a contiguous block of memory prior to transmission.

 Firmware is software that is encoded directly onto read-only memory chips hosted by the adapter.

The *Media Access Control (MAC) layer processing* module is perhaps the most important module in the network adapter. It performs the following important functions:

❖ **Encapsulation/decapsulation functions.** *Encapsulation* is performed by the transmitting station and includes the generation of correct address, control, and frame-check sequence (CRC) fields. *Decapsulation* is performed by the receiving station and includes processing of the address, control, and frame-check sequence fields. Error-detection is also performed by the decapsulation function.

❖ **Implementation of the MAC algorithms.** This is the Carrier Sense Media Access/Collision Detect (CSMA/CD) access mechanism for Ethernet and the Token Access mechanism for token ring.

These functions require processing power. Earlier network cards borrowed this processing power from the station's CPU. Needless to say, these network cards were extremely slow. Today, all network adapters have their own processing functions, which are special microprocessors that have their own ROM or microcode containing the MAC algorithms. These network controller chips have their own RAM to process the MAC algorithms.

Understanding Bus-Mastering and the Host-Bus Interface

The exchange of control and data information between the network adapter and the station takes place through the host-bus interface. The *host-bus interface module* must have a built-in understanding of the nature of the host bus. Because there are many bus standards, network cards are classified by their design. They can be designed for an ISA (Industry Standard Architecture) bus, an EISA (Extended Industry Standard Architecture) bus, or a MCA (Micro Channel Architecture) bus. Apple's Macintosh machines use Nu-Bus and must have their own network cards.

The width of a bus is defined by the number of data bits it can transmit in parallel. The wider the data bus, the more efficient the network adapter is. For IBM PCs, eight-bit network cards are quite common. Although they are more expensive, 16-bit cards provide better performance. 32-bit network cards for EISA and microchannel buses are also available. Another important consideration is the speed of the bus, measured in Mhz (megahertz), and the data transferred per cycle of the bus.

The EISA and microchannel buses have a bus-mastering capability. Network adapters designed for these buses can do data transfer into the computer at high data rates with minimal interaction from the CPU. ISA bus network adapters can be placed in on an EISA bus, but these do not benefit from the bus-mastering capability of the EISA bus. In other words, EISA buses are downwardly compatible with ISA buses. ISA network adapters, on the other hand, cannot interoperate with microchannel buses. Microchannel buses require specially designed network adapters.

The data-transfer rate of a bus can be characterized by the following formula:

$B = S * (D/C)$

B = Bus-transfer rate (bus throughput)

S = Speed of bus (Mhz)

D = Width of data transferred

C = Cycles to transfer D bits

For the ISA bus, the bus speed is 8.33Mhz; 16 bits are transferred in two cycles. Therefore, the ISA bus throughput is calculated as follows:

B (ISA) = 8.33Mhz * (2 bytes/2 cycles) = 8.33M/sec

For the EISA bus, the bus speed is 8.33 Mhz; 32 bits are transferred in per cycle. Therefore, the EISA bus throughput is worked out in the following way:

B (EISA) = 8.33Mhz * (4 bytes/1 cycle) = 33.32 M/sec

For the MCA bus, the bus speed is 10 Mhz; 32 bits are transferred in per cycle. Therefore, the MCA bus throughput is as follows:

B (MCA) = 10Mhz * (4 bytes/1 cycles) = 40M/sec

A new type of bus, the local bus, has become popular for bypassing the ISA, EISA, or MCA bus for video traffic between the CPU and the video adapter. The purpose of this bypass is to avoid the bus bottleneck. The local bus on many systems operates at 33 Mhz and transfers 32 bits-per-cycle. By using the formula shown, the throughput of the local bus works out to be the following:

B (local bus) = 33 * (4 bytes/1 cycle) = 132M/sec

Understanding Network Adapter Performance

Which network adapter is faster: token ring, Ethernet, or ARCnet? The answers are not always obvious because studies can be biased or skewed in favor of one adapter. The studies all conclude that 10Mbps Ethernet and 16Mbps token ring are faster than ARCnet at 2.5Mbps. These results are not so surprising, considering the data rates. ARCnet Plus at 20Mbps can be expected to be faster than both Ethernet and ARCnet, and FDDI is the fastest. Thomas-Conrad has a 100Mbps fiber-optic proprietary LAN that is a combination of ARCnet and FDDI.

In designing a network interface card, a vendor makes several design choices that affect the price/performance tradeoff. The four major characteristics that contribute to NIC performance are the following:

- ❖ Media-access scheme
- ❖ Raw bit rate
- ❖ Onboard processor
- ❖ NIC-to-host transfer

These characteristics are discussed in the next section.

Media-Access Scheme

The media-access scheme, such as CSMA/CD Token Access, is an important parameter in NIC performance. Token Access gives a deterministic performance; CSMA/CD does not. On the other hand, CSMA/CD is simpler and faster under light loads compared to Token Access.

Raw-Bit Rate

The *raw-bit rate* is the maximum bit rate that is possible on a given medium. The actual effective bit rate, taking into account protocol overhead and timing delays, is much less. Nevertheless, the raw-bit rate represents an upper limit for the given media.

Fiber optic media can be used for data rates in hundreds of Mbps range. FDDI at 100Mbps is only the beginning; you can expect higher-speed LANs based on fiber optic cables.

Coaxial cable can generally accommodate data rates up to 50Mbps and shielded twisted-pair wiring yields 20Mbps.

ARCnet Plus uses a 5Mhz sine wave. By using special encoding techniques, however, it can pack four bits of information in every cycle, yielding a maximum of 20Mbps.

Onboard Processor

Effective use of an onboard processor can speed up an NIC. If the firmware for the NIC is poorly written, however, it can have the opposite effect. Some vendors implement upper layer protocol processing on the NIC card itself for better overall throughput. An example of such an NIC is the Federal Technologies EXOS series board that has onboard TCP/IP processing. (The EXOS product line was sold by Excelan to Federal Technologies after the merger of Excelan with Novell).

When NetBIOS was created by IBM for the IBM PC Broadband LAN, it was implemented in firmware on the NIC itself. Due to inefficient implementation, however, it ran more slowly than NetBIOS implemented in software.

NIC-to-Host Transfer

The NIC-to-host channel can be implemented in several ways: shared memory, DMA, or I/O ports. NICs can use any of these methods or a combination of them. Shared memory is the fastest, I/O ports are next, and DMA is the slowest.

The data width of the bus interface has a dramatic effect on NIC-to-host transfer speeds. This width can be 8, 16, or 32 bits. The wider the data width, the faster the data transfer.

The type of host bus also affects the transfer rate. EISA and Micro Channel NICs are faster than ISA NICs.

Understanding IEEE LANS

The IEEE (Institute of International Electrical and Electronic Engineering) undertook Project 802 in February of 1980 to identify and formalize LAN standards for data rates not exceeding 20Mbps. Their standardization efforts resulted in the IEEE 802 LAN standards. The number 802 was chosen to mark the calendar when IEEE undertook the LAN standardization efforts (80 represents 1980, 2 represents February, the second month).

Figure 7.2 shows the IEEE LAN standards in relationship to the OSI model. You see that the primary emphasis of the IEEE committee was to standardize the hardware technologies used at the physical and data-link layer. Such an emphasis is not surprising, considering the fact that networking hardware such as network interface cards (NICs) and LAN wiring, can be modeled completely by the two lower OSI layers.

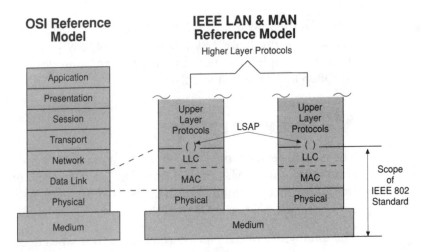

Figure 7.2:
IEEE 802 reference model.

The data-link layer is divided into two sublayers: the Media Access Control (MAC) and the Logical Link Control (LLC). The MAC layer deals with media-access techniques to access shared physical media. Token ring and Ethernet have different implementations of the MAC layer because their methods of sharing the physical media are different.

 All IEEE LANs have the same LLC layer. The advantage of a common sublayer such as the LLC is that upper-layer mechanisms can be the same, regardless of which kind of networking hardware is used.

IEEE has identified a number of LAN technologies for standardization. The most important of these technologies are the following:

- ❖ IEEE 802.3. Standardization of Ethernet technology
- ❖ IEEE 802.4. Token-bus standard
- ❖ IEEE 802.5. Token-ring standard

❖ IEEE 802.6. Metropolitan Area Network (MAN)

Each of the IEEE LAN standards discussed earlier has its own rules for LAN wiring. You can lay out the wiring in a number of ways. The geometrical arrangement of the wiring scheme is called the *topology*. The topologies that are common in LANs are the star, bus, and ring topologies.

In the *star topology*, communication between any two nodes must go through a central device or switching element. The devices that connect to the central switch tend to be simple, with all the complexity residing in the central switch. Classic examples of star topology are the mainframe and minicomputer architecture, in which the host is the central switch. Star-wiring topology is vulnerable to a single point of failure: if the host breaks down, the entire system goes down.

 You should have a central switching element that is reliable and provides signal isolation between ports so that failures at any one port are not propagated to other ports.

If failures at any one port are not propagated to other ports, the *physical star topology* is one of the best topologies (it is used in ARCnet, token ring, FDDI, and 10 BASE-T LANs). It is easy to connect or remove stations from a central location. In many LANs, these central elements (*hubs*) come with advanced network-management features, such as SNMPs (Simple Network Management Protocols).

The *bus topology* consists of a linear cable to which stations are attached. Signals sent by a station on the bus propagate in both directions. A classic example of a bus topology is Ethernet.

The *ring topology* consists of cable in the form of a loop with stations attached to it. Signals are sent in one direction only; therefore, the ring can be implemented by point-to-point simplex (one-direction flow) links. An example of a ring topology is the token ring LAN.

Making LAN Choices

To manage such diversity, you must understand the basic operation of each of these LAN technologies. NetWare alone runs on over 180 different types of NICs. The predominant LAN technologies of today are Ethernet, token ring, and ARCnet. These technologies offer a number of wiring choices and are discussed in the following sections.

Ethernet LANS

In 1973, Robert Metcalfe wrote his Ph.D. thesis at MIT on the subject of LANs. He later on went to work for Xerox Corporation where he, along with David Boggs and others, developed a LAN based on carrier-sensing mechanisms. This LAN spanned a distance of 1km, supported 100 personal stations, and achieved data rates of 2.94Mbps. This system was called *Ethernet*. It was named in honor of that elusive substance called ether, through which electromagnetic radiation was once thought to propagate.

Ethernet was proposed as a standard by Digital Equipment (DEC), Intel, and Xerox. Digital Equipment (DEC) is a computer manufacturer, Intel is a chip manufacturer, and Xerox is a research organization. The combination produced good results. The first Ethernet standard was published in September, 1981. This standard was called the DIX 1.0. (DIX, of course, stood for Digital, Intel, and Xerox). DIX 1.0 was followed by DIX 2.0, published in November, 1982.

Meanwhile, Project 802 from IEEE had undertaken LAN standardization efforts. Not surprisingly, Digital, Intel, and Xerox proposed the adoption of Ethernet as a standard. IBM proposed the Token Ring as a standard, based on prototypes built at IBM's Zurich Lab. General Motors and others interested in factory automation proposed the token bus as a standard. The IEEE committee probably saw the futility of convincing everyone to adopt only one LAN standard and decided to adopt all of them! The Ethernet proposal became known as the IEEE 802.3; the Token Bus proposal became the IEEE 802.4; the Token Ring proposal became the IEEE 802.5.

 True to the nature of committee design (a standards committee cannot adopt a standard without modifications because the new standard must discriminate equally among all vendors), the IEEE 802.3 standard is not quite the same as the Ethernet standard. Important differences exist—for example, an Ethernet node does not talk to an IEEE 802.3 node.

Ethernet Operation

Before an Ethernet station transmits, it listens for activity on the transmission channel. In fact, all stations are constantly engaged in listening for any activity on the channel (*activity* is defined as any transmission caused by other Ethernet stations). The presence of a transmission is called a *carrier*; station electronics can sense the presence of a carrier.

If a carrier is detected (a busy channel), the station refrains from transmission. After the last bit of the passing frame, the Ethernet data-link layer continues to wait for a minimum of 9.6 microseconds to provide proper interframe spacing. At the end of this time, if a data frame is waiting for transmission, the transmission is initiated. If the station has no data to transmit, it resumes the *carrier-sense* operation (listening for a carrier). The interframe gap provides recovery time for other Ethernet stations.

If a station transmits when the channel is busy, you get garbled transmission. Garbled transmissions are called *collisions*.

If the channel is free, that is, if no carrier is detected, the station can transmit. Multiple stations attached to the Ethernet channel use the carrier-sense mechanism, which is called a Carrier Sense with Multiple Access (CSMA). Carrier-sense mechanisms belong to a general class of techniques called LBT (LBT stands for Listen Before Talking).

A collision occurs if two stations decide to transmit at the same time and there is no activity on the channel. Collisions occur in Ethernet LANs because stations transmit based on one fact: the presence of a carrier on the channel. These stations do not have any knowledge of packets that are queued for transmission on other stations.

The CSMA operation is also complicated by propagation delay in LANs. In Ethernet, signals propagate at 0.77 times the speed of light for standard (thick) cables and 0.65 times the speed of light on Thin Ethernet cables. Because of this difference, there is a delay before a transmission is heard by all stations, and a station may decide to transmit because it has yet to hear another station's transmission.

Collisions are a fact of life in Ethernet LANs. Ethernet stations minimize the effects of collision by detecting the collision. The name CSMA/CD describes the Ethernet media-access mechanism (CD stands for Collision Detect). The stations involved in the collision abort their transmissions. The first station to detect the collision sends out a special jamming pulse, and all stations are then alerted that a collision has taken place. When a collision occurs, all stations set up a random interval timer; transmission takes place only after this interval timer expires. Introducing a delay before transmission can lessen the probability of collisions.

 What happens when successive collisions occur? The average random timeout value is doubled. This doubling continues up to 10 consecutive collisions. Beyond that, doubling the average random timeout value does not improve the performance of the network to any significant degree. The doubling gives an exponential effect; stopping after 10 consecutive collisions truncates the exponential effect. This mechanism is called the *truncated binary exponential back-off algorithm*.

How long does a station have to wait under heavy load conditions to transmit a frame? A station may experience a string of bad luck in which some other station has the bus every time it transmits. When collisions occur, stations introduce a delay using the random timer. What if a station has the misfortune of timing out after the other stations have already timed out? In the worst-case scenario, a station may have to wait indefinitely. Ethernet is thus not suited for real-time applications because this wait is not acceptable.

The next section examines different Ethernet options.

Ethernet Options

The coaxial cable serves as the medium for two variations of Ethernet: Standard Ethernet and Thin Ethernet. One version of Ethernet runs on unshielded twisted-pair wiring. This version is called the 10BASE-T standard. These options are shown in relationship to the IEEE/OSI model, shown in figure 7.3.

Although the packet structures for Ethernet and IEEE 802.3 are different, many vendors now manufacture cards that can operate in both modes by changing the network driver setting. In the case of NetWare, the workstation and server software can be configured to operate a NE2000 or SMC (previously Western Digital) network card with either the Ethernet packet structure or IEEE 802.3 packet structure.

Standard (Thick) Ethernet Wiring Design Rules

Another name for Standard Ethernet is *Thick Wire Ethernet* because the coaxial cable it uses is much thicker than that used for Thin Wire Ethernet. The IEEE version of Standard Ethernet is called 10BASE5 (10 stands for 10Mbps operation; BASE stands for baseband operation; 5 stands for 500 meters-per-segment).

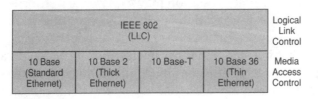

Figure 7.3:
IEEE 802.3 options.

Stations are connected to Standard Ethernet cable by using a *transceiver*, also known as a *media attachment* (MAU). The transceiver illustrated in figure 7.4 can be attached to the coaxial cable by using a connector or by tapping directly into the cable.

The *transceiver* is connected to the station by using the DIX connector socket, which is a D-shaped connector that is specific to Ethernet. The DIX connector is equipped with a sliding lock that clamps the mating connectors together. A *transceiver cable* connects the DIX connector on the transceiver with a DIX connector on the network-interface card in the station.

Stations on Thick Ethernet communicate to the external network through *external transceivers* attached to the shared media. The shared media is called the *trunk segment* cable, or just *segment*. Because of signal attenuation, a segment cannot be longer than 500 meters.

The connection between the external transceiver and the NIC is done by a *transceiver cable*. The DIX connector plug mates with the DIX connector socket on the NIC. A *slide lock* is used to secure this connection. The other end of the transceiver fits into a connector on the external transceiver.

Figure 7.4:
An Ethernet transceiver. Courtesy of AMP, Harrisburg, PA.

Figure 7.5 shows the Thick Ethernet cable used to make up the trunk segments. Thick Ethernet cable is a 0.4-inch diameter, 50-ohm cable, and it is available in various pre-cut lengths with a 0.4-inch diameter *N-series connector* plug attached to each end. Thick

Ethernet cable can also be purchased in spools or in bulk quantities, which come without the N-series connector attached at the ends.

Figure 7.6 shows the N-series barrel connectors that can be used to join two lengths of Ethernet cable. A trunk segment must be terminated with an *N-series terminator*. The N-series terminator is a 50-ohm terminator that blocks electrical interference on the segment. Additionally, it cancels out any signal reflections caused by signals reaching the end of the cable. The N-series terminator is attached to the male N-series terminator on the end of the segment. N-series terminators come with grounding wire. Only one end of the cable must be grounded; the other end must remain ungrounded. This electrical rule is necessary to avoid ground-loop currents.

Figure 7.5:
Standard Ethernet cables and connectors. Courtesy of AMP, Harrisburg, PA.

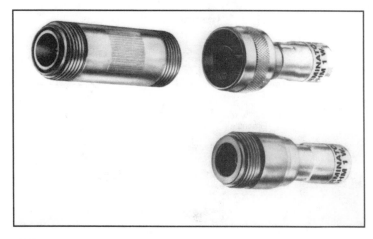

Figure 7.6:
Standard Ethernet barrel connectors and terminators. Courtesy of AMP, Harrisburg, PA.

Figure 7.7 shows an example of a Thick Ethernet network. In this network, two trunk segments are joined together by a device called a *repeater*. A repeater is an active device that enables an Ethernet LAN to be expanded beyond a single segment by linking two segments together. The repeater amplifies and regenerates the signal so the signal can be transmitted over longer distances. The repeater in figure 7.7 has two ports to attach a maximum of two segments. A multiport repeater, such as a DEMPR (DEC multiport repeater), can link a number of Ethernet segments together.

Thick Ethernet wiring involves a number of rules, which are summarized in table 7.1.

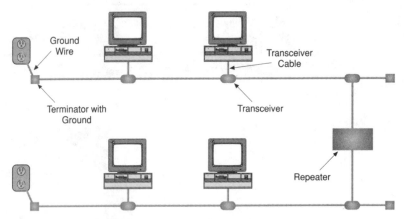

Figure 7.7:

Example of a Thick Ethernet cable network.

Table 7.1

Thick Ethernet Parameters and Wiring Rules

Thick Ethernet Parameters	Value
Max data rate	10Mbps
Max repeaters without IRLs	2
Max repeaters with IRLs	4
Max coaxial segment	500 meters
Max transceiver cable length	50 meters
Max number of link segments	2
Max combined link segment length	1000 meters
Max stations per segment	100
Max number of stations	1024
Distance between stations	Multiples of 2.5M

To go from one station to another station on an Ethernet LAN that consists of coaxial trunk segments only (see fig. 7.8), a signal cannot travel through more than two full repeaters. A *full repeater* joins two coaxial segments together directly. (A coaxial segment is defined to be distinct from a link segment.)

A *link segment* made of fiber optic or twisted-pair cable can be used to join two coaxial segments over a longer distance. The purpose of a link segment is to extend the range of an Ethernet LAN. There can be a maximum of two link segments on an Ethernet LAN. Link segments do not have any stations attached to them; they are connected to coaxial segments by repeaters. Another name for link segments is Inter Repeater Link-segment (IRL).

A *half-repeater* joins a coaxial segment to a link segment. Another name for a half-repeater is a *remote repeater.*

The trunk coaxial segment length cannot exceed 500 meters. The combined lengths of the two link segments cannot exceed 1000 meters. By using these wiring parameters, you can deduce the maximum length of an Ethernet LAN, as shown in figure 7.9.

Some people add the transceiver cable lengths to transceivers T1, T2, T3, T4, T5, and T6, shown in figure 7.8. Because the maximum transceiver cable length is 50 meters, this gives a combined transceiver length of 300 meters. Thus, by cheating a little, the maximum Ethernet length becomes 2500 meters plus 300 meters, totalling 2800 meters.

The maximum number of stations that can be attached to a Thick Ethernet segment is 100, and the total number of stations cannot exceed 1024. The repeater attachment to a segment counts as one station. The minimum distance between any two stations is 2.5 meters. Stations should be separated at distances of multiples of 2.5 meters. This rule minimizes interference caused by standing waves that are formed on an Ethernet segment.

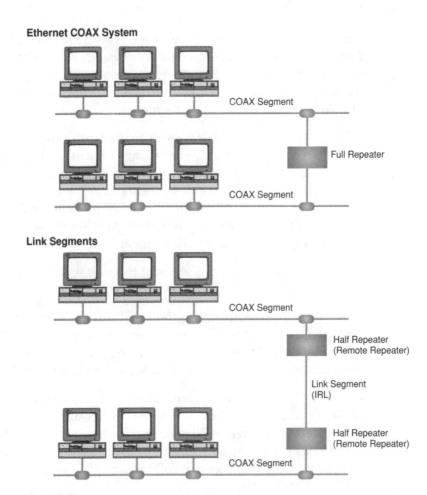

Figure 7.8:
Ethernet coaxial segments versus link segments.

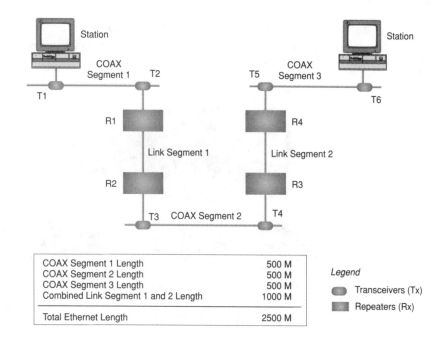

Figure 7.9:
Longest possible Ethernet.

Thin Wire Ethernet Wiring Design Rules

Another name for *Thin Wire Ethernet* is Cheapernet because it is less expensive than Standard Ethernet (its coaxial cable is much thinner). The IEEE version of Thin Wire Ethernet is called 10BASE2 (10 stands for 10Mbps operation; BASE stands for baseband operation; 2 stands for approximately 200 meters—actually, 185 meters—per segment).

Figure 7.10 illustrates a Thick Ethernet connector, known as a *BNC connector*. Stations can be connected to thin coaxial by using a transceiver similar to a Standard Ethernet connection.

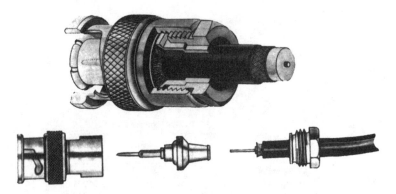

Figure 7.10:
A BNC connector. (Courtesy of Trompeter, Inc.)

More typically, however, Thin Ethernet connections are made by using a BNC connector that is built into the station's network-interface card. The cable itself is connected to the crossbar of a T-connector, shown in figure 7.11. The base of the T-connector is connected directly to the BNC jack on the network-interface card. When this type of connection is used, the transceiver functions are performed by the circuitry on the network-interface card.

The shared media is called the *trunk segment* cable, or just *segment*. Because of signal attenuation, a thin wire segment cannot be longer than 185 meters. Thin Ethernet cable is a 0.2-inch diameter, RG-58 A/U 50-ohm cable, and is available in various pre-cut lengths with a standard BNC plug attached to each end. Thin Ethernet cable can also be purchased in spools or in bulk quantities, which come without the BNC connectors attached at the ends.

Figure 7.11:
A BNC T-connector. Courtesy of AMP, Harrisburg, PA.

A trunk segment must be terminated with a *BNC terminator*. The BNC terminator is a 50-ohm terminator that blocks electrical interference on the segment. Additionally, it cancels out any signal reflections caused by signals bouncing off the end of the cable. The BNC terminator is attached to one of the two jacks on a T-connector when no cable will be attached to that jack. You can obtain a grounded BNC terminator, which has a grounding wire. Only one end of the cable must be grounded; the other end must remain ungrounded. This electrical rule is necessary to avoid ground-loop currents.

Figure 7.12 shows an example of a Thin Ethernet network. In this network, there are two trunk segments that are joined together by a device called a *repeater*. A repeater is an active device that enables an Ethernet LAN to be expanded beyond a single segment by linking two segments together. The repeater amplifies and regenerates the signal so that it can be transmitted over longer distances. The repeater in figure 7.10 has two ports to attach a maximum of two segments. A multiport repeater can link a number of Ethernet segments together.

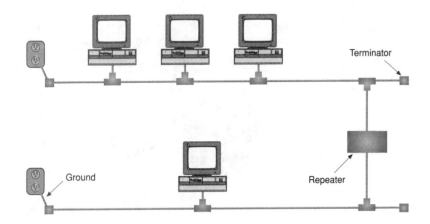

Figure 7.12:
Example of a Thin Ethernet network.

Thin Ethernet wiring involves a number of rules, which are summarized in table 7.2.

Table 7.2
Thin Ethernet Parameters and Wiring Rules

Thin Ethernet Parameters	Value
Max data rate	10Mbps
Max repeaters without IRLs	2
Max repeaters with IRLs	4
Max coaxial segment	185 meters
Max number of link segments	2
Max stations per segment	30
Max number of stations	1024
Min distance between stations	0.5M

NOTE The repeater rules for Thin Ethernet are the same as for Thick Ethernet.

The trunk coaxial segment length for Thin Ethernet cannot exceed 185 meters. The maximum number of stations that can be attached to a Thin Ethernet segment is 30, and the total number of stations cannot exceed 1024. The repeater attachment to a segment counts as one station. The minimum distance between any two stations is 0.5 meters.

10BASE-T Wiring Design Rules

An upsurge of interest in 10BASE-T began in 1990 because of the lower-cost components and the ease of configuring networks based on unshielded twisted-pair wiring (10 stands for 10Mbps operation; BASE stands for baseband operation; T stands for twisted-pair wiring).

A 10BASE-T NIC uses a telephone-type RJ-45 port (an RJ-45 connector is illustrated in figure 7.12). The NIC shown in the figure also has a DIX connector. The DIX connector is used to connect to Thick Wire Ethernet. This particular card can be used with both 10BASE-T and Thick Ethernet. Many NICs require a switch setting to enable either the 10BASE-T or DIX port; others, such as the SMC Elite16T card, have an auto-sense mechanism.

The transceiver functions for a 10BASE-T are performed by the on-board NIC electronics.

The 10BASE-T uses a physical star topology with the 10BASE-T concentrator serving as the central switching element (the 10BASE-T connector is shown in fig. 7.13). Unshielded twisted-pair wiring is used to connect a 10BASE-T concentrator to the workstation. This wiring normally consists of 0.4mm to 0.6mm diameter (26 to 22 AWG) unshielded wire in a multipair cable. The performance specifications are generally met by 100 meters of 0.5mm telephone twisted-pair.

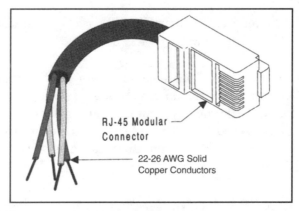

Figure 7.13:
Unshielded twisted-pair (UTP) cable.

Each station on a 10BASE-T network is connected to a wiring hub with an individual twisted-pair cable. Typically, each hub is equipped with connectors to support twelve workstations. For larger networks, hubs may be interconnected by cables in a variety of configurations. Also, a variety of advanced cabling systems, known as *structured wiring systems*, allow multiple hubs to be housed in a *wiring concentrator.* The concentrator provides power to the hub modules and provides the necessary interconnections through a bus. A typical network, consisting of local concentrators and a wiring concentrator, is illustrated in figure 7.14.

The 10BASE-T concentrator serves the role of a repeater. It performs the following functions:

- ❖ Data-packet retiming (IEEE 802.3 standard)
- ❖ Per-port Link Integrity Test ("Good Link Test")
- ❖ Per-port autopartitioning, which disconnects the port in the event of 30 consecutive collisions, an excessively long single collision, or jabber input

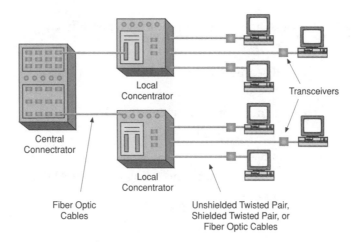

Figure 7.14:
Example of a 10BASE-T network (courtesy of Synoptics Communications, Inc.).

The proper operation of the CSMA/CD 10BASE-T network requires network size to be limited in order to control round-trip propagation delays (the time it takes a signal to reach the extremity of the network and come back). The configuration rules for more than one concentrator are the following:

❖ Maximum of four concentrators in the data path between any two stations

❖ UTP segments should be no longer than 100 meters

Mixed Media Ethernet Networks

You can combine the different media (coaxial, twisted pair, and fiber optic) into an Ethernet LAN. When combining mixed-media networks, a fiber optic, twisted pair, or coaxial cable can be used to implement the link segment.

The following network topology constraints apply for mixed media networks.

1. All segments (coaxial or link) must be connected by repeaters.

2. The maximum transmission path between any two stations may consist of up to:

    5 segments

    4 repeater sets (including optional AUIs)

    2 MAUs

    AUIs

3. If the path between a pair of stations consists of five segments and four repeaters, then no more than three segments can be coaxial segments. The remaining segments must be link segments. Link segments can be either FOIRL (Fiber Optic Inter-Repeater Link) or 10 BASE-T (twisted pair wire cables). If two FOIRL link segments are used, each should not exceed 500 meters.

4. A network path can consists of four segments and three repeaters. If FOIRL is used as link segments, its maximum length cannot exceed 1000 meters.

Rule 2, concerning the maximum transmission path, is illustrated in figure 7.15. Notice that this rule does not tell you how many segments are coaxial trunks with multiple station attachments and how many are link segments with no station attachments. Rule 3 will clarify this.

Rule 3, concerning maximum segments and repeaters, is illustrated in figure 7.16. This figure shows a multimedia Ethernet network. The media used in this network are a combination of coaxial, fiber, and twisted-pair. In figure 7.16, there are five repeater sets. This arrangement may seem to contradict the rule of a maximum of four repeater sets, but between any two stations there are no more

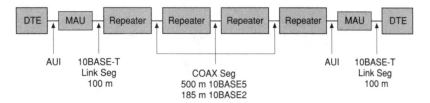

Figure 7.15:

Maximum transmission path with three coaxial segments.

than four repeaters in the transmission path. The total of the segments is 10: seven twisted pair, two fiber optic, and one coaxial segment. However, there are no more than five segments between any two stations. Also, there is a maximum of one coaxial segment, which is within the rule of a maximum of three coaxial segments. When the coaxial segment is included in the transmission path, the remaining four segments are link segments: four-twisted pair segments and one fiber optic link segment.

Because there are a maximum of five segments and four repeaters in the transmission path, the maximum FOIRL length is 500 meters — which follows from Rule 3. The maximum span of this network is 1300 meters, not including AUI drops.

Rule 4, concerning four segments and three repeater sets, is illustrated in figure 7.17. The figure shows three repeater sets and six segments: four twisted pair and two fiber optic. This figure shows no coaxial segments. Between any two stations, there is a maximum of four segments and three repeaters. The four segments consist of two fiber optic and two twisted-pair cables. Each of the FOIRL links has a maximum length of 1000 meters. The maximum span of this network is 2200 meters, not including AUI drops.

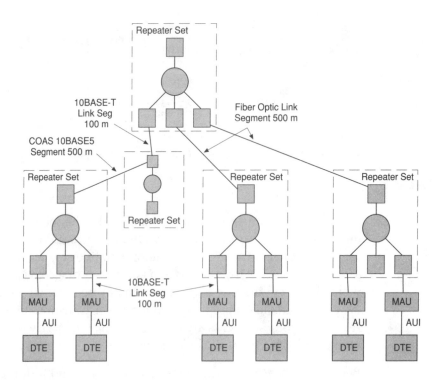

Figure 7.16:

Maximum transmission path.

Thin/Thick Cable Combined in a Segment

You can combine thin and thick Ethernet cable in a single segment, using as much thin cable as possible. The rationale for doing this is that thin cable is cheaper and easier to install than thick cable. Figure 7.18 illustrates a network layout using segments made up of a combination of thin and thick cable.

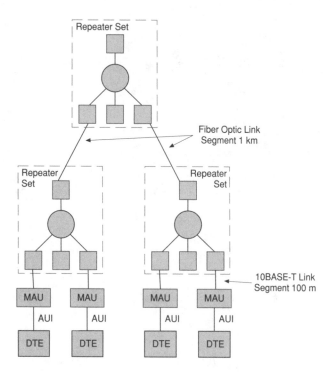

Figure 7.17:

Example of a maximum transmission path with three repeater sets and four link segments.

Combined thin/thick cables are between 185 meters and 500 meters long. The minimum length is 185 meters because coaxial segments shorter than 185 meters can be built with thin cable exclusively. The maximum of 500 meters is the limit for a segment made out of thick coaxial cable exclusively.

To compute the maximum amount of thin cable you can use in one combination trunk segment, use the following equation:

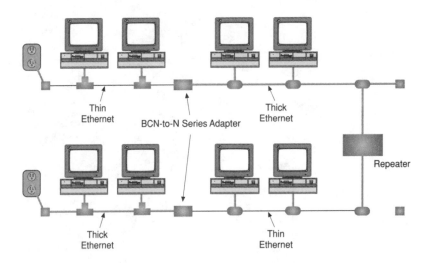

Figure 7.18:

Example of a combination thin/thick cable network layout.

thinLen = (500 - trunkLen)/3.28 meters

(trunkLen = Length of trunk segment you want to build and thinLen = Maximum length of thin length cable you can use)

For example, if you want to build a trunk segment of 400 meters, the maximum length of thin coaxial cable you can use is:

thinLen = (500 - 400)/3.28 = 30.48 meters

You can use 30.48 meters of thin coaxial cable with 400 - 30.48 = 369.52 meters of thick cable.

Thin and thick coaxial cable must be connected through an N-series to a BNC jack.

IEEE 802.3 versus Ethernet-II (DIX 2.0)

Both Ethernet-II and IEEE 802.3 have a minimum frame size of 64 bytes and a maximum frame size of 1518 bytes. There are differences between Ethernet-II and IEEE 802.3. Before examining these differences, study their respective frame structure.

The Ethernet frame (see fig. 7.19) begins with a preamble of eight octets (1 octet = 8 bits), consisting of an alternating pattern 1010 that ends in 101011. At 10 Mbps, this preamble is of 6.4-microsecond duration, which is sufficient time for the receiving station to synchronize and get ready to receive the frame.

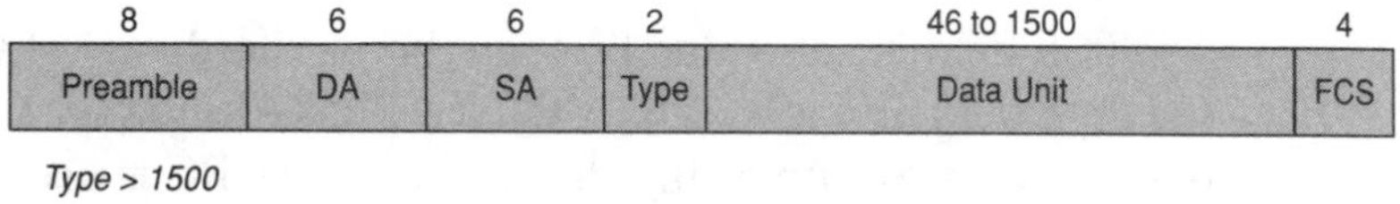

8	6	6	2	46 to 1500	4
Preamble	DA	SA	Type	Data Unit	FCS

Type > 1500

Figure 7.19:
Ethernet frame structure.

The Destination Address (DA) and the Source Address (SA) fields follow this preamble. Each address field is six octets long. The first three octets represent a manufacturers' code and the remaining three octets are assigned by the manufacturer. This assignation is made so that any two Ethernet cards have a unique six-octet address. This address is usually "burned" into a ROM chip on the Ethernet card. The least significant bit (LSB) of the first octet is the Physical/Multicast bit, which is 0 for Ethernet address. A value of 1 for this LSB indicates a multicast address. For instance, a hex value of FFFFFFFFFFFF, all 1's, for the DA field represents a broadcast. The manufacturer code, formerly assigned by Xerox, is now assigned by IEEE.

The Type field, also referred as Ethertype, is a two-octet field used to indicate the type of data in the data field. Thus, if the Ethernet frame is used to carry NetWare data, the Ethertype value will be 8137 hex. If it is used to carry DoD Internet Packet (IP) data, it will have the value 0800 hex. XNS packets used in 3COM networks will have the value 0600hex. This field is used by network drivers or the network layer to demultiplex data packets to the appropriate protocol stack. It allows multiple protocol stacks to run on a single Ethernet card.

The Data Unit field is a variable length field that can range from 46 to 1500 bytes. The remaining fixed length fields add up to 18 bytes. Hence the limit of 64 to 1518 bytes for an Ethernet packet.

The FCS field is generated by the Ethernet hardware at the end of the data field and is a 32-bit CRC (Cyclic Redundancy Checksum) over the address, type, and data fields. The CRC is used to detect errors in transmission. Bad frames are retransmitted.

The IEEE frame (see fig. 7.20) begins with a preamble of seven octets (1 octet = 8 bits), consisting of an alternating pattern 1010. At 10 Mbps, this preamble is of 5.6-microsecond duration, which is sufficient time for the receiving station to synchronize and get ready to receive the frame.

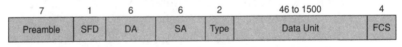

Length ≤ 1500

Figure 7.20:
IEEE 802.3 frame structure.

The SFD (Start Frame Delimiter) follows after the preamble and is defined by the pattern 10101011. The alert reader notices the following:

IEEE 802.3 preamble + SFD = Ethernet preamble

The IEEE 802.3 preamble and the SFD field combined are identical to the eight-octet Ethernet preamble.

The Destination Address (DA) and the Source Address (SA) fields follow the SFD. Each address field can be six octets or two octets long. (Six-octet addressing is the most common.) The first three octets represent a manufacturer's code, and the remaining three octets are assigned by the manufacturer. This assignation is made so that any two Ethernet and IEEE cards have a unique six-octet address. This address is usually "burned" into a ROM chip on the IEEE 802.3 card. The least significant bit (LSB) of the first octet represents the Individual/Group field and is similar to the Physical/Multicast field in Ethernet. The next bit is the Universe/Local (U/L) field and indicates whether the addressing is global or local.

The Length field follows the address fields and is two octets long. It indicates the data size of the LLC layer. A minimum of 46 octets of LLC is required to make up the minimum size of 64 octets. The maximum value of this field is 1500 to make a maximum frame size of 1518 octets.

The Data Unit field is a variable length field containing 46 to 1500 octets of LLC data.

The FCS field is generated by the IEEE 802.3 hardware at the end of the data field and is a 32-bit CRC (Cyclic Redundancy Checksum) over the address, type and data fields. The CRC is used to detect errors in transmission. Bad frames are retransmitted.

There are differences between Ethernet-II and IEEE 802.3. You can see that Ethernet-II uses a two-byte type field to indicate the type of data. The type-field values were at one time assigned by Xerox; they are now assigned by IEEE. Instead of the type field, IEEE 803.3 has a two-byte length field. The length field for Ethernet Packets is supplied by a higher layer such as the network layer. In some cases, the NIC is able to determine the length of the frame based on signal duration and passes this information to upper layers. For IEEE 802.3 frames, the type information is supplied by the IEEE 802.2 (Logical Control Layer) frame that is part of the Data Unit field (see fig. 7.21). The IEEE 802.2 frame consists of a DSAP and SSAP field that are used as "type" fields. These fields have unique assignments.

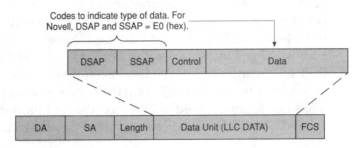

Figure 7.21:
"Type" information in IEEE 802.3.

Ethernet has no provision to pad the data to make a minimum Ethernet frame of 64 bytes. IEEE 802.3 frames have a length field to encode the pad information. In Ethernet, the padding has to be performed by upper layers.

Token Ring LANS

Token-ring-based networks have been around for many years. Many researchers, such as those at UC Irvine and Cambridge University, built ring LANs in the early 1970s.

Token-ring LANs are a concatenation of point-to-point links, and as such are not really a broadcast LAN such as Ethernet. They may be considered to be sequential broadcast LANs with the point-to-point links forming a circle. The technology of ring LANs is digital, unlike that of Ethernet LANs, in which the carrier-sense mechanism may be analog. Another attractive feature of ring-based

LANs is their deterministic response time even under heavy load conditions. This feature is of interest for real-time applications.

 The token-ring LAN you see most often is the IEEE 802.5. In the industry, this is often referred to as the IBM Token Ring because IBM was the prime mover behind the IEEE 802.5 standard. IEEE 802.5 plays an important role in IBM's SAA (Systems Application Architecture), which is IBM's grand theme to integrate their entire product line. From IBM's perspective, the Token Ring will be used to network desktop machines. The desktop machines running an operating system such as OS/2 will be able to access IBM mainframes through SNA (System Network Architecture) gateways.

IBM makes its own proprietary chips to implement Token Ring NICs. Other vendors such as 3COM, Madge, and Proteon make use of the TMS 380 chip set from Texas Instruments.

Token-Ring Operation

Figure 7.22 illustrates token-ring operation. The token-ring LAN can be seen as a concatenation of point-to-point links. Each station acts like a repeater, providing the necessary amplification and correcting for signal jitter. The links can be made up of any media such as coaxial, twisted-pair, and fiber optic cable. For the IBM Token Ring, twisted-pair cable is the medium of choice. Fiber optic links can be used to extend token-ring operations over longer distances. The following section describes the IEEE 802.5 operation.

A special group of bits, called the *token* (shown in figure 7.22), is used to arbitrate access to the ring. If a station wants to transmit a frame, it must seize this token. While the station is holding on to the token, it can transmit a frame. At the end of the transmission, it must release the token so other stations can access the ring.

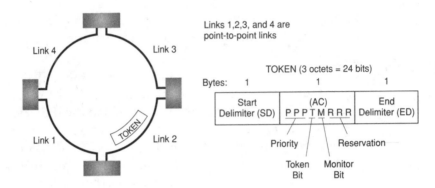

Figure 7.22:
Token-ring operation.

For proper operation of the ring, the token must circulate continuously even if there is no activity on the ring. Now, there are 24 bits (3 octets) in the token, and therefore the ring must have enough latency or delay to hold 24 bits. If the bit rate on the ring is 4 Mbps, the ring must have a latency of 24/4 Mbps = 6 microseconds. Six microseconds may seem like a short delay, but consider a twisted-pair medium in which the propagation velocity is 0.59 times the speed of light. To compute the size of the ring that has a latency of 6 microseconds, use the following formula:

Size of Ring = Latency × Propagation speed of media

Size of Ring = 0.0000006 x 0.59 x 3 x 100000000 meters

Size of Ring = 1062 meters

Size of Ring = 1.062 km

Thus, the minimum size of the ring would be one km! This size is enormous, considering that you may want to install a few stations in a single room. For this reason, a special station that is designated as the Active Monitor adds a 24-bit delay buffer to the ring. This buffer also compensates for any accumulated phase jitter on the ring. The Active Monitor, is the important for maintaining the normal operation of the ring.

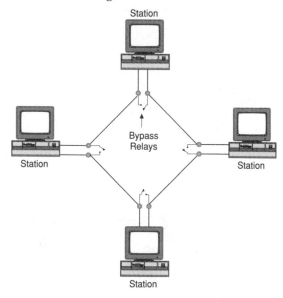

Figure 7.23:
Token-ring relay operation.

Under normal operation of the ring, stations may be powered down. What happens to the bits that need to go across an inactive station? Token-ring networks are wired as physical star networks with a hub or wiring center. In figure 7.23, the relays are held open by power from the station. When a station is powered down, the relay closes and bypasses the inactive station.

A token-ring station operates in one of four modes:

Transmit mode

Listen mode

Bypass mode

Receive mode

Figure 7.24 shows stations operating in these modes.

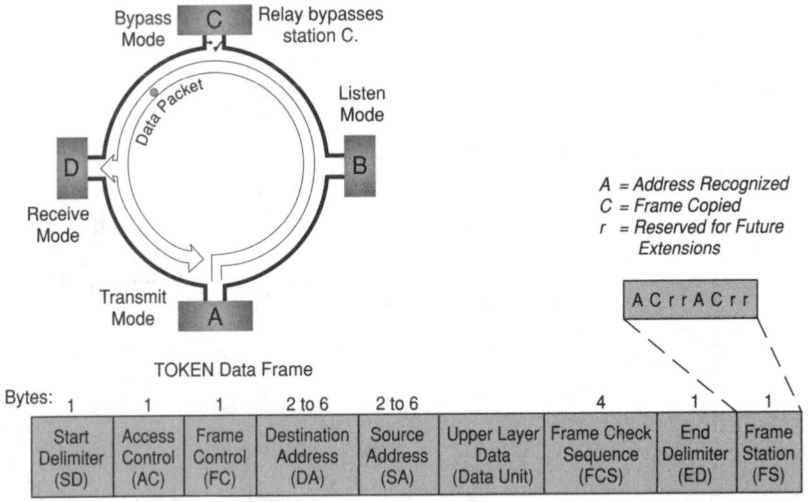

Figure 7.24:
Token-ring station modes.

Station A is in the *transmit mode*. To enter this mode, it seizes a free token. The token has a token bit, called the *T bit*. This T bit has the value of one in a free token. The transmitting station changes this T bit to a 0, indicating a busy token, and transmits the data frame. In figure 7.24, station A is sending this data frame to station D, and therefore the destination address field holds station D's address; the source address field holds station A's address.

Station B is operating in the *listen mode*. It checks the destination address field of the frame to see if it holds its address (station B's address). Because the frame is addressed to station D, it enters the listen mode. In listen mode, a station copies the incoming bits to the output link.

Station C has been powered down and is therefore in the *bypass mode*. The bits flow through the bypass relay.

Station D examines the destination address field. It discovers that it is indeed the addressed station, and it enters the *receive mode*. In receive mode, the data frame is copied into the station's memory, and also sent along the ring. A number of flags, called the *frame status flags*, are modified to indicate proper reception of the data frame. Station A receives the data frame that it sent and examines the frame status flags. The frame status flags serve the purpose of a hardware-based acknowledgment. The sending station can see these flags and determine if the frame was received correctly. The frame status flags are the Address-recognized (A) flag, Frame-copied (C) flag, and the Error (E) flag. The E flag is computed and set by every station. The A and C flags are set by the destination station only. Table 7.3 shows the flags and their values and meanings.

Table 7.3
Frame Status Flags

Frame Flags	Value	Meaning
A	1	Address recognized
A	0	Address not recognized
C	1	Frame copied successfully
C	0	Frame not copied
E	1	Bad frame (CRC error)
E	0	Good frame

The legal combinations of these flags are the following:

❖ **AC = 00.** The address was not recognized, so the copy operation did not take place.

❖ **AC = 10.** The station exists, but the frame was not copied. The E flag is examined to see if it were set to 1. If E = 1, it shows that a bad frame was received. This is the equivalent to a Negative Acknowledgement (NAK). If the E flag is 0, the frame was not copied for unknown reasons.

❖ **AC = 11.** Station exists and frame is copied to station. This is the equivalent to a Positive Acknowledgement (ACK). What if the E flag is set to 1? If the destination station receives a frame with E=1, it never copies the frame, and therefore AC is never 11. If ACE = 111, it indicates that an error was introduced after the destination frame had already copied the frame. If E = 0, no errors occurred on the ring for the transmission of the frame.

The only illegal combination is AC = 01, which indicates that the station was not recognized, but somebody still copied the frame. In other words, some station illegally copied the data frame!

As the bits that were sent by station A come back to station A, that station removes the bits from the ring.

What if station A is powered down before the frame that it sent came back? Because it is the responsibility of the sending station to remove the frame that it sent, this frame would circulate endlessly! Many similar scenarios could disrupt the normal ring operation. What if the token is destroyed by noise on the ring? Would stations wait for the token indefinitely? The token ring operation contains "self-healing" mechanisms to correct for these and many other possibilities. These situations are detected and handled by special control frames called MAC frames. The self-healing capability is one of the reasons that the IEEE 802.5 operation is more complex than IEEE 802.3. The following paragraphs describe just a few of these self-healing mechanisms.

Although all stations are equal, some stations are more equal than others. One such station is the Active Monitor. It contains a *monitor bit* (*M-bit*) in the token that is set to 0 by the transmitting station. The Active Monitor examines this M-bit and changes it to a 1, if it is a 0. If the Active Monitor bit sees an M-bit value of 1 it concludes that this data frame has been circulating around once too often! This occurrence could be due to a crash of the transmitting station, which failed to remove the data frame from the ring.

If the token is lost because it got mangled by noise on the ring, the Active Monitor times out and generates a new token. The Active Monitor keeps track of this Token Rotation Time (TRT) and times out if it exceeds a threshold value. For small token-ring networks, a typical value of TRT is eight microseconds. Under heavy load conditions, this value may rise slightly.

The Active Monitor is not a station with special networking hardware. Any station on the token ring can become an Active Monitor. All other stations act as Standby Monitors. The choice of which station becomes an Active Monitor is made through a ring-initialization procedure. If the Active Monitor fails, one of the Standby Monitors becomes the Active Monitor.

When no data frames are circulating around the ring, the Active Monitor issues an Active Monitor Present (AMP) MAC frame. This frame is sent at regular intervals of seven seconds. Other stations in the role of Standby Monitors send Standby Monitor Present (SMP) MAC frames. Standby monitors detect the AMP frame and conclude that the Active Monitor is doing its job. But the Standby Monitors are waiting for the Active Monitor to fail! If the Active monitor does not send out the AMP frame when it should, one of the Standby Monitors takes over the role of the Active Monitor. The Standby Monitor that detects the failure of the Active Monitor sends its claim on the token ring in the form of Claim Token (CL_TK) MAC frames. The Standby Monitor stops sending these frames if any of the following conditions occurs:

❖ Another CL_TK frame is received and the sender's address is greater than this station's address. In this situation, if two or more stations send out CL_TK, the decision about who becomes the Active Monitor is made in favor of the station with the higher address.

❖ A Beacon (BCN) MAC frame is received. This frame is sent as a result of a major ring failure, such as a ring break. The BCN frame is used to locate and isolate the fault. In this case, the ring needs to be healed before deciding the winner of this contest.

❖ A Purge (PRG) MAC frame is received. This frame is sent out at the end of the Claim Token procedure by the station who has become the new Active Monitor. In this situation, the race has already been won by another station, so there is no point in continuing.

In any of the preceding cases, the Standby Monitor backs off. If a station receives the CL_TK frame it generated, it becomes the Active Monitor and issues a Purge MAC frame to inform other stations that there is a new Active Monitor. At this point, the new Active Monitor adds the 24-bit latency buffer to the ring and commences monitoring the network.

Before joining a ring, a new station sends out the Duplicate Address Test (DAT) MAC frame as part of the ring-initialization procedure. The DAT frame is sent with its own address in the Destination Address field. If another station responds with the AC bits set to 11, another station has the same address. In this case, the new station returns an appropriate status code. Network monitoring software can detect this code and process it with an appropriate error message.

Another feature of the IEEE 802.5 is the priority-access mechanism. The token has two fields, called the Priority field and the Reservation field, each consisting of three bits. A total of eight priority values can be defined (0 to 7). The Reservation field is set to 0 by the transmitting station. If a station wants priority access, it can place its priority value in the Reservation field. When the transmitting station receives the frame it sent, it copies the Reservation field value in the Priority field of the new token that it generates. The token now has the requested Priority value. Only stations with higher or equal priority can access this token. The next section examines token-ring options.

Token-Ring Options

The IEEE 802.5 specifies token-ring options at data rates of 1, 4, and 16Mbps. The 1Mbps uses unshielded twisted-pair wiring. Initially the 4Mbps and 16Mbps used shielded twisted-pair wiring. There has been a demand in the industry to have the 4Mbps and 16 Mbps run on UTP wiring. Several products have become available to support UTP wiring for 4 and 16Mbps token ring. For a long time, a 16Mbps UTP version was not available from IBM. IBM has teamed up with Synoptics Communications to propose a 16Mbps UTP standard to the IEEE 802.5 committee. These options are shown in relationship to the IEEE/OSI model, in figure 7.25.

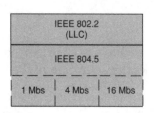

Figure 7.25:
IEEE 802.5 options for token ring.

The 16Mbps stations do not wait for the return of the data frame to place the token on the network. This is called the *early release token mechanism*. This failure to wait allows up to two data frames to be transmitted on a token ring LAN at a time.

Token Ring LAN Components

Figure 7.26 illustrates the IBM 8228 Multistation Access Unit, also called MAU (but not to be confused with the Media Attached Unit in IEEE 802.3.) This MAU is a wiring center that allows up to eight stations to be connected to it. The two end ports, called RI (Ring In) and RO (Ring Out), are not used to connect token-ring stations. These ports are used to connect multiple MAUs together. Four port Wiring Centers (also called hubs) are also available. MAUs are also available that contain a number of network-management features. These MAUs are called smart or intelligent MAUs.

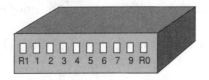

Figure 7.26:
The IBM 8228 Multistation Access Unit (MAU).

The IBM 8228 Setup Aid is used to test each port in the IBM 8228 before it is installed. It checks the operation of the bypass relay mechanism for each port.

The IBM Token Ring network adapter cable is made of eight feet of IBM cable. One end of this cable connects to the token-ring adapter, and the other end is a dual-gender connector that plugs into one of the station ports in the IBM 8228 MAU.

Type 3 cabling, which refers to conventional telephone wiring (UTP), can also be used.

IEEE 802.5 Design Rules

Token-ring wiring involves a number of rules, which are summarized in table 7.4.

Table 7.4
Token Ring Wiring Rules

Token Ring Parameters	Type 1, 2	Type 3
Max devices per ring	260	96
Tested data rates	16 Mps	4 Mps
Station to single MAU LAN	300 M	100 M
Station to multiple MAU LAN	100 M	45 M
Max MAUs per LAN	12	2
MAU to MAU distance	200 M	120 M

The following list describes the general guidelines for token-ring cabling:

1. Stations located within eight feet of the MAU can be connected by using 8-foot adapter cable.

2. Stations farther than eight feet from the MAU can be connected by using extension cords, or you can build longer adapter cables.

3. To form a ring using multiple MAUs, connect a patch cable from the RO (Ring Out) of the first MAU to the RI (Ring In) of the second MAU. Continue doing this for all the MAUs until you reach the last MAU. Connect the RO of the last MAU to the RI of the first MAU.

4. You cannot connect stations to the RI and the RO port. The RI and RO ports are only used for interconnecting multiple MAUs.

5. Patch cables (IBM Type 6) should not be spliced.

6. Patch cables (IBM Type 6) should not be used in any duct, plenum, or other space used for air handling. IBM Type 9, which is a plenum-rated cable, can be used instead.

ARCnet LANS

In 1976, a group of four engineers from Datapoint Corporation embarked on a project to build a LAN that evolved into a widely used but relatively unknown LAN in the industry—ARCnet. (ARCnet stands for Attached Resource Computer Network.) The goal of the design team was to develop network links between Datapoint's computer systems so that customers could share resources while still retaining the benefits of stand-alone processing.

A data rate of 2.5Mbps was selected, primarily because that was the transfer rate of the disks that Datapoint was using at the time. A small frame size of 508 bytes maximum was chosen, because a study done by ARCnet's designers revealed that more than 90 percent of all messages transmitted on a network were small. The designers wanted to make the network reliable so that failures in stations and cables had a minimum impact on the rest of the network. Another requirement was to make ARCnet work with a variety of media such as coaxial, twisted pair, and fiber optic cable. Today, products exist that support these media.

By fall of 1977, the project was complete but did not make a big splash in the industry, primarily because ARCnet was not a separate product; rather, it was embedded in Datapoint's computing machines.

ARCnet technology predates Ethernet technology, even though many people feel that Ethernet technology was the first. The reasons for ARCnet being relatively unknown are many. One reason is that Datapoint kept the technology proprietary. It was not until 1982 that Datapoint allowed SMC (Standard Microsystems Corporation) to market an ARCnet chip set to other OEMs. Ethernet had already become popular by this time. Also, Datapoint — unlike Digital, Intel, and Xerox — did not propose ARCnet to the IEEE committee and it had less market influence compared to other companies behind Ethernet and the token-ring standard. The SMC chip set developed in 1982 started a grass-roots movement. More than a dozen vendors have used this chip set to manufacture ARCnet network cards.

ARCnet uses the RG/62 93-ohm coaxial cable used with IBM 3270 terminals. This coaxial cable is cheaper than the 50-ohm coaxial cable used in Ethernet. Additionally, many older office buildings and airport complexes are wired with this type of cabling, making the transition to ARCnet easy.

ARCnet uses the token passing bus mechanism, which makes ARCnet deterministic. There is a fixed upper limit on the amount of time a station has to wait before it can transmit.

Despite its many advantages, ARCnet has the disadvantage of a low data rate of 2.5Mbps. A number of ARCnet vendors have banded together to form the ARCnet Trader's Association (ATA), which disseminates information to users about ARCnet technology. Membership in ATA is open to vendors, system integrators, and users. ATA is located at 3413 North Kennicott, Suite B, Arlington Heights, IL; and their telephone number is (312) 255-3003. Under its auspices, a new ARCnet standard is in the works. Called ARCnet Plus, it has a designed data rate of 20 Mbps.

ARCnet Operation

Figure 7.27 shows an ARCnet LAN. Station transmission is broadcast in the same manner as for a bus LAN, but access to the bus is determined by a token; hence the name, Token Passing Bus.

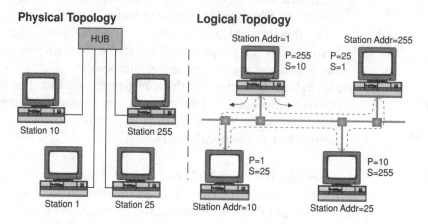

Figure 7.27:
ARCnet LAN operation.

Figure 7.27 shows stations with node address 1, 25, 50, and 255 on a bus. At startup time, a logical ordering is made so that these stations form a logical ring. Each station keeps track of two pieces of information: who is its successor and who is its predecessor? This information is shown by the letters S (successor) and P (predecessor) for each station. A *successor* for a station is defined as the station on the ring with the next highest address. A *predecessor* for a station is defined as the station with the next lowest address. A maximum of 255 stations are allowed in ARCnet, with the lowest station address being 1. Station address 0 is used for broadcast. The successor for station 255 is 1 and the predecessor for station 1 is 255. The predecessor and successor information for the stations is shown in table 7.5.

Table 7.5
Table of Station Numbers

Station	Predecessor(P)	Successor (S)
1	255	10
10	1	25
25	10	255
255	25	1

A special frame, called the *token frame* is passed from a station to its successor. The passing of this frame from station to station forms a logical ring. The token frame is called the Invitation To Transmit (ITT) frame. Its structure is shown as follows:

```
ITT =    ALERT   EOT   DID   DID
ITT =  | ALERT | EOT | DID | DID |
***
```

All ARCnet frames are preceded by an ALERT burst, similar to the preamble for Ethernet. An ALERT burst is six-bit intervals of mark (1). A *mark* (1) is represented by a dipulse pulse that consists of a positive pulse, followed by a negative pulse. A space (0) is represented by the absence of a pulse. The EOT is the ASCII EOT (04 hex) and is followed by two bytes. Each of the bytes contains the successor information called *The Destination Identification (DID) number* in ARCnet terminology. The DID field is repeated for reliability.

A station that has the ITT frame can transmit at most one frame before passing the frame to its successor (the next DID).

Before a data frame is sent to a destination node, it must be queried to see if it has enough buffer space to accept the frame. A special frame called the Free Buffer Enquiry (FBE) performs this function.

```
FBE =   ALERT   ENQ   DID   DID
```

The ENQ is the ASCII ENQ (05 hex), which means enquiry and is followed by two bytes. Each of the bytes contains the destination address (DID) of the station whose free buffer status is desired. The DID field is repeated for reliability. If the destination node sends a positive response, an ACK frame, the sending node can send the data frame.

A positive ACK frame consists of the following two bytes:

```
ACK =   ALERT   ACK
```

The ACK is the ASCII ACK (06 hex), which means acknowledgment. When ACK is sent in response to a FBE frame, it indicates the availability of buffer space at the receiver. There is no DID field, because it is sent as a broadcast frame.

A negative acknowledgment (NAK) frame consists of the following two bytes:

```
NAK =   ALERT   NAK
```

The NAK is the ASCII ACK (15 hex), which means negative acknowledgment. It indicates non-availability of buffer space at the receiver. It is not sent to indicate improper data-frame reception. There is no DID field because it is sent as a broadcast frame.

After an ACK frame is received in response to a FBE frame, a data frame can be sent. Data frames are transmitted by the PAC frame.

```
PAC =   ALERT   SOH   SID   DID   DID   CP   DATA
CRC   CRC
```

The SOH is the ASCII SOH (01 hex), which means start of header. The source and destination address are indicated by the SID (Source ID) and DID (Destination ID) fields. Again, the DID field is repeated for reliability. The CP is the Continuation Pointer field and indicates where in its memory the station finds the beginning of the transmitted data. The data field, DATA, varies in length between 1 to 508 bytes. A two-byte CRC determined by the DATA field is appended by the sender for error-checking purposes.

In normal ARCnet operation, there are a number of situations in which a fault may occur. A *fault* in ARCnet is defined as any situation that disrupts the logical ring. Its end result is that the token-frame (ITT) is lost. This token frame needs to be regenerated. The process of detecting and recovering from a fault is called *reconfiguration* or *resequencing*. Reconfiguration can also occur when a new station is added or removed from a ring.

A timeout mechanism detects faults. Each active node on the logical ring keeps track of the last time it saw the ITT token frame. If the active node does not see the ITT token frame within 840 milliseconds (timeout period), it generates a special signal pattern that is distinct from any data frame. This special signal pattern informs all nodes that something has gone wrong on the ring, and that a reconfiguration is in progress to correct this problem. This special signal pattern, called the RECON (RECONfiguration), consists of eight mark intervals, followed by one space repeated 765 times. The RECON signal is also generated when a station is first powered on.

This RECON burst lasts for 2754 microseconds; it is long enough to disrupt any token-frame transmission that is under way. The result is that the token frame is lost. The stations wait for another 78 microseconds, and if no activity occurs, you can assume that a reconfiguration is in progress.

Each station then sets its successor (NID) to its own address (ID) plus 1 initially, and sets a timeout value according to the following equation:

```
TIME-OUT = 146 x (255 - ID) microseconds
```

The node with the highest address will timeout first and issue an ITT to its successor (NID). The station with address 255 will have a timeout value of 0. If no activity occurs after 74 microseconds (less than 78 microseconds), the highest address station assumes that the node with the successor address of NID does not exist. It will increment the NID value and send another ITT with the DID field set to the new NID value. This procedure is repeated until the highest address station discovers its successor. At that time, the token is transferred to the successor, and the successor will repeat this process.

After all active nodes are found, the normal token-passing operation is resumed. Reconfiguration can take between 24 to 61 milliseconds, depending on the number of active nodes and the value of their node addresses. To minimize the initial timeout value to 0 and reduce the reconfiguration time, set at least one ARCnet node to address 255.

Deletion of a node is a simpler process under ARCnet and does not invoke the full reconfiguration mechanism. In figure 7.28, if station 10 drops from the ring and does not respond to the ITT sent from station 1 for a period of 74 microseconds, station 1 assumes that station 10 is no longer active. Node 1 then increments its NID value (new value 11), and sends an ITT to station 11. If there is no response, the process repeats in another 74 microseconds. In figure 7.28, the next station address is 25. Therefore, within $(25 - 10) \times 74$ microseconds = 1.1 milliseconds, station 1 figures out that its successor is station 25.

If station 10 wants to re-enter the network, it waits for a period of 840 milliseconds for the token. If it has not been invited to transmit through an ITT frame sent to it, itinvokes the full reconfiguration mechanism.

ARCnet Components

Figure 7.28 shows some typical ARCnet components. A RG-62/U 93-ohm cable is used to connect the components of an ARCnet LAN. BNC twist-lock connector plugs are attached to both ends of the cable. BNC connector jacks mate with the BNC connector plugs and are located on several pieces of ARCnet hardware such as active and passive hubs, network cards, and active links.

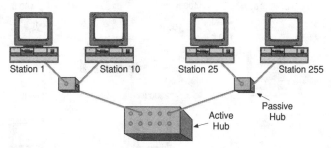

Figure 7.28:
ARCnet LAN operation.

Active hubs serve the role of a repeater in other LANs. Active hubs amplify and recondition the signal. They usually have eight ports, although active hubs with more ports are available. Terminating unused ports on an active hub is recommended but not necessary because of the isolation circuitry used in most ARCnet active hubs.

Passive hubs usually come with four ports to which network cables such as the RG-62/U can be attached. Unused ports in passive hubs must be terminated. Unlike the active hubs, they do not have special isolation circuits.

ARCnet Star Wiring Design Rules

Figure 7.29 illustrates the design rules for an ARCnet LAN using distributed star topology. These rules are summarized in table 7.6.

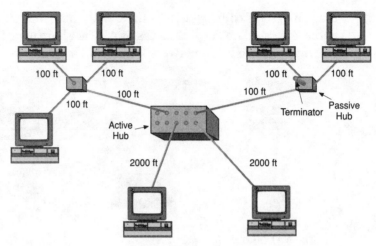

Figure 7.29:
ARCnet LAN using star-wiring rules.

Table 7.6
Cable Distance Limitations

From	To	Max Distance (feet)
One network end	The other end	20,000
Network station	Active hub	2,000
Network station	Passive hub	100
Active hub	Active hub	2,000
Active hub	Passive hub	100
Passive hub	Passive hub	Does not work

The maximum span of an ARCnet network is 20,000 feet (3.8 miles). ARCnet LANs can often handle installations that have longer distances between active components. They have been known to span distances of 4.5 miles, even though this is outside the ARCnet specification. When passive hubs are employed, the distances cannot exceed 100 feet. Also, a passive hub cannot be connected in series with another passive hub. The signal attenuation is too great for this to work.

General rules for ARCnet networks:

1. Active hubs can connect to other hubs (active and passive) and ARCnet stations.

2. Passive hubs can connect to active hubs and ARCnet stations. They cannot connect to other passive hubs directly.

3. Do not create loops in an ARCnet LAN. A loop is created when a cable coming from a hub goes through other hubs and then connects back into the original hub.

4. Always terminate unused ports in a passive hub.

5. Keep a log of station addresses. Two stations cannot have duplicate addresses. No automatic mechanism exists to prevent this from occurring as is the case in IEEE 802.5.

6. To minimize reconfiguration time, set your most reliable station that is active most of the time to station address 255. This station can be your file server.

ARCnet Coaxial Bus Design Rules

ARCnet can be used in a bus topology in which up to eight stations can be daisy-chained with RG-62/U cables over a maximum distance of 1000 feet. In the bus topology, a T-connector is used to connect the workstations and a single bus segment must be terminated with a 93-ohm impedance at both ends.

ARCnet coaxial bus topology can be mixed with the distributed star topology provided by an active hub. One end of the bus can be connected to an active hub. The total number of workstations that can be connected to a single eight-port active hub in this manner is $8 \times 8 = 64$. If two active hubs are to be connected, one port in each active hub is used for connecting the active hubs. Therefore, each active hub supports 56 stations, and the two active hubs support a total of 112 stations.

Table 7.7 summarizes the configuration rules for coaxial bus.

Table 7.7

Configuration Rules for ARCnet Coaxial Bus

Parameters	Value
Max stations per bus	8
Max length of bus	1000 feet
Max stations on single	64 8-bit active hubs

ARCnet Twisted-Pair Wiring Design Rules

Twisted-pair wiring can be used for ARCnet LANs.

With ARCnet, twisted-pair bus topology is functionally and logically equivalent to the coaxial bus topology. Only one pair of twisted-pair wiring is needed. The twisted-pair ARCnet board has two six-pin modular jacks. The two jacks can be used to daisy-chain the ARCnet board unless the board is at the beginning or end of the daisy-chain segment. Terminators must be placed on unused plugs. A maximum of 10 stations can be used in the twisted-pair daisy chain whose length cannot exceed 400 feet. The minimum spacing between stations in the daisy chain is six feet.

Twisted-pair bus topologies can be mixed with the distributed star topology provided by an active hub. One end of the bus can be connected to an active hub. Table 7.8 summarizes the configuration rules for twisted-pair bus.

Table 7.8

Configuration Rules for ARCnet Twisted-Pair Bus

Parameters	Value
Max stations per TP bus	10
Max length of TP bus	400 feet
Min distance between nodes	6 feet
Max stations on single	80 8-port active hubs

Large ARCnet Networks

The total number of stations in a single ARCnet LAN cannot exceed 255, and its maximum span is 20,000 feet. Within these limitations, any combination of distributed star, coaxial bus, and twisted-pair bus can be used.

20 Mbps ARCnet Plus

One of the most amazing features of the 20Mbps ARCnet Plus is that it improves the performance of ARCnet by a factor of eight and yet retains downward compatibility with the 2.5Mbps ARCnet.

Nodes on standard ARCnet signal a logical 1 by a single cycle of a 5-Mhz sine wave, followed by a silence of equal length. A logical 0 consists of two intervals of silence. The duration of the interval is $1/5\text{Mhz} = 200$ nanoseconds. Two such intervals are necessary to send 1 bit (0 or 1) of information, which works out to a duration of 400 nanoseconds. This results in a maximum data rate for ARCnet of $1/400$ nanoseconds = 2.5Mbps. ARCnet sends data in integral multiples of bytes. Each byte is preceded by a three-bit calibration pattern (110) to keep the receiver in pace with the transmitter. There is an overhead of three bits for every eight bits of data.

Therefore, the effective data rate for ARCnet is $8/11 \times 2.5$Mbps = 1.82Mbps. This rate leaves a lot of wasted bandwidth. The periods of silence are wasteful, and the calibration overhead takes up 27 percent of the bandwidth.

ARCnet Plus uses the bandwidth more effectively. As you can guess, one way of achieving higher data rates is to cut out the periods of silence. Another way is to send calibration patterns once every eight bytes. The most ingenious technique is to use Amplitude Modulation to squeeze four bits of information into every 200-nanosecond interval. A pulse can be either a positive or a negative sine wave with eight possible amplitudes, from 0 to 12 volts. This definition gives a total of $2 \times 8 = 16$ combinations of pulses, enough to represent four bits of data.

Thus, the total ARCnet Plus data rate = 4 bits $\times$ 5 million pulses per second = 20Mbps, excluding overhead. When you take into account the calibration overhead, this yields an effective data rate of 16.84Mbps, which is faster than Ethernet and 16Mbps token ring.

During initialization, the ARCnet Plus node sends a special signal, informing others that it can operate at higher speeds. This signal is also sent when an ARCnet Plus node passes the token. An ARCnet Plus node communicates to another ARCnet Plus node at 20Mbps, but will step down to 2.5Mbps to communicate with a 2.5Mbps ARCnet node.

The new standard allows packet lengths of up to 4096 bytes and a maximum of 2047 nodes. IEEE 802.2 or DoD IP addressing mechanism can be used for easier integration with Ethernet, token ring, and TCP/IP networks.

Upgrading to ARCnet Plus

To mix the two types of cards together, the cabling can remain the same but the active hubs have to be replaced with ARCnet Plus active hubs. If older active hubs were used, the high-speed ARCnet Plus signals will be filtered out.

 Another way of solving this problem is to use older ARCnet active hubs, but make sure that you do not put two ARCnet Plus nodes on opposite sides of the older active hub.

Understanding FDDI

FDDI (*Fiber Distributed Data Interface*) is regarded by many as a high-speed LAN (100Mbps). Because it can span a distance of 100 km, however, it can be used as a WAN to interconnect LANs or serve as a backbone to LANs. A number of chip sets are becoming available that implement FDDI protocols. FDDI spans layers 2 and 1 of the OSI model and can be used to provide IEEE 802.2 or LLC services to upper layers (see fig. 7.30). This means that FDDI can be used to run client/server applications that rely on IEEE 802.2 services. NetWare, which provides IEEE 802.2 encapsulation, supports FDDI. The FDDI physical station address follows the IEEE 48-bit (six octet) addressing convention.

FDDI is based on the token-ring access method that runs at 100Mbps. A token is used to control access to the ring but the details of token management are different from IEEE 802.5 LANs. Maximum length of FDDI is 200 km (100 km for dual rings) and the distance between two nodes on a FDDI LAN cannot exceed 2 km. The distance parameters are based on a maximum latency (delay) of 1.617 milliseconds. Maximum FDDI frame size is 4500 bytes. This size makes it suited for high-speed file transfers such as graphic, image, and other data files. The total number of connections to an FDDI ring cannot exceed 2,000 (1,000 for dual-attached stations).

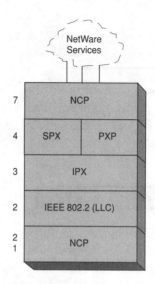

Figure 7.30:
FDDI for netware servers.

A full FDDI configuration consists of a dual-fiber ring. The primary ring is used for data transfer, and the secondary ring serves as a backup ring in case the primary ring fails. If the primary ring fails, an auto-sense mechanism causes a ring wrap so that traffic is diverted to the secondary ring (see fig. 7.31). Only stations that have a dual-attachment station (they are connected to primary and secondary rings) are tolerant to this type of failure. Some single-attachment stations have cheaper interfaces but do not enjoy this level of fault tolerance.

Normally, PC workstations are not attached directly to the FDDI network, but are attached by a FDDI concentrator or router (see fig. 7.32). PC workstations are powered on and off quite often in their normal usage. If they were connected to the FDDI ring directly, their powering on and off would cause frequent ring

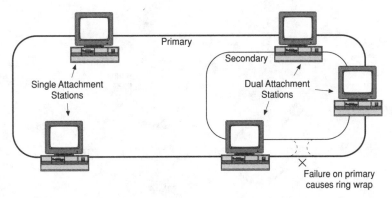

Figure 7.31:
FDDI ring with dual and single attachments.

reconfigurations that could become costly in a large FDDI network. Another reason for not connecting PC workstations to FDDI networks directly is that they may not be able to keep up with the high data rates in FDDI. The newer ATs, based on Intel 80386, 80486, and 80586 chips, may be able to keep pace with the FDDI data rates, but they are hampered by slow I/O buses.

The FDDI concentrators, or MAUs, also serve in the role of a fan-out box, enabling multiple stations to be connected. Several FDDI concentrators can be cascaded to increase the fan-out. Although the FDDI concentrator has a dual attachment (DA), the stations attached to the concentrator have a single attachment (SA), thus saving on FDDI NIC costs.

 FDDI concentrators should be powered on all the time to reduce ring reconfigurations.

The FDDI token management permits several FDDI frames to be resident on the ring at a time, which makes for better utilization of the data bandwidth on the ring.

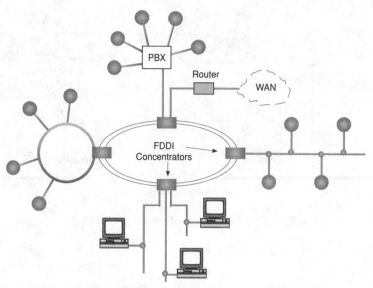

Figure 7.32:
PCs on an FDDI LAN.

The FDDI ring operates in two modes: synchronous and asynchronous. In *synchronous mode* operation, stations are guaranteed a percentage of total bandwidth available on the ring. This bandwidth allocation is done in terms of percentage of Target Token Rotation Time (TTRT). The TTRT is the token rotation time for the expected traffic on the network, and is negotiated during ring initialization. A station with synchronous bandwidth allocation can transmit data for a period of time not to exceed the percentage of TTRT allocated to it. Any leftover time, after all stations finish their synchronous transmission, is allocated to remaining nodes that are considered to operate in the *asynchronous mode*. Thus, if the actual Token Rotation Time (TRT) is less than TTRT, the leftover time of (TTRT - TRT) is used for asynchronous transfer.

Asynchronous mode transfer can take place in two modes: restricted and non-restricted. In the *restricted asynchronous mode*, a station can perform an extended transfer. The Station Management (SMT) negotiates a maximum restricted time. It would be unfair for a station in the restricted asynchronous mode to tie up the entire ring for a period of time greater than TTRT.

In the *non-restricted asynchronous mode*, the leftover time is divided among any nodes that want to send data — this is the normal mode of operation. The division of time can be based on priority schemes in which stations have a threshold TRT. Stations with lower threshold TRT are cut off earlier.

FDDI uses multimode fiber. Extensions to FDDI are being considered that use single-mode fiber. Although multimode can use a mix of light frequencies, single-mode fiber uses laser and a smaller core diameter fiber. Single-mode fiber has smaller signal attenuation and can be used over longer distances. These FDDI extensions allow up to 60 km between two stations. FDDI-II allows circuit switching in the synchronous mode, in which there can be up to 16 synchronous channels of 6.144Mbps each.

Many vendors are interested in running the FDDI protocols over copper media. Some vendors have proposed unshielded-twisted pair; others favor shielded-twisted pair.

 The goal of the ANSI committee on FDDI is to have one unifying protocol rather than separate protocols for shielded and unshielded twisted-pair. The reason for the interest in copper-based FDDI is that it would be much cheaper than the fiber-based products. One problem in using twisted pair wiring is compliance with FCC regulations and signal attenuation that limits the distance between a workstation and the FDDI concentrator. The goal for copper-based FDDI is to have distances of at least 100 meters between workstations and FDDI concentrators.

Some vendors, such as Crescendo Communications, Inc., of Sunnyvale, California, have copper-based FDDI products. Crescendo Communications calls their product CDDI (Copper Distributed Data Interface), and it runs on UTP wiring. Crescendo currently offers an eight-station MAU (1000 Workgroup Concentrator) that connects workstations at distances of 50 meters. A SBus CDDI adapter can be used as the FDDI interface for Sun Microsystems, Inc. Sparcstation.

Summary

This chapter has examined important considerations that affect network I/O. The choice of the technology one needs is determined by the distance spanned by these networks, the number of nodes that can be attached to them, and the data rates that are possible on these LANs. To explain these parameters, the internal operation of these LAN technologies has been discussed at some length.

Topics covered in this chapter:

Understanding the Importance of SCSI

Creating Multipartition Volumes

Evaluating Intelligent Drive Arrays

Configuring Server Volume

Chapter 8

Customizing the NetWare Installation for Large-Scale DP

A NetWare server provides the type of support—in terms of users and storage capacity—that IS professionals have grown to expect from their computer systems. The NetWare documentation was not written, however, for the IS professional who is downsizing. Therefore, you face some decisions when installing your NetWare servers for which you have inadequate information. This chapter attempts to fill in the "holes" when it comes to setting up NetWare volumes and configuring your storage systems. This chapter is not designed as a substitute for the NetWare documentation; rather, it is a supplement to the documentation.

In this chapter, you learn how to accomplish the following tasks during the NetWare installation procedure:

❖ Creating multipartition NetWare volumes

❖ Adding partitions to a NetWare volume at run time

❖ Mirroring and unmirroring partitions

❖ Evaluating intelligent drive arrays

❖ Deciding on a volume block size

❖ Adding and removing volume name space support

Before reading on, note the following assumptions that this chapter makes about you, the user:

❖ You are installing at least 1G (or more) of disk storage

❖ You are using SCSI disk subsystems

❖ Data integrity and performance are both important, but data integrity is more so

Understanding the Importance of SCSI

In case you have not yet "gotten the message" (after reading Chapter 6) about the importance of SCSI drive subsystems, the following is another "pitch" for SCSI.

SCSI systems provide the most intelligent and rich command set to operating systems for device input/output (I/O) among all the standard device interfaces for microcomputers. Certain SCSI commands are critical to multithreaded operating systems such as NetWare. SCSI also enables an operating system to deal with multiple devices in the most efficient manner. These attributes of SCSI are especially important for operating systems that have a multithreaded, asynchronous file system, as NetWare does.

 An *asynchronous file system* enables the operating system to continue to perform I/O processing while physical storage systems are busy performing physical I/O. NetWare's file system is highly asynchronous. The intelligence of the storage device controller is critical to the success of an asynchronous file system because the device must have a way to notify the operating system of the completion or failure of individual I/O commands.

Although NetWare works well with non-SCSI systems, it works better when you use SCSI storage systems. This is particularly true when you install multipartition volumes on your NetWare server.

 The advantages of SCSI over other types of device interfaces on the market are too great to ignore. Therefore, your only choice when it comes to storage subsystems for NetWare should be SCSI.

 If you are curious about how you can use NetWare's asynchronous file system in your data-processing applications, read Chapter 14!

Creating Multipartition Volumes

A *multipartition volume* is a volume that spans more than one physical storage device. Multipartition volumes are created for the following reasons:

❖ Using multiple partitions, the volume size is practically unlimited

❖ You can enlarge volumes while the server is running

❖ Multipartition volumes automatically enables split-seeking

These advantages are discussed in the following sections.

Unlimited Volume Size

Although it is true that the hard limit on volume size is in the terabyte range, the actual limit depends on the amount of RAM in your server. The server must be able to cache the entire FAT table of the volume. For all practical purposes, however, NetWare does not place any real limits on volume size, given today's technology.

Chapter 4 explains how to calculate server RAM requirements, based on volume size.

Disk drives for microcomputers continue to become larger. Today, the common size of a "large" drive suitable for NetWare is 1.2G. By creating a NetWare volume that spans two such drives, the volume size is 2.4G.

Note that you can enlarge such a volume "on the fly" while the server is still running. You can, for example, add yet another drive to the volume, bringing its capacity up to 3.6G. (You can continue to add drives to a volume in this manner, up to 32 drives.)

Drive Partitions and Segments

When you create or enlarge a NetWare volume, you do so by adding segments to that volume. A *segment* is nothing more than a NetWare partition that resides on a physical storage device. You create a partition (and hence a segment) by using the INSTALL.NLM utility.

A *NetWare partition* is a contiguous group of storage sectors on a device that have been set aside for use by NetWare, and which include control information used by NetWare.

A *segment* is a NetWare partition that has been added to a NetWare volume, either as the entire volume or as one of two or more parts of the volume.

Before loading and running INSTALL.NLM, however, you must be certain that you have loaded NetWare v3.11 disk drivers for the drives you want to work with. *Disk drivers* are NLMs that have a DSK file-name extension (instead of NLM).

After loading the appropriate disk drivers, you can load INSTALL.NLM by typing the following command at the server console and pressing Enter:

```
LOAD INSTALL
```

When INSTALL.NLM loads, your server console should display the screen shown in figure 8.1.

Figure 8.1:
The INSTALL.NLM opening screen.

The Installation Options menu, shown in figure 8.1, provides all the features you need to configure, maintain, and enlarge NetWare volumes, including the implementation of drive mirroring.

Right now, however, you want to create one or more NetWare partitions and use them to create a volume. To do so, select the Disk Options item on the Installation Options menu by highlighting the item and pressing Enter.

Your server should display a screen similar to that shown in figure 8.2.

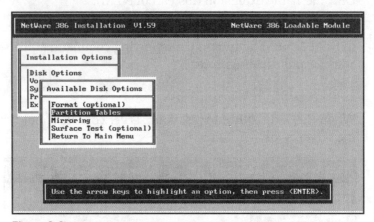

Figure 8.2:
The INSTALL.NLM Available Disk Options menu.

Within the Available Disk Options menu, there are five options: Format, which is an optional step you should only have to use for older disk drives; Partition Tables, which allows you to create NetWare partitions; Mirroring, which allows you to associate partitions for redundant operation; and Surface Test, which allows you to perform both destructive and non-destructive tests on a

NetWare partition. Finally, the last item on the menu enables you to exit to the INSTALL.NLM opening screen.

To create one or more NetWare partitions, highlight the Partition Tables option and press Enter. When you do so, the Available Disk Drives window appears. This window should list every physical disk drive you have installed in your server machine.

 INSTALL.NLM discovers which disk drives are installed on your server machine by querying the device subsystem that is part of the NetWare operating system. There are two cases in which a device will not show up in the Available Disk Drives window: if you have not loaded the appropriate disk driver for that device or if the device is faulty.

 If you find yourself viewing an Available Disk Drives window that does not display a device that you know is installed on your server machine, first check to see if you loaded the device driver. If you have, the device or its controller is probably faulty.

To create a NetWare partition on a storage device, you must highlight the appropriate device in the Available Disk Drives window, and then press Enter. INSTALL.NLM displays a window showing partition information for the drive, similar to that shown in figure 8.3.

Once you have INSTALL.NLM displaying the partition information for a specific storage device, you can choose any of the options shown in the Partition Options menu by highlighting the option of your choice and pressing Enter.

For example, to create a NetWare partition, highlight Create NetWare Partition, and press Enter. INSTALL.NLM displays a screen similar to that shown in figure 8.4.

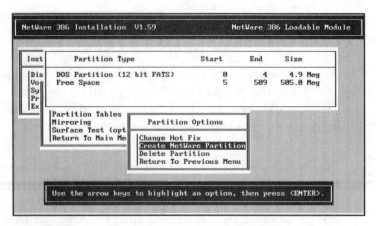

Figure 8.3:

The INSTALL.NLM partition information window.

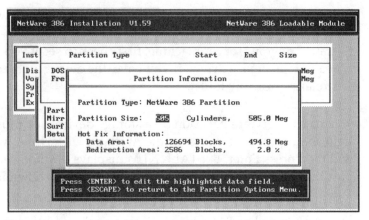

Figure 8.4:

The INSTALL.NLM Partition Information window.

To actually create a NetWare partition, press Esc. INSTALL.NLM prompts you to confirm or cancel the creation of a new NetWare partition, as shown in figure 8.5.

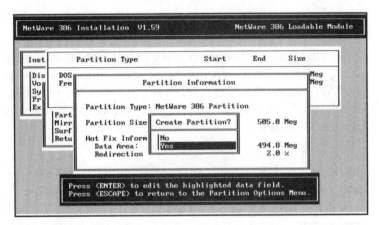

```
 NetWare 386 Installation   V1.59              NetWare 386 Loadable Module

┌─────────────────────────────────────────────────────────────────────┐
│ Inst │    Partition Type           Start      End      Size          │
│ Dis   DOS                                                      Meg    │
│ Vo    Fre┌──────────────────────────────────────────┐         Meg    │
│ Sy       │            Partition Information          │                │
│ Pr       │                                           │                │
│ Ex       │  Partition Type: NetWare 386 Partition    │                │
│     Part │                                           │                │
│     Mirr │  Partition Size┌─Create Partition?─┐ 505.0 Meg             │
│     Surf │                │No                 │                       │
│     Retu │  Hot Fix Inform│Yes                │                       │
│          │    Data Area:  └───────────────────┘ 494.8 Meg             │
│          │    Redirection                        2.0 %                │
│          └──────────────────────────────────────────┘                │
│     ┌─────────────────────────────────────────────────────┐          │
│     │ Press <ENTER> to edit the highlighted data field.    │          │
│     │ Press <ESCAPE> to return to the Partition Options Menu.│         │
│     └─────────────────────────────────────────────────────┘          │
└─────────────────────────────────────────────────────────────────────┘
```

Figure 8.5:
Confirming the creation of a new NetWare partition.

That is all there is to creating a new partition, except that there are a few rules you need to know. First, only one NetWare partition can reside on a single physical device. Second, other types of partitions (such as DOS partitions) may also reside on a device, alongside a NetWare partition. The most frequent use of a non-NetWare partition is to serve as a DOS boot partition, which enables you to boot NetWare directly from a hard drive.

Finally, you can increase or reduce the amount of partition storage set aside for hot-fix by editing the data in the Partition Information window. You can also change the size of the hot-fix redirection area for a particular volume segment (in other words, a partition that has been added to a volume) after you create a volume, even while the volume is in use.

For more information about the hot-fix feature, refer to Chapter 5.

Partition Mirroring and Duplexing

Mirroring and duplexing enable you to associate two or more partitions, thus creating redundant physical storage devices on your NetWare server. Once two or more partitions are mirrored or duplexed, NetWare can survive physical faults on mirrored or duplexed partitions without having those faults affect the operation of the server.

Mirroring and duplexing are not the same thing. *Mirroring* associates two or more devices that share the same controller; *duplexing* associates two or more devices that have different controllers. Obviously, duplexing is the preferred approach, because mirroring does not protect against controller failure.

 This book refers to *mirroring* when discussing both mirroring and duplexing. The differences between the two are invisible when it comes to configuring partitions and volumes.

You can mirror up to fifteen partitions together, which provides far more redundancy than you need. In most cases, mirroring two partitions is more than sufficient. Remember, however, that you should mirror partitions that have different controllers (in other words, you should duplex partitions).

Note that you can mirror two partitions that reside on different types of devices. You can also mirror partitions of different sizes, although the size of the resulting logical "partition" always resolves to the size of the smallest mirrored partition.

 You should mirror partitions that are of approximately the same size. They do not need to be exactly the same size, and they do not have to be located on devices of the same type.

To actually mirror partitions, select Mirroring from the INSTALL.NLM Available Disk Options menu. INSTALL.NLM displays the Partition Mirroring Status window, shown in figure 8.6.

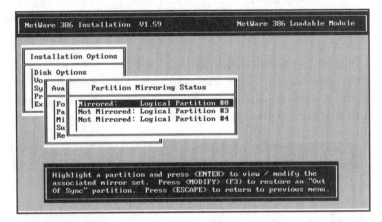

Figure 8.6:

The INSTALL.NLM Partition Mirroring Status window.

Figure 8.7 shows one mirrored partition and two partitions that are not mirrored. The mirrored partition actually consists of two or more actual (physical) partitions that are associated logically into one single "partition."

In a mirrored set of partitions, one partition is always the primary partition; the others (one or more) are secondary partitions that shadow all activity of the primary partition. NetWare treats the primary partition as if it were the only real partition among the mirrored set. If NetWare experiences an error writing or reading data to or from the primary partition, it disables it and promotes one of the secondary partitions to primary status.

To create the mirror from this point, you must select an unmirrored partition as the primary partition of the mirrored set. Next, select one or more available partitions to serve as secondary partitions to the primary one (*available* means that it is not currently a volume segment and it is not currently in a mirrored set.) Finally, you must explicitly join all the partitions you have selected into a mirrored set.

To select an unmirrored partition to be the primary partition of a mirrored set, highlight that partition in the Partition Mirroring Status window, and press Enter. INSTALL.NLM displays a screen similar to that shown in figure 8.7.

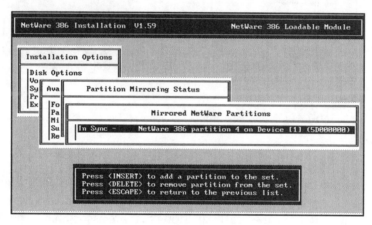

Figure 8.7:
Selecting a partition for mirroring.

Select one or more partitions for mirroring to the primary partition, which is shown in the Mirrored NetWare Partitions window. (You always mirror secondary partitions *to* the primary partition, not *with* the primary partition.)

To select one or more secondary partitions for mirroring with the primary partition, press Ins. INSTALL.NLM displays a list of all partitions that are candidates for mirroring to the primary partition (see fig. 8.8).

 To be a candidate, a partition must not currently be part of a mirrored set, and it must not currently be a segment on a NetWare volume.

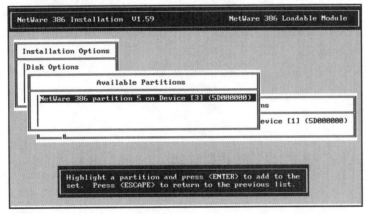

Figure 8.8:
INSTALL.NLM, displaying a partition available for mirroring.

To add a candidate partition to a mirrored set, highlight that partition in the Available Partitions window, and press Enter. You can verify that you actually created a new mirrored set by exiting back to the INSTALL.NLM Available Disk Options menu and selecting Mirroring. If your attempt at creating a mirrored partition worked, you should see a brand new mirrored partition listed in the Partition Mirroring Status window, as shown in figure 8.9.

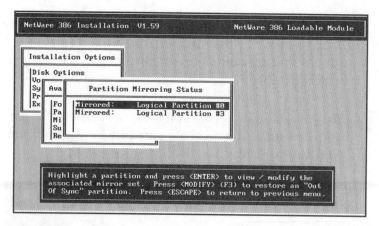

Figure 8.9:

Verifying the creation of a mirrored partition.

Notes on Mirroring

Now that you have seen how to create an actual mirrored partition, there are several things to keep in mind. First, you can mirror and unmirror partitions while the server is running, and even when volume segments associated with partitions are servicing a mounted NetWare volume. Although you are learning about mirroring prior to reading about volume creation, you can actually create volumes before you perform mirroring.

Mirroring decreases performance slightly for I/O operations that write data *to* disks. On the other hand, mirroring can increase performance for I/O operations that read data *from* disks. When writing data, NetWare always attempts to write data to a primary mirrored partition. After writing data to a primary mirrored partition, it mirrors that data by writing it to secondary partitions that are part of the same mirrored set as the primary partition. On read operations, however, NetWare reads data from the first available partition of a mirrored set. Thus, write operations are slower and read operations are faster for mirrored sets.

Disk mirroring has been part of the NetWare operating system since the late 1980s. As a result, it is a mature and robust technology that adds significantly to the integrity of your data. There is no reason not to use NetWare's disk-mirroring capabilities.

A multisegment volume should always be built from mirrored partitions. Multisegment volumes have more potential for failure because their underlying physical storage spans multiple disk drives. One failed disk drive can render a multisegment volume corrupt unless you build the multisegment volume using mirrored partitions.

How To Create NetWare Volumes

You create NetWare volumes by associating partitions together into a logical file system. (A *volume* is a file system, consisting of a directory table and a File Allocation Table.) Once you add a partition to a volume, that partition becomes a segment of the volume to which you added it. A multisegment volume, of course, is a volume to which you have added two or more partitions.

The first volume you create on a NetWare server is always called SYS. The SYS volume contains the NetWare *bindery*, which is a database maintained by the NetWare operating system for maintaining users, groups, security, and other information. The SYS volume also contains some default directories, such as the SYSTEM directory, which contains supervisor utilities; the PUBLIC directory, which contains user programs; the LOGIN directory, which contains programs for logging in, attaching, and discovering servers on an internetwork; the MAIL directory; and the DELETED.SAV directory, which contains deleted (but not purged) files that have had their original parent directory deleted.

To create a NetWare volume, you must first have created one or more NetWare partitions by using the techniques described earlier in this chapter. From the INSTALL.NLM Installation Options menu, select Volume Options, and press Enter. INSTALL.NLM displays its Volumes window, which shows all volumes currently created for the server (see fig. 8.10).

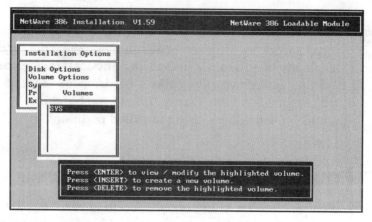

Figure 8.10:
The INSTALL.NLM Volumes window.

In figure 8.10, the server already has a SYS volume. To create a volume, press Ins when the Volumes window is active. INSTALL displays a New Volume Information window, which allows you to name and configure the new volume. You can alter the volume's name and block size by editing the fields in the New Volume Information window. You can also add segments to the volume by selecting the Volume Segments field of the Volume Information window.

Figure 8.11 shows the way to alter a volume's block size from within the New Volume Information window.

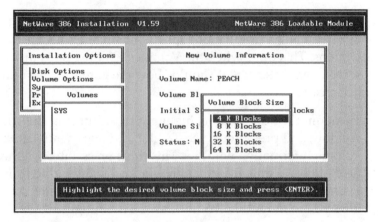

Figure 8.11:

Creating a new volume by using INSTALL.NLM.

Once you have edited the fields in the New Volume Information window to your satisfaction, you can create the new volume by pressing Esc. When you do so, INSTALL.NLM asks you to verify or cancel the creation of the volume, as shown in figure 8.12.

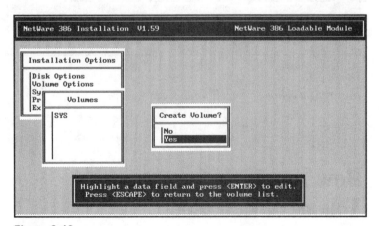

Figure 8.12:

Confirming the creation of a new NetWare volume.

You can verify the creation of the new volume by returning to the INSTALL.NLM Installation Options menu and selecting Volume Options. This time, when the Volumes window pops up on the server console screen, it should show the name of the volume you just created.

To mount the new volume, highlight the volume in the Volumes window, and press Enter. INSTALL.NLM once again displays the Volume Information window. This time, press Tab until the Status field of the Volume Information window is highlighted, and press Enter. INSTALL.NLM displays a Volume Status menu, which allows you to mount the volume, as shown in figure 8.13.

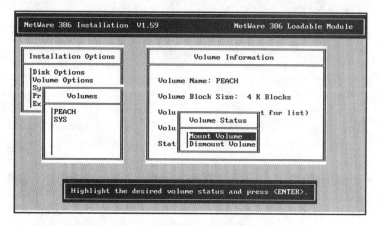

Figure 8.13:
Mounting a volume from within INSTALL.NLM.

How To Add Segments to a Volume at Run Time

If one of your NetWare volumes becomes full after running your server for a time, you can increase the size of that volume while the server is still running (and while the volume is still mounted).

All you have to do is add an additional segment to the volume by using the techniques described previously. Before you can add a segment to a volume, however, there must be a free NetWare partition on the system, which may require you to bring down the server and install a new hard drive.

Even if you have to bring down the NetWare server to install a new hard drive, you can do everything else while the server is running, including formatting the new drive (if necessary), performing a surface test, creating a NetWare partition, and extending the volume.

How To Decide on Volume Block Size

Volume block size determines the smallest storage-allocation unit for a given volume. The capability you have to select a specific block size is designed so you can optimize file-system performance for specific database applications.

The default block size for a volume is always 4K. A file, no matter how many bytes of data it contains, always occupies at least one block. If your volume block size is 4K, a one-byte file consumes 4K (one block) of volume storage. Obviously, the larger the block size of a volume, the more storage space you waste for each small file stored on that volume.

You should always accept the default volume block size of 4K unless you are dedicating a volume to a DP application that performs most of its reads and writes in chunks that are larger than 4K.

For example, if you have a DP application that defines its physical database in terms of 8K "pages," and you are dedicating a volume to storage for that DP application, you should set the volume block size to be 8K. This size optimizes the volume for your specific application. With the right application and the right block size, you can increase performance up to 100% or greater by customizing the volume block size.

If you choose an inappropriate block size for a volume, you can waste lots of storage space and slow performance at the same time. As a result, you should choose a volume block size other than 4K reluctantly, and only when you are certain you know what the (larger) block size should be.

Data Striping

When you create a multisegment volume using SCSI partitions, NetWare automatically performs data striping whenever it writes or reads data to or from that volume, which increases NetWare's file-system performance dramatically. For this reason, you should prefer multisegment volumes over single-segment volumes.

 For more information about striping data, refer to Chapter 5.

Volume Name Spaces

Name spaces are alternate entries in the NetWare Volume Directory Table that store non-DOS file-name and attribute information. NetWare uses name spaces to enable support for non-DOS file systems on a NetWare server. For example, to store Macintosh files on a NetWare server, the Macintosh name space creates an extra directory entry for each file. In that directory entry, NetWare stores the long Macintosh name of the file, points to the file's resource fork, and stores the file's Finder information. The actual file data is stored only once on the volume.

Different network clients gain access to the file's data differently, however. For example, a DOS client gains access to the file's data by reading the primary directory entry for that file. A Macintosh client, on the other hand, gains access to that file's data by reading the Macintosh directory entry for that file.

NetWare supports name spaces for Macintosh, OS/2 HPFS, UNIX NFS, and OSI FTAM file formats. You must add support for a specific name space to a NetWare volume explicitly by using the ADD command from the NetWare server console. To add Macintosh name space, for example, you issue the following command at the server console:

```
ADD NAME SPACE MAC TO VOLUME PEACH
```

From the moment you issue the ADD command, NetWare maintains extra Directory Table entries for every file stored on the volume. These extra entries decrease the amount of space available for storing file data on that volume and always increases the amount of server RAM required to mount the volume.

To enable non-DOS clients to gain access to files by using their native formats, you must make specific name spaces *active*. To make a name space active, load the appropriate name space module by using the LOAD command at the server console, as follows (this example loads the Macintosh name space module):

```
LOAD MAC.NAM
```

Name space modules are NLMs with the special file-name extension NAM. When you have added name-space support to a volume, and you have activated that name space by loading its support module, non-DOS clients can read and write files in their native format. Name spaces are an elegant way for NetWare to support multiple file systems.

If you ever need to remove name-space support from a volume, you can do it by using VREPAIR.NLM (see the *NetWare System Administrator's Guide*).

 Removing a name space from a volume deletes all Directory Table entries for that name space. DOS clients still have normal access to the volume's files.

Evaluating Intelligent Drive Arrays

Intelligent Drive Arrays (IDAs) are hardware-only storage subsystems that consist of multiple disk drives. Although IDAs appear to NetWare as a single physical device, they perform data striping as an integral part of their operation. IDAs also offer hardware-level fault tolerance by allowing mirroring of individual disk drives within the array or by generating parity drives.

 A *parity drive* allows data recovery when one—but only one—drive in the array fails.

 Because IDAs do not add anything to NetWare, do not consider an IDA as a requirement for your server. IDAs make more sense for other operating systems, such as OS/2 and UNIX, which do not support mirroring and data striping.

On the other hand, IDAs work well with NetWare. The important thing is that you purchase excellent storage subsystems from a reliable vendor.

Configuring Server Volumes

You should follow these recommendations for your server's volume configuration:

❖ All drive subsystems are SCSI

❖ All partitions are mirrored (preferably duplexed)

❖ All volumes consist of multiple segments

❖ Volume Block Size is 4K unless dedicated to a DP application

❖ Name spaces are installed only when required

❖ Intelligent Drive Arrays are not required

If you follow these simple guidelines, your NetWare server will work very well, even with multigigabyte volumes and hundreds of users. The entire key to configuring a NetWare server for downsizing lies in taking advantage of the features already resident in the NetWare operating system.

Summary

This chapter discussed the customization of the NetWare installation for large-scale data processing. You learned the importance of SCSI and how to create multipartition volumes. The chapter also discussed ways to evaluate intelligent drive arrays, as well as to configure server volume.

Topics covered in this chapter:

Bringing Mainframe Capabilities to PC Networks

Understanding NetWare's Cache System

Handling File and Record Locking

Protecting Data with the Transaction Tracking System

Chapter 9

Customizing NetWare for Large-Scale Data Processing

NetWare is a high-performance operating system designed to support large-scale data processing. Because many of NetWare's default settings assume a moderately sized network, however, it may be appropriate for you to customize NetWare for your particular configuration. This chapter helps you do that. It also helps you understand how NetWare manages memory and protects data.

Bringing Mainframe Capabilities to PC Networks

Just as the 386 CPU represents a quantum leap in processing power, NetWare 386 opens a new world of possibilities for LAN users. With dynamic resource configuration and support for larger disk volumes, NetWare 386 brings mainframe capabilities to the PC-network arena. NetWare 386 is a 32-bit operating system that supports the following:

❖ 250 workstations

❖ 100,000 concurrently open files

❖ 4 gigabytes of memory

❖ 32 terabytes of disk storage

❖ 2,048 physical disk drives

❖ 25,000 concurrent Transaction Tracking System (TTS) transactions

NetWare 386 thus convincingly demonstrates that the client-server architecture can handle tasks previously reserved for mainframes and minicomputers. Of course, the dual hallmarks of mainframe computing are reliability and security. Whether they are used for banking transactions, airline reservations, or stock trading, mainframe systems often support mission-critical operations. In these situations, two things are imperative: that the computer system stay up and running, and that the data be secure from unauthorized use and loss (whether the loss is intentional or accidental).

 This chapter assumes that a reliable, secure network is of prime importance. Although performance is also important, no fine-tuning that compromises reliability or security is

recommended. This chapter further assumes that you support a large-scale data-processing operation with large, frequently accessed database files, 1G or more of storage, more than 100 users, and 16M or more of RAM.

Understanding NetWare's Cache System

To customize an installation, you must first know something about NetWare's cache system, which is a key to NetWare's excellent performance.

NetWare uses random-access memory (RAM) for a variety of purposes. A minimum of 2M of RAM is required for any NetWare server, and NetWare v3.11 needs at least 4M. As previously mentioned, NetWare can address up to 4G of RAM. Generally, the more RAM you have, the better the server performs.

NetWare uses four different memory pools: kernel memory, permanent memory, alloc memory, and file-cache memory. *Kernel memory* allows the operating system to be initialized and loaded into high memory (memory above 1M). *Permanent memory* handles long-term memory needs, such as communications buffers and directory information. *Alloc memory* provides memory for short-term needs, such as drive mappings, user-connection information, and file locking. It also provides memory to NetWare Loadable Modules (NLMs). *File-cache memory* improves system performance by holding frequently accessed data and instructions in memory.

Just as one might hide valuables in a cache, the NetWare file system stores valuable files and other information in its cache. Accessing a file already in cache memory is up to one hundred times faster than retrieving that same file from the hard disk. It is not hard to see why file-server performance is so closely linked to the amount of cache memory available.

For additional information about file caches and how the file system, Directory Tables, and File Allocation Tables use the file-cache buffers, refer to Chapter 5.

The file-cache buffer does not receive memory from any of the other three memory pools. Kernel memory remains static and is unavailable for other uses. Permanent memory is semi-dynamic and can draw memory from the cache as the need arises, but that memory is not returned to the cache (at least not until the server is reinitialized). Similarly, alloc memory has varying requirements but does not return any memory borrowed from cache.

File-cache memory is more dominant than the other types of memory—often accounting for 70 percent or more of total memory—and is also more dynamic. Along with allocating memory to the permanent and alloc memory pools, the file-cache buffer also sends memory to the cache-movable pool (used for system tables that change size, such as Hash Tables) and the cache-nonmovable pool (used for loadable modules). Both of these pools, however, return memory to the file-cache buffer when they no longer need it.

The file-cache buffer reserves most of its memory to store frequently used files, but it also allocates space for the following:

❖ Each volume's complete File Allocation Table (FAT). The FAT is an index that tells where a file is located on the hard disk. Because a file can cover several disk-allocation blocks, the FAT includes an entry for each block and links blocks in the proper order. When a user requests access to a file, NetWare checks the FAT for all the information it needs to retrieve the complete file from the hard disk.

❖ A Turbo FAT Index for opening files larger than 64 blocks. For these large files, the Turbo FAT Index links all corresponding FAT entries. The first entry in the Turbo FAT Index is the file's first FAT number; the second entry is the file's second FAT number, and so on. Turbo FAT indexing enables the file server to quickly access large files.

❖ Parts of each volume's Directory Table. Directory entries most frequently requested are cached. The file server checks the directory cache to find a file's address. When users stop requesting a given file, the respective directory entry may be moved out of cache to make room for another directory entry. (Because the FAT is used for a variety of purposes and the directory entry is used simply for file addresses, caching the FAT is more important than caching the directory entry.)

❖ A Hash Table for all directory entries. Because not all directory entries are cached, a process called *hashing* predicts a file's address both in cache and on the hard disk. When a user attempts to retrieve a file, the server uses a hash algorithm to calculate an address on the Hash Table. The Hash Table in turn predicts an entry in the Directory Table. The hash algorithm finds the entry on the first try about 95 percent of the time (if it does not, it finds the entry on the second try). Hashing is a highly accurate means of locating files and contributes significantly to overall system performance.

Figure 9.1 presents a graphic representation of the way cache memory is divided.

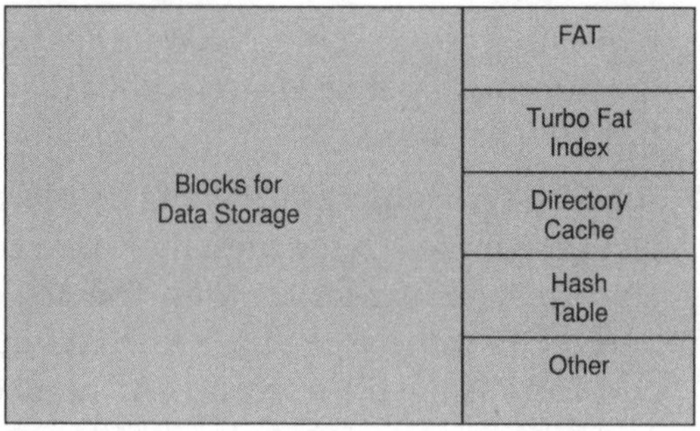

	FAT
Blocks for Data Storage	Turbo Fat Index
	Directory Cache
	Hash Table
	Other

Figure 9.1:
The file-cache buffer pool.

Reading Files from Cache

When a user makes a read request, the hash algorithm first calculates a file address on the Hash Table. The Hash Table address points to the first and second probable locations of the file's directory entry in the directory cache. When the server finds the entry, it checks the cache for a copy of the file. If the file is already in cache, the file server routes it directly to the workstation. If the file is not in the cache, the file is retrieved from the disk and then sent to the user requesting it.

As available cache buffers fill up, NetWare must determine which buffers to overwrite. To do this, NetWare uses the Least Recently Used (LRU) algorithm. The buffer that has not been used for the longest time is recycled. This way, the most requested files remain in cache.

Writing Files to Cache

When a user makes a write request, the server first executes the hash algorithm to find the cache buffer for the file. The file is written to the proper location, and the Directory Table is updated. The cache buffer is now *dirty*, which means that the version of the file in cache is different from the version of the file on the hard disk. The file in cache is dirty until the new version of the file is copied to the disk (and checked against the cache version). Next, the workstation receives a message indicating that the file was written to disk, and the application is free to perform other tasks.

 To reduce the number of times it has to access the hard disk, NetWare often combines several small write requests into one larger write request. Because of this grouping of write requests, NetWare sometimes "tricks" the application into concluding that a file was written to disk before it actually happens. The application is then free to do something else, even though the file is still in cache.

By default, the file is written to disk as soon as all the sectors in the cache buffer are updated or after 3.3 seconds. "Tuning NetWare with the SET Command," later in this chapter, explains how to change the default time of 3.3 seconds.

Managing Memory with the MONITOR Utility

The MONITOR utility enables you to see how efficiently the network is operating. This utility offers valuable information on the following aspects of the network:

- ❖ Resource utilization and network activity
- ❖ Cache memory
- ❖ Active connections
- ❖ System hard disks
- ❖ Mounted volumes
- ❖ LAN drivers
- ❖ System modules
- ❖ File open and lock activity
- ❖ Memory statistics

Load MONITOR at the file-server console by using the following syntax:

```
LOAD [path]MONITOR [parameter]
```

If MONITOR is already loaded, press Alt-Esc or Ctrl-Esc to display the main menu. For the *path* variable, enter the complete path, beginning with a DOS drive letter or a NetWare volume name. If you do not enter a path, NetWare uses the default SYS:SYSTEM directory.

Although the *parameter* entry is not required, you can use ns (no saver) to turn off the screen saver or nh (no help) to turn off on-line help.

The opening screen for MONITOR is shown in figure 9.2. The following chart describes each item in the information screen:

Screen Element	Description
File Server Up Time	The amount of time the server has been running since it was last initialized
Utilization	The percentage of time the CPU is occupied

Screen Element	Description
Original Cache Buffers	The number of free buffers when the system is booted or the total number of blocks of RAM available (some of these blocks are routed to kernel, permanent, and alloc memory)
Total Cache Buffers	The number of blocks actually available for caching; this number varies as modules are loaded or unloaded
Dirty Cache Buffers	The number of blocks in memory not yet written to the hard disk
Current Disk Requests	The number of disk requests waiting to be handled by the server
Packet Receive Buffers	The number of buffers set aside in RAM to handle packets arriving from workstation network interface cards (the default is 10)
Directory Cache Buffers	The number of buffers set aside for the directory cache
Service Processes	The number of task handlers set aside for workstation requests; when necessary, the server uses extra memory to handle requests (once this memory is loaned out, however, it is not returned to cache)
Connections In Use	The number of nodes currently connected to the server
Open Files	The number of files currently being accessed by the server or by workstations

```
┌─────────────────────────────────────────────────────────────────────┐
│ NetWare 386 V3.10 Rev. A - 6/13/90        NetWare 386 Loadable Module │
├─────────────────────────────────────────────────────────────────────┤
│                    Information For Server IGOR                        │
│                                                                       │
│  File Server Up Time:     0 Days  0 Hours 17 Minutes  5 Seconds       │
│  Utilization:                   1     Packet Receive Buffers:     10  │
│  Original Cache Buffers:       679     Directory Cache Buffers:    22  │
│  Total Cache Buffers:          421     Service Processes:           2  │
│  Dirty Cache Buffers:            0     Connections In Use:          2  │
│  Current Disk Requests:          0     Open Files:                  7  │
│                                                                       │
│                  ┌──────────────────────────┐                        │
│                  │      Available Options     │                       │
│                  ├──────────────────────────┤                        │
│                  │ Connection Information    │                        │
│                  │ Disk Information          │                        │
│                  │ LAN Information           │                        │
│                  │ System Module Information │                        │
│                  │ Lock File Server Console  │                        │
│                  │ File Open / Lock Activity │                        │
│                  │ Resource Utilization      │                        │
│                  │ Exit                      │                        │
│                  └──────────────────────────┘                        │
└─────────────────────────────────────────────────────────────────────┘
```

Figure 9.2:
The opening information screen for the MONITOR utility.

Understanding the Available Options Menu

The Available Options menu, which is part of the MONITOR utility's opening screen, lists the following options, each of which has several additional options:

❖ **Connection Information**. List active connections, List physical record locks for a user, Clear a connection, List open files.

❖ **Disk Information**. List system hard disks, List volume segments per hard disk, Change the Read After Write Verify status of the hard disk, Flash the hard disk light, Activate/deactivate a hard disk, Mount/dismount a removable media device, Lock/unlock a removable media device.

❖ **LAN Information**. List LAN drivers and statistics.

❖ **System Module Information** List system modules, List resources used by system module.

❖ **Lock File Server Console** Lock the file server console, Unlock the file server console.

❖ **File Open/Lock Activity** Check file status, View mounted volumes.

❖ **Resource Utilization** View memory statistics, View tracked resources.

 MONITOR handles a wide variety of tasks and is a valuable tool for managing the network. It is to the advantage of a network manager to become well acquainted with all of MONITOR's options.

Using MONITOR To View Memory Statistics

To check memory statistics, select the Resource Utilization option from the Available Options menu. A screen similar to the one in figure 9.3 appears.

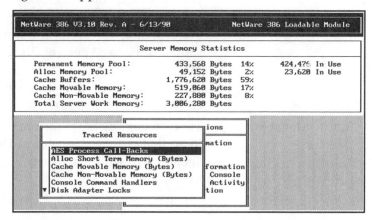

Figure 9.3:
Viewing memory statistics.

The second column of the Server Memory Statistics screen specifies the number of bytes of RAM that are set aside for the various categories. The third column lists the percentage of total memory allocated to each category. The fourth column lists the number of bytes actually being used. The following chart describes each of the memory categories listed on this screen:

Memory Category	Description
Permanent Memory Pool	This category includes both permanent and semipermanent memory. The permanent pool takes memory from cache but does not return it.
Alloc Memory Pool	The complete name for this category is *Alloc Short Term Memory Pool*. Like permanent memory, this pool takes memory from cache but does not return it.
Cache Buffers	This category includes all the items listed in figure 9.1 (blocks for data storage, FAT, Turbo FAT Index, directory cache, Hash Table, and others). As an absolute minimum, 20 percent of total memory should be reserved for the cache buffers. For best performance, however, the number should be 60 to 80 percent. To achieve this percentage, add memory to the server rather than limit the amount of cache used for other purposes.
Cache Movable Memory	This category includes memory used for items that change size, such as Hash Tables; returned to cache when no longer needed.

Memory Category	Description
Cache Non-Movable Memory	This category lists the amount of memory sent out temporarily to modules and returned to cache when no longer needed.
Total Server Work Memory	This is the total memory installed on the server minus memory set aside for ROM BIOS, DOS, and SERVER.EXE.

Now that you understand how to use the MONITOR utility and what the different statistics mean, you can use the SET command to customize your configuration.

Tuning NetWare with the SET Command

SET is a versatile command that can be used for many different purposes, including allocating services, setting memory parameters, setting limits for file and directory caching, locking files, and tracking transactions. You can use SET to either view or change parameters.

 Remember that you always have trade-offs when you change parameters. Setting aside more memory for a certain category may increase system reliability, but it takes memory from cache and therefore decreases overall performance. On the other hand, reserving too much memory for cache can wreak havoc with other network functions. You must continually weigh conflicting needs as you allocate memory. The more you understand about the intricacies of

NetWare—including which services need how much memory and why—the better prepared you are to make these decisions.

Remember also that permanent memory is more important than cache memory; permanent memory is used for vital server functions such as file-control blocks and transaction tracking.

Finally—and this cannot be overemphasized—remember that the best way to solve memory problems is to add memory to the system.

You can use the SET command with nine different categories. Type **SET** with no parameters to view these categories. Select a category to see the parameters for that category. If you use the SET command with a parameter, the current setting for that parameter displays. If you use the SET command with a parameter value, the operating system is reconfigured to the selected value.

You can execute most SET parameters from the file-server console command line. In addition, you can save these parameters permanently in the AUTOEXEC.NCF file. (Changes made at the command line are temporary and are erased when you reboot the server.) Certain parameters, however, must be set in the STARTUP.NCF file. These include the following:

❖ Auto Register Memory Above 16 Megabytes

❖ Auto TTS Backout Flag

❖ Cache Buffer Size

❖ Maximum Physical Receive Packet Size

❖ Maximum Subdirectory Tree Depth

❖ Maximum Packet Receive Buffers

Changes made to STARTUP.NCF or AUTOEXEC.NCF do not take effect until you reboot the server. Edit both of these files with the INSTALL utility.

Setting Memory Parameters

Of the nine categories that you can alter with the SET command, two are memory parameters. You can use SET to change the Cache Buffer Size and Maximum Alloc Short Term Memory parameters, as described in the following paragraphs.

The Cache Buffer Size parameter refers to the block size of the cache buffer. The default is 4,096 bytes (4K); other possible settings are 8,192 (8K) and 16,384 (16K). This parameter is closely related to volume disk block size, which also has a default of 4K and the possible settings of 8K, 16K, 32K, and 64K.

Follow these rules when working with cache-buffer size:

- ❖ If you use volumes with varying sizes of disk blocks, make sure that the cache-buffer size matches the smallest disk-block size.

- ❖ If you use disk blocks larger than 4K (8K, for example), set the cache buffer for that larger size.

- ❖ Never set the cache-buffer size larger than the disk block size. In fact, NetWare does not mount a volume with such parameters.

 With a large-scale data-processing operation, you probably use large database files. If the files are generally about 16K, for example, setting a similar size for blocks and cache buffers increases performance because the network handles data more efficiently. (On the other hand, if you generally use small files and set blocks and cache buffers to a large size, network performance decreases.)

You can change the Cache Buffer Size parameter by using the SERVER command or by adding a line to the STARTUP.NCF file with the SET command. To boot the server with a cache-buffer size of 8K, for example, enter the following:

```
SERVER -C8K
```

Adding the following line to the STARTUP.NCF file makes the change permanent:

```
SET cache buffer size = 8192
```

The Maximum Alloc Short Term Memory parameter sets a limit on how much cache can be set aside for Alloc Short Term Memory. The default is 2,097,152 bytes (2M), with a possible range of 50,000 to 16,777,216. If you store a gigabyte or more of data on the server, you should probably increase this default. Alloc memory is used for a variety of short-term but important needs, including drive mappings, service-request buffers, file locking, and loadable module tables. It is therefore important that this pool has sufficient memory.

Use the Resource Utilization option from the MONITOR utility's Available Options menu to check how much Alloc Memory is being used. If this number is often at or near the limit (of 2M, for example) increase the limit by 1,000,000 bytes. Use the SET command to make the change. To increase the default by 1,000,000 bytes, for example, enter the following:

```
SET maximum alloc short term memory: 3097152
```

Add this same line to the AUTOEXEC.NCF file to make the change permanent.

Setting Caching Parameters

Of the nine categories you can alter with the SET command, four are caching parameters. You can use SET to change the Maximum Concurrent Disk Cache Writes, Dirty Disk Cache Delay Time, Minimum File Cache buffers, and Reserved Buffers Below 16 Meg parameters, as described in the following paragraphs.

The Maximum Concurrent Disk Cache Writes parameter determines how many write requests can be placed in the queue before the disk head moves across the disk. The default is 50, with a range of 10 to 100. A large-scale data-processing operation may mean a good deal of database activity, which in turn may require an increase in this number.

To know whether you should change this parameter, check the MONITOR utility's main information screen. If the number of dirty cache buffers is more than two-thirds of the number of total cache buffers, increase the Maximum Concurrent Disk Cache Writes number. To change the number to 60, for example, enter the following:

```
SET maximum concurrent disk cache write = 60
```

The Dirty Disk Cache Delay Time parameter determines how long the cache holds a write request before writing it to the hard disk. The default is 3.3 seconds, with a range of 0.1 to 10 seconds.

To make data more secure, some network managers may be tempted to decrease this number. Doing so, however, has a negative effect on performance because the server accesses the hard disk more often; furthermore, decreasing this setting does not make data that much more secure. Instead, use TTS (discussed later in this chapter) to maintain data integrity.

Experienced system managers may actually want to increase this number for large networks experiencing high-load conditions. Performance increases if write requests can be written to disk a complete block at a time.

The Minimum File Cache buffers parameter sets the number of cache buffers that cannot be allocated for other purposes. The default is 20, with a range of 20 to 1,000. You may want to increase this number for a large-scale data-processing operation (which is likely to require high-performance, cached file service). At the same time, however, be careful not to reserve too many buffers for the cache. Doing so can negatively affect loadable modules and transaction tracking, among other things.

 Check the memory requirements of the NLMs you run; also estimate memory requirements for connections, receive buffers, and directory cache buffers. Subtract this total from the Total Server Work Memory (found on the Server Memory Statistics screen) and divide the remainder by the size of the file-cache buffer (for example, divide by the default of 4,096). Multiply the resulting number by 70 percent to determine an appropriate minimum number of file-cache buffers.

The Reserved Buffers Below 16 Meg parameter sets aside a certain number of cache buffers below the 16M level for device drivers that are unable to access cache above 16M. The default is 16, with a range of 8 to 200. To change the default to 30, for example, enter the following in the STARTUP.NCF file:

```
SET reserved buffers below 16 meg: 30
```

N_{OTE} You must use the STARTUP.NCF file to change the Reserved Buffers Below 16 Meg parameter.

Setting the Directory Caching Parameter

Of the nine categories you can alter with the SET command, one is a directory-caching parameter. You can use SET to change the Minimum Directory Cache Buffers parameter, as described in the following paragraphs.

The Minimum Directory Cache Buffers parameter determines the minimum number of buffers set aside for directory caching. The default is 20, with a range of 10 to 2,000. If you access a large number of directories, you may need to increase this number.

Check the number of directory cache buffers listed on the MONITOR utility's main information screen. If that number is higher than the minimum limit, increase the Minimum Directory Cache Buffers limit. Do so judiciously, however, because taking unnecessary memory away from the cache decreases network performance.

To change the minimum number of directory cache buffers to 100, for example, enter the following:

```
SET minimum directory cache buffers = 100
```

Setting Packet Receive Buffers

Of the nine categories you can alter with the SET command, two are packet receive buffer parameters. You can use SET to change the Minimum Packet Receive Buffers and Maximum Packet Receive Buffers parameters, as described in the following paragraphs.

Packet receive buffers are reserved areas in memory that hold data packets arriving from network interface cards. The default for the Minimum Packet Receive Buffers parameter is 10, with a range of 10 to 1,000. Use the MONITOR utility to check the server's use of packet receive buffers. If the server uses more than 10 and responds slowly right after booting, increase the Minimum Packet Receive Buffers number.

 If you use EISA or Micro Channel bus master boards in the server and see a NO ECB Available Count message after booting the file server, increase the Minimum Packet Receive Buffers parameter so that you have at least five packet receive buffers for each board.

The default for the Maximum Packet Receive Buffers parameter is 100, with a range of 50 to 2,000. Check the server's use of packet receive buffers with the MONITOR utility. If the number is at its maximum, increase this parameter, in increments of 10, until you have one packet receive buffer for each workstation on the network.

TIP

If you use EISA or Micro Channel boards in the server and see a NO ECB Available Count message after booting, increase the Maximum Packet Receive Buffers number so that you have 10 packet receive buffers for each board.

To change either of the packet receive buffer parameters, add the appropriate SET command to the STARTUP.NCF file. Use a syntax similar to this:

```
SET maximum packet receive buffers = 200
```

Controlling the Read After Write Verify Field

The Read After Write function ensures that data written to the hard disk matches the data still in the cache. If the two match, the data in the cache is recycled and the server is ready to process the next operation. If the data on disk does not match the data in the cache, NetWare identifies the disk-storage block in question as defective. The hot-fix feature then sends the data in cache to a good block location.

SEE ALSO

For more information about the hot-fix feature, refer to Chapter 5.

You can use the MONITOR utility to change the Read After Write Verify status of the hard disk. From the MONITOR utility's Available Options menu, select Disk Information. Select a hard disk, and a screen similar to the one shown in figure 9.4 appears.

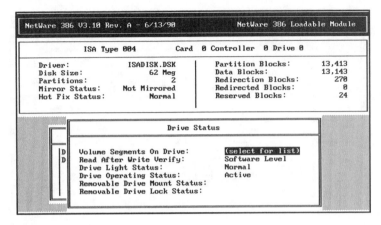

Figure 9.4:
The Drive Status screen.

If a Not Supported message follows the Read After Write Verify line, you cannot change this field. That does not mean, however, that Read After Write Verify is not being performed. Rather, it probably means that the driver is not configurable. (To be Novell-certified, a driver must ensure that data is always checked after it is written to the hard disk.)

If the Read After Write Verify line is followed by something other than Not Supported, select this field. A menu similar to the one shown in figure 9.5 appears.

The Software Level Verify option means that the disk driver handles read-after-write verification. The Hardware Level Verify option means that the controller handles verification. The Disable Verify option does not mean that data written to disk is not verified. Rather, it means that neither the driver nor the controller verifies the write. Use this option for disks that provide internal verification. Check the disk documentation to see whether this is the case. For all three options, hot-fix redirects any data not verified to a good location on the disk.

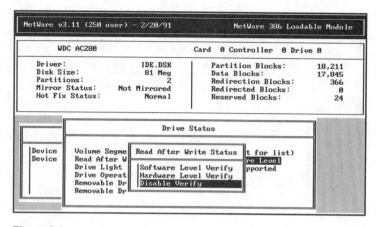

Figure 9.5:
The Read After Write Status menu screen.

Under normal circumstances, read-after-write verification and hot-fix take place automatically (and are transparent to the user). The Enable Disk Read After Write Verify parameter is set to ON by default. To disable read-after-write verification for any reason, enter this line at the file-server console:

```
SET enable disk read after write verify = OFF
```

Handling File and Record Locking

File and record locking ensure that files or parts of files are correctly updated and written to disk before another user or process can change them. These features thus play an important role in maintaining data integrity.

Once a user opens a file, that file is locked to other users. Although other users may be able to read it, they cannot write to it. The initial user "owns" the file until he or she gives up ownership by exiting the file. That user's changes are then written to the disk (if the user so elected), and the file is unlocked until another user opens it.

Record locking follows the same pattern, except that only parts of the file (records) are locked. Record locking is particularly applicable to database files, which can be large and often store records in separate portions of the file. Figure 9.6 shows a two-block, 8K file with a file lock. Figure 9.7 shows the same file with a record lock.

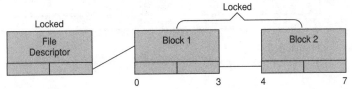

Figure 9.6:
A file lock.

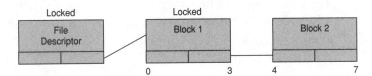

Figure 9.7:
A record lock.

The MONITOR utility offers a variety of useful information related to locks. To see whether a given file is locked or unlocked, select the File Open/Lock Activity option from the Available Options menu. Use the Select an Entry menu to identify the path of the file in question. Once a file is selected, a screen similar to the one in figure 9.8 appears.

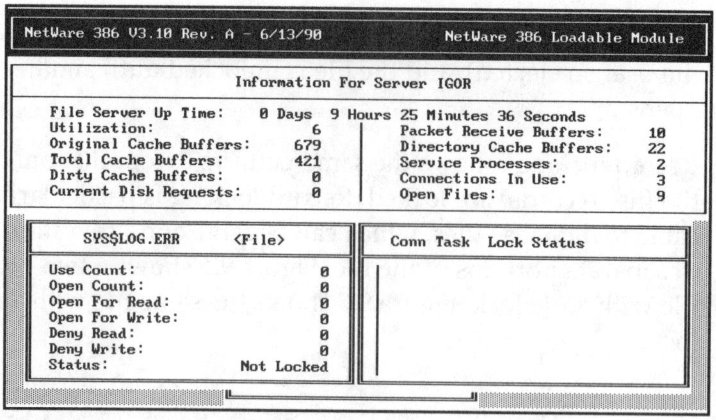

```
┌──────────────────────────────────────────────────────────────────┐
│ NetWare 386 V3.10 Rev. A - 6/13/90          NetWare 386 Loadable Module │
│  ┌──────────────────────────────────────────────────────────────┐  │
│  │                 Information For Server IGOR                   │  │
│  │  File Server Up Time:    0 Days  9 Hours 25 Minutes 36 Seconds │  │
│  │  Utilization:              6      Packet Receive Buffers:   10 │  │
│  │  Original Cache Buffers:  679     Directory Cache Buffers:  22 │  │
│  │  Total Cache Buffers:     421     Service Processes:         2 │  │
│  │  Dirty Cache Buffers:       0     Connections In Use:        3 │  │
│  │  Current Disk Requests:     0     Open Files:                9 │  │
│  └──────────────────────────────────────────────────────────────┘  │
│  ┌──────────────────────────┐  ┌──────────────────────────────┐  │
│  │   SYS$LOG.ERR    <File>  │  │  Conn Task  Lock Status      │  │
│  │                          │  │                              │  │
│  │  Use Count:           0  │  │                              │  │
│  │  Open Count:          0  │  │                              │  │
│  │  Open For Read:       0  │  │                              │  │
│  │  Open For Write:      0  │  │                              │  │
│  │  Deny Read:           0  │  │                              │  │
│  │  Deny Write:          0  │  │                              │  │
│  │  Status:     Not Locked  │  │                              │  │
│  └──────────────────────────┘  └──────────────────────────────┘  │
└──────────────────────────────────────────────────────────────────┘
```

Figure 9.8:
The SYS$LOG.ERR screen.

The Status line is followed by Not Locked if the file is accessible by other users; it is followed by Locked if the file is not accessible. The Conn column shows which connections are using the file; the Task column lists the number that an application assigns to the shell. The Lock Status column displays one of the following attributes for each connection:

Attribute	Description
Exclusive	No other users can read or write to the file
Shareable	Other users can read the file but not change it
TTS Holding Lock	Although the application has unlocked the file, TTS has locked it because transactions are not yet complete
Logged	The server is preparing a set of records for locking
Not Logged	This is the normal status—no requests are pending for a set of locks

You also can use the MONITOR utility to check record-lock information for individual users. From the Available Options menu, choose Connection Information. Then select the appropriate user and an open file. A screen similar to the one shown in figure 9.9 appears.

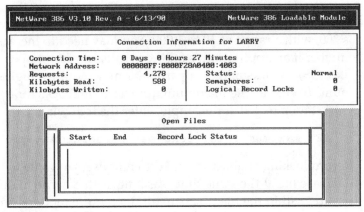

Figure 9.9:
Open Files screen.

Setting Parameters for File and Record Locks

You can set parameters for file and record locks with the SET command. This section describes the two parameters you can change to customize NetWare to your configuration.

The Maximum File Locks parameter enables you to set a limit on the number of concurrent file locks that the operating system allows. The default is 10,000, with a range of 100 to 100,000. Increase this number if the number of open files is frequently at or near the maximum. Even for a large network, however, the default is likely to be sufficient.

To change the file-locks limit to 20,000, for example, enter the following:

```
SET maximum file locks = 20000
```

The default number of maximum file locks for a single workstation is 250, with a range of 10 to 1,000. You may need to increase this number if an application is failing because it cannot open enough files. OS/2 workstations in particular may require a higher maximum. To change the maximum number of file locks for a single workstation to 350, for example, enter the following:

```
SET maximum file locks per connection = 350
```

Record locking enables several different users to write to the same database file at the same time—as long as they write to different records within the file. Users naturally require more record locks than file locks, so the default for the Maximum Record Locks parameter is 20,000 (with a range of 100 to 200,000), which is much higher than the file-lock default of 10,000.

Increase the Maximum Record Locks number if applications display error messages, saying that insufficient record locks are available. To change the default to 30,000, for example, enter the following:

```
SET maximum record locks = 30000
```

Increase the maximum number of record locks per connection if an application fails because it cannot lock enough records. The default number of record locks per workstation is 500, with a range of 10 to 10,000. To change the default to 1,000, for example, enter the following:

```
SET maximum record locks per connection = 1000
```

Solving Problems with File and Record Locking

If file or record locking fails to function properly with a certain application, try the following troubleshooting methods:

1. Make sure that the workstation boots with the same version of DOS that the application uses for file locking. You run into problems, for example, if the application requires DOS 3.1 or above and the workstation boots with DOS 2.2.

2. Make sure that the application is NetWare-compatible.

3. Log in directly to the server running the application rather than attaching to the server from another server.

4. In a multiserver environment, map regular drives to the application rather than using search drives.

Protecting Data with the Transaction Tracking System

The Transaction Tracking System (TTS) ensures database integrity by tracking transactions. If a transaction fails for any reason, TTS returns the database to the state it was in before it started the transaction (this action is also called *backing out* the transaction). Mainframe database systems have had this capability for some time, usually as part of the database software. TTS, however, is tightly integrated with NetWare. This integration brings two distinct benefits:

❖ High performance. Because the *server* tracks transactions, network traffic is reduced. In addition, the server's file-cache buffer is available for transactions.

❖ Protection for database programs lacking built-in transaction tracking. As soon as the application opens a file, TTS begins its tracking process. That process ends when the database closes the file.

 For additional information about TTS, refer to Chapter 5.

TTS protects data from hardware errors (whether they occur at the server, the workstation, or in transmission), software errors, and power failures. If the server fails, TTS restores the database to its original state after you reboot the server. If a workstation or other network component fails, TTS restores the database immediately. TTS protects any file that uses record locking; it does not protect nonrecord-locking files, such as word processing files. TTS tracks bindery files by default. To track other files, make sure that you flag the file as transactional.

Flagging Files as Transactional

The basic rule for determining which files you should flag as transactional is simple: flag all database files but no other files.

The FLAG command, which supports wild cards, enables you to view or change a file's attributes. Use the following syntax to flag a file as *transactional* (to make sure that the file is protected by TTS):

```
FLAG filename +T
```

To remove the transactional flag from a file, use this syntax:

```
FLAG filename -T
```

Once you flag a file as transactional, TTS tracks that file. If a network failure occurs while that file is being written to, TTS ensures that either all changes are made to the file or that no changes are made.

You cannot flag an open file. You cannot rename or delete a file flagged as transactional.

Disabling and Enabling TTS

By default, transaction tracking is enabled and takes place automatically. Rarely, if ever, must you disable it. One exception is the case of a programmer who needs to test database applications with TTS disabled.

 You should not disable TTS to gain more server memory. TTS does not require much cache (only 40 bytes initially and 400K at most). Any possible performance benefits are far outweighed by the risk of database corruption.

To disable TTS, enter the following at the file-server console:

```
DISABLE TTS
```

The following message appears:

```
TTS disabled by operator
```

To re-enable tracking, enter **ENABLE TTS** or reboot the server.

The file server automatically disables TTS if the SYS volume runs out of disk space. When this happens, the following message appears:

```
TTS disabled because of error allocating more disk
space for the backout file
```

The server also disables TTS if not enough memory is available. When this happens, the following message appears:

```
TTS cannot allocate sufficient memory
```

Solve the first problem by freeing up at least 1M of disk space on the SYS volume. Solve the second problem by unloading unnecessary modules, dismounting unused volumes, or adding more memory to the file server.

To enable TTS, enter the following at the file-server console:

```
ENABLE TTS
```

You see the following message if TTS is successfully executed:

```
Transaction tracking system enabled
```

If TTS is not successfully enabled, you may see this error message:

```
TTS cannot be enabled because the TTS work volume
is not mounted
```

To solve this problem, use the MOUNT command to mount the SYS volume before enabling TTS.

Using SETTTS

Certain database applications may require you to set new transaction beginning points. An example is dBASE III PLUS v1.0 (later versions of dBASE, however, do not require you to use SETTTS). Make any adjustments to the beginning-point parameter before entering the application. To set this parameter, use the SETTTS command with the following syntax at the workstation in which you want to run the database:

```
SETTTS [logical level [physical level]]
```

This command tells TTS how many logical or physical record locks to ignore before tracking a transaction. Replace each of these variables with a number and leave a space between the two numbers.

For example, if you want TTS to ignore two logical record locks and three physical record locks, enter this command:

```
SETTTS 2 3
```

 Logical and physical locks prevent multiple users from accessing the same record. With *logical locks*, the application locks a record when it is accessed; with *physical locks*, the operating system enforces the lock.

To set a physical level, you must first set a logical level. If no logical level is necessary, enter **0** as the logical-level value. You can change the setting by entering another SETTTS command, logging out, or rebooting. Most database applications do not require you to use this command. However, applications that use logical record locks may require changes with SETTTS. Check the application documentation or contact the vendor if you are uncertain whether to use SETTTS.

Use the following command to check the current setting:

```
SETTTS
```

Once you change parameters with SETTTS, the new paramaters remain until you choose new ones or reboot the server.

Setting TTS Parameters

You can change five TTS parameters with the SET command. You generally do not change these parameters, however; only an experienced network manager should do so when it is necessary.

The Maximum Transactions parameter tells NetWare how many transactions can take place at the same time. The default is 10,000, with a range of 100 to 10,000. To change the upper limit to 5,000, for example, enter the following:

```
SET maximum transactions = 5000
```

The TTS Unwritten Cache Wait Time parameter specifies how long the cache holds a block of transactions before writing it to disk. The default is 1 minute, 5.9 seconds; it has a range of 11 seconds to 10 minutes, 59.1 seconds.

Use this syntax to change the default:

```
SET TTS unwritten cache wait time = time
```

The TTS Backout File Truncation Wait Time parameter specifies how long unused, allocated blocks remain available for the TTS backout file. The default is 59 minutes, 19.2 seconds; it has a range of 1 minute, 5.9 seconds to 1 day, 2 hours, 21 minutes, 51.3 seconds.

Use this syntax to change the default:

```
SET TTS Backout File Truncation Wait Time = time
```

Use the Auto TTS Backout Flag parameter if you want the server to automatically back out failed transactions when it boots. The default is OFF; add the following line to the STARTUP.NCF file to change the setting to ON:

```
SET auto TTS backout flag = ON
```

You cannot execute this command at the console; it must be added to the STARTUP.NCF file. If you do not change this parameter, you see the following message when the server boots with incomplete transactions:

```
Incomplete transaction(s) found. Do you wish to
back them out?
```

The TTS Abort Dump Flag parameter specifies whether transaction backout data is saved to the TTS$LOG.ERR file (found in the root directory of the SYS volume). The default value is OFF. Setting this parameter to ON causes NetWare to copy backed out information to the TTS$LOG.ERR file (which in turn causes the TTS$LOG.ERR file to grow much more quickly than normal).

Enter the following to turn the flag on:

```
SET TTS abort dump flag = ON
```

 The TTS$LOG.ERR file is a valuable troubleshooting tool because it records all backed-out transactions. View or print this file when you have questions about failed transactions. You should also monitor the size of this file. When it grows too large, you can delete part of it with an ASCII text editor. You also can archive a copy and delete the original. NetWare automatically creates a new copy when necessary.

Summary

In this chapter, you learned ways to bring mainframe capabilities to PC networks. You now understand NetWare's cache system, how to manage memory by using the MONITOR utility, and how to turn NetWare with the SET command.

The chapter also discussed the Read After Write Verify field, how to handle file and record locking, and ways to protect your data with the Transaction Tracking System (TTS).

Topics covered in this chapter:

Understanding Login Security

Understanding Attribute Security

Understanding Rights Security

Understanding File and Print Server Security

Understanding Accounting

Using the NetWare Bindery

Chapter 10

NetWare Security

When networks were first imagined and implemented, the designers envisioned a computing environment that would allow users to share programs, data files, and other network resources. The hope was that this utopian style would encourage greater productivity and cooperation among users.

Unfortunately, there are those who would take advantage of such flexibilities for personal gain. The news media is full of stories of people breaking into corporate networks and either stealing information or mischievously altering it. Contrary to popular belief, these *crackers*, as they are called, are not particularly clever; instead, they are knowledgeable about network-security vulnerabilities. Often, they succeed in compromising a system because the system administrator overlooked the need for enabling security features.

Novell carefully considered security when implementing NetWare 386. They took into account that the malicious cracker, as well as the innocent user, can cause damage if granted too much access. Laying out the system with this in mind, Novell designed its network operating system in layers. A user must cross various layers before accessing files. These security layers are as follows:

❖ Login security

❖ Rights security

❖ Attribute security

❖ File and print server security

The following sections explain each of these security layers in detail.

Understanding Login Security

To use a Novell network, you must first *log in* to a file server. The login process incorporates a username and password. When you enter the LOGIN command, you are prompted for a username. The *username* uniquely identifies a computer account belonging to you. After typing the username, you are prompted for a password. It is this password that provides a majority of the login level of security. The *password* is a combination of letters, digits, and punctuation. NetWare checks the password against an entry in its internal database corresponding to the password field of the user's account. If the passwords match, the login process continues.

Selecting a Password

Password protection of user accounts is often the only security feature utilized at many sites. Because of this, the selection of secure passwords is extremely important. Suppose that a cracker wants to break into a user's account. If the cracker does not know the password, he has to try a number of combinations.

IBM-compatible computers have 69 printable characters that can be typed from the keyboard: 26 letters (uppercase and lowercase are considered the same), 10 digits, and 33 punctuation characters. If the cracker assumes that a user's password is one to six characters in length and writes a program that attempts 100 passwords-per-second, it would take almost 35 years to try all the possible combinations.

Clearly, accessing a user's account with this method is unrealistic. Instead, most crackers try a variety of options that typically return quicker results. The basic premise they follow is that users select passwords that can easily be remembered. The cracker first tries variations on the user account name. Following this, the cracker tries any information known about the user, including variations on the user's first or last name, initials, social security number, or spouse's first name. The cracker often tries common first names, nicknames, and slang words. If all these methods fail, the cracker may use a dictionary file, hoping that the user chose a password commonly found in the English language. If the user is from a foreign country, a dictionary from that country might also be used.

An amazing number of passwords can be broken with this method. Many users consider passwords a hassle and select one that is short and easy to remember. The problem is that once a cracker has access to even one account, he or she can compromise the entire network. Most users won't realize the significance of this until it happens to them. It falls to the system administrator to take steps to prevent any compromise from occurring.

The system administrator must first decide whether to allow users to select their own passwords. In many organizations, the system administrator chooses secure passwords when creating user accounts and restricts the ability of users to change their passwords. Unfortunately, many users resort to writing down their passwords to remember them and often keep them in an easily accessible location where anyone can find and use them.

If the system administrator allows users to change their passwords, the following guidelines should be set to aid users in selecting secure ones:

❖ The password should be a minimum of six characters in length. A shorter password gives an automated attack a higher probability of success.

❖ The password should be neither all the same character or number (for example, *aaaaaa* or *111111*) nor a pattern found on the keyboard (for example, *qwerty*). This sort of password is easy to remember and type, which is why a cracker tries it early in the attack.

❖ The password should not be any variation of the user's account, initials, first or last name, or any information easily obtainable about the user, such as a social security number.

❖ The password should not be anyone's first name. Many crackers use dictionaries that contain long lists of men's and women's first names.

❖ The password should not be one found in any dictionary, including nonEnglish ones.

❖ Passwords can be selected that are several words connected by punctuation characters, such as *mop&top* and *book$mark*, or alternating characters and vowels to make a nonsense word pronounceable like *penmal* or *boksed*.

Setting Default User Account Security

NetWare provides the menu-driven utility, SYSCON, to enable the system administrator to easily set and maintain login security options. SYSCON handles security parameters in two ways: default account restrictions and user account restrictions. When setting up the network, the system administrator should decide how to implement login security for all users. This is done by logging in as the Supervisor and typing **SYSCON** at the MS-DOS prompt. Then select the Default Account Balance/Restrictions option from the Supervisor Options submenu. This action displays the screen shown in figure 10.1.

```
SYSCON  3.66                          Monday  September 14, 1992  9:55 am
                    User SUPERVISOR On File Server ETFACULTY

              ┌──────────────────────────────────────────────────┐
              │        Default Account Balance/Restrictions       │
              ├──────────────────────────────────────────────────┤
 Account Has Expiration Date:              Yes
     Date Account Expires:                 January 24, 1993
 Limit Concurrent Connections:             Yes
     Maximum Connections:                  1                            ctions
 Create Home Directory for User:           Yes
 Require Password:                          Yes
     Minimum Password Length:              6
 Force Periodic Password Changes:          Yes
     Days Between Forced Changes:          40
     Limit Grace Logins:                   Yes
         Grace Logins Allowed:             6
 Require Unique Passwords:                 Yes
 Account Balance:                          3000
 Allow Unlimited Credit:                   No
     Low Balance Limit:                    0
```

Figure 10.1:
The Default Account Balance/Restrictions screen.

The following list explains each of the fields pertaining to the login security architecture. To adequately implement login security for users, the system administrator must thoughtfully fill out this screen according to the security plan.

❖ **Date Account Expires**. When an account is only to be used for a specific amount of time, the system administrator can put an expiration date on it. The account remains active until the expiration date, at which time the account is automatically disabled.

❖ **Limit Concurrent Connections**. At many sites, the system administrator may want to restrict the number of machines that a user can log in from at a given time. This prevents a user from taking up resources that other users may need. In many cases, the concurrent-connection number is set to 1; the system administrator can be alerted to a cracker who is trying to access a broken account at the same time the actual user is logged in.

A *broken account* is an account for which a cracker has already broken (found) the password.

❖ **Create Home Directory for User.** When a user is added, the home directory is created with the security also set up, keeping the user's files safe from access by others.

❖ **Require Password and Minimum Password Length**. Passwords are essential to the security of the network. Without them, anyone can use an account and access every file for which the account user has permissions. By setting the Require Password field to Yes, any user must first enter a valid password to access files on the system. Simply requiring a password is not enough. The longer the password length, the less likely the account can be broken into by brute-force methods. For the Minimum Password Length field, a good minimum length to specify is six.

❖ **Force Periodic Password Changes**. Even if users select more secure passwords, these passwords have a way of becoming discovered. Often a user gives a password to another person because it is easier to allow others to access files directly instead of copying the files to disk and giving the disk to the other people. Although the system administrator cannot prevent this sort of situation, he or she can minimize the severity of it by requiring users to change their passwords periodically. This is known as *password aging*. Password aging can also reduce the long-term threat of crackers who break into a system. When the password on a broken account expires, the user changes it and the cracker loses access to the system. The ideal period between password changes should be short enough that there is little security risk and long enough that users do not find it a hindrance. Forty days is the default setting.

 Rather than give out passwords to provide others with access to files and directories, you can temporarily change users' access rights or files' attributes. Both of these methods have the advantage of being temporary (you can return both the access rights and attributes to their original states). More about these methods later in this chapter.

❖ **Limit Grace Logins**. Once a password expires, the user is notified at each login. Many users become attached to their passwords and ignore this warning. To prevent users from continuing to access accounts with expired passwords, NetWare allows the system administrator to limit the number of times a user can log into the system before changing his or her password. These logins are known as *grace logins*. If the user attempts to enter an account with the old password beyond the number of grace logins allowed, the user finds the account locked and must contact the system administrator to regain access. The default number of grace logins allowed is six.

❖ **Require Unique Passwords**. Many users dislike the thought of changing passwords periodically. To avoid remembering a new password each time the old one expires, some users try to alternate back and forth between two passwords. NetWare allows the system administrator to prevent this by requiring users to replace expired passwords with unique ones. NetWare stores the last 10 passwords that each user has provided for an account. If a user tries to reset the password to one previously entered, the user is notified that the password is invalid. Along the same line, some users try to change their passwords a number of times on the day that their password expires, hoping that they can eventually reuse the original one. NetWare stops this ploy by allowing a user to change the password a maximum of 10 times per day.

❖ **Account Balance and Credit Limits**. A user's access can be limited if the current balance reaches established credit limits. If the user is granted unlimited credit, that user can use the server resources without any limitations. Otherwise, the user is charged for various services that the file server performs. The user is initially given a credit balance. As the user continues to use the server, charges are subtracted from the balance. The details of the charges are discussed later in this chapter. If the account balance equals or drops less than the established limit, the user is denied further access. By enabling accounting features, users are prevented from abusing server resources by remaining continually logged in to a file server.

Modifying User Account Security

When new users are created, NetWare checks the default security settings and applies them to the new user account. However, the default security settings are not always desirable. The system administrator can change these settings by entering SYSCON and selecting the User Information option. A list of all user accounts is displayed.

Highlight the user to be changed and press Enter to display a menu for viewing and changing that user's information. The second option on the menu is Account Restrictions; selecting it reveals the screen shown in figure 10.1.

In a large network, you may want to change the security for many users at the same time: highlight all the users you want to change and press Enter.

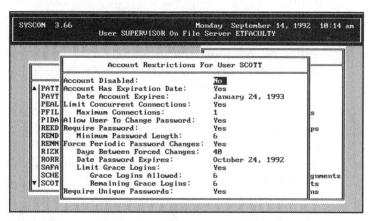

Figure 10.1:

The Account Restrictions screen.

❖ **Account Disabled**. Frequently, the accounts broken in to by crackers are not active accounts at all but old accounts no longer being used. Such crackers are unlikely to be discovered because the original user is not around to notice anything peculiar about the account. If an account is not to be used for a while, the Account Disabled field enables the system administrator to disable the account without actually removing it. When the account is needed again, it can be reactivated, still possessing the same privileges and password as it did before.

❖ **Allow User To Change Password**. Some users are notorious for choosing insecure passwords. The system administrator can reduce this problem by selecting more secure passwords for these users and by setting the Allow User To Change Password option to No. Although this arrangement greatly minimizes the risk of accounts getting broken into, educating users to choose more secure passwords is the preferred and more popular solution to password-selection problems.

❖ **Date Password Expires**. If a password-aging policy is active, the Date Password Expires option contains the date on which the current password expires. When password aging is activated for an account—as well as whenever the password changes—NetWare calculates the new expiration date based on the value set in the Days Between Forced Changes option. Every time the user logs in, NetWare compares the current date with the expiration date to determine whether the user should be notified that the password has expired.

❖ **Remaining Grace Logins**. The Remaining Grace Logins option is the number of times a user can log in to a file server with an expired password. When a user changes his or her password, this option is set to the value specified in the Grace Logins Allowed option. When a user's account expires, the Remaining Grace Logins option is checked; if it is zero, NetWare denies the user access.

Restricting User Access

Even when a user has a valid password, he or she is not necessarily granted access. Additional factors are considered before a user can log in: At what times are users allowed to log in and from which computers? Have users exceeded the disk-storage quota limits imposed on them? Depending on resources available and security policies implemented, the answers to these questions may determine whether or not users are granted access.

Restrictions Based on Login Times

The NetWare operating system limits the number of connections that can be active at one time. In large organizations, servers can have more user accounts than available connections. If users can log in concurrently, the number of requests can grow exponentially larger than the limits. By restricting the times at which users can access the file server, the system administrator can manage user access to prevent the NetWare limit from being reached. Another reason for restricting access times is to allow the system administrator to schedule maintenance without inconveniencing users.

Time restrictions can be set up in two ways: default and user. Both are set up through the SYSCON utility and use the same screen, shown in figure 10.2. Default time restrictions are applied to every newly created user account. Default time restrictions are specified by selecting the Default Time Restrictions option from the SYSCON Supervisor Options submenu. The screen shown in figure 10.2 then appears. To alter the default time restrictions for an individual user, the system administrator chooses the User Information option from the Available Options main menu, highlights the user, and presses Enter. From the resulting menu, the administrator selects Time Restrictions to change the time settings in a screen similar to the one shown in figure 10.2.

To alter the default time restrictions for more than one user, use the F5 key to highlight all the users you want to change and then press Enter.

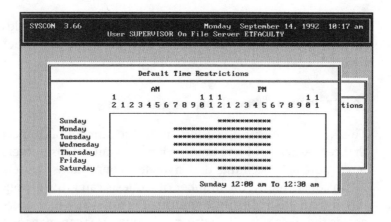

Figure 10.2:
The Time Restrictions screen.

Each asterisk represents a 30-minute time period. If the asterisk is present, users can log in during that time. Figure 10.3 shows that users can log in to the file server from 7:00 a.m. to 6:00 p.m. on Monday through Friday and from noon to 6:00 p.m. on Saturday and Sunday. To change the settings, locate the cursor at one corner of the block of time you want to change, press the F5 key, and use the arrow keys to define the highlighted block. Once the block is defined, press Ins to enable access or press Del to deny access during those times.

Station Restrictions

Another way to restrict access is to allow users to access file servers from only selected machines. The server can tell one machine from the other through a combination of network and node addresses. The network address is an eight-digit hex number that a NetWare server associates with a particular network segment. A file server can have several network interface cards installed, and each card is associated with a unique network address assigned by the system administrator. Node addresses are 12-digit hex numbers incorporated into each network interface card. In Ethernet networks, the numbers are set by the card manufacturers. Interface card addresses are unique. The first six digits refer to the manufacturer's code; the remaining six digits are the manufacturer's internal number.

Station access is restricted by choosing User Information from the Available Topics main menu, highlighting the user whose access you want to limit, and pressing Enter. From the resulting menu, select the Station Restrictions option to reveal the screen shown in figure 10.3. In this example, the user can only log in to the server from the machine with a network address of 86440700 and node address of 02608C848732. Add new stations by pressing Ins; when prompted for the network and node address, use the arrow keys to highlight a particular station. Delete a station from the allowed login list by pressing Del.

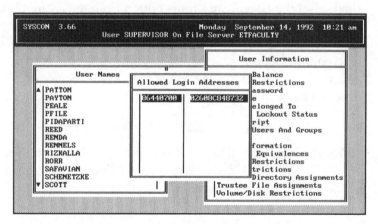

Figure 10.3:

Restricting access to specific stations.

Disk-Storage Restrictions

One of the most precious resources on a file server is disk space.
Depending on the number of users and amount of disk space
available on the server, limiting the amount of disk space a user
can have access to on the server may or may not be a concern. On
servers with many user accounts, some users have a tendency of
storing everything. This is particularly true in college and university environments. The system administrator must track the
amount of space used and project limits based on the physical storage present on the server. Because budgets may not allow for the
purchase of additional disks, the system administrator can limit
the maximum amount of disk storage any user can utilize.

The DSPACE utility enables the system administrator to limit the
amount of disk storage a user can access on a volume-by-volume
basis. This gives the system administrator more flexibility when
setting up the file system. To restrict the user's access to a volume,
log in as the Supervisor and type **DSPACE** at the MS-DOS prompt;
then select the User Restrictions option from the Available Options
main menu. A list of users is displayed. With the arrow keys, highlight the user to be restricted and then press Enter; a list of available volumes appears. Select the volume or volumes to be
restricted, press Enter, answer Yes to the Limit Space option, and
type the amount of space this user is limited to in kilobytes (see
fig. 10.4).

You can also limit a user's accessible disk space with the
SYSCON utility by selecting Volume/Disk Restrictions from
the User Information screen.

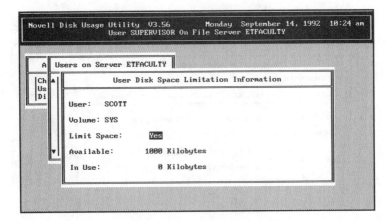

```
Novell Disk Usage Utility  V3.56        Monday  September 14, 1992  10:24 am
                    User SUPERVISOR On File Server ETFACULTY

    ┌A┌ Users on Server ETFACULTY ┐
     │Ch│▲┌        User Disk Space Limitation Information        ┐
     │Us│ │
     │Di│ │
          │   User:    SCOTT
          │
          │   Volume: SYS
          │
          │   Limit Space:     Yes
     │ │▼│
          │   Available:      1000 Kilobytes
          │
          │   In Use:            0 Kilobytes
```

Figure 10.4:
The User Disk Space Limitation Information screen.

Often, multiple users can store files in common directories. These directories are usually set up so that users can share their work without having to put the files on floppy disks and exchange them. Unfortunately, stored files are rarely removed once the users are finished with them; the directory frequently becomes unmanageable. DSPACE enables the system administrator to limit the amount of disk storage to be used by a directory and any subdirectory under it. Once the directory has reached the storage limit, no user can store files in that directory without first removing files. To enable this feature, the system administrator enters the DSPACE utility and selects the Directory Restrictions option from the Available Options main menu. After selecting the volume and directory, the screen in figure 10.5 appears. At the Limit Space option, type **Yes** and press Enter. Then type the maximum amount of disk storage to be used by the directory in kilobytes.

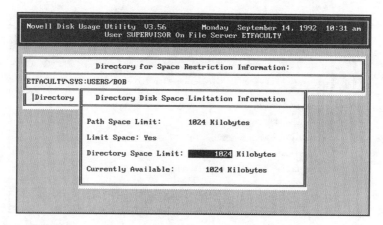

Figure 10.5:
The Directory Disk Space Limitation Information screen.

Applying Account Security when Creating Many Users

When a new file server is installed, it has two accounts: SUPERVISOR and GUEST. If the file server is to support a large number of users, it would take some time to use SYSCON to create the accounts correctly. NetWare provides the utility MAKEUSER to automate this process. MAKEUSER reads in a text file (also called a *script*) and creates users based on the user names and security defaults set in the file.

 The MAKEUSER script is an ASCII text file. Once the file is created and saved with a file name, implement it by typing **MAKEUSER** *scriptname*.

The following is a typical MAKEUSER script file. Descriptions of some of the more commonly used entries are given after the sample file.

```
#Rem A Sample MAKEUSER file to Create Users
#Rem
#Rem Staff Accounts
#Rem
#PASSWORD_REQUIRED
#PASSWORD_LENGTH 6
#PASSWORD_PERIOD 40
#UNIQUE_PASSWORD
#ACCOUNT_EXPIRATION January 24, 1993
#ACCOUNTING 3000,0
#CONNECTIONS 1
#MASK_DISK_SPACE SYS,250
#RESTRICTED_TIME mon, 6:00 p.m., 7:00 a.m.;+
   tue, 6:00 p.m., 7:00 a.m.;+
   wed, 6:00 p.m., 7:00 a.m.;+
   thu, 6:00 p.m., 7:00 a.m.;+
   fri, 6:00 p.m., 7:00 a.m.;+
   sat, 6:00 p.m., 11:00 a.m.;+
   sun, 6:00 p.m., 11:00 a.m.
#STATIONS 86440800, all; 86440700, 2608C848732
#GROUPS staff
#HOME_DIRECTORY sys:users
#CREATE jones;Lisa Jones;milrad;;
#CREATE grubbs;Debbie Grubbs;saqwel;;
#CREATE carter;Vickie Carter;jutzef;;
#CREATE orr;Robert Orr;capnul;;
#REM
#REM System Administrator Accounts
#REM
#CLEAR
#PASSWORD_REQUIRED
#PASSWORD_LENGTH 6
#PASSWORD_PERIOD 40
#UNIQUE_PASSWORD
#MASK_DISK_SPACE SYS,250
#RESTRICTED_TIME everyday, 6:00 p.m., 7:00 a.m.
#STATIONS 86440800, all; 86440700, all
#GROUPS staff;sysadmin
#HOME_DIRECTORY sys:users\admin
#CREATE damon;Damon Beals;mukweh;;
#CREATE jon;Jon Burgoyne;xafgob;;
#CREATE rita;Rita Mateos;firvup;;
#CREATE scott;Scott Orr;lokqad;;
```

#ACCOUNT_EXPIRATION *month day, year*. Use this option to set up an expiration date on the accounts created with the MAKEUSER script.

#ACCOUNTING *balance,limit*. Only use this option if accounting is already installed on the file server.

#CONNECTIONS *number*. This option limits users to a specified maximum number of concurrent connections. Security-conscious sites limit users to only one connection.

#MAX_DISK_SPACE *volume, blocks[;...]*. This option limits disk storage to a specified number of blocks per volume.

 The size of a block in bytes depends on the way the block size was specified when the volume was created. A block size of 4096 bytes is frequently used, so that 10 megabytes translates to 250 blocks.

#PASSWORD_LENGTH *number*. This option specifies the minimum length of a user's password.

#PASSWORD_PERIOD *days*. If password aging is employed, this option specifies the number of days a password is valid before expiring.

#PASSWORD_REQUIRED. This option prevents users from not having a password. If passwords are required on the system, this option must precede the #PASSWORD_LENGTH, #PASSWORD_PERIOD, or #UNIQUE_PASSWORD options.

#RESTRICTED_TIME *day, start, end[;...]*. This option restricts the user from logging in to the file server during the times specified. The variable *day* specifies the day of the week to which this restriction applies. The *start* and *end* variables specify the period during which the user cannot log in to the file server. If the same time restrictions apply to every day of the week, the keyword EVERYDAY can be used in place of the day of the week. (Refer to the sample MAKEUSER script file for examples of how to enter times.)

#STATIONS *network, node[;...]*. This option restricts the user to log in to the file server from selected machines. The *network* number is the eight-digit hex address the system incorporated for the network interface card in the file server. The *node* number is the 12-digit hex address set by the manufacturer of the network interface card installed in the workstation. If all nodes can access the file server from a particular network, replace the *node* number with ALL.

#UNIQUE_PASSWORD. This option requires that the user select a different password each time it is changed.

Detecting and Locking Out Intruders

Once the security measures described in the first part of this chapter are in place, it is difficult to break into any of the accounts on the file server. However, no system is completely secure; a cracker may eventually succeed in breaching even these defenses. The key problem that faces the system administrator is how to discover these attempts.

NetWare provides an Intruder Detection and Lockout feature; when enabled, it locks an account when someone unsuccessfully tries to log in to it. This option is activated from the SYSCON utility by selecting the Intruder Detection/Lockout option from the Supervisor Options submenu. The Intruder Detection/Lockout screen that appears is shown in figure 10.6.

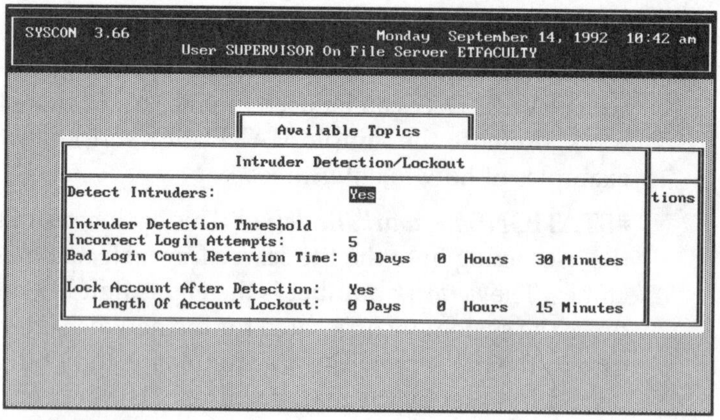

```
SYSCON 3.66                          Monday  September 14, 1992  10:42 am
                        User SUPERVISOR On File Server ETFACULTY



                        ┌─────────────────────────┐
                        │    Available Topics      │
                  ┌─────┴──────────────────────────┴─────┐      ┌──┐
                  │      Intruder Detection/Lockout       │      │t ions│
                  │Detect Intruders:          Yes         │
                  │                                       │
                  │Intruder Detection Threshold           │
                  │Incorrect Login Attempts:      5        │
                  │Bad Login Count Retention Time: 0  Days    0  Hours    30 Minutes │
                  │                                       │
                  │Lock Account After Detection:  Yes      │
                  │  Length Of Account Lockout:   0  Days    0  Hours    15 Minutes │
                  └───────────────────────────────────────┘
```

Figure 10.6:

The Intruder Detection/Lockout screen.

After activating this option, you set the Intruder Detection Threshold information. This information includes the number of times someone can unsuccessfully attempt to log in to an account before being considered an intruder. These attempts need not be in rapid succession. The system administrator can set a time period during which unsuccessful attempts are kept track of before resetting the count of incorrect logins. The default settings detect an intruder if there are five unsuccessful login attempts in a 30-minute span. NetWare enables you to lock an account if an intruder is detected. Once enabled, NetWare can keep the account locked for a specific time period; the default is 15 minutes.

When Intruder Detection and Lockout is triggered, several things happen. If the Intruder lock feature is enabled, the account is locked and a timer is started to determine when to unlock the account. On the system console, a message is displayed, indicating which account is locked, at what time the lock occurred, and from which network and node address. This message is also saved in the System Error Log and in the NET$ACCT.DAT file.

The NET$ACCT.DAT file stores all the accounting information and can be extracted with the PAUDIT utility.

Understanding Rights Security

Once a user successfully logs into a file server, the Rights level of security controls which files and directories the user can access and change. This access is based on a combination of user and group trustee rights and is compared to the Inherited Rights Mask of the directory or file. *Rights* consist of a group of options that correspond to a particular privilege associated with a file or directory. (Trustee rights and the Inherited Rights Mask are described in detail later in this chapter.)

 Rights often appear in brackets with a spaces left for rights that are not granted. The complete rights list is represented as follows:

[SRWCEMFA]

The order of the rights in the brackets does not change; if a right is not assigned, a space is left where that right's letter usually appears. For example, in the designation [R F], the Read and File Scan rights are assigned; the Supervisory right (S), Write right (W), Create right (C), Erase right (E), Modify right (M), and Access Control right (A) have not been granted.

There are eight individual rights that control access to directories and files. Although each right carries the same name when assigned to files and directories, its meaning is slightly different. The following rights control directory and file access:

❖ **Access Control right**. This right enables a user to modify the trustee rights and the Inherited Rights Mask for directories and files. When viewing the rights list, this right appears as the letter *A*.

When you grant the Access Control right to a user, that user then can grant access to any other user. Assign this right with caution.

❖ **Create right**. For directories, this right enables a user to create files and subdirectories in that directory. If this is the only right associated with a directory, a user can create a file in the directory but cannot view it afterwards. This is roughly what happens with the SYS:MAIL directory: users have Create and Write privileges to that directory; a user can mail a file to another user but cannot go to that user's mail subdirectory and view the mail. If the Create right is assigned to a particular file, a user can salvage the file after inadvertently erasing it. When viewing the rights list, this right appears as the letter *C*.

❖ **Erase right**. For directories, this right enables a user to delete files and subdirectories. When this right is assigned to a file, a user can delete the file, even if the directory itself does not have this right. When viewing the rights list, this right appears as the letter *E*.

❖ **File Scan right**. For directories, this right enables a user to see file and subdirectory names. When the right is assigned to a file, a user can see the file, even though the directory does not have this right. When viewing the rights list, this right appears as the letter *F*.

❖ **Modify right**. For directories, this right enables a user to rename subdirectories and files. In addition, a user can change any subdirectory and file attributes. When the right is assigned to a file, a user can rename or change the attributes of that file, even though the directory does not have this right. Directory and file attribute are discussed later in the chapter. When viewing the rights list, this right appears as the letter *M*.

❖ **Read right**. For directories, this right enables a user to open subdirectories, view the contents of files, and run programs. When the right is assigned to a file, a user can read the file if it is data or run it if it is a program, even though the directory does not have this right. When viewing the rights list, this right appears as the letter *R*.

❖ **Supervisory right**. The system administrator uses a special account named SUPERVISOR. With this account, the administrator can access every file and directory in the file system. With the Supervisory Right on a directory, a user has complete access to all files and subdirectories in the directory that have this right. This access supercedes any restrictions imposed by the Inherited Rights Mask. The Supervisory right cannot be revoked in any file or subdirectory. The only way to revoke this right is to remove it from the directory itself. If this right is assigned to a file, a user has complete access to that file, regardless of the Inherited Rights Mask settings. A user possessing the Supervisory right to a directory or file can also grant others this right. When viewing the rights list, this right appears as the letter *S*.

❖ **Write right**. For directories, this right enables a user to open and write data into files. When this right is assigned to a particular file, the user can open and write to the file, even though the directory does not have this right. When viewing the rights list, this right appears as the letter *W*.

Understanding Trustee Rights

When users and groups need to access directories and files, they must have permission before access can be granted. Permission comes in the form of trustee rights. A *trustee right* consists of the full path to a file or directory and the rights associated with it. For example, a user possesses [RWCEMF] rights to his or her home directory. In the SYS:PUBLIC directory, a user typically has only [R   F] rights. If rights are granted to a directory, they also apply to all subdirectories and files. The only way to change access rights to files and subdirectories below a directory is to add another trustee right for the file or subdirectory in question. By default, [R   F] rights are granted when a new trustee is added.

When determining whether a user can access a file or directory, the system first checks the user's effective trustee rights. This is accomplished by discovering what trustee rights are possessed by the user and every group he or she belongs to. The *effective trustee rights* are the combination of all rights granted to the file or directory. For example, if a user has [R   F] rights to SYS:TEST and is member of group PROGRAMMER that has [WC   ] rights to that directory, the effective trustee rights the user has to the directory are [RWC F].

Assigning Trustee Rights

You can assign trustee rights to users and groups in several ways. To prevent the uncontrolled assigning of trustee rights, no user other than the system administrator should possess the Supervisory or Access Control right. In this way, no user is granted privileges he or she should not have.

The SYSCON utility enables groups and users to be granted trustee rights. The system administrator can follow these steps to assign trustee rights to a group:

1. Type **SYSCON** at the MS-DOS prompt and press Enter.

2. Select the Group Information option from the Available Topics main menu. This action displays the list of groups available.

3. Using the arrow keys, highlight the group whose accesses you want to change; press Enter.

4. Select the Trustee Directory Assignments or the Trustee File Assignments option, depending on which trustee rights you want to add. A list of currently assigned trustee rights is displayed.

5. To add trustee rights, press Ins ; a screen prompts for the trustee volume and directory. If a file trustee right is being assigned, a second screen prompts for the file name.

6. To remove a trustee right, highlight the right and press Del.

7. To change a trustee right, highlight it and press Enter. A second screen appears, containing a list of currently assigned rights. To add additional rights, press Ins; a third screen displays (see fig. 10.7). The third screen lists the remaining unassigned rights. Highlight the unassigned right to be added and press Enter. To remove a currently assigned right, highlight it and press Del.

To assign trustee rights for a user, select the User Information option from the Available Topics main menu and follow the same steps used for assigning group trustee rights.

The GRANT command is used to add trustee rights for users and groups without parsing a menu. GRANT is entered from the MS-DOS prompt with the following syntax:

```
GRANT Rights_List [FOR Path] TO [USER | GROUP] Name [/Options]
```

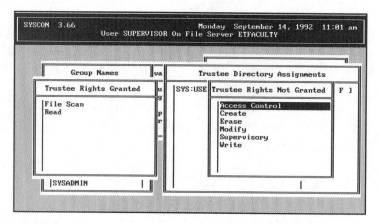

Figure 10.7:
The Directory Trustee Rights Not Granted screen.

In this syntax, the following variables are used:

Variable	Description
Rights_List	This list consists of the rights letters to be assigned, separated by spaces. If all rights are to be assigned, replace *Rights_List* with *ALL*. Use the letter *N* (for No Rights) to take all privileges away. To grant all rights except one, use *ALL BUT* and the letter of the right to be revoked. Use *ONLY* and the letter of a single right to revoke all rights except for the one specified.
Path	This variable refers to the directory path to the subdirectory or file to which the rights are being granted. If FOR *Path* is not specified, the current directory is used.
Name	This variable corresponds to the user or group name to which you want to assign the trustee

| | rights. The keyword USER or GROUP is only used if the name exists for both a user and a group. |
| */Options* | Two options can be added to this command line: /S applies the rights to all subdirectories; /F applies the rights to all files that match the *path* parameter when wild cards are used. |

To remove trustee rights from a user or group, use the REVOKE command. The syntax for REVOKE is as follows:

```
REVOKE Rights_List [FOR Path] FROM [USER | GROUP] Name [-Op-
tions]
```

In this syntax, all the variables are the same as those used with the GRANT command, except for the N, ALL BUT, and ONLY options which do not exist for the *Rights_List* variable. In addition, the /S option is replaced by -SUB; the /F option is replaced by -F.

The REMOVE command is similar to REVOKE, but is used to delete users and groups from file and directory trustee lists. This command uses the following syntax:

```
REMOVE [USER | GROUP] Name [[FROM] Path] [-Options]
```

In this syntax, *Name* is the user or group name and is preceded by *USER* or *GROUP* only if the name belongs to both a user and a group. The *FROM* keyword is completely optional, and *Path* is specified only if the current directory is not the one to be changed. Like REVOKE, the -SUB and -F options are available.

If a user has the Access Control right for a file or directory, he or she can find out what trustee rights have been assigned to users and groups for that file or directory. The command to do this is TLIST and has the following syntax:

```
TLIST [Path [USERS | GROUPS]
```

In this syntax, *Path* is the directory path to the file or directory to be checked. If the USERS or GROUPS keyword is used, only user or group trustee rights are displayed.

Changing the Inherited Rights Mask

When a file or directory is created, an Inherited Rights Mask is associated with it. This mask is a group of rights that represents the maximum rights any user or group may possess. Every effective trustee right granted to a file or directory must have the corresponding right in the Inherited Rights Mask, or else that right is not granted. Initially, every file and directory has all the rights in the Inherited Rights Mask when created.

You can change the Inherited Rights Mask in several ways, but a user can change it only if he or she has been assigned the Access Control right for that file or directory. The first way to change the Inherited Rights Mask is to use the FILER utility. To use FILER, follow these steps:

1. Type **FILER** at the MS-DOS prompt and press Enter.

2. Select the Current Directory Information option for the current directory. For files and subdirectories in the current directory, choose the Directory Contents option instead. A screen with the file and subdirectory names is displayed. Highlight the file or directory whose mask you want to change and press Enter. If you selected a subdirectory, choose the View/Set Directory Information option from the Subdirectory Options menu; the screen shown in figure 10.8 appears.

3. Select the Inherited Rights Mask field by highlighting it and pressing Enter. The currently assigned rights are displayed.

4. To add a right to the mask, press the Ins key; the screen shown in figure 10.9 appears, listing the unassigned rights. Highlight the right to be added, and press Enter.

5. To remove a right from the list, highlight the right and press Del.

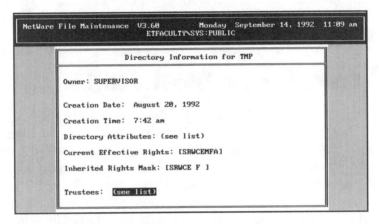

Figure 10.8:
The Directory Information screen.

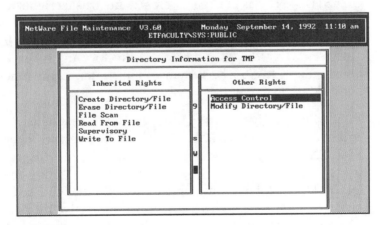

Figure 10.9:
Adding rights to the Inherited Rights Mask.

The ALLOW command enables you to view or change the Inherited Rights Mask without parsing a series of menu options. The syntax of the ALLOW command is as follows:

```
ALLOW [Path [TO INHERIT] [Rights_List]]
```

In this syntax, *Path* is the path to the file or directory. The TO INHERIT keyword is optional and precedes the *Rights_List* to be assigned.

Understanding Effective Rights

Effective rights are the actual rights a user has to a file or directory. These rights are determined by trustee rights and the Inherited Rights Mask. The trustee rights that the user possesses for a directory or file consist of a union of all trustee rights assigned to the user, as well as rights assigned to each group of which the user is a member. The effective rights are those rights that result from an intersection of the effective trustee rights and the Inherited Rights Mask. The following example demonstrates the application of effective rights.

User STUDENT has not been assigned any trustee rights to the SYS:HANDOUT directory but is a member of group CLASS that has [R   F] trustee rights to the directory. User PROFESSOR possesses [WCEM A] rights to the directory and is also a member of group CLASS. The system administrator set the Inherited Rights Mask to [SRWCEMF].

To find the effective rights of user STUDENT, first determine the effective trustee rights STUDENT has to the directory. The union of STUDENT's user trustee rights, [   ], and the group trustee rights, [R   F], result in [R   F] trustee rights for STUDENT. Intersecting these rights with the Inherited Rights Mask, [SRWCEMF], gives STUDENT the effective rights of [R F]. STUDENT can view and read files and directories but cannot change them. This is the arrangement of rights that would allow a student to pick up course handouts.

PROFESSOR, on the other hand, is assigned [WCEM A] trustee rights; the union of CLASS's rights [R   F] gives PROFESSOR [RWCEMFA] trustee rights to the SYS:HANDOUT directory.

The intersection with the Inherited Rights Mask, [RWCEMF], limits PROFESSOR to [RWCEMF] effective rights. PROFESSOR can create files and directories and put course material in them for STUDENT's use. The rights [A] are taken away from PROFESSOR to prevent him from altering the type of access granted to other users and groups.

To discover what effective rights a user has to a directory or file, use the RIGHTS command. The syntax for this command is as follows:

```
RIGHTS [Path]
```

In this syntax, *Path* is the full path to the file or directory. If the path is not included, the current directory is used.

Understanding Attribute Security

Attribute security is actually an extension of a feature present in MS-DOS. Security attributes control file and directory access and can override privileges assigned by effective rights. Unlike trustee rights, attributes assigned to files and directories apply to every user. Only a user with the Modify (M) right can change security attributes.

Fourteen different attributes can be assigned to files; five of these attributes also can be assigned to directories. Definitions for these attributes follow.

❖ **Archive Needed attribute**. When the contents of a file change, NetWare automatically sets the Archive Needed attribute. Backup systems often look for files with this attribute when doing incremental backups. After the file is copied to the backup device, most systems reset the attribute. When viewing a list of file attributes, this attribute appears as the letter *A*.

❖ **Copy Inhibit attribute**. If the Copy Inhibit attribute is set, a file cannot be copied. However, this only applies to Macintosh users. When viewing a list of file attributes, this attribute appears as the letter *C*.

 The Macintosh operating system displays each file as an icon. By clicking on the icon, a user can drag and copy the icon anywhere in the system. The Copy Inhibit attribute prevents this.

❖ **Delete Inhibit attribute**. The Delete Inhibit attribute can be set for both files and directories. If set for a file, the file cannot be erased, regardless of what rights the user has. If set for directories, this attribute prevents all the files and subdirectories in the directory from being erased. When viewing a list of file attributes, this attribute appears as the letter *D*.

❖ **Execute Only attribute**. The Execute Only attribute can be assigned only by the system administrator to *.COM and *.EXE files. The purpose of the attribute is to prevent users from copying the files. Unfortunately, once this attribute is assigned, it cannot be removed. An alternative way to achieve this goal is for the system administrator to set the Read Only and Hidden attributes instead. NetWare can find and run files with these two attributes through search mappings, but because MS-DOS commands like COPY cannot see the files, users cannot copy them. When viewing a list of file attributes, this attribute appears as the letter *X*.

❖ **Hidden attribute**. The Hidden attribute prevents a file from being viewed with standard MS-DOS commands such as COPY and DIR. By setting this attribute, a file cannot be copied or deleted. When viewing a list of file attributes, this attribute appears as the letter *H*.

❖ **Indexed attribute**. If a file takes more than 64 FAT entries, NetWare automatically indexes the file. Indexing improves the speed at which the file can be accessed. When viewing a list of file attributes, this attribute appears as the letter *I*. (This attribute is internal only; system administrators cannot assign it.)

❖ **Purged attribute**. This attribute can be set for both files and directories. When a file or directory is erased, NetWare maintains a record of it until the space it occupied is needed by another file or directory. By setting the Purged attribute, the file or directory is completely removed when erased, preventing the SALVAGE command from restoring it. When viewing a list of file attributes, this attribute appears as the letter *P*.

❖ **Read Only attribute**. With the Read Only attribute set, a file cannot be changed, renamed, or erased, regardless of what effective rights a user has. When this attribute is set, NetWare also sets the Delete Inhibit and Rename Inhibit attributes. When viewing a list of file attributes, this attribute appears as *Ro*. If the attribute is not set, *Rw* (for Read/Write) appears. The R and D attributes are automatically removed if the Ro attribute is changed to Rw.

❖ **Rename Inhibit attribute**. The Rename Inhibit attribute can be set for both files and directories. Setting the attribute prevents a user from renaming a file or directory, regardless of what effective rights he may possess. When viewing a list of file attributes, this attribute appears as the letter *R*.

❖ **Shareable attribute**. The Shareable attribute allows multiple users to access a file concurrently. The Read Only attribute is usually also set to prevent the risk of a race condition from occurring. When viewing a list of file attributes, this attribute appears as the letter *S*.

In a race condition, several users can open a file to add or change information. If one person makes changes and saves the file, those changes are lost if a second user opened the file for writing before the first user finished.

❖ **System attribute**. This attribute is generally used by MS-DOS to indicate which files are internal parts of the operating system. Using it in NetWare has the same effect as setting the Hidden attribute. When viewing a list of file attributes, this attribute appears as *Sy*.

❖ **Transactional attribute**. When this attribute is set, the file is controlled by the Transaction Tracking System (TTS). TTS prevents files from becoming corrupted by a system failure. The way the system works is that when a file with this attribute is being saved, either all the changes are saved or none of them are. TTS is useful to protect large database files. When viewing a list of file attributes, this attribute appears as the letter *T*.

The Transaction Tracking System and its impact on large database files is discussed in Chapter 5.

❖ **Read Audit and Write Audit attributes**. The Read Audit and Write Audit attributes are not used by NetWare but can still be set. The Read Audit and Write Audit attributes are represented by *Ra* and *Wa*, respectively.

In future releases of NetWare, the accounting system will be able to charge users who read or write to files with the Ra and Wa attributes.

Assigning File and Directory Attributes

You can change attributes to files and directories in several ways. To prevent users from changing attributes that other users need, no user other than the system administrator should possess the Modify trustee right. In this way, no user can alter the privileges others may need.

The FILER utility enables you to view or change file and directory attributes from the same screen as the Inherited Rights Mask. To use FILER to view or change attributes, follow these steps:

1. Type **FILER** at the MS-DOS prompt and press Enter.

2. Select the Current Directory Information option for the current directory. For files and subdirectories in the current directory, choose the Directory Contents option instead. A screen listing the file and subdirectory names is displayed. Highlight the file or directory to be changed and press Enter. If a subdirectory is selected, choose the View/Set Directory Information option from the Subdirectory Options menu that appears. If a file is selected, choose the View/Set File Information option from the File Options menu that appears.

3. Select the Directory Attributes or Attributes field by highlighting it and pressing Enter. The currently assigned attributes are displayed.

4. To add an attribute, press Ins; the screen shown in figure 10.10 appears, listing the unassigned attributes. Highlight the attribute to be added, and press Enter.

5. To remove an attribute from the list, highlight the attribute and press Del.

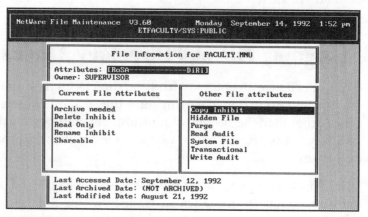

Figure 10.10:
Adding file/directory attributes.

The FLAG and FLAGDIR commands enable a user to view or change the attributes of files and directories, respectively. The syntax for the two commands is the same:

```
FLAG(DIR) [Path [TO INHERIT] [Attribute_List]]
```

In this syntax, *Path* is the directory path for the file or directory. The TO INHERIT keyword is completely optionally and precedes the *Attribute_List* to be set.

Using the Effective Rights Example

This example builds on the example first presented in the discussion of effective rights. User PROFESSOR possesses effective rights of [RWCEMF] in the SYS:HANDOUT directory. In this directory is a file called INTRO.DOC with the `[RoS          DR]` attributes assigned. PROFESSOR reads the file and discovers a misspelled word. When PROFESSOR tries to change the file using an editor, an error results. Even though PROFESSOR has the Write (W) trustee right, PROFESSOR still cannot change the contents of the file because the file has the Read Only attribute. Because PROFESSOR has the Modify (M) right to the directory, he or she uses the FLAG command to change the file attributes to `[RwS                ]`. This time, PROFESSOR can correct the spelling and save the file without errors. Once again, PROFESSOR uses FLAG and returns the attributes to their original status.

Remember that the R and D attributes are automatically removed when the Ro attribute is changed to Rw.

Implementing Security Equivalence and Workgroup Management

When a user is on vacation, there always seems to be another person who needs access to the first user's files. The worst thing the system administrator can do is to reveal the user's password. Instead, the administrator can make the second user *security equivalent* to the first user. When security equivalence is granted, the second user not only possesses his or her own trustee rights, but also the trustee rights of the first user.

The system administrator should be very careful when giving security equivalence to users: the second user may not need access to certain files and directories. To prevent this sort of situation from arising, assign each group trustee rights to a directory so that members can share files.

Security equivalences are assigned through the SYSCON utility. To assign security equivalences, the system administrator follows these steps:

1. Type **SYSCON** at the MS-DOS prompt, and press Enter to start the SYSCON utility.

2. From the Available Topics main menu, select the User Information option.

3. When the list of all users appears, select the user whose rights are to be changed by highlighting the user and pressing Enter.

4. From the menu of user options, select the Security Equivalences option. A screen with the current security equivalences assigned to that user is displayed.

5. To add new security equivalences, press Ins; the screen shown in figure 10.11 appears, listing all users and groups not already assigned. Highlight the user whose rights you want to assign to the user selected in step 3 and press Enter. If several users are to be selected, use the F5 key to mark them before pressing Enter.

6. To remove assigned security equivalences, highlight the currently assigned security equivalence and press Del. Several equivalences can be removed at the same time by using the F5 key to mark them before pressing Del.

Large sites with many users may have several system administrators. Instead of all administrators using the SUPERVISOR account, each can have his or her own account, set to be security equivalent to the SUPERVISOR account. With several administrators arranged in this way, however, many inconsistencies may exist with the way the server is managed. An easier way to manage a large number of users is through the workgroup manager concept.

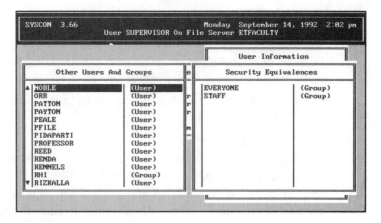

Figure 10.11:
Adding security equivalences.

The system administrator can delegate the responsibility of managing user accounts to workgroup managers. Each department can have its own workgroup manager who is responsible for managing all the user accounts in that department. The responsibilities of the workgroup manager include creating new users, modifying user trustee rights, and assigning Inherited Rights Masks for those files and directories belonging to the department. Because each department has different requirements, the department workgroup manager can customize the user accounts as needed.

The system administrator can set up workgroups and workgroup managers using the following steps:

1. Type **SYSCON** at the MS-DOS prompt, and press Enter to start the SYSCON utility.

2. Select the Group Information option from the Available Topics main menu. A list of available groups is displayed.

3. If one of the these groups is the one to be managed, highlight it and press Enter. Otherwise, press Ins to create a new group and select it afterwards. The group options appear as shown in figure 10.12.

4. Select the Managed Users and Groups option. A list of current group members is displayed.

5. To add new members, press Ins; a second list is displayed. This list contains all the user and group names not currently part of the selected group. Highlight the user or group to be included and press Enter. If multiple users and groups are to be added, mark them with the F5 key before pressing Enter.

6. To remove group members, highlight the user or group, and press Del. If multiple users and groups are to be excluded from membership, use the F5 key to mark them before pressing Del.

7. Return to the Group Information menu and select the Managers option. A list of current group managers is displayed. Adding or removing managers is done in the same way as group members (see steps 5 and 6).

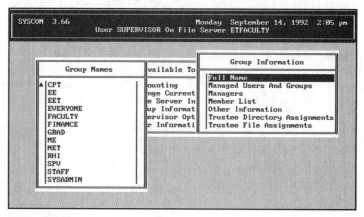

Figure 10.12:
Assigning managed users and groups.

Understanding File and Print Server Security

NetWare provides additional security features that control the management of user accounts, access to the file-server console, and print queues and servers. These features often aid the system administrator in the management of the network as a whole or enable the administrator to delegate responsibility to other users.

File-Server Security

The physical security of the network and the file server are of prime importance. Anyone who gains access to either can upset the operation of the network. Physical security of the network refers to controlling what nodes are attached to it. One way some crackers gain unauthorized access to a user's account is to physically connect a machine to the network and capture network packets to local hard-disk storage. If a user logs into the file server while this machine is active, the cracker can replay the login session to discover the user's password.

Older versions of NetWare offered no way to prevent unencrypted passwords from being transmitted. Because of this problem, the NetWare workstation shell was updated to always encrypt the password before transmitting it to the file server. The cracker trying to capture the password is unable to decrypt the passwords, but can simply replace the LOGIN command with an older version. Clearly, the new version of LOGIN could not eliminate this problem. NetWare minimizes the risk by setting the file server to reject any login attempts that do not encrypt the password first. This is accomplished by typing the following command at the file-server console or by including it in the AUTOEXEC.NCF file:

```
SET ALLOW UNENCRYPTED PASSWORDS = OFF
```

If everyone can get to where the file server is kept, a person can reset the file server to accept connections without encrypted passwords. In addition, that person may have written loadable modules or may try to use the NetWare debugger to extract user account information. The file server, therefore, should be in a location to which few people have access. NetWare also provides the console command, SECURE CONSOLE, to prevent anyone from trying these tricks.

Some file-server settings can be accomplished with the FCONSOLE utility. Before users other than the Supervisor can use this utility, they must be assigned as a file-server console operator. As a console operator, a user can get connection information, enable/disable logins for all users, enable/disable the Transaction Tracking System, and set the file server's time and date.

One of the drawbacks of putting the file server in a secure location is that it is inconvenient for the system administrator to change the console settings or check server statistics unless the administrator uses the Remote Console feature. RCONSOLE enables the system administrator to connect to the file-server console from any workstation on the network. To prevent other users from accessing the console in this way, the RCONSOLE module running on the file server can require that a password be entered first. In addition, the system administrator can load the MONITOR module which locks the file-server console until its password is entered.

Print-Queue and Print-Server Security

Printing is one of the most important resources in a network. If users cannot get their printouts, they quickly complain to the system administrator. In large networks, many printers may be connected to a variety of print servers. For the system administrator to timely check every printing problem could more than fill each working day. Instead, the administrator can designate print-queue and print-server operators who can fix most problems that arise.

Print-queue operators control access to print queues. They can delete jobs or change the order of the jobs in the queue. They also can change the status of jobs. If the printers supporting a queue must be shut down and worked on, the queue can be disabled. Once the printer is back on-line, the queue operator can enable the queue once again.

Print-server operators control the print server that supports the print queues. They can change the queues serviced by the print server or change the priority of queued print jobs if more than one queue is serviced by a printer. If problems arise with the printers connected to the print server, the operator can designate which users are sent a broadcast message. The operator can issue commands to the attached printers and change forms if needed. In the event that the print server must be worked on, the operator can shut down the print server. The print-server operator can set a password that must be entered each time the print server is restarted.

 In many large systems, each department has its own print server. Only users within a department can print to one of the departmental printers. To make coordination easier, the print-queue operator and print-server operator are usually the same person. Often, the user who is the workgroup manager may also serve as the print-queue and print-server operator.

The system administrator can use the PCONSOLE utility to set print queue and server information. Print-queue users are set using the following steps:

1. Type **PCONSOLE** at the MS-DOS prompt, and press Enter.

2. Select the Print Queue Information option from the Available Options main menu. A list of currently defined queues is displayed.

3. Highlight the queue you want to change and press Enter. The Print Queue Information menu appears.

4. Select the Queue Users option to display a list of users and groups that are currently queue users. By default, when a queue is created, group EVERYONE is granted queue usage.

5. To enable users or groups to be queue users, press Ins. A list of all users and groups not having access to the print queue is displayed. Highlight the user or group to add and press Enter. To add multiple users and groups, use the F5 key to mark them before pressing Enter.

6. To remove users or groups from print-queue access, highlight the user or group and press Del.

Print-queue operators are assigned using the following steps:

1. Type **PCONSOLE** at the MS-DOS prompt, and press Enter.

2. Select the Print Queue Information option from the Available Options main menu. A list of currently defined queues is displayed.

3. Highlight the queue you want to change, and press Enter. The Print Queue Information menu appears.

4. Select the Queue Operators option to display a list of users and groups that are currently queue users. By default, when a queue is created, the Supervisor is the only queue operator.

5. Add or remove queue operators in the same way as queue users (refer to steps 5 and 6 in the preceding instructions for print-queue users).

Print-server operators are assigned using the following steps:

1. Type **PCONSOLE** at the MS-DOS prompt, and press Enter.

2. Select the Print Server Information option from the Available Options main menu. A list of currently defined servers is displayed.

3. Highlight the queue you want to change, and press Enter. The Print Server Information menu appears.

4. Select the Print Server Operators option to display a list of users and groups that are currently queue users. By default, when a print server is created, the Supervisor is the only print-server operator.

5. Add or remove print-server operators in the same way as queue users (refer to steps 5 and 6 in the instructions for print-queue users).

Understanding Accounting

Although accounting services are not normally considered part of NetWare security, they help control access of file-server resources. The accounting services not only enable the system administrator to charge for resources used, but also to monitor file-server resource usage. If accounting services are activated, users are given initial balances and credit limits. Based on charge settings, the users' balances start approaching the credit limit. Once a user's balance matches the credit limit, the user is locked out of the account.

When charges are assessed by the accounting system, the charges are recorded in the NET$ACCT.DAT file. Because login and logout times are also recorded, this file can later be used to track file-server usage. The accounting services charge for the following resources:

❖ **Blocks Read**. This is the number of data blocks read from the server. The size of these blocks is determined by the system administrator when the NetWare volume is set up. Typically, the block size is four bytes.

- ❖ **Blocks Written.** This is the number of data blocks written to the disk.

- ❖ **Connect Time.** This is the amount of time a user is connected to the file server.

- ❖ **Disk Storage.** This is the amount of disk storage, in blocks, used by a user.

- ❖ **Service Requests.** This is the number of requests a user makes. Examples include requesting a directory listing or viewing the connections active on the file server.

  Charges for using resources are assessed in half-hour blocks. These charges are calculated by the following formula:

Total Charge = (Multiply Factor / Divisor Factor) × Used Resource Amount

For example, if the system administrator wants to charge $.50 for every half-hour block a user is connected to the file server, set the charge multiplier to 1 and the divisor to 2.

Charges for a resource do not have to be the same throughout the day and week. Each half-hour of the week can have its own charge factor. For example, the system administrator can decide that if a user decides to work past 5:00 p.m. during the week or at any time on the weekend, that user is charged only $.25 per half-hour block.

The system administrator installs accounting charges by following these steps:

1. Type **SYSCON** at the MS-DOS prompt, and press Enter.

2. Select the Accounting option from the Available Topics main menu.

3. Select the resource to be charged for. A screen similar to the one in figure 10.13 is displayed.

4. Using the arrow and the F5 keys, highlight the block of time to be charged for, and press Enter. A menu with the currently defined charge rates is displayed.

5. Highlight the desired rate with the arrow keys and press Enter. The number associated with the charge now fills the previously highlighted box.

6. To define a new rate, select the Other Charge Rate option. A second screen appears. Enter the multiplier and divisor values in the appropriate fields. Once defined, this charge rate can be selected, as in step 5.

```
SYSCON  3.66                         Monday  September 14, 1992  2:13 pm
                    User SUPERVISOR On File Server ETFACULTY

                                     Sun  Mon  Tue  Wed  Thu  Fri  Sat
         Connect Time Charge Rates   8:00am   1    1    1    1    1    1    1
                                     8:30am   1    1    1    1    1    1    1
                                     9:00am   1    1    1    1    1    1    1
Sunday                               9:30am   1    1    1    1    1    1    1
8:00 am To 8:29 am                  10:00am   1    1    1    1    1    1    1
                                    10:30am   1    1    1    1    1    1    1
Rate  Charge     Rate  Charge       11:00am   1    1    1    1    1    1    1
  1   No Charge   11                11:30am   1    1    1    1    1    1    1
  2               12                12:00pm   1    1    1    1    1    1    1
  3               13                12:30pm   1    1    1    1    1    1    1
  4               14                 1:00pm   1    1    1    1    1    1    1
  5               15                 1:30pm   1    1    1    1    1    1    1
  6               16                 2:00pm   1    1    1    1    1    1    1
  7               17                 2:30pm   1    1    1    1    1    1    1
  8               18                 3:00pm   1    1    1    1    1    1    1
  9               19                 3:30pm   1    1    1    1    1    1    1
 10               20                 4:00pm   1    1    1    1    1    1    1
        (Charge is per minute)       4:30pm   1    1    1    1    1    1    1
```

Figure 10.13:
Assigning charges.

In most organizations, the accounting system is not used to actually charge for resources but to track resource usage. The system administrator can discover when, during the week, the file server is used the most. With this information, the administrator can project what resources are needed and when.

The system administrator extracts this information from the NET$ACCT.DAT file using the PAUDIT and ATOTAL commands. PAUDIT creates a detailed log of which user was charged some value for what resource. Also included in this log are login and logout times and account lockouts. ATOTAL calculates daily and weekly resource usage totals.

 One way to keep track of resource reports is to run these commands once a month and save the output to files. After generating the reports, either rename the NET$ACCT.DAT file or delete it. The next time a resource entry is to be added, a new NET$ACCT.DAT file is created.

Using the NetWare Bindery

The *bindery* is the heart of the NetWare security system. It is a database that maintains information on users, groups, workgroups, file servers, and print servers. The bindery is a three-tier structure created to promote an organized and secure working environment. The components of this database are known as objects, properties, and property values and are stored in the NET$OBJ.DAT, NET$PROP.DAT, and NET$VAL.DAT files of the SYS:SYSTEM directory.

Bindery *objects* are the actual users, groups, and other named resources. Each object has a name, type, identification number, static/dynamic flag, and security byte. The identification number uniquely identifies one object from the other. Because remembering a user or group by identification number is very difficult, objects are also assigned names. The object type specifies what sort of object it is. Some common object types are user, group, and print queue. These objects are known as *static objects*—objects that must be physically removed. *Dynamic objects* include those resources that can be added or deleted without any user interaction, such as file servers tracked by the internal routing mechanism. The object-security byte controls who can view or write to the object. The byte is broken into two parts. The high-order nibble controls who can write to this object. The low-order nibble controls reading.

Each object has associated properties. *Properties* define what sort of information is stored about the object. Sample properties a user object might possess include GROUPS_I'M_IN, IDENTIFICA-TION, PASSWORD, and SECURITY_EQUALS. Like objects, prop-erties also have flags and the security byte.

If a property is used, one or more values are assigned to it. These values are either set property values or item property values. A *set property value* refers to a list of object identification numbers. If a user object has the GROUPS_I'M_IN property, the values associ-ated with the property consist of a list of group object-identification numbers. The *item property value* stores whatever type of data the property requires. The item value for the PASS-WORD property is an ASCII string corresponding to the object's password.

 A user logging into the file server provides a good example of the way the bindery is consulted. When prompted, the user enters his or her account name. NetWare looks in the NET$OBJ.DAT file to see whether an object of type user has a name that matches the account name. Once NetWare finds the object, it consults the NET$PROP.DAT file to see whether the PASSWORD property has been defined for that user. When it finds the property, NetWare requests that the user enter a password. The password is compared to the value of the PASSWORD property corresponding to the user object in the NET$VAL.DAT file. If they match, access is granted.

With the exception of attribute rights and Inherited Rights Masks, the bindery stores all the security information about the system. The command SECURITY scans the bindery for network security holes. The following problems are reported, if found:

❖ Objects not requiring a password.

❖ Objects with insecure passwords. This catches users with passwords identical to their usernames, users who have passwords of fewer than six characters, users who have not changed their passwords in the last 60 days, users who do not have unlimited grace logins, and users who do not have unique passwords.

❖ Objects that are security equivalent to SUPERVISOR.

❖ Objects with access to the root directory of any volume.

❖ Objects without login scripts.

❖ Objects with excess privileges in the standard directories.

The following list shows the default privileges for the standard directories:

```
SYS:PUBLIC    [ R     F ]
SYS:SYSTEM    [         ]
SYS:LOGIN     [ R     F ]
SYS:MAIL      [  WC    ]
```

Summary

Of course, not every security feature is always necessary. Security and flexibility of use are often at opposite ends of the spectrum. The balance point varies from site to site. The system administrator and corporate management need to find that point to ensure a secure and productive environment in which to work.

Once the security policy is decided on, the system administrator can break it down and apply the features described in this chapter. With these settings, the system administrator can discover whether users are restricted too much or too little, and can fine tune the system to reach the security balance point.

Part Four: Developing "Downsized" Software for NetWare 386

The NetWare Development Environment

Thread Control

Interprocess Communication

Working with the NetWare File System

IPX Message-Passing Architecture

NLM Reliability

Chapter 11

The NetWare Development Environment

This chapter introduces the NetWare development environment. NetWare Loadable Modules (NLMs), which are applications that run on NetWare, are different from most programs in several important ways: They have equal status with the operating system, capability to link to system call libraries at run time, and remarkable flexibility (derived from the first two items).

This chapter describes the NetWare application programming interface (API), and the NetWare linker and loader, which are two components of the NetWare development environment that help make NLMs powerful. The chapter discusses NLMs as distributed applications and the different types of NLMs you may create; it also explains why you create them and what makes them different from regular applications. Finally, you learn how create an actual NLM.

The purpose of this chapter is not to provide a developer's guide to NetWare but to enable you—whether you are a software engineer or an information systems (IS) executive—to evaluate the application development potential that NetWare offers. Most IS departments must perform at least some in-house development. Because downsizing doesn't change this reality, information about NetWare's development environment is valid and important to all IS decision makers, regardless of their technical inclinations.

Comparing Client Development and Server Development

Before discussing the NetWare development environment in depth, it is important first to distinguish between client development and server development. In this discussion, *client development* refers to developing applications that run on network workstations. Client applications do not call the NetWare operating system directly. Rather, they request services from the operating system by sending request information to the server over the network. The server responds by sending response information to the client.

Client applications run on the client workstation's operating system, whether it is DOS, OS/2, Macintosh, UNIX, or some other operating system. The applications, developed in the client's development environment using the client's operating system interfaces, can communicate with the server because the developer has linked the application with a NetWare client library. The client library handles the network communications.

Server-based applications, on the other hand, run on the NetWare operating system. They are written to use NetWare interfaces—not the interfaces from another operating system.

A client-server application usually is effective only if the server-based component is powerful and performs well. The server-based component performs all the heavy work, and the client-based component provides an interactive interface with the user. Some exceptions exist (as you read later in this chapter), but the critical component of a client-server application is primarily the server-based component.

 Because this chapter focuses specifically on the server-based component of NetWare application development, terms such as *API* or *development environment* refer specifically to server-based applications running on NetWare v3.11.

Rating the NetWare Environment

A hallmark of a good operating system is a rich API and a development environment that enhances programmer productivity. *API* refers collectively to system calls, function calls, and interfaces that developers can use to construct applications. An operating system's API provides developers with the building blocks to create applications. If the API is strong enough, developers can use it to create spectacular applications. An operating system's development environment is a collection of tools that developers use to piece together the building blocks the API offers—a compiler, linker, and debugger, for example.

 Think of a *development environment* as a miniature "code factory" that provides an assembly line that the developer uses to build programs. The developer is always in charge; he or she decides how to use the factory. Although the developer's talent is always the most important factor in determining the quality of the application, a better factory can help the developer to produce good applications faster and more efficiently.

Rating the Development Environment

Although NetWare's API is rich, its development environment is uneven. The development environment is powerful but difficult to learn, at least in comparison to other operating system environments, such as UNIX.

Some of the difficulty in learning NetWare's development environment is the result of NetWare's uniqueness as a specialized network operating system. Perhaps the most difficult task in developing applications on NetWare involves the prominence of network communications in all aspects of NetWare application development. Although most IS programmers are not familiar with network programming techniques, NetWare's network communications API is so well-designed and powerful that these programmers can eventually be unusually productive.

Rating the API

In the area of data-processing (DP) application development, NetWare's API rates very highly. NLMs may take complete advantage of the NetWare file system, including all aspects of concurrency control and transaction control; and may take control over how applications read and write files and how the operating system caches files. Furthermore, most APIs (including the file system API) are coded to work equally well on a remote server—the developer does not have to worry whether he or she is targeting a particular function call to the local server or a remote server because NetWare handles the details.

The NetWare development environment is compliant with most major programming standards, including ANSI C andPOSIX. In addition, the NetWare API supports standard communications libraries such as Berkeley Sockets, the IP Transport Interface Library (TLI), and AT&T STREAMS. Support for these standards entails most aspects of development, including file and device I/O, network communications, string and character manipulation, floating-point arithmetic, and memory allocation.

Most nonstandard areas of the NetWare API involve operating-system-oriented areas such as thread control, record locking, IPX communications, Queue Services, and the Bindery. These NetWare services are not available on other operating systems.

Understanding Language Support

The bad news about language support is that NetWare's operating system API supports only C, C++, and Intel assembler. Do not confuse the operating system API with the workstation (client) API, which supports all popular programming languages.

The good news is that C is the most popular and widely used programming language. A good C programmer can outcode programmers working in most similar programming languages. In addition, C produces efficient code, and programmers can use C to explore even the most arcane and low-level aspects of the host operating system.

Alternatively, developers can write NLMs in a non-C (and non-assembly) language if that language supports C-style calling conventions and the 32-bit Phar Lap EZ-OMF object file format. Calling conventions dictate the way function parameters are passed to the operating system; the object file format determines the way the program is loaded into memory and executed.

A non-C approach can become tedious and counterproductive because developers must spend most of their time calling routines that are not part of their language's standard API library.

Understanding Multithreaded Programming

NetWare provides an unmatched multithreaded API. Developers have several different ways to design and code multithreaded applications, and the NetWare operating system rewards them well. Threads may communicate with each other in several ways, and may communicate also with threads belonging to other applications. The only problem is that threads adhere to NetWare's nonpreemptive nature by frequently relinquishing control of the CPU.

 You learn how to relinquish control of the CPU in Chapter 12.

The NetWare development environment, including APIs, is peerless; the development environment is powerful, but requires time to learn. In addition, network programming techniques may require experienced programmers to retool their skills, but the payoff for such retooling can be rewarding for both the programmer and his or her employer.

The NetWare operating system has no API for an interactive user interface. Although NetWare supports standard device-oriented I/O, including screen I/O, you must build interactive, menu-driven interfaces. (You can build them effectively with NetWare, but it requires work.)

The reason that NetWare lacks a modern user interface API is simple: that component is supposed to run on network workstations; NetWare is supposed to provide the back-end server component. (The back-end component is defined in Chapter 2.) NetWare servers usually reside in closets or utility rooms, and users gain access to server resources through their own client workstation. Most client operating systems provide effective and modern user interface libraries.

Categorizing APIs

The NetWare API consists of all function calls, system calls, and interfaces that applications may use to gain services from the operating system. Because the API has so many specific calls and interfaces, Novell organizes them into groups, based on their general purpose. These groups are discussed in this section in alphabetical order.

The *Accounting Services* interface enables applications to submit resources for the operating system's accounting system to track. The accounting system tracks each client's use of submitted resources and generates account balances for each client. The accounting system can track, for example, each client's use of volume blocks. In addition, the accounting system can generate billings for individual clients based on information you specify. The Accounting Services interface enables your application to track its resources (by client) and to bill clients.

The *Advanced Services* API set is a mixed bag of low-level system calls that are either more specialized or more powerful (or both) than other similar APIs provided in other categories of the NetWare API.

The *AppleTalk Filing Protocol (AFP) Services* interface enables NetWare server-based applications to manipulate Macintosh files, including long Macintosh file names, Macintosh resource forks, and Macintosh Finder information.

The *Asynchronous I/O (AIO) Services* interface enables server-based applications to control the server's serial ports. Examples of applications that use the AIO interface include modem servers and data-acquisition modules.

The *Bindery Services* database is maintained by every NetWare server that manages information about users, security, server resources, and so on. Applications can use the Bindery for a variety of purposes, including maintaining application-specific information and providing information to network clients. The Bindery Services API provides applications with complete access to the NetWare Bindery.

Bit Array Services provide a small set of routines that make it easy for an application to maintain large bit fields. Occasionally, applications must maintain a large amount of information in RAM. Bit fields are an extremely efficient method of maintaining a large amount of information in a small amount of RAM. (Bit fields are difficult to manipulate, however.)

Character Manipulation Services are the ANSI C routines for manipulating characters.

NetWare's native network communications protocol is IPX/SPX. The *Communication Services* API enables server-based applications to have access to the entire range of IPX/SPX services.

The *Connection Number and Task Management Services* group of APIs enables server-based applications to assume the "identity" of client workstations for gaining access to operating system resources. When a server-based application is maintaining network connections to other servers, this API enables the server-based applications also to toggle among servers to which they are connected when they are making remote calls, thus targeting a call to a specific server.

As a group, the *Device I/O Services* APIs provide for input and output from and to physical devices installed on the NetWare server, including the keyboard, the monitor, CPU-based hardware ports, and the CPU flags register (specifically the interrupt flag). Most of these APIs are part of the ANSI C standard for device input and output, but some are specific to Intel CPUs.

A NetWare server may be configured with a DOS boot partition. This partition enables you to store startup files (such as the NetWare loader and executable image) on a DOS floppy disk or a DOS partition on an internal hard disk. The *DOS Partition Services* APIs enable NLMs to read files from or write files to a DOS partition or floppy disk if one is resident on the server machine. Most users keep the volume repair NLM (VREPAIR.NLM) also on the server's DOS partition so that it is readily available if the server's SYS volume is damaged.

NetWare supports non-DOS file systems through a name spaces architecture. *Name spaces* are extra directory entries that contain information about non-DOS files (such as long file names) that are not contained in the standard NetWare file format. Because of the way that name spaces work, any file is universally available to all clients, regardless of their operating systems. *File Engine Services* are most useful to NLMs that implement non-DOS file systems. These services provide some features relevant to DP applications, however, such as enabling an application to open a file in write-through mode.

The *File Server Environment Services* APIs enable a server-based application to obtain information about the server and to manipulate the server environment, for example, disabling or enabling login, and disabling or enabling TTS.

The NetWare file system is rich and robust; the *File System Services* APIs provide applications with complete access to the file system. Some of these APIs are ANSI C, but most of them are specific to the NetWare file system. (ANSI stream I/O APIs are in a different category.)

When TCP/IP is loaded on a NetWare server, the *Internet Network Library Services* APIs enable applications to control IP communications.

 A *library* is a special type of NLM that exports functions to other NLMs. The *Library* API enables you to create library NLMs.

Mathematical Computation Services are a full-fledged math library, including having floating-point functions and all ANSI C math functions.

The *Memory Allocation Services* API includes the standard ANSI C `alloc` and free calls, in addition to other, more specialized memory-management routines.

Most of the *Memory Manipulation Services* APIs are ANSI C memory-manipulation routines.

The *Message Services* API enables you to send console messages to other stations on the network.

Miscellaneous Services are an eclectic set of general and low-level APIs that defy categorization. They include several ways to parse or concatenate NetWare path strings.

Operation System I/O Services are low-level (mostly POSIX) file I/O services.

NetWare provides a complete system for creating job queues and queue servers. A *job queue* is a list of jobs, each of which consists of a file or files. A *job server* reads a queue, interprets its contents, and performs some type of processing based on the contents of the job.

(NetWare's print server software uses the Queue Management API.) The *Queue Management Services* APIs provide server-based applications with full access to NetWare queues. You may use them to implement a queue server or to perform some other type of processing on queues and jobs.

The *Screen Handling Services* APIs enable applications to create multiple screens and manipulate screen displays.

Server-based applications frequently must advertise their services to network clients. The *Service Advertising Protocol (SAP)* API provides an easy way to advertise.

Stream I/O Services are the ANSI C stream I/O functions. Streams may be files or devices such as screens and the keyboard.

String Conversion Services are ANSI C string-manipulation APIs, with the addition of two calls to convert strings to and from non-C format.

String Manipulation Services are more ANSI C string functions.

The *Synchronization Services* APIs are a rich set of routines that enable multithreaded applications to communicate, share resources, and lock files and records. NetWare implements these critical routines well.

Threads are instances of an executing application. Multithreaded applications are critical to using NetWare effectively. The *Thread Services* APIs provide applications with access to the NetWare operating system scheduler. You may control the scheduling of threads and applications using Thread Services.

The *Time Conversion and Manipulation Services* APIs are a mixture of ANSI C routines and routines for manipulating the time in DOS format and converting output from the PC timer to ANSI format.

Transaction Tracking Services are an easy-to-use group of APIs for operating system-level transaction control.

The *Transport Interfaces Services* API set implements a fully compliant version of the Berkeley Sockets IP network interface.

The *Transport Layer Interface Services* API set implements a fully compliant version of TLI, a standard UNIX network programming interface.

UNIX STREAMS Services are an implementation of AT&T STREAMS, which is a standard interface for moving data among different modules running both in the same computer and among different computers.

Linking and Loading

Two key components of any development environment are the linker and the loader. Applications must be "linked" to APIs that they call, and they must be "loaded" into memory by the operating system.

A *linker* binds references made by an application to external procedures (APIs) to the addresses of those APIs. It does this either by combining the application's file image with external code files (libraries) or by binding such references to memory addresses. A *loader* reads an application's file image into memory, ensures that linkage occurred successfully, and begins executing the application's code.

Linking at Load Time

NetWare makes use of *load-time linkage*, an advanced technology in which linkage occurs when the application is loaded. Rather than combine code libraries with the application's file image before loading (as DOS does), NetWare leaves references to external procedures unresolved in the NLM file. When you load the NLM,

NetWare performs linkage directly to the addresses of external procedures in server RAM.

In load-time linkage, linkage is performed by the program loader. Developers benefit from two important advantages. First, it is easier to change applications because linkage (in the traditional sense) is not part of the development process. Conversely, Novell may change the NetWare operating system, but your application runs as before without recompilation. The second advantage is that it enables different applications to call the same memory addresses. This capability makes APIs "shared libraries," in which only one copy of an API resides in memory, regardless of how many applications call it. The memory requirements of applications then are reduced significantly.

Linking with the Operating System

The second important aspect of the NetWare linker and loader is that, at load time, they link the application directly to the operating system and make the application, in effect, part of the operating system. This process makes applications equal with the operating system. Equal status with the operating system allows careless programmers to corrupt system memory; it gives careful programmers, however, an unusual degree of freedom in designing their applications. Good programmers can use this freedom to create better, more efficient, and more powerful applications than would be possible otherwise.

 Because of the way applications are linked to NetWare, applications can "export" their own procedures and make them linkable by other applications at load time. Not only can your application call operating system routines (APIs), but also other applications can call your application's routines.

Using 32-Bit Development Tools

NetWare is a 32-bit, protected-mode operating system. Application development for NetWare therefore requires 32-bit development tools that create executable formats that are compatible with Intel protected-mode execution. (Intel *protected mode* is the technical name of the 386 and 486 CPU's 32-bit execution mode.)

The 32-bit requirement for NLMs makes some of the more popular PC development products inadequate, such as Borland C and C++ and Microsoft C and C++. Several excellent PC development products, however, produce 32-bit protected-mode executable formats that you may use to create NLMs.

The two best packages for 32-bit C language development are High C, from MetaWare Inc., and Watcom C. For Intel Assembler development, the best product is Phar Lap's 386 | ASM.

Using Cross-Platform Tools

Developing server-based applications for NetWare requires *cross-platform development*. You use this technique to write, compile, and link applications on one platform for execution on a different platform. Cross-platform development is a widely used technique for developers of embedded control systems (such as factory automation and airline avionics), but it is used also for mainstream computer development. Many programmers of Microsoft Windows products, for example, use cross-platform development techniques.

When you develop applications for NetWare, you write, compile, and link the NLM on a DOS workstation (the development tools run on DOS), but you load and run the NLM on a NetWare server.

You also debug the NLM using a NetWare server (NetWare has a resident debugger).

Linking at Compile Time

This chapter has stated that NetWare features load-time linkage. Compile-time linkage refers only to combining different object modules in a single NLM and to building an "import list" of external functions that is stamped on the NLM file as a header. The import list is necessary for NetWare's loader to provide load-time linkage to the correct NetWare APIs. Compile-time linkage of an NLM, therefore, is only a cursory and partial linkage, and it happens very quickly. The NetWare tool NLMLINK accomplishes this cursory compile-time linkage (see the section on NLMLINK).

Using Watcom C

When you purchase the NLM Software Developer's Kit (SDK) from Novell, you receive the NetWare operating system, NLMs that provide the API discussed earlier, NLMLINK, and Watcom C. Watcom C produces 32-bit protected mode code and creates executable files compliant to the Phar lap EZ-OMF object format (required by NLMLINK.)

Watcom C provides full ANSI C compliance, but its other strong points make it especially good for developing NLMs. These strengths include the following items:

❖ Optimization of C code to produce efficient and high-performance executable code

❖ The capability to align structures on byte, word, and `dword` boundaries

❖ Compliance with the DOS Protected Mode Interface (DPMI) enables large source files to be compiled

❖ Support for embedded SQL statements (see Chapters 18 and 19)

❖ The Watcom Disassembler helps debug NLMs

❖ Excellent integration with assembly-language modules

Integrating with Assembly Language

Good integration with assembly-language modules is a requirement for any C compiler you use to produce NLMs, even if you do not do any development work in assembly language. The reason is that approximately 20 percent of the NetWare operating system is written in assembly language. Because of the way the NetWare loader links NLMs at load time, you are by default integrating your code with other assembler modules.

Although no official standards exist for calling assembly-language routines from a C program, the following de facto standards exist for Intel 32-bit protected mode programs:

❖ The calling routine pushes parameters on the stack in reverse order.

❖ The called routine preserves the values of the EBX, EBP, ESI, and EDI registers.

❖ The called routine passes its return value back to the calling routine in the EAX register.

Like any C compiler you use to produce NLMs, Watcom C follows the C-to-Assembler calling convention shown in this list. All routines in NetWare, even internal routines that never get called by modules other than the operating system, follow these C-to-Assembler conventions. Any routine in NetWare, therefore, can be called by a C module.

Using NLMLINK

Although the NetWare loader performs load-time linkage of an NLM to external routines (server APIs), certain information must be resident in the first part of the NLM file image in order for the NetWare loader to be capable of doing its work. The placement of this information, which includes a list of external routines for the loader to resolve, is the job of NLMLINK.

Because NLMLINK is a DOS program, it fits in well with the cross-platform development environment, as discussed earlier in this chapter. Novell includes with the NetWare SDK two different NLMLINK versions: NLMLINKR.EXE and NLMLINKP.EXE. NLMLINKR.EXE executes under DOS in real mode, and NLMLINKP.EXE executes under DOS in protected mode using the DOS Protected Mode Interface (DPMI). The only difference between NLMLINKR and NLMLINKP is the amount of memory they can address and, consequently, the size of the object files they are processing. In other words, most NLMs are small enough for NLMLINKR to process. For very large NLMs, however, you may process them using NLMLINKP.

 Although a slight difference in performance exists between the two NLMLINK versions—NLMLINKP performs slightly better—you probably do not notice the difference because the amount of work NLMLINK must do is not very large relative to the C compiler or the Assembler.

You use NLMLINK just as you use link utilities in other microcomputer operating-system development environments, such as DOS or UNIX. That is, after compiling source code to produce object files (they usually have the OBJ file-name extension), you run the link utility.

NLMLINK is slightly easier to use than most microcomputer link utilities, however, because you do not have to specify any information to NLMLINK using the DOS command line. Rather, you create a special text file containing information about the NLM you are creating and the NetWare APIs it calls. NLMLINK automatically opens this file and uses the information contained in it to perform its job.

When you run NLMLINK, it always looks for a text file with the file-name definition DEF. This information file is for the NLM you are creating, and it should have the same file name as the NLM. If you are creating an NLM called HELLO.NLM, for example, you should create an information file called HELLO.DEF. To run NLMLINKR on the file, type the following command at the DOS command line:

```
NLMLINKR HELLO
```

If you have included the necessary information in the file HELLO.DEF, NLMLINK produces the NLM for you; after NLMLINK completes its execution, the directory should have a file called HELLO.NLM—that is your NLM. All you have to do is load it on the NetWare server using the console LOAD command.

Understanding the DEF File Syntax

The key words described in this section can be used in a definition file to direct NLMLINK in creating NLMs. The DEF file key words are case-insensitive, except for symbol names used with the import and export directives. You can place key words in the file in any order. A key word is required, unless it is indicated as optional in the description.

TYPE specifies the type of loadable module, as shown in the following list, and implicitly determines the extension to append to the output file.

1 LAN driver (LAN)

2 Disk driver (DSK)

3 Name space module (NAM)

0 Utility (NLM)

DESCRIPTION specifies a string that describes the loadable module to be created. The console command MODULES outputs this description string. The description, which can be between one and 127 bytes long, must be enclosed in double quotes and cannot include a null, double quote, carriage return, or newline. The description should contain the indicated fields in the following order:

```
"Company (or product) name, description, version
M.mm, (yymmdd)"
```

The v in version must be in lowercase. M indicates a major version and mm indicates a minor version (all digits must be present). yymmdd is the year, month, and day. July 17, 1992, for example, is represented as (920717).

OUTPUT specifies the name of the output file. The extension is added by the linker, as specified by the TYPE key word.

INPUT specifies the name of the input OBJ file or files.

The optional START specifies the name of the loadable module's initialization procedure. When the operator uses the LOAD console command to load the module, NetWare calls this procedure.

The optional EXIT specifies the name of the loadable module's exit procedure. This procedure is called when the operator uses the UNLOAD console command.

The optional CHECK key word specifies the name of the loadable module's check procedure. The console command UNLOAD calls an NLM's check procedure (if it exists) before unloading the module or shutting down the server. The check procedure is optional for drivers; it provides an opportunity to warn the user what may happen if unloading continues.

The optional MAP key word directs the linker to create a map file.

DEBUG, which is optional, specifies that the linker is to include debug information in the output file. Be sure to remove this key word when you are ready to build your production driver.

IMPORT specifies a list of variables and procedure names that are external to the object files. These variables and procedures are operating-system variables and procedures from NetWare (or from other loadable modules that previously have been loaded) that are linked to the module after it has been loaded but before it begins initialization.

The optional EXPORT key word specifies a list of variables and procedure names resident in the loadable module to be made available to other loadable modules.

MODULE, which is optional, specifies loadable modules that must be loaded before the current loadable module is loaded. The loader attempts to find and load any modules not already in the server memory. If it cannot find and load them, the current module cannot be loaded.

The optional @ operator can be used with the input, import, and export directives. It indicates that the list is to be read from a file. This list can be nested; that is, the file may include another @ operator. The file specifier, including the path, must immediately follow the @ operator, as in the following example:

```
import @file.txt
```

CUSTOM, which is optional, specifies the name of a custom data file to be appended to the output file. A driver may have to use this feature if its hardware device, for example, contains special customized firmware.

The optional COPYRIGHT key word tells the linker to include a copyright string in the output file. An ASCII string that is from one to 252 bytes long, is in double quotes, and follows the key word `copyright` is displayed whenever the MSL driver is loaded. To start a new line within the displayed string, use `\n`. If the copyright key word is used but no string is entered, the linker includes the Novell default copyright message.

VERSION specifies the version of the module that should be placed in the header field. The format for this key word is as follows:

```
version MajorVersion, MinorVersion[, Rev]
```

The version fields must be separated by commas: `MajorVersion` is one digit, and `MinorVersion` is two digits. The last comma and `Rev` are optional. `Rev` is a number from one through 26, representing a letter from *a* through *z*. VERSION 3,10,1 in the DEF file, for example, produces the version field 3.10a in the header of the output file.

Looking at a Sample NLM Definition File

In the following example, NLMLINK produces an output file that is the final (NLM) form of the application, which is ready to load into an active NetWare environment. Although line numbers have been added here to help you understand the discussion of the DEF file, they produce linker errors in a DEF file.

```
1    type 0
2    description "Sample DP Application NLM
3    copyright "Copyright 1992 ABC Company"
4    version 1, 00, 1
5    output DPAPP
6    input
7      DPAPP.OBJ
8      PRELUDE.OBJ
```

```
 9      map
10      debug
11      import
12         printf
13            sprintf
14            fopen
15            fread
16            fwrite
17            fclose
```

This short DEF file provides NLMLINK with information necessary for creating the loadable driver. This DEF file creates an imaginary NLM called DPAPP.OBJ.

Line 1 instructs NLMLINK to create a type 1 NLM. Application NLMs always should be of type 1; the other types are for device drivers or name space (alternative file system) modules.

Line 2 provides a description of the module. NLMLINK places this description in the resulting NLM, and the operating system displays this description whenever an operator issues a CONFIG command at the server console.

Line 3 provides a copyright message that is displayed whenever the NLM loads.

Line 4 provides version information, which is displayed also when the NLM loads. The line `version 1, 00, 1` causes the version information—as displayed on the server console at load time—to be `Version 1.00a`.

Line 5 indicates the name of the resulting NLM. Note that the file extension is not included on line 5. The file extension (NLM, LAN, DSK, and so on) is a function of the NLM type.

Line 6 lists the input files required to build the NLM. In this case, there are two input files: DSAPP.OBJ and PRELUDE.OBJ. PRELUDE.OBJ is a standard object file you use to build all your

NetWare applications. It contains start-up code for the NLM and establishes a standard ANSI C environment, in which the NLM may run. To build NLMs with many input modules, it may be appropriate to list those modules in a text file and include the text file in the DEF file, as follows:

```
input @objs.txt
```

Lines 9 and 10 instruct the linker to include debugging symbols in the NLM file and to create a MAP file. When you are building a production NLM, you should remove these two lines from the DEF file.

Line 11 indicates the beginning of the NLM's import list. The *import list* defines which routines and data items the NLM must link to when it is loaded. Because the imaginary NLM imports only a few items, including the imported items directly in the DEF file is appropriate. For an NLM that imports many items, it may be appropriate to list those items in a separate text file and to refer to that file as follows:

```
import @DPAPP.IMP
```

Understanding the NetWare Internal Debugger

Clearly, the most difficult aspect of developing server-based applications for NetWare is debugging them. This statement is true for two reasons. First, NLM development is, by definition, cross-platform development. You write and compile your application using DOS tools, but you run and debug your application on a NetWare server. Second, the NetWare internal debugger is an assembly-oriented debugger.

To use the NetWare debugger successfully, you must have an understanding of Intel assembly language, Intel registers, and the NetWare operating system run-time environment.

Programmers can be very productive when they debug NLMs if they have learned how to use the NetWare debugger. The NetWare debugger can open up even the lowest-level internal aspects of the NetWare operating system.

After discussing the commands available within the NetWare debugger, this section discusses some programming conventions you can use to make the debugging process more efficient.

The internal debugger enables a developer to do any of the following tasks:

- ❖ Trap into the debugger from an assembler or C program
- ❖ Trap into the debugger from the server console keyboard (either dynamically or following a server abend or General Protection Interrupt)
- ❖ Trap into the debugger by way of an NMI board
- ❖ Identify the cause and the point in a program's execution at which it trapped into the debugger
- ❖ Single-step
- ❖ Proceed to the next instruction
- ❖ Continue until a specified address is reached
- ❖ Set or clear breakpoints (including read-write breakpoints with conditional statements); a maximum of four breakpoints can be set at one time
- ❖ Unassemble code
- ❖ Display or modify registers
- ❖ Display or modify memory, including the stack
- ❖ Read from and write to ports
- ❖ Search memory for a byte pattern

- ❖ Traverse a linked list that has been built dynamically
- ❖ Display loaded modules
- ❖ Display current server processes
- ❖ Display process control blocks
- ❖ Display screens, including the file server's screen
- ❖ Display debugger help screens
- ❖ Exit from the debugger and return to either normal server operation or DOS

You can enter the debugger in one of four ways:

From the server console keyboard:

1. Press Alt, Right-Shift, Left-Shift, and Esc simultaneously at the server console keyboard. This method does not work if the server is hung up in an infinite loop with interrupts disabled or if the server console is secured.

2. After the server suffers an abend or GPI, either press Alt, Right-Shift, Left-Shift, and Esc simultaneously, or type **386debug** at the server console.

 An *abend* is an abnormal end.

From an NLM:

3. Call the `Breakpoint()` routine from any C program. (Assembly-language modules can execute an INT 3 instead.)

Manually:

4. Generate a Non-Maskable Interrupt with an NMI board. This step causes the server to reach an abend, after which you can perform step 2. This step may be required if the software being debugged is in an infinite loop with interrupts disabled.

When the debugger is entered, it displays the following information:

❖ The location at which the trap occurred

❖ The cause of the trap into the debugger

❖ The contents of general registers and the flags

 You can call up the following five help screens in the NetWare debugger:

h   Displays help for general commands

hb   Displays help for breakpoints

he   Displays help for grouping operators

.h   Displays help for "dot" (.) commands

.m   Displays modules that are loaded and their code and data-segment addresses

The Debugger Commands

The commands in this section are supported by the NetWare internal debugger. You may have noticed that some of the commands begin with a period, or dot (.). You must issue these "dot commands" to the debugger by typing a period and then the letter or letters associated with the command.

As the debugger command summary shows, there is little that cannot be done with the NetWare debugger—if you have a working knowledge of it.

Table 11.1
The Debugger Commands

Command	Purpose
.A	Displays the abend or break reason
B	Displays all current breakpoints
BC number	Clears the specified breakpoint
BCA	Clears all breakpoints
B = address {condition}	Sets an execution breakpoint at address
BW = address {condition}	Sets a write breakpoint at address
BR = address {condition}	Sets a read-write breakpoint at address
C address	Changes memory in interactive mode
C address=number(s)	Changes memory to the specified number or numbers
C address="text"	Changes memory to the specified text ASCII values
.C	Does a diagnostic memory dump to disk
D address {length}	Dumps memory for optional length
DL{+linkOffset} address {length}	Dumps memory starting at address for optional length and traverses a linked list (default link field offset is 0)
REG=value	Changes the specified register to the new value in which REG is EAX, EBX, ECX, EDX, ESI, EDI, ESP, EBP, EIP, or EFL

Table 11.1—continued

Command	Purpose
F Flag=value	Changes the FLAG bit to value (0 or 1) in which FLAG is CF, AF, ZF, SF, IF, TF, PF, DF, or OF
G {break address(s)}	Begins execution at current EIP and sets optional temporary breakpoint or breakpoints
H	Displays basic debugger command help screen
HB	Displays breakpoint help screen
HE	Displays expression help screen
.H	Displays dot help screen
I {B;W:D} PORT	Inputs byte, word, or dword from PORT (default is byte)
M start {length} pattern-byte(s)	Searches memory for pattern; length is optional and, if it is not specified, the rest of memory is searched
.M	Displays loaded module names and addresses
N name address	Defines a new symbol name at address
N -name	Removes defined symbol name
N—	Removes all defined symbols
O {B;W;D} PORT=value	Outputs byte, word, or dword value to PORT
P	Proceeds over the next instruction
.P	Displays all process names and addresses
.P <address>	Displays <address> as a process control block

Table 11.1—continued

Command	Purpose
Q	Quits and exits to DOS
R	Displays registers and flags
.R	Displays the running process control block
S	Single-steps
.S	Displays all screen names and addresses
.S <address>	Displays <address> as a screen structure
T	Single-steps (same as S)
U address {count}	Unassembles count instructions starting at address
V	Views server screens
.V	Displays server version
Z expression	Evaluates the expression
? {address}	If symbolic information has been loaded, the closest symbols to address are displayed (default is EIP)

Public Variables

When you include debugging information in your NLM (by specifying the debug key word in the NLM's definition file), you may use the names of public variables, both functions and data items, in the place of memory addresses when you are using the NetWare debugger. This capability can be tremendously helpful because specifying memory addresses at the debugger command prompt is meticulous work, and typing errors are possible.

Debugging Tips

You can do a few things before entering the NetWare debugger that make debugging your NLM easier, including using the Watcom disassembler, the ANSI `assert` macro, and the NetWare global error variable.

The Watcom Dissambler WDISASM.EXE

You should always disassemble your NLM's object (OBJ) files to create a list (LST) file. The list file may include the NLM's C source code and the unassembled assembly-language code. Listing 11.1 shows unassembled code for the C function `DoOperation`. The original C source code is listed, in addition to the assembled machine code (along the left column) and the unassembled assembly-language code (along the right column). The source code in listing 11.1 was produced by WDISASM.EXE, the disassembler shipped as part of the NetWare NLM SDK.

Listing 11.1:

An excerpt from a WDISASM list file.

```
void DoOperation(ENGINE_OP_NODE *callBackNode)
{
   int ccode;
 0000  b8 14 00 00 00   DoOperation     mov     eax,00000014H
 0005  e8 00 00 00 00                   call    __STK
 000a  55                               push    ebp
 000b  89 e5                            mov     ebp,esp
 000d  50                               push    eax
   switch(callBackNode->packet.operation)
     {
     case 0x07: /* mark an existing record as deleted */
     case 0xf6: /* edit an existing record */
 000e  8b 45 08                         mov     eax,+8H[ebp]
 0011  8a 40 20                         mov     al,+20H[eax]
 0014  2c 02                            sub     al,02H
```

```
0016   3c 00                          cmp     al,00H
0018   74 14                          je      L1
001a   fe c8                          dec     al
001c   3c 00                          cmp     al,00H
001e   74 1b                          je      L2
0020   2c 04                          sub     al,04H
0022   3c 00                          cmp     al,00H
0024   74 08                          je      L1
0026   2c ef                          sub     al,0efH
0028   3c 00                          cmp     al,00H
002a   74 02                          je      L1
002c   eb 1a                          jmp     L3
     case 0x02: { AddRecord(callBackNode); break; }
002e   ff 75 08           L1          push    +8H[ebp]
0031   e8 00 00 00 00                 call    AddRecord
0036   83 c4 04                       add     esp,0004H
0039   eb 0d                          jmp     L3
     case 0x03: { FindRecordKey(callBackNode); break; }
     default: break;
        }
003b   ff 75 08           L2          push    +8H[ebp]
003e   e8 00 00 00 00                 call    FindRecordKey
0043   83 c4 04                       add     esp,0004H
0046   eb 00                          jmp     L3
   callBackNode->packet.operation = 0;
0048   8b 45 08           L3          mov     eax,+8H[ebp]
004b   c6 40 20 00                    mov     byte ptr +20H[eax],00H
   ExitThread(EXIT_THREAD, 0);
004f   6a 00                          push    00H
0051   6a 00                          push    00H
0053   e8 00 00 00 00                 call    ExitThread
0058   83 c4 08                       add     esp,0008H
}
```

Why do you need a disassembler? When you are debugging an
NLM using the NetWare debugger, all instructions are shown as
unassembled code, and not as C source code. By viewing the
NLM's list file, therefore, you can match C source code to the
unassembled instructions displayed by the NetWare debugger. On
entry to the function DoOperation, for example, the NetWare
debugger shows the unassembled code listed in the right column

of figure 11.1. The list file provides a convenient "road map" that enables you to associate unassembled code and register values with the original C source code.

```
WATCOM C/SQL Optimizing Compiler Version 9.0
Copyright by WATCOM Systems Inc. 1989, 91. All
rights reserved.
WATCOM is a trademark of WATCOM Systems Inc.
hello.c: 8 lines, included 301, 0 warnings 0 errors
Code size: 31
```

The ANSI assert Macro

Another tip to use in debugging NLMs is the ANSI C assert macro. It enables you check the values of variables for consistency during the execution of your NLM. Using assert, you make an assertion that a logical statement should be true or false. If the assertion fails, the NLM exits and displays the source file line of the assertion. Listing 11.2 shows an example.

Listing 11.2:

The ANSI C assert *macro enables you to include checks for consistency within the body of your NLM.*

```
int variable1 = 0;
int variable2 = 1;
assert(variable1 != variable2);
```

When your NLM executes the assert macro, if variable1 is equal to variable2 (which should be an error condition), the NLM exits and prints a message similar to the following:

```
Assertion Failed!: <filename> <linenumber>
    variable1 != variable2
```

The assert macro is simply a convenient way to include code for checking consistency in your NLM. Checking for consistency among data structures and variables is an excellent programming practice, and it is one that the NetWare operating system employs heavily. Because the `assert` macro is implemented in the C preprocessor, you can effectively remove it from your production NLM after the debugging cycle by redefining it as follows:

```
#define assert(condition)
```

This redefinition makes the `assert` macro produce a null statement, which removes it from your production NLM.

The NetWare Global Error Variable

All ANSI-compliant C programming environments maintain a global error variable called `errno` that contains the error code of the last error that occurred. Your NLM always can print a string describing the last error by using the ANSI `strerror` function. The `strerror` function returns a string describing the error indicated by the value of `errno`. Listing 11.3 shows how to use the NetWare global error variable.

Listing 11.3:
An example of using the NetWare global error variable.

```
#include <errno.h>
#include <stdio.h>
FILE *fileHandle;
fileHandle = fopen("file", "rw+");
if (fileHandle == NULL)
   printf("Error opening file: %s", strerror(errno));
```

If the call to `fopen` fails, the NLM prints a string showing the reason the call failed, such as a bad file name or insufficient access rights. Used together, the `strerror` function and the global `errno` variable can provide much-needed information about the source of the error.

When you are programming an NLM, you always should include error-checking code that is similar to the code shown in listing 11.3. You should include it, even though you may not normally do so, because errors occur for many reasons in NetWare. Opening a file, for example, may fail for several reasons: insufficient access writes occur, the target volume is not mounted, or the operating system cannot find the target server. (An NLM can open a file on a remote server as easily as it can on a local server.) When you encounter an error, you always should know (or have a good idea) what caused the error before entering the NetWare debugger.

Writing and Linking Your First NLM

Now that you have read about the NetWare development environment, let's look at the standard "Hello World" program as an NLM. (Hello World is traditionally the first program that C programming students write.) Listing 11.4 shows the source code for HELLO.NLM.

Listing 11.4:
Source code for HELLO.NLM.

```
/* Source file name: hello.c */
#include <stdio.h>
int main(void)
{
   printf("\nHello Downsizing World!");
   return(0);
}
```

To compile the source file HELLO.C, enter the following command at your DOS development station:

```
WCC386P /mf /3s /d2 /ez hello.c
```

The Watcom compiler compiles the file HELLO.C and prints a message similar to the one shown in figure 11.1.

A file called HELLO.OBJ now should be in your directory. This file is the object file (in Phar Lap EZ-OMF format) compiled from your source code. The next step is to run NLMLINK on the object file. Listing 11.5 shows the definition file for creating HELLO.NLM.

Listing 11.5:

The definition file for HELLO.NLM.

```
## This file is named HELLO.DEF
copyright "This program is not copyrighted"
debug
description "First NLM"
import
  @i:\public\nwcnlm\imp\clib.imp
input
  i:\public\nwcnlm\imp\prelude.obj
  hello.obj
map
module clib
output hello
screenname "Hello Screen"
type 0
version 1, 00, 0
```

This definition file is self-explanatory. Notice, however, the `input`, `module`, and `output` key words. The `input` key word specifies two object files: HELLO.OBJ and PRELUDE.OBJ. HELLO.OBJ is the object file you created earlier by running the Watcom compiler on the source code file HELLO.C. PRELUDE.OBJ contains start-up code for the NLM and establishes a standard ANSI C environment (including command-line argument processing, `stdin`, `stdout`, and `stderr`).

The `module` key word in listing 11.5 specifies that CLIB.NLM, the NetWare C interface run-time library, should be loaded before HELLO.NLM. If you attempt to load HELLO.NLM before loading CLIB.NLM, NetWare first loads CLIB.NLM automatically, and then loads HELLO.NLM.

To perform partial linkage of HELLO.NLM, you must run
NLMLINK. Type the following command at your DOS development station:

```
NLMLINKP HELLO
```

If the partial linkage is successful, you should see the following
message on your DOS station:

```
Novell Loadable Module Linker, Version 2.66 P
Linking HELLO.NLM
    Version 1.00 (08\30\92)
```

The file HELLO.NLM now should be in your directory. To load
and run HELLO.NLM, type the following command at the server
console:

```
LOAD HELLO
```

You should see the following message on your server's console:

```
Hello Downsizing World!
<Press any key to close screen>
```

When you load HELLO.NLM, the server displays some of the information from the definition file HELLO.DEF, as follows:

```
Loading module HELLO.NLM
    First NLM
    Version 1.00   August 30, 1992
    This program is not copyrighted
    Debug symbol information for HELLO.NLM loaded
```

Working with the Server
Environment and Diagnostic NLM

Now that you are familiar with an extremely simple NLM, look at
a more sophisticated (but still simple) NLM that does something

useful. FSENV.NLM displays important diagnostic information on the server's console.

FSENV.NLM calls three important NetWare APIs: `GetServerInformation` retrieves key information about the server's environment; `GetFileServerLoginStatus` indicates the login state of the server (whether login is enabled or disabled); and `TTSIsAvailable` indicates the transaction control state of the server (whether TTS is enabled or disabled).

FSENV.NLM is structurally *elegant* (a programming euphemism for *simple*): it executes in an endless loop. Every time it goes through the loop, it collects server information by calling `GetServerInformation`, `GetFileServerLoginStatus`, and `TTSIsAvailable`. After collecting the information, FSENV.NLM prints the information on its console screen. After printing the information, FSENV.NLM "sleeps" for five seconds by calling the delay API.

To load FSENV.NLM, you must be certain first that the NLM is located in the server's SYS:SYSTEM directory. If it is, enter the following command at the server's system console screen:

```
LOAD FSENV
```

After loading FSENV.NLM, you must switch to its screen by pressing Alt-Esc until a screen similar to the following appears:

```
        NetWare Server Environment Information
--------------------------------------------------------
-------
Server Name:              BULLET
NetWare Version:          3.11
Max. Supported Connections: 120
Connections now in use:   2
Maximum Volumes Supported: 64
SFT Level:                2
TTS Level:                1
Peak Connections Used:    2
```

```
CLIB Version:                3.11
Login State:                 Login Enabled
Transaction Control State:   TTS Enabled
```

 If you are accustomed to a single-threaded environment such as DOS, you may be wondering how to exit from FSENV, executing in an endless loop. Because NetWare is a multithreaded environment, when you want to do something else at the server console, you can switch to another screen by pressing Alt-Esc.

When you want to unload FSENV.NLM, you can switch to the server's system console screen (press Alt-Esc until the system console screen appears) and enter the following line:

UNLOAD FSENV

Until you explicitly unload FSENV.NLM, however, it remains resident in server RAM and remains an active process. FESENV.NLM consumes CPU cycles, however, only when it is not "sleeping" as the result of the call to delay. During the time FSENV.NLM is "asleep," it does not consume any CPU cycles. As a result, FSENV.NLM is efficient in its use of server resources (see the section "Using the Server Effectively").

Listing 11.6 contains the entire C source code for FSENV.NLM. There is not much source code—most of the work is accomplished by the NetWare operating system with calls to GetServerInformation, GetFileServerLoginStatus, and TTSIsAvailable.

Listing 11.6:

The entire C source code for FSENV.NLM.

```
/******************************************************************
* filename    :   fsenv.c                                        *
* date        :   August 31 1992                                 *
```

```
* version       :  1.0                                              *
* description   :  Server environment and diagnostic NLM            *
* compiler      :  Watcom C 386                                     *
* cc options    :  wcc386p /mf /3s /ez fsenv.c                      *
*                                                                   *
*******************************************************************/
#include <stdio.h>
#include <nwenvrn.h>
#include <process.h>
#include <conio.h>
#include <nwtts.h>
typedef struct envStruct {
  char serverName[48];
  BYTE netwareVersion;
  BYTE netwareSubVersion;
  WORD maxConnectionsSupported;
  WORD connectionsInUse;
  WORD maxVolumesSupported;
  BYTE revisionLevel;
  BYTE SFTLevel;
  BYTE TTSLevel;
  WORD peakConnectionsUsed;
  BYTE accountingVersion;
  BYTE VAPVersion;
  BYTE queingVersion;
  BYTE printServerVersion;
  BYTE virtualConsoleVersion;
  BYTE securityRestrictionLevel;
  BYTE internetBridgeSupport;
  BYTE reserved[60];
  BYTE CLibMajorVersion;
  BYTE CLibMinorVersion;
  BYTE CLibRevision;
} SERVER_INFO;
int main(void)
{
  int ccode;
  SERVER_INFO info;
  int loginFlag, ttsFlag;
  while(1)
    {
    ccode = GetServerInformation(sizeof(FILE_SERV_INFO), &info);
```

```
    if (!ccode)
        {
    clrscr();
    printf("\n                    NetWare Server Environment Information");
    printf("\n--------------------------------------");
    printf("--------------------------------------\n\n");
    printf("Server Name:                %s\n", info.serverName);
    printf("NetWare Version:           %i.%i\n",
      info.netwareVersion, info.netwareSubVersion);
    printf("Max. Supported Connections: %i\n",
      info.maxConnectionsSupported);
    printf("Connections now in use:    %i\n", info.connectionsInUse);
    printf("Maximum Volumes Supported: %i\n",
      info.maxVolumesSupported);
    printf("SFT Level:                 %i\n", info.SFTLevel);
    printf("TTS Level:                 %i\n", info.TTSLevel);
    printf("Peak Connections Used:     %i\n",
      info.peakConnectionsUsed);
    printf("CLIB Version:              %i.%i\n",
      info.CLibMajorVersion,
      info.CLibMinorVersion);
}
    ccode = GetFileServerLoginStatus(&loginFlag);
    printf("Login State:               %s\n",
    loginFlag ? "Login Enabled" : "Login Disabled");
        ttsFlag = TTSIsAvailable();
    printf("Transaction Control State: %s\n",
        (ttsFlag == 0xff) ? "TTS Enabled" : "TTS Disabled");
    if (ccode)
       return(-1);
    delay(5000);
        }
  return(0);
}
/****************************************************************
*       END OF FILE                                           *
****************************************************************/
```

Listing 11.7 shows the linker definition file for FSENV.NLM.

Listing 11.7:
The linker definition file for FSENV.NLM.

```
## filename: FSENV.DEF
## definition file for FSENV.NLM
debug
description "Server Environment Display"
import
   @i:\public\nwcnlm\imp\clib.imp
input
   i:\public\nwcnlm\imp\prelude.obj
   fsenv.obj
map
module  clib
output  fsenv
screenname "FSENV"
type 0
version 1, 00, 0
threadname "FSENV"
```

Distributing DP Applications

Turning a conventional DP application into a distributed client-server application is truly an art rather than a science. A good place to start splitting the application is between the logical database and the conceptual schema, particularly between the user interface and the remainder of the program (refer to Chapter 3). A good start, then, means that you implement the user interface as a client program and implement the remainder of the application as a back-end, server-based engine.

Achieving a split, however, is not the equivalent of achieving a well-distributed application. You should consider many subtle characteristics of both machine and software. The facts are different for each distribution project.

Using the Server Effectively

The purpose of all distributed applications should be to use the server effectively (and therefore also the client). Splitting an application into client and server components is the means toward the end, and not the end itself.

The key to making effective use of the server in a distributed application lies in following these simple rules:

1. Use the server only to do tasks it can do faster or more efficiently than can the client

2. Minimize network traffic

3. When you can do something once on the server, rather than once on each client, do it once on the server

4. Minimize the use of server RAM; using server RAM depletes file-cache buffers

5. Do as much as possible on the client without breaking the first three rules

Rule 1 requires intelligent decision-making on the part of the programmer because few hard-and-fast rules exist. You can use some rules of thumb, however. When the NetWare operating system is performing file I/O, it almost always is faster and more efficient than the client (whatever the client may be). Also, the NetWare operating system is fully 32 bits wide: All registers, instructions, and operands are 32-bit values rather than 16-bit values, as in other operating systems such as DOS. This capability makes almost any CPU-intensive processing performed by a DP application faster when NetWare performs that processing.

Rule 1 must be balanced, however, against rules 2 through 5. Remember that the NetWare operating system is multitasking and multithreaded: other applications may require resources of the operating system concurrently with your application. Concentrating on rule 1 to the exclusion of the other rules creates a tendency to overload the server and dilute the benefits you seek by following rule 1.

You usually can implement rule 2 and minimize network traffic by simply building NetWare awareness into your application. Consider the difference, for example, between a DOS-only file manager running on a DOS NetWare client and a server-based distributed file manager.

When a DOS-only file manager needs to read a record, it issues a DOS file I/O command. The NetWare shell (DOS client software) intercepts the I/O command and translates it into a series of NetWare Core Protocol requests for file data. The NetWare Core Protocol resolves into a series of request packets and a corresponding series of reply packets. The DOS-only file manager obtains the data it requested, but only after causing a storm of IPX network activity.

Contrast the DOS-only file manager with a NetWare-aware distributed file manager. When the DOS client requests a file record, it sends one packet to the server. (The format of the packet is predefined and is understood by both the DOS client and the NetWare back-end code.) The server interprets the packet to mean that the client is requesting a file record. The server then sends the file record data back to the client.

The distributed approach results in only two packets. Moreover, the DOS client does not force the NetWare client shell to intercept and redirect a DOS file I/O call to the NetWare server. Markedly fewer IPX packets (only two total) then travel between the client and the server over the network.

Rule 3 restates the notion of leveraging often-repeated tasks (refer to Chapter 2).

Consider a DP application, for example, in which each client maintains a memory cache of recently accessed record data. If each client gains access to common records, each client (separately) maintains a cache of data from those common records. Alternatively, a back-end, NetWare-based engine can provide the common file data cache for all of its clients. Data for a record then may be cached once by the engine, but the benefit of that cached data accrues to every single client. The engine may cache a record's data once, to the benefit of multiple clients, rather than have each client cache the same record data, which results in multiple caching operations.

Tip
The NetWare file system cache buffers provide the most obvious example of leveraging often-repeated tasks. Others exist, however, such as the methods used by the operating system to maintain global memory structures such as LAN receive buffers. Depending on the design of your distributed application, you probably can identify many opportunities for leveraging often-repeated tasks by placing the code for performing them on the server-based component of the distributed application.

Rule 4—minimize the use of server RAM—introduces a conflict with rule 1 because the NetWare operating system features a 32-bit, flat memory space. For this reason alone, memory management in NetWare is faster and more efficient than in DOS. NetWare's memory management is faster and more efficient than in other 32-bit operating systems also, such as UNIX, because NetWare does not implement virtual memory or memory protection. Why use rule 4 then? You should use it because allocation of memory by NLM applications depletes NetWare file system cache buffers, which slows file service. The importance of this rule is exaggerated or diminished by the amount of RAM in your server. Rule 4 is more important, for example, for a server with 8M of RAM than for a server with 16M of RAM.

Tip
In DP applications, an especially useful technique minimizes use of server RAM: perform indexing using files rather than memory data structures. An index file becomes cached by the NetWare file system as clients use the application, which offers performance gains nearly equal to maintaining an index in server RAM. By using a file-based index, however, you enable the operating system to manage the cache, which

makes programming the application easier and balances the needs of the DP application with other requirements of the server operating system.

Rule 5 leads to an interesting discussion of the characteristics of a networked system. The fact that the server machine is the most powerful machine on the network does not mean that the server machine has the most free capacity.

The server machine always has work to do, such as network routing and bridging, managing file-cache buffers, and service advertising, even when network clients are idle. Network clients, on the other hand, usually have much free capacity, depending on their operating system and applications. Do not, therefore, blindly dump all the heavy work on the server when you are creating a distributed client-server application.

As you have read about the downsizing rules and their implications, you probably have noticed their ambiguity and conflicts. For this reason, distributing applications is still more of an art than a science. Although becoming a true artist requires experience and a thorough understanding of the NetWare operating system, you can achieve acceptable (and even excellent) results in your downsizing effort without being a true artist; the NetWare environment is more forgiving than this discussion reveals. Downsizing efforts by experienced programmers who are new to NetWare can produce rewards more quickly than you may expect at first.

Summary

This chapter evaluated the NetWare development environment by discussing the NetWare API categories and comparing client development and server development. You learned to write, link, and load NLMs and saw a simple server diagnostic NLM.

The chapter also discussed the NetWare debugger and gave you practical programming tips.

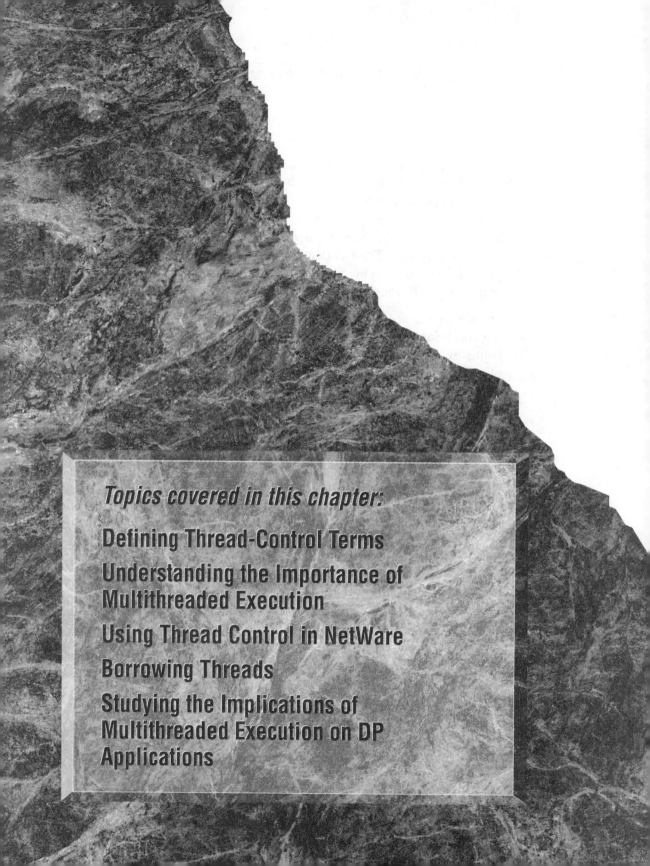

Topics covered in this chapter:

Defining Thread-Control Terms

Understanding the Importance of
Multithreaded Execution

Using Thread Control in NetWare

Borrowing Threads

Studying the Implications of
Multithreaded Execution on DP
Applications

## Chapter 12

Thread Control

As a multithreaded operating system, NetWare makes the most of the server machine's computing resources. *Multithreaded* refers to NetWare's capability to maintain and execute multiple instances of programs or parts of programs concurrently.

This chapter discusses what multithreaded execution means to a data processing application. It also provides specific details of NetWare's environment for multithreaded applications, and explains how you can control that environment.

Defining Thread-Control Terms

Before discussing the implications of NetWare's multithreaded architecture on your downsizing efforts, this section defines some terms you should understand.

A *multitasking* operating system enables more than one program to be active at a single instant.

An *active* program is loaded into memory and receives regular *time slices*, or periods of execution, from the operating system.

A *scheduler* is a group of low-level routines within the operating system that control the order of execution among multiple active programs. A scheduler "dishes out" time slices.

A *multithreaded* operating system allows not only programs, but also subroutines within programs, to be scheduled and active concurrently. A multithreaded operating system also is multitasking, and to a higher degree than an operating system that is multitasking but not multithreaded. In a multithreaded operating system, its scheduler offers a higher degree of control over the process of "dishing out" time slices.

A *thread* is an instance of active code that gains access to the computer's CPU by being scheduled. A thread in NetWare can be a single function, a sequential group of functions, or an entire application. The programmer controls the creation of threads—how many and for what purpose.

A *thread group* is a group of threads that share important global data items such as file handles, screens, and semaphores. An NLM is always a thread group. An NLM that starts additional threads after it is loaded becomes a thread group containing more than one thread; an NLM that does not start threads after it is loaded is a thread group containing only one thread.

Understanding the Importance of Multithreaded Execution

A downsizing platform must be based on a multithreaded operating system because a downsizing platform always has a large amount of work to do: it must read and write records, open and close data bases, sort, index, check constraints in the application schema, check security, and control transactions.

Most of the responsibilities of a downsizing platform can be broken down into groups of *functionally associated tasks*. These tasks are related to each other in their purpose, in the subject of their responsibilities, or in the data structures to which they must gain access. Depending on its design, the typical DP application has from 10 to more than 100 functionally associated tasks.

Designers of DP applications usually organize functionally associated tasks into threads, or processes. (In NetWare, the correct term is "thread," not "process.") By organizing functionally associated tasks into threads, the designer of the application minimizes sequential dependencies within the application. A *sequential dependency* occurs when one job has to be fulfilled, but it must wait on the fulfillment of another job before the first job can be fulfilled.

 The application designer should organize threads so that sequential dependencies do not exist among threads. When sequential dependencies are unavoidable, they should exist *within* threads rather than among threads. The reason is that each thread may go about its work without having to wait on other threads to complete their work.

If there are no sequential dependencies among threads in a DP application, the application as a whole spends less time waiting for jobs to be fulfilled and more time actually fulfilling jobs. In a well-designed multithreaded application, sequential dependencies exist only at a *base level* (a level that must occur, regardless of the application's design).

A well-designed multithreaded application always outperforms a single-threaded application, and also always outperforms a poorly designed multithreaded application. The reason is that a well-designed multithreaded application reduces sequential dependencies to a minimum.

Imagine an application with two threads, for example. Thread A is responsible for reading records, and thread B is responsible for writing records. Each thread has *housekeeping* duties (a programming term for maintaining the thread's environment in a known state) and logical duties, such as enforcing the database schema. Thread A has issued a write request and is waiting for the storage media to fulfill the request. While thread A is waiting for fulfillment of the write request, the operating system's scheduler puts thread A to *sleep* by unscheduling it, or taking it off the run queue. In the meantime, the operating system *wakes* thread B by scheduling it, or placing it on the run queue. While thread A is awaiting the fulfillment of its read request, thread B may perform housekeeping or logical duties, or issue a read request. When the physical media has fulfilled thread A's read request, the operating system wakes thread A and puts thread B to sleep.

If the application has only one thread, the read routine (thread B) must await the fulfillment of the write routine's (thread A's) write request before it may perform any of its responsibilities. This process introduces a sequential dependency, which implies that the application would perform better if it were organized into two threads.

This example provides a glimpse into the advantages of multithreaded application design. In a working DP application, thousands of potential sequential dependencies, if they are not addressed properly by the designer, may have a negative effect on the application's performance.

A multithreaded operating system provides application designers with a powerful set of tools for removing sequential dependencies from a complex application. An experienced programmer may use multithreaded techniques to achieve sparkling performance from NetWare. In addition, NetWare provides an excellent set of tools.

Using Thread Control in NetWare

When you are designing a DP application for NetWare (or porting an application to NetWare), you should understand the different methods NetWare provides for controlling threads. *Thread control* refers to beginning threads, scheduling the execution of threads, and ending threads. The NetWare scheduler enables you to gain a high degree of control over when and how frequently threads gain access to the server machine's CPU.

Understanding Threads and Thread Groups

A *thread group* consists of one or more threads that share access to common system data structures such as screens, file handles, and network connections. If one thread within a thread group creates a NetWare console screen, for example, all threads within that thread group may display output on that screen.

When you load an NLM, the C run-time library establishes a thread group that consists of the NLM's initial thread. Whenever the NLM creates threads afterward, those threads also may gain access to global data structures maintained by the NLM. By default, a new thread started by an NLM belongs to the NLM's thread group.

An NLM may create an entirely new thread group, however, by calling the API `BeginThreadGroup`. This capability is most useful when the NLM creates a new thread that in turn creates more threads. The threads that belong to an entirely new thread group still have access to global data structures that have an NLM-wide scope. Figure 12.1 illustrates the concepts of NLMs, thread groups, and threads, and shows data structures they have in common.

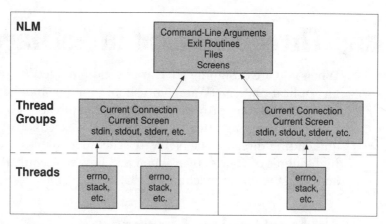

Figure 12.1:

Thread groups and threads have access to common data structures.

Each thread—regardless of how it was started by the NLM—has its own stack. (A *stack* is an area of memory the thread uses to store temporary variables and return addresses.) Because each thread has its own stack and other threads are not allowed to reference the thread's stack, NLM functions are *re-entrant*: multiple threads may execute the code of a function concurrently. Re-entrancy is a requirement for any application that makes use of multithreaded programming techniques.

Starting Threads

A server-based DP application for NetWare can create threads in several ways, including the following:

❖ Start a single thread by calling `BeginThread`

❖ Start a new thread group by calling `BeginThreadGroup`

❖ Load an NLM by calling `spawnlp` or `spawnvp`

❖ Borrow a worker thread from the operating system by calling `ScheduleSleepAESProcessEvent`

When an NLM calls `BeginThread`, the operating system creates a new thread that becomes part of the calling thread's thread group. When an NLM calls `BeginThreadGroup`, the operating system creates a new thread group, consisting of only one thread. If the newly created thread later creates more threads by calling `BeginThread`, those threads become part of the calling thread's thread group.

Both `BeginThread` and `BeginThreadGroup` require a function as a parameter. When the operating system creates the new thread (or thread group), it calls this function, which must be part of the NLM creating the new thread.

Introducing THREAD.NLM

Because the APIs `BeginThread` and `BeginThreadGroup` both have the same *prototype* (calling convention), if you know how to call one of them, you know how to call both. THREAD.NLM is a demonstration NLM that shows how to use `BeginThread`. By necessity, THREAD.NLM demonstrates some other thread-control APIs, such as `OpenLocalSemaphore`, `WaitOnLocalSemaphore`, `CloseLocalSemaphore`, `delay`, and `ThreadSwitch`. The C source code for THREAD.NLM is shown in listing 12.1. Listing 12.2 shows the linker-definition file for THREAD.NLM.

Listing 12.1:
C source code for THREAD.NLM.

```
/***************************************************************************
*                                                                         *
*    filename      :      thread.c                                        *
*    date          :  September 5 1992                                    *
*    version       :      1.0                                             *
```

```
*   description    :   Demonstration of thread control              *
*    compiler      :   Watcom C 386                                 *
*   cc options     :   wcc386p /mf /3s /ez fsenv.c                  *
*                                                                   *
*   usage          :   load thread <number>                         *
*                                                                   *
*********************************************************************/
#include <stdio.h>
#include <nwenvrn.h>
#include <process.h>
#include <conio.h>
#include <signal.h>
#include <nwsemaph.h>
/*---- GLOBAL VARIABLES ----*/
int shutdown = 0, screen = 0;
LONG shutdownSem;
/*******************************************************************
* ChildMain                                                       *
*-----------------------------------------------------------------*
* This function is started as an independent thread by main       *
*                                                                 *
*******************************************************************/
void ChildMain(void *data)
{
   if (data)  // get rid of compiler warnings
      ;
   /* The child thread stays alive until the user UNLOADS THREAD.NLM */
   /* at the server console. During the course of its execution,    */
   /* the thread spins to gain control of the NLM screen. As soon    */
   /* as it gains control of the NLM screen, the thread prints its   */
   /* thread ID on the screen, relinquishes control of the screen,   */
   /* and puts itself to sleep for 1/10 of a second by calling       */
   /* delay.                                                         */
   while(!shutdown)
      {
      while(screen)                // spin until the screen is free
         ThreadSwitch();
      screen++;                    // lock the screen by incrementing
      gotoxy(20, 12);              // the global variable
      printf("%i", GetThreadID());
      screen--;                    // release the screen
      delay(100);                  // go to sleep for 1/10 second
```

```
        }
   return;
}
/************************************************************************
* UnloadCleanUp                                                        *
*----------------------------------------------------------------------*
* The NetWare operating system calls this function as soon as the      *
* operator issues the UNLOAD THREAD.NLM command at the server console. *
* This function sets the global shutdown variable to 1, which causes   *
* the child threads to fall out of their loop and then die. This       *
* function then signals the shutdownSem semaphore, which awakens main  *
* and causes main to die.                                              *
*                                                                      *
************************************************************************/
void UnloadCleanUp(int sig)
{
   sig = sig;  // get rid of compiler warnings
   shutdown = 1;
   SignalLocalSemaphore(shutdownSem);
   return;
}
/************************************************************************
* ShutdownCleanUp                                                      *
*----------------------------------------------------------------------*
* The NetWare operating system calls this function after all the threads *
* have killed themselves. At this point, all you can do is free OS     *
* resources you have allocated, such as semaphores.                    *
*                                                                      *
************************************************************************/
 void ShutdownCleanUp(void)
{
   int ccode;
   ccode = CloseLocalSemaphore(shutdownSem);   // close the semaphore
   return;
}
/************************************************************************
* usage                                                                *
*----------------------------------------------------------------------*
* print a help screen                                                  *
*                                                                      *
************************************************************************/
void usage(void)
```

```c
{
   printf("\nUsage: LOAD THREAD <number>");
   printf("\n\nWhere <number> is the number of child");
   printf("\nthreads to spawn.");
   return;
}
/*************************************************************************
 * main                                                                 *
 *----------------------------------------------------------------------*
 * get command-line arguments, allocate semaphore from operating system,
 *
 * begin child threads                                                  *
 *                                                                      *
 *************************************************************************/
int main(int argc, char **argv)
{
   int i, y, ccode;
   /* Check command-line args */
   if (argc != 2)
     {
     usage();              // incorrect command line args, print help
     return(0);
     }
   i = atoi(argv[1]);  // save number of threads argument
   shutdownSem = OpenLocalSemaphore(0L);  // open semaphore
signal(SIGTERM, UnloadCleanUp);  // register unload functions
atexit(ShutdownCleanUp);
gotoxy(0, 12);
printf("Inside thread:");
/* start the child threads */
for (y = 0; y < i; y++)
   ccode = BeginThread(ChildMain, NULL, 0x1000, NULL);

/* go to sleep until the operator issues the UNLOAD THREAD.NLM */
/* command. */
WaitOnLocalSemaphore(shutdownSem);
return(1);
}
/*---- END OF FILE ----*/
```

Listing 12.2:
Linker definition file for THREAD.NLM.

```
## LINKER DEFINITION FILE "THREAD.DEF"
copyright "Copyright 1992"
debug
description "Thread control demonstration"
import
   @i:\public\nwcnlm\imp\clib.imp
input
   i:\public\nwcnlm\imp\prelude.obj
   thread.obj
map
module  clib
output  thread
screenname "THREAD DEMO"
type 0
version 1, 00, 0
threadname "THDEMO"
## END OF FILE ##
```

Building and Running THREAD.NLM

To build THREAD.NLM, enter the following commands from your DOS development station:

```
WCC386P /MF /3S /EZ /D2 THREAD.C
NLMLINKP THREAD
```

Next, copy the resulting THREAD.NLM file to your server's SYS:SYSTEM directory. Then load THREAD.NLM by activating the server console and entering the following command:

```
LOAD THREAD 5
```

The NetWare loader loads THREAD.NLM after also loading CLIB.NLM and STREAMS.NLM, if they are not loaded already.

You should see a display on the THREAD DEMO server screen. The number that is displayed changes rapidly as the different threads gain access to the server's CPU.

 Notice that the LOAD THREAD 5 command causes THREAD.NLM to start five child threads.

As THREAD.NLM is running, you should see the thread ID number change rapidly (too rapidly to see which thread is active at any specific moment). To see what happens among the child threads, you must run MONITOR.NLM with the *undocumented profiling option*. To load MONITOR.NLM with the undocumented profiling option, enter the following command at the server console:

```
LOAD MONITOR -P
```

If MONITOR.NLM is loaded already, you should unload it and then reload it with the -p argument as part of the command line.

When the NetWare loader is finished loading MONITOR.NLM, the server displays the Monitor Screen.

Now select Processor Utilization from the Monitor Available Options menu and press Enter. MONITOR.NLM displays a dialog box containing the names of all the server's active threads. The thread names are in alphabetical order; scroll through them until you see a series of thread names beginning with THDEMO. The THDEMO threads all are part of THREAD.NLM. Highlight the thread called THDEMO 0 Process and press F5. This action "marks" the THDEMO 0 Process thread. Mark all threads that have a name beginning with THDEMO by highlighting them and pressing F5.

After you have highlighted all the threads that have names beginning with THDEMO, press Enter. MONITOR displays a pop-up window showing all the threads you marked and their names, execution times, instructions executed, and CPU load relative to total server load.

The first thread, THDEMO 0 Process, is consuming no time, in-structions, or load. The 0 process is the `main` function from THREAD.C. Remember that you put `main` to sleep by calling `WaitOnLocalSemaphore`. All the remaining threads, however, are consuming an equal number of instructions, although they all do not necessarily consume an equal amount of time or load.

Because NetWare is not a preemptive operating system, thread timing and load are uncertain, and thread instructions are defined by the code image of the thread and are certain. Threads 1 though 5, however, all are consuming a relatively equal amount of time and load. Under a preemptive operating system, you could expect each of the threads to consume an equal time slice, and perhaps a different number of instructions.

Going Inside the THREAD.NLM Source Code

Although THREAD.C is a short and straightforward C source code file, it demonstrates all the basic NetWare thread-control methods. (Some advanced thread-control methods are discussed later in this chapter.) The first thing to look at in the file THREAD.C are the global variables:

```
/*---- GLOBAL VARIABLES ----*/
int shutdown = 0, screen = 0;
LONG shutdownSem;
```

Good programming practice dictates that you declare variables you will use to control threads globally. Temporary variables (declared within the body of a function) are available only within the function that declares them. If you want a variable to be available from within multiple threads, therefore, declare it globally.

The variable `shutdown` controls the lifetime of the child threads created by `main`. The child threads execute a repeating loop as long as the value of `shutdown` is 0. The value of `shutdown` remains 0 until you unload THREAD.NLM by issuing the UNLOAD command at the server console, when the function `UnloadCleanup` sets the value of `shutdown` to one. This action causes the child threads to fall from their repeating loop and return to `main`, which is the equivalent of killing themselves.

The `screen` variable is a home-grown semaphore for controlling access to the THREAD.NLM's screen. Whenever a child thread wants to display its thread ID on-screen, it must wait until the value of `screen` is 0. When the value of `screen` is 0, the child thread quickly increments it, thereby locking the NLM screen and preventing other child threads from gaining access to it. As soon as the child thread is finished with the NLM screen, it decrements the value of the `screen` variable, and enables other child threads to gain access to it.

For simple contention problems in which you must lock an NLM resource for short periods, and in which contention for the resource is limited within the scope of the NLM, you may implement "home grown" semaphores by declaring a public variable and controlling it as THREAD.C does. This method of controlling contention has a low overhead, although it's not as powerful as using operating-system semaphores.

The variable `shutdownSem` is an operating system semaphore handle, which controls the execution of `main`. The `main` variable opens the `shutdownSem` semaphore by calling `OpenLocalSemaphore`. (A *local semaphore* is one that has a scope of NLM; normal semaphores have a scope of server, and network semaphores have a multiserver scope.)

When `main` is finished starting all the child threads, it puts itself to sleep by calling `WaitOnLocalSemaphore`. `main` remains asleep until you issue the UNLOAD THREAD command at the server console, and then the function `UnloadCleanUp` wakes `main` by calling `SignalLocalSemaphore`. By definition, when `main` wakes, it is time to exit; `main`, therefore, kills itself by returning.

The two functions that execute as the result of the UNLOAD THREAD command, `UnloadCleanUp` and `ShutdownCleanUp`, are called by the operating system's console-command handler during the course of the UNLOAD code. The operating system knows to call these two functions because `main` registered them using the following code:

```
signal(SIGTERM, UnloadCleanUp);  // register unload
functions
atexit(ShutdownCleanUp);
```

The `signal` API is an ANSI standard C library function. Its purpose is to enable applications to be called back when certain system events occur. The parameter `SIGTERM` means that the function `UnloadCleanUp` wants to be called before a termination event (`SIGTERM` is shorthand for *term*ination *sig*nal). The operating system's console-command handler, therefore, calls `UnloadCleanUp` before the operating system terminates the NLM. The code for `UnloadCleanUp` is as follows:

```
void UnloadCleanUp(int sig)
{
    sig = sig;  // get rid of compiler warnings
    shutdown = 1;
    SignalLocalSemaphore(shutdownSem);
    return;
}
```

By setting the global variable `shutdown` to 1, `UnloadCleanUp` causes all the child threads to exit their repeated loop and kill themselves by returning to `main`. By calling `SignalLocalSemaphore`, `UnloadCleanUp` causes `main` to return, which is logically equivalent to `main` killing itself.

The `atexit` API enables an NLM to register a cleanup function with the operating system. The operating system calls this cleanup function after all of the NLM's threads are terminated. (The function registered by `atexit` executes under the context of an operating system thread.) At this point, the NLM can only free resources that it allocated from the operating system during initialization. One such resource is the semaphore `shutdownSem`, which is released during the body of `ShutdownCleanUp`, as follows:

```
void ShutdownCleanUp(void)
{
    int ccode;
    ccode = CloseLocalSemaphore(shutdownSem);    //
close the semaphore
    return;
}
```

The child threads are started within `main`, as follows:

```
ccode = BeginThread(ChildMain, NULL, 0x1000, NULL);
```

The first parameter is a pointer to a function that executes under the context of the new thread—`ChildMain`, in this case. This function can be as simple or as complex as you want. In THREAD.C, the `ChildMain` function is a simple one. Nothing, however, prevents you from starting very large and complex functions as new threads.

The second and third parameters define the stack of the thread to be created. The second parameter is a pointer to memory allocated by the NLM. If the second parameter is `NULL`, the third parameter defines a stack size that the operating system should allocate and assign as stack to the new thread.

The fourth parameter is a pointer to data that the operating system passes back to the NLM when the operating system calls the first parameter. Because `ChildMain` doesn't require any parameters (all the information it needs is contained either in global variables or obtained at run time by making function calls to APIs), `main` passes a `NULL` for the fourth parameter.

Note that each child thread is executing the function `ChildMain` concurrently. Remember that all functions started as a new thread are automatically re-entrant because each thread has its own private stack.

Two more thread control APIs are important to discuss: `delay` and `ThreadSwitch`. Both of these APIs are called during the child thread's loop, as follows:

```
while(!shutdown)
   {
   while(screen)            // spin until the screen
is free
      ThreadSwitch();
   screen++;                // lock the screen by
incrementing
   gotoxy(20, 12);          // the global variable
   printf("%i", GetThreadID());
   screen--;                // release the screen
   delay(100);              // go to sleep for 1/10
second
   }
```

The `ThreadSwitch()` API causes the calling thread to relinquish control of the CPU. The operating system then places the calling thread at the end of the run queue. Other threads then get a chance to execute before the calling thread reaches the front of the run queue and regains control of the CPU. The use of `ThreadSwitch` in this case is critical because it is called only when some other child thread has the screen locked. The calling thread therefore must "get out of the way" so that the "locking" thread can finish using the screen and release its lock.

The `delay` API goes further than `ThreadSwitch`. `delay` not only causes the calling thread to relinquish control, but it also forces the thread to be suspended for a period of milliseconds before the operating system places the calling thread at the end of the run queue. The `delay` API therefore is a harsher method of relinquishing control than the `ThreadSwitch` API because `delay` essentially "kills" a thread briefly. When `delay` "resurrects" the thread, it places the thread at the end of the run queue.

Borrowing Threads

You may find it useful for advanced applications to "borrow" worker threads from the operating system. The operating system maintains a pool of worker threads for short-term, low-overhead tasks such as establishing client connections and servicing client requests. You can put these special threads to work for your application by calling the following APIs:

```
ScheduleSleepAESProcessEvent
ScheduleNoSleepAESProcessEvent
```

`AES`, or Asynchronous Event Scheduler, refers to NetWare's nonpreemptive scheduler. A *sleep process* can call *blocking routines* (routines that relinquish control of the CPU); a *no sleep process* cannot call blocking routines.

What is the advantage of borrowing an operating system thread over creating your own thread? Borrowing a thread consumes less overhead and housekeeping than creating an entirely new thread. When you create a thread, the NetWare operating system must create a thread-control structure, place it on the scheduler's run queue, and allocate a stack for the thread. (You may allocate a stack for the thread yourself, but the overhead is the same.) Borrowing an already existing thread is a simple way to eliminate the overhead associated with creating an entirely new thread. The added efficiency of borrowing an operating system thread, however, has some limits:

❖ The stack size is set at 4K

❖ Routines are executed under the context of the borrowed thread

❖ NLM global variables are out of scope during the execution of the borrowed thread (you can pass parameters to a borrowed thread using a memory pointer)

When efficiency is critical, borrowing a thread (rather than creating an entirely new thread) can increase the performance of your application. Be certain, however, that you know what you are doing if you choose these advanced thread-control methods.

Studying the Implications of Multithreaded Execution on DP Applications

As this chapter has stated, the entire purpose of a multithreaded architecture is to eliminate sequential dependencies from an application. DP applications, which usually are based around a database management system, present many opportunities for multithreaded programming techniques. The primary implication of multithreaded execution on a DP application, therefore, is increased performance.

Multithreaded programming techniques are difficult for programmers to grasp, however. The APIs are not difficult—you have seen a simple demonstration NLM that uses all the basic thread-control APIs in Netware. The conceptual framework of multithreaded execution is difficult, however. Most programmers are accustomed to thinking sequentially because computers are sequential-state machines. Multithreaded programs, however, are decidedly nonsequential. Execution among threads occurs nonsequentially. Each active thread is "in scope" concurrently with all other active threads. Programmers must master the concepts of threads: going to sleep, blocking, being wakened, and getting killed.

 Perhaps the multithreaded architecture of NetWare contributes to the perception that NLM programming is difficult. NLM programming is no more difficult than other types of programming. Multithreaded programming techniques, however, are difficult to master.

Summary

Now you should know all the basics of thread control in NetWare. Specifically, you have learned how to accomplish the following operations:

- ❖ Start new threads
- ❖ Control thread execution by using global variables
- ❖ Control thread execution using semaphores
- ❖ Force threads to relinquish control of the CPU
- ❖ Register cleanup functions for execution when the operating system unloads the NLM

Using the basic thread-control methods demonstrated in THREAD.NLM, you can build some sophisticated multithreaded DP applications. The complexity of the multithreaded design of your application is ultimately your decision.

Chapter 13 continues your NetWare programming education by presenting information about interprocess communication.

Topics covered in this chapter:

Introducing Semaphores

Exploring Shared Memory

Working with Shared Files (Pipes)

Chapter 13

Interprocess Communication

C hapter 12 discussed thread control in NetWare and explained how multithreaded design can increase your DP application's performance. This chapter describes *interprocess communication*, or *IPC*.

IPC refers specifically to methods that threads can use to communicate among themselves. In THREAD.NLM from Chapter 12, for example, only one thread at a time was allowed to print its thread ID to the screen. When a thread had to print to the screen, it had to "lock" the screen, thereby informing other threads that the screen was in use and that they must wait before printing their thread ID to the screen. THREAD.NLM used a simple type of semaphore to communicate this information among threads. NetWare provides other methods of IPC, including the items in the following list:

- ❖ Local (NLM-wide) semaphores
- ❖ System (server-wide) semaphores
- ❖ Shared memory
- ❖ Shared files (pipes)

This chapter bases examples on the THREAD.NLM file presented in Chapter 12. If you are not already familiar with this file, refer to Chapter 12 before you continue.

Before you learn about NetWare's IPC mechanisms, you should understand a couple of concepts. First, IPC is a generic term used by programmers to refer to communication among running processes. In NetWare, a more appropriate term is *interthread communication*. Because IPC is somewhat of a standard acronym, however, this chapter uses IPC to refer to interthread communication. Second, NetWare provides an effective method of IPC that is not available on other operating systems: message-passing using IPX. As a network-transport protocol, IPX typically is used to send messages among computers over a network. You can use IPX, however, as a method of IPC among threads running *on the same computer*. This method, in fact, is often the preferred method of IPC for NetWare server-based applications.

 Because IPX message-passing is a relatively complicated topic, it deserves a chapter of its own; IPX message-passing designs are discussed in Chapter 15.

Introducing Semaphores

The term *semaphore* most often is associated with a flag or trackside sign used on a railroad system to reserve a section of railroad track. When an engine enters a section of track, it *signals* (turns on) a semaphore to inform other engines that they should not enter that section of railroad track. When the engine exits from the section of track, it turns off the semaphore to inform other engines that the section of track is free, or available for entry. Railroad semaphores prevent train collisions.

In the computer world, a semaphore is a global (usually system-wide) variable that programs can use to lock sections of code or other computer resources. Semaphores are only as effective as the programmer makes them be, however. Just as railroad semaphores are effective only when a train engineer turns them on (or observes their status), computer semaphores are effective only when a software engineer uses them correctly.

The primary purpose of semaphores in NetWare is to temporarily reserve system resources and thereby prevent other active threads from gaining access to those resources for a short time. You may use semaphores also, however, to announce the availability of dynamic resources to other threads. You may use semaphores, for example, to inform other threads of new client connections or the arrival of a network packet. Also, you may use semaphores to control the execution of NetWare threads by putting them to sleep and waking them.

Using semaphores is appropriate in many instances in a typical DP application—for example, controlling access to NLM screens (as in THREAD.NLM), controlling access to shared memory, and waiting for or announcing the creation of dynamic resources. An example of using semaphores inappropriately is in locking files.

  NetWare has a complete set of file-locking routines, which are discussed in Chapter 14.

Local Semaphores

Local semaphores are available only to threads within the same NLM. (You cannot use local semaphores for system-wide semaphores; rather, you must use *normal*, or system, semaphores, discussed later in this chapter.)

The primary advantage of a local semaphore over a normal semaphore is that a local semaphore is a resource with lower overhead. Local semaphores are slightly easier to open and maintain, but you must also close local semaphores before your NLM terminates (if you do not close them, the server abends). THREAD.NLM uses a local semaphore to control the execution of the `main` function. THREAD.NLM had to register a special function with the NetWare operating system for closing the local semaphore, in case an operator unloaded THREAD.NLM.

Opening Local Semaphores

Listing 13.1 demonstrates how to open a local semaphore.

Listing 13.1:

Opening a local semaphore.

```
#include <nwsemaph.h>
LONG semaphoreHandle;
semaphoreHandle = OpenLocalSemaphore(1L);
```

The sole parameter to `OpenLocalSemaphore` sets the initial value of the local semaphore (in listing 13.1, the initial value is 1). The *initial value* determines how many threads may gain access to resources associated with the semaphore. An initial value of 1 means that only a single thread may gain access to resources associated with the semaphore.

Waiting on and Signaling Local Semaphores

When a railroad engineer waits on a semaphore, he checks to determine whether a section of railroad track is clear and, if not, waits for it to clear. If the engineer determines that the section of track is clear, he proceeds to the section of track without waiting; otherwise, he waits.

In NetWare, *waiting on a local semaphore* involves checking the value of the semaphore. Each semaphore has a value associated with it, and this value determines whether the NetWare thread must "wait" or proceed. If the value of the local semaphore is 0 or negative, the waiting thread cannot proceed until some other thread or threads increase the value of the local semaphore to the point at which the value is positive. Furthermore, the act of waiting on a local semaphore causes the value of that semaphore to be decremented automatically by 1 (see listing 13.2).

Listing 13.2:

A code segment that demonstrates WaitOnLocalSemaphore.

```
#include <nwsemaph.h>
LONG semhandle;
semHandle = OpenLocalSemaphore(1L);   // value of semaphore is
1
WaitOnLocalSemaphore(semHandle);      // execution proceeds,
but
                                      // value of semaphore is
                                      // decremented to 0
WaitOnLocalSemaphore(semHandle);      // execution DOES NOT
proceed;
                                      // value of semaphore is
                                      // decremented to -1
/*—thread is now asleep—*/
```

The thread in listing 13.2 is put to sleep by the operating system as a result of the second call to WaitOnLocalSemaphore. The second call, which occurs when the value of the local semaphore becomes equal to 0, causes a "wait." The first call, with the value of the local semaphore equal to 1, decrements the value of the semaphore but does not cause the thread to wait.

What happens at the operating system level when a thread calls WaitOnLocalSemaphore (and the value of the semaphore is 0 or less)? First, the operating system takes the calling thread off the scheduler's run queue, thereby putting the calling thread to sleep. Second, the operating system links the calling thread's ID to a list of threads that are waiting on the semaphore. In this way, the operating system knows which threads to waken when another thread eventually signals the semaphore.

The thread in listing 13.2 remains asleep until some other thread signals the local semaphore on which the thread in listing 13.2 is waiting. Listing 13.3 shows the way to signal a local semaphore.

Listing 13.3:
Signaling a local semaphore.

```
#include <nwsemaph.h>
LONG semHandle;
SignalLocalSemaphore(semHandle)
```

You should note in listing 13.3 that the "signaling" thread does not have to open a local semaphore to signal it. A thread must have opened the semaphore, however, before another thread can wait on it or signal it; otherwise, the operating system protests violently.

 Good programming practice involves opening all local semaphores early in the main function, and always before starting child threads.

Closing Local Semaphores

NLMs that open local semaphores must *always* close those local semaphores. This stipulation becomes slightly more complicated because an NLM does not know exactly when it will be terminated. Why? Because an operator can terminate a loaded NLM at any time by issuing the UNLOAD *<NLM name>* command at the server console. NLMs that open local semaphores, therefore, always should register an unload function with the operating system. Furthermore, the unload function must (among other things) close local semaphores used by the operating system. (See listing 13.4. Note the registration of *UnloadFunction*: the operating system calls *UnloadFunction* when the NLM is terminated.)

Listing 13.4:

A template for NLM that uses local semaphores.

```
#include <nwsemaph.h>
#include <process.h>
LONG semHandle1, semHandle2, semHandle3;
void UnloadFunction(void)
{
   CloseLocalSemaphore(semHandle1);
   CloseLocalSemaphore(semHandle2);
   CloseLocalSemaphore(semHandle3);
   return;
}
int main(int argc, char **argv)
{
   /* process command line options, etc. */
   semHandle1 = OpenLocalSemaphore(1L);
   semHandle2 = OpenLocalSemaphore(1L);
   semHandle3 = OpenLocalSemaphore(3L);
   atexit(UnloadFunction);       // register unload function
   /* do further initialization */
   /* start child threads, thread groups, and so on */
   /* sleep or loop until unloaded */
   return(0); }
```

The code segment in listing 13.4 is a template that demonstrates how a multithreaded NLM that uses local semaphores should close those local semaphores. Note that, although large portions of code are missing from the template, the basic technique for closing local semaphores remains intact.

System Semaphores

System semaphores work much like local semaphores. Unlike local semaphores, however, system semaphores are available to all NLMs running on a NetWare server. System semaphores are also different from local semaphores in that they have a name in addition to a semaphore handle. The semaphore name enables multiple NLMs to gain access to a single system semaphore.

System semaphores require slightly more overhead on the part of the operating system to create and maintain. The extra overhead is relatively slight, however, and certainly is worth the system-wide access they provide.

Opening System Semaphores

To open a system semaphore, an NLM calls the API `OpenSemaphore`. The prototype for `OpenSemaphore` is as follows:

```
int    OpenSemaphore(
        char * __semaphoreName,
        int __initialValue,
        long * __semaphoreHandle,
        WORD * __openCount );
```

The first parameter, `semaphoreName`, is a character string that contains the name of the semaphore to be opened. The second parameter, `initialValue`, indicates how many threads (or NLMs) may gain access to the resource associated with the semaphore. The final parameter, `openCount`, contains the number of threads (or NLMs) that currently have the semaphore open.

The identity of the system semaphore is determined solely by its name. The first time an NLM opens a specific system semaphore (as determined by its name), the operating system creates that semaphore and returns a handle for it to the calling NLM. Subsequent openings of a specific semaphore cause the operating system to return a handle to the calling NLM but do not cause the operating system to create the system semaphore (it has been created already). The second parameter, `initialValue`, is effective only when the operating system creates a new system semaphore. When an NLM calls `OpenSemaphore` to open an existing system semaphore, the operating system ignores the second parameter. Listing 13.5 demonstrates the way to open a system semaphore.

Listing 13.5:

Opening a system semaphore.

```
#include <nwsync.h>
LONG semHandle;
WORD openCount;
int ccode;
ccode = OpenSemaphore("SemaphoreOne",
                      1,
                      &semhandle,
                      &openCount);
if (ccode != 0)
   {
   printf("\nError opening system semaphore");
   return(-1);
   }
printf("\nThreads which have opened SemaphoreOne: %i",
        openCount);
```

In listing 13.5, the name of the opened system semaphore, `SemaphoreOne`, is a global value: all NLMs (or threads) that open this specific semaphore must specify the name exactly as it appears in listing 13.5. The system semaphore handle (parameter 3) returned by the call to `OpenSemaphore`, however, is a local handle, available to only the calling NLM. With system semaphores, therefore, NLMs use local handles to gain access to system-wide resources.

Waiting On and Signaling System Semaphores

Waiting on and signaling system semaphores is much like waiting on and signaling local semaphores. The prototype for WaitOnSemaphore is as follows:

```
int    WaitOnSemaphore(
          long __semaphoreHandle,
          WORD __timeoutLimit );
```

The first parameter, semaphoreHandle, is the same handle returned by the call to OpenSemaphore (refer to listing 13.5). The second parameter, timeoutLimit, establishes an upper time limit for how long the calling NLM (or thread) sleeps while waiting for the resource associated with the system semaphore to become available. When you are calling WaitOnSemaphore, you specify timeoutLimit in *system ticks* (there are approximately 18 system ticks in every second). To wait one second for a resource to become available, you pass 18 as the timeoutLimit parameter.

If the call to WaitOnSemaphore returns 0, the calling NLM knows that the resource has become free, and it can start to gain access to the resource. If the call to WaitOnSemaphore returns "254," however, the calling NLM knows that it reached the time limit indicated by the parameter timeoutLimit and that the resource is not yet available. In this case, the calling NLM must decide what to do next: try again or give up attempting to gain access to the resource. The prototype for signaling a system semaphore is as follows:

```
int    SignalSemaphore(long __semaphoreHandle );
```

The only parameter, semaphoreHandle, is the same handle that was returned to the NLM when it opened the semaphore.

Closing System Semaphores

Closing system semaphores is much like closing local semaphores. Closing a system semaphore, however, does not necessarily cause the operating system to delete that system semaphore; rather, it deletes the calling NLM's handle to the system semaphore. Only the last NLM to have the system semaphore open causes the operating system to delete the system semaphore.

Three NLMs, for example, open a system semaphore. NLM 1 then closes the system semaphore, which causes the operating system to delete NLM 1's handle, but the system semaphore remains open. Next, NLM 2 closes the system semaphore, with the same consequences. Finally, NLM 3 closes the system semaphore, and the operating system deletes the system semaphore.

The prototype for `CloseSemaphore` is as follows:

```
int    CloseSemaphore(
        long __semaphoreHandle );
```

The single parameter, `semaphoreHandle`, is the same handle that was returned when the NLM called `OpenSemaphore`. NLMs should use the same method for closing system semaphores as for closing local semaphores—that is, to register an unload function that closes system semaphores.

Exploring Shared Memory

Shared memory is a basic, powerful form of IPC. It is simply an area of memory that is addressable by multiple NLMs. The NetWare operating system uses shared memory heavily, including screen buffers, file-cache buffers, and much more. NLMs may also use shared memory to provide IPC.

Some uses of shared memory in a multithreaded DP application include buffering user data, buffering file-access information, buffering portions of the data dictionary, and storing global data structures such as transaction information. Perhaps the simplest use of shared memory implements a "home-grown" semaphore, as in THREAD.NLM. As you may recall, THREAD.NLM uses a global variable called `screen` to control interthread contention for the single NLM screen. In this case, the global variable `screen` is a simple instance of shared memory masquerading as a semaphore.

NLM Shared-Memory Mechanics

Because NetWare has no memory protection, implementing shared memory is exceedingly simple. Other operating systems, such as OS/2, require a special shared memory API because—under normal conditions—memory sharing is an error condition. The following procedure for implementing shared memory in an NLM involves both exporting and importing the address of the memory to be shared.

To export shared memory:

1. Declare the address of shared memory as a global variable

2. In the linker-definition file, include the name of the global variable in the NLM's export list

To import shared memory:

1. Declare the address of shared memory as an external variable

2. In the linker-definition file, include the name of the global variable in the NLM's import list

Listings 13.6 and 13.7 use code segments and a linker-definition file template to demonstrate the mechanics of shared memory.

Both listings share a global data structure that contains user information.

Listing 13.6:
The mechanics of exporting a shared memory variable.

```
typedef struct userInfo {
    LONG        userID;
    char        userName[48];
    BYTE        networkAddress[12];
    time_t      loginTime;
}USER_INFO;
USER_INFO users[24];    // Declare globally an array of
userInfo
                        // structures. This is the address of
                        // shared memory.
/* Remainder of NLM maintains array of userInfo structures,
/* tracking user logins and filling in the rest of the user */
/* information. */
/* end of C code segment */
## segment of linker definition file
copyright "Copyright String"
debug
description "description string"
import
    @i:\public\nwcnlm\imp\clib.imp
input
    i:\public\nwcnlm\imp\prelude.obj
    nlmname.obj
map
module  clib
output  <name of nlm>
screenname "NLM Screen"
type 0
version 1, 00, 0
threadname <name of nlm>
## export the address of shared memory
export users
## END OF FILE ##
```

In the C code segment in listing 13.6, notice that a user info structure is defined as a complex type. Notice also that an array of user information structures is declared as a global variable. Missing from the code segment in listing 13.6 is the body of the exporting NLM, including the code that fills in the userInfo array elements.

In the linker-definition file template in listing 13.6, notice the addition of the export key word at the end of the file. This key word informs the linker that it should make the address of the globally declared variable users "importable" by other NLMs.

Listing 13.7:

The mechanics of importing a shared memory variable.

```
typedef struct userInfo {
    LONG        userID;
    char        userName[48];
    BYTE        networkAddress[12];
    time_t      loginTime;
}USER_INFO;
extern USER_INFO users[];    // allow external linkage to
                             // structure declared globally
                             // in listing 13.6
/* code for displaying user info array elements */
int i;
for (i = 0; i < 24; i++)
{
    if (users[i].userID)
        {
        printf("\nUser name: %s; user ID: %#08lx",
                users[i].userName, users[i].userID);
        }
}
/* end of C code segment */
## segment of linker definition file
```

```
copyright "Copyright String"
debug
description "description string"
import
   @i:\public\nwcnlm\imp\clib.imp
## import the shared memory address
   users
input
   i:\public\nwcnlm\imp\prelude.obj
   nlmname.obj
map
module  clib
output  <name of nlm>
screenname "NLM Screen"
type 0
version 1, 00, 0
threadname <name of nlm>
## END OF FILE ##
```

Look at the differences between listings 13.6 and 13.7. Both C code segments require the type definition of the `userInfo` structure. (Typically, this type definition is part of a header file.) Near the top of listing 13.6, the importing NLM declares `users`—the array of `userInfo` structures—as an external variable. This declaration lays the groundwork for the external linkage that ultimately is accomplished by the NetWare linker and loader. Finally, the linker-definition file template in listing 13.7 imports `users`, which is the same variable exported in listing 13.6.

Additional Shared-Memory Information

By following the simple steps outlined for exporting and importing shared memory, NLMs can communicate with each other by using shared memory. Because the NLM programmer determines the size, format, and meaning of shared-memory areas, you have total freedom when you are implementing shared memory. It means also, however, that both the exporting and the importing

NLM must agree on the format and meaning of shared-memory areas.

The importing NLM, however, does not have to know the size of a shared-memory area until run time. In listing 13.7, the importing NLM does not have an array size operand in its declaration of the external variable `users`. The importing NLM has to have some way of discovering the end of the shared-memory area.

After an exporting NLM makes a memory address available for importing by other NLMs, there is no limit on the number of NLMs that import the shared memory. This capability is both a powerful and a potentially dangerous feature. For this reason, an NLM that exports shared memory may have to limit the methods that other NLMs use to gain access to the first NLM's exported memory area. Perhaps the easiest way of limiting the methods is to implement an exported semaphore (or an exported variable masquerading as a semaphore) that importing NLMs must check before gaining access to the shared-memory area.

T̲I̲P If you want to be extra careful when you are using shared memory, you can implement an API that importing NLMs must call to gain access to shared memory. Most experienced C programmers can quickly implement this type of API if they understand NetWare's shared-memory mechanics.

Working with Shared Files (Pipes)

The last method of NetWare IPC described in this chapter is shared files, or pipes. *Pipes* are widely used in UNIX for IPC, but perhaps are most well-known as an OS/2 IPC method called named pipes. (In OS/2, *named pipes* are shared files available across a network.)

Although NetWare has no specific API for implementing pipes, implementing them is simple, even for network-wide pipes, because NetWare's file system API is designed for network-wide access. A server-based DP application, for example, may open files that reside on a remote server by using the same API used for opening files that reside on the local server.

How Pipes Work

Pipes are similar in principle to shared memory. Although shared memory uses system RAM as a medium for IPC, pipes use secondary storage in general, and the file system in particular, as a medium for IPC.

You can think of pipes as having a head and a tail. Data is introduced at the *head* of the pipe and extracted at the *tail* of the pipe. A good analogy is the Alaska oil pipeline. Wells and pumps fill the pipeline with oil. The oil courses through the pipeline until it reaches the terminal. At the terminal, operators choose the location where the oil goes next: a super tanker or a storage tank. The wells and pumps are analogous to the pipe head, and the super tankers and storage tanks are analogous to the pipe tail.

In NetWare, an NLM wanting to export shared data opens a file only for writing (the pipe head). An NLM waiting to import the shared data opens the same file only for reading (the pipe tail). To export data, the first NLM writes data to the file, and the second NLM imports data by reading it from the same file. This process is all there is to implementing pipes in NetWare, except for some important details, as shown in this list and discussed in the remainder of this chapter:

❖ Controlling access to the pipe by locking the file

❖ Message format for exported (and imported) data

❖ Naming conventions for pipes

How To Control Access to Pipes

Because NetWare has no predefined API for implementing pipes, you make your own rules. One of the first things you have to decide about a specific pipe is a convention for writing data to the pipe. Do you want only one NLM to be capable of writing to the pipe, or do you want multiple NLMs to be capable of writing to the pipe?

If you want only one NLM to be capable of writing to the pipe, you must have that NLM (the exporting NLM) lock the pipe file with a shareable lock. A *shareable lock* enables other NLMs to read the pipe; only the locking NLM, however, can write data to the pipe.

If you want multiple NLMs to be capable of writing data to the pipe, you must ensure that only one NLM at a time can write data to the pipe—you must implement *record locking* (that is, lock a specific portion of the pipe file exclusively). When an NLM wants to export data by writing to the pipe, it first must gain a record lock for the portion of the pipe to which it wants to write data. After writing data to the pipe, the exporting NLM must release the lock and enable other NLMs also to export data to the pipe.

Chapter 14 discusses the specific file-system APIs you must use to implement these record and file locks.

Enabling only one NLM to export data to a pipe is much simpler than enabling multiple NLMs. The pipe becomes a much more powerful IPC medium, however, if you enable multiple NLMs to export data to the pipe. (Your decision is a result of the IPC requirements of your DP application.)

Writing and reading data to and from a pipe is similar to writing and reading data to and from a database file. Some of the same issues come into play—most notably concurrency control (record and file locking). Performance and transaction control, however, are rarely as important for pipes as they are for database files.

The Message Format for Exported and Imported Data

Another issue to consider when you are implementing pipes is the message format for pipe data. Just as in designing a database, the most important decision you make involves whether pipe data resides in fixed- or variable-length messages. Fixed-length messages are preferred because they make pipe-file maintenance much easier. Fixed-length pipe messages introduce other issues, however—specifically, what to do with pipe messages that are longer than a fixed-length pipe record. Listing 13.8 shows a simple (yet effective) format for fixed-length pipe messages.

Listing 13.8:
A simple, effective format for fixed-length pipe messages.

```
#define MESSAGE_SIZE 512
typedef struct pipeMessage {
   int     messageNumber;
   LONG    nextMessage;
   int    messageSize;
   BYTE   message[MESSAGE_SIZE];
}MESSAGE
```

The first element of the complex type `MESSAGE` (`messageNumber` in listing 13.8) is a control variable you can use to set and clear the status of the message. By placing a positive number in the `messageNumber` element, an exporting NLM marks this message as "active," which means that it contains new data. Later, when an importing NLM reads the data from an active message, it may clear the `messageNumber` element by setting it to 0. This action, in turn, marks the message as "cleared," which means that the exporting NLM can write a new message over the "cleared" message.

The second element of the `MESSAGE` type, `nextMessage`, provides a mechanism for exporting data that is larger than a single message. If an exporting NLM wants to export more data than will fit in a single message, it must split the data into multiple messages. The first `MESSAGE` node of a multimessage export contains the offset (within the pipe file) of the next node in the message. The exporting NLM therefore can chain a multinode message. The last message in the chain should contain a 0 in its `nextMessage` element. Also, single-node messages should contain a 0 in their `nextMessage` element.

When an importing NLM reads a multinode message, it reads and clears the first node and then moves to the offset position specified by `nextMessage`. It then reads the next node (from the offset contained in the preceding node's `nextMessage` element), clears the next node, and continues the process until it has read all nodes of the multinode message (and therefore has imported all the message data).

The third element of the `MESSAGE` type, `messageSize`, gives the length of data in a specific message node. Although the data field of a message node formatted as in listing 13.7 is 512 bytes, a specific message may contain far less than 512 bytes of exported data. The importing NLM therefore should not be forced to read the entire 512 bytes of data. The `messageSize` element informs the importing NLM exactly how many bytes it must read from the pipe file to obtain all the exported data for that message node.

The final element of the `MESSAGE` type, `message`, is an array of bytes that comprise the exported data contained by the message node. Using the C preprocessor, you can change the size of a message node data field by changing the definition of MESSAGE_SIZE.

Feel free to place other information that is useful to your DP application in the format for a message node. You may want to include a time stamp in each message node, for example. In that way, you can clear old messages from a pipe file, which may be necessary if no importing NLM passes through the pipe and clears exported messages. Another item you may want to include is the name of the thread that exported the message to the pipe.

Naming Conventions for Pipes

For an importing NLM to open a pipe for reading, it first must know the name of the pipe file. The NLM learns the name of the pipe file in several ways, including using shared memory. Regardless of how you choose to notify importing NLMs, however, you should develop a naming convention for pipes.

The first rule in your pipe-naming convention is that all pipe file paths contain a server name because using a server name in a NetWare file path automatically makes it possible to open that file, even if it resides on a remote server. Therefore, if you want your pipes to be readable and writeable from and to remote servers, include the server name in your pipe-naming convention.

The second rule is that all pipe files go in a special directory. For example, the file name

```
BULLET\SYS:PIPES
```

tells the system that BULLET is the name of the server, SYS is volume zero (all NetWare servers name their first volume SYS), and PIPES is a special subdirectory. Placing all pipes in a single directory makes it easier to secure pipes from access to users. You can make the PIPES directory inaccessible by users by making it out of bounds for everyone but the SUPERVISOR user.

Finally, all pipe files should have a common file-name extension, such as PIP. You should place non-alphabetic characters in pipe-file names, as shown in the following example:

```
BULLET\SYS:PIPES\$PIPE001.PIP
```

This convention reduces the likelihood that another user or application will try to create a file with the same name as a pipe file maintained by your DP application.

You can make your pipe-naming convention as simple or as complex as you want. You may want to include access information in the name of a pipe file, for example, such as whether multiple NLM can export data to the pipe.

Summary

This chapter discussed NetWare's IPC capabilities: local and system semaphores, shared memory, and pipes. NetWare provides a powerful yet easy-to-use semaphore API. You can choose to use local semaphores, which have a scope limited to a single NLM, or system semaphores, which have a server-wide scope. The primary purpose of semaphores in NetWare is to control access to shared resources such as NLM screens. You can also use semaphores to control thread execution, such as by putting threads to sleep and waking them.

Implementing shared memory in NetWare is exceedingly simple, primarily because NetWare has no memory protection. The mechanics of implementing shared memory include defining the address of shared memory as a global variable (exporting NLM) and defining the address of shared memory as an external variable (importing NLM). The exporting NLM must use in its linker-definition file the `export` key word and the name of the exported variable. Also, the importing NLM should use the `import` key word and the name of the imported variable in its linker-definition file.

Both the importing and exporting NLMs should agree to the format and meaning of shared-memory areas. The best way to do this is to define a common structure for shared-memory areas. Remember that multiple NLMs may import any shared-memory variables. You may need to implement some type of API by which NLMs can gain access to exported-memory areas.

Pipes, or shared files, are simple to implement in NetWare. Because NetWare has no predefined API for implementing pipes, you can implement them any way you want. Some of the factors you should consider when you are implementing pipes are how to control access to pipes (file and record locking), the message format for pipe data, and naming conventions for pipes. Because pipes are NetWare files, they are automatically available across the network.

Topics covered in this chapter:

Using Advanced File System APIs

Looking at the FILE10.NLM Source Code

Using Transaction-Tracking APIs

Chapter 14

Working with the NetWare File System

Much about the NetWare file system and its suitability for downsizing database applications has been discussed in this book. Chapter 5 described NetWare's advanced file system capabilities; Chapters 6 and 8 explained how to configure your NetWare server for heavy-duty file system I/O. This chapter looks "under the hood" to show you how to take advantage of NetWare's file system when you are creating DP applications.

Chapter 11 explained that NetWare's development environment has a full suite of ANSI C and POSIX run-time libraries. These libraries include standard file I/O APIs such as `fopen`, `open`, `fread`, `read`, `fwrite`, `write`, `fseek`, and `lseek`. All of these standard I/O APIs are completely compliant in their calling conventions, behavior, and return values.

NetWare also provides a set of advanced file I/O APIs. These advanced file I/O APIs do not conform to any industry-wide standards; rather, they make use of specific features of the NetWare file system.

As a group, NetWare's advanced file I/O APIs provide greater performance than do the standard file I/O APIs—performance is the name of the game in NetWare's file system.

Before discussing NetWare's advanced file I/O APIs in depth, you should understand a couple of concepts. First, you can safely ignore advanced file I/O APIs if you are porting an existing C program to NetWare. When you are porting an application from one operating system to another, your first priority should be to achieve operational status. NetWare's standard file I/O APIs are good performers and are completely portable. You therefore should consider implementation of NetWare's advanced file I/O APIs as optimization tools rather than as requirements for a true NetWare implementation of an existing DP application.

NetWare's advanced file I/O APIs are not portable. They have no direct counterparts on other operating systems. If you use them, remember that they do not transfer to other systems.

The centerpiece of this chapter is the demonstration program FILEIO.NLM. This program performs timed I/O operations using all of the advanced APIs discussed in this chapter. Furthermore, FILEIO.NLM performs advanced I/O operations, both with and without record locking. FILEIO.NLM demonstrates how to use NetWare's advanced I/O APIs and their record-locking techniques.

The C source code for FILEIO.NLM is shown later in this chapter, in listing 14.1.

Using Advanced File System APIs

NetWare's advanced file I/O APIs are a set of nonstandard, performance-oriented routines for reading from and writing to files on a NetWare volume. The following two routines are the advanced routines for writing to files:

❖ qwrite

❖ gwrite

The following two routines are the advanced routines for reading from files:

❖ qread

❖ AsyncRead

Using qwrite

The qwrite API routine is a lower-level version of the POSIX standard write API. qwrite is faster than write because it does not maintain a *file position* (the position within the file at which the next read or write operation will take place). The following code shows the prototype for qwrite:

```
#include <advanced.h>
int qwrite(int handle, void *buf, LONG size, LONG
position)
```

The first parameter to qwrite, handle, is a POSIX file handle, which you can obtain by calling the standard POSIX open API. The second parameter, buf, is a pointer to a (type void) memory address that contains the data you want to write to the file. (In ANSI C, a *pointer to type void* means that the memory address pointed to is of no particular C type.)

The third parameter, size, specifies how many bytes of data you want to write to the file. The final parameter, position, indicates the offset within the file in which you want the write operation to begin. The write operation begins at the offset indicated by `position` and continues for `size` bytes.

The calling convention for `qwrite` is the same for the POSIX `write` API, except that you must specify the position. (Standard file I/O APIs maintain the file position for you.)

Using `gwrite`

The `gwrite` API is one of NetWare's two most spectacular advanced file I/O APIs (the other one is `AsyncRead`). `gwrite` enables you to write data from a number of different memory addresses directly to a file by making a single call. Your DP application, for example, maintains changes to the data dictionary in a series of change records, which are buffered in a *linked list* of memory addresses. By definition, a *linked list* consists of a chain of uncontiguous memory locations. Using `gwrite`, you can flush all the change records from their uncontiguous memory addresses to the data dictionary file by making one call. This process is not only a fast way of transferring data from memory to file, but also it is simpler than transferring the data using multiple calls to `write`. The following code shows the prototype for `gwrite`:

```
typedef struct mwriteBufferStructure
    {
    char *mwriteBufferPointer;
    LONG  mwriteBufferLength;
    int   reserved;
    } T_mwriteBufferStructure;
#include <advanced.h>
int gwrite(int handle,
           T_mwriteBufferStructure *bufferP,
           LONG numberOfBuffers,
           LONG *numberOfBuffersWritten);
```

The first parameter to `gwrite`, `handle`, is a standard POSIX file handle you can obtain by calling `open`. The second parameter, `bufferP`, is a pointer to an array of type `T_mwriteBufferStructure`. Each element in the array pointed to by `bufferP` contains a pointer to a memory address of data you want to write to the file. To write data from 100 separate memory addresses to a file, for example, you declare an array of 100 `T_mwriteBufferStructure` elements. Each element points to a memory address of data to be written, and indicates the length of data to write from that address to the file.

The third parameter to `gwrite`, `numberOfBuffers`, indicates the size of the `T_mwriteBufferStructure` array pointed to by the second parameter (`bufferP`). The fourth parameter, `numberOfBuffersWritten`, receives the number of buffers `gwrite` was able to flush to the data file.

The `gwrite` API is considerably more difficult to call than a standard API. It is also incredibly fast, however, and can be easier to call generally because it has the potential to replace hundreds of separate calls to `write`, `fwrite`, or `qwrite`.

If you do not understand how to set up and call `gwrite`, be patient: `gwrite` is shown in FILEIO.NLM (the C source code is shown in listing 14.1).

Using `qread`

The `qread` API is a direct counterpart of `qwrite`, and has the same characteristics. Specifically, `qread` is faster than the POSIX standard `read` API, but it doesn't maintain a file position. The following code shows the prototype for `qread`:

```
#include <advanced.h>
int qread(int  handle, void *buf, LONG size, LONG
position)
```

Each parameter to `qread` corresponds to the same parameter in `qwrite`.

Using AsyncRead

`AsyncRead`, another advanced I/O API, enables you to read file data directly from NetWare's file-cache buffers. When a file is cached (it becomes cached through normal access), using `AsyncRead` is essentially as fast as performing memory-to-memory copies of data. This capability translates into performance that is faster than standard APIs such as `read` and `fread`. When you must perform record locking before reading data, however, `AsyncRead` performs as well as other APIs. The prototype for `AsyncRead` is as follows:

```
typedef struct cacheBufferStructure
    {
    char *cacheBufferPointer;
    LONG  cacheBufferLength;
    int   completionCode;
    } T_cacheBufferStructure;
#include <advanced.h>
extern int AsyncRead(int handle,
                    LONG startingOffset,
                    LONG numberOfBytesToRead,
                    LONG
*numberOfBytesActuallyRead,
                    LONG localSemaphoreHandle,
                    T_cacheBufferStructure
**cacheBufferInformation,
LONG *numberOfCacheBuffers );
```

As in all of the advanced I/O APIs discussed in this chapter, the first parameter to `AsyncRead`, `handle`, is a standard POSIX file handle that you can obtain by calling `open`. The second parameter, `startingOffset`, indicates the position within the data file from which you want the read operation to begin. The third parameter, `numberOfBytesToRead`, indicates how many bytes you want to read from the data file.

The fourth parameter to `AsyncRead`, `numberOfBytesActuallyRead`, receives the number of bytes read from the data file as a result of your call to `AsyncRead`. You can use this parameter to determine the success of the call. This success, by its nature, is not an all-or-nothing proposition.

The fifth parameter to `AsyncRead`, `localSemaphoreHandle`, is the handle of a local semaphore. You must open a local semaphore before calling `AsyncRead`. After calling `AsyncRead`, you must wait on the local semaphore: The operating system awakens your thread when it has fulfilled all the requests you made by calling `AsyncRead`.

SEE ALSO Local semaphores are described in detail in Chapter 13.

The sixth parameter to `AsyncRead`, `cacheBufferInformation`, is a pointer to a pointer to an array of type `T_cacheBufferStructure`. The array contains the information you need to copy data directly from file-cache memory to its ultimate destination.

The final parameter to `AsyncRead`, `numberOfCacheBuffers`, receives the size of the array pointed to by the sixth parameter (`cacheBufferInformation`). You need the information returned in `numberOfCacheBuffers` to control the retrieving of file data from cache memory.

After calling `AsyncRead`, you should call `AsyncRelease`, which frees the array of cache-buffer structures allocated by the operating system as a result of your call to `AsyncRead`. Notice, however, that if you call `AsyncRelease` before you have retrieved the information you need from cache-buffer memory, you lose access to that information.

`AsyncRead` and `AsyncRelease` are shown in FILEIO.NLM, in the C source code shown in listing 14.1.

Looking at the FILEIO.NLM Source Code

Listing 14.1 displays the complete source code for FILEIO.NLM, which is a demonstration program that performs NetWare advanced file I/O APIs with and without record locking. It displays also the times required to execute the various APIs.

Listing 14.1:

The source code for builFILEIO.NLM.

```
/***********************************************************************
*        FILEIO.NLM                                                    *
*                                                                      *
*  Special test NLM to gauge performance of advanced file I/O APIs     *
*----------------------------------------------------------------------*
*                                                                      *
* filename       : fileio.c                                            *
* date           : Aug 25 1992                                         *
* version        : 1.0                                                 *
* compiler       : Watcom C 386 (see makefile for cc options)          *
*                                                                      *
* Copyright 1992, Michael Day. This work (and portions of it)          *
* may be freely copied, altered, and distributed, either in source     *
* or binary form, provided that it is not used for commercial purposes,*
* except as a teaching tool to demonstrate network programming.        *
*                                                                      *
***********************************************************************/
#include <stdio.h>
#include <time.h>
#include <nwsemaph.h>
#include <string.h>
```

```c
#include <errno.h>
#include <stddef.h>
#include <io.h>
#include <fcntl.h>
#include <share.h>
#include <sys\stat.h>
#include <nwsync.h>
#include <advanced.h>
typedef struct ioBuf {
   struct ioBuf *next;
   BYTE *buf;
}IOBUF;
IOBUF iobufs[300];
T_mwriteBufferStructure gBufs[300];
T_cacheBufferStructure *aBufs;
LONG blocksize, operations, semHandle, handle, switchFlag;
void usage(void)
{
printf("\nUSAGE: FILEIO <blocksize> <operations> [-s]");
printf("\n\tWhere <blocksize> is the size of each I/O operation");
printf("\n\tin bytes, and <operations> is the number of reads");
printf("\n\tand writes performed for each type file I/O API\n");
printf("\n\n-s causes a ThreadSwitch after every I/O operation");
}
void cleanup(void)
{
   CloseLocalSemaphore(semHandle);
   return;
}
int main(int argc, char **argv)
{
   int index, ccode, i, bufIndex;
   LONG position, gwrites, areads;
   time_t start, end, total;
   BYTE buf[25];
   char *p;
   if (argc < 3)
      {
      usage();         // print help screen if not enough
      return(0);       // command-line arguments
      }
   atexit(cleanup);
```

```
/*** process command-line arguments ***/
blocksize = atol(argv[1]);        // get the block size
operations = atol(argv[2]);       // get the number of operations
if (operations > 300)             // maximum operations: 300
   operations = 300;
p = strchr(argv[3], '-');         // check for ThreadSwitch
if (p != NULL)                    // option
   if (*(p + 1) == 's' || *(p + 1) == 'S')
      switchFlag = 1;
   else
      switchFlag = 0;
/*** Open a local semaphore for use with AsyncRead ***/
semHandle = OpenLocalSemaphore(0L);
/*** Allocate buffers for I/O operations ***/
for (index = 0; index < operations; index++)
   {
   iobufs[index].buf = (BYTE *)malloc(blocksize);
   if (!iobufs[index].buf)
      {
      printf("\nUnable to allocate working buffer");
      goto Exit;
      }
   memset(iobufs[index].buf, '1', blocksize);
   }
/*** Try to open a test file. If you get an ***/
/*** error, try again with a different name ***/
for(i = 0; i < 100; i++)
   {
   sprintf(buf, "SYS:file%i.dat", i);
   handle = creat(buf, 0);
   if (handle != -1)
      break;
   }
if (i == 99)
   {
   printf("\nUnable to open test file: %s", strerror(errno));
   goto Exit;
   }
/****************************************************************
* WRITE TESTS                                                  *
****************************************************************/
   /* To get a baseline, you do some normal writes. */
```

```
/* First, you get a time with no record locking. */
start = clock();              // get beginning time
for (i = 0; i < 100; i++)
   {
   for (index = 0; index < operations; index++)
      {
      ccode = write(handle, iobufs[index].buf, blocksize);
      if (switchFlag)
         ThreadSwitch();
         }
   ccode = lseek(handle, 0L, SEEK_SET);
   }
end = clock();               // get ending time
total = end - start;
printf("\nwrite() no locks; %li bytes: %li hundredths of \
      a second", ((blocksize * operations) * 100),
         total);
/* Now you get a time with record locking. */
/* You set read/write exclusive locks.     */

start = clock();
for (i = 0; i < 100; i++)
   {
   position = 0;
   ccode = lseek(handle, 0L, SEEK_SET);
   for (index = 0; index < operations; index++)
      {
      ccode = LogPhysicalRecord(
                handle,
                position,
                blocksize,
                0x01,          // read/write exclusive
                18);           // timeout in 18 ticks
      ccode = write(handle, iobufs[index].buf, blocksize);
      ccode = ClearPhysicalRecord(   // clear the lock
                handle,
                position,
                blocksize);
      position += blocksize;
      if (switchFlag)
         ThreadSwitch();
         }
```

```
      }
   end = clock();
   total = end - start;
   printf("\nwrite() with locks; %li bytes: %li hundredths of \
         a second", (blocksize * operations * 100),
          total);
   /* Now that you have a baseline, try qwrite().    */
   /* Note: qwrite does not maintain a file position, */
   /* so you have to do that yourself.                */
   /* get a time without record locking */
   start = clock();
   for (i = 0; i < 100; i++)
      {
      position = 0;
      for (index = 0; index < operations; index++)
         {
         ccode = qwrite(handle, iobufs[index].buf, blocksize,
                      position);
         position += blocksize;
         if (switchFlag)
            ThreadSwitch();
         }
      }
   end = clock();
   total = end - start;
   printf("\nqwrite() no locks; %li bytes: %li hundredths of \
         a second", (blocksize * operations * 100),
          total);
   /* get a time with record locking */
   start = clock();
   for (i = 0; i < 100; i++)
      {
      for (index = 0, position = 0;
          index < operations;
          index++, position += blocksize)
            {
            ccode = LogPhysicalRecord(
                       handle,
                       position,
                       blocksize,
                       0x01,
                       18);
```

```
        ccode = qwrite(handle, iobufs[index].buf, blocksize,
                    position);
        ccode = ClearPhysicalRecord(
                    handle,
                    position,
                    blocksize);
        if (switchFlag)
          ThreadSwitch();
        }
    }
end = clock();
total = end - start;
printf("\nqwrite() with locks; %li bytes: %li hundredths of \
      a second", (blocksize * operations * 100),
        total);
 /* gwrite no locks */
for (index = 0; index < operations; index++)
    {
    gBufs[index].mwriteBufferPointer = iobufs[index].buf;
    gBufs[index].mwriteBufferLength = blocksize;
    }
start = clock();
 for (i = 0; i < 100; i++)
    {
    ccode = lseek(handle, 0L, SEEK_SET);
    ccode = gwrite(handle, &gBufs[0], operations, &gwrites);
    }
 end = clock();
total = end - start;
printf("\ngwrite() no locks; %li bytes: %li hundredths of \
      a second", (blocksize * operations * 100),
        total);
 /* gwrite with locks */
 for (index = 0; index < operations; index++)
    {
    gBufs[index].mwriteBufferPointer = iobufs[index].buf;
    gBufs[index].mwriteBufferLength = blocksize;
    }
start = clock();
for (i = 0, position = 0; i < 100; i++)
    {
    ccode = lseek(handle, 0L, SEEK_SET);
```

```
    ccode = LogPhysicalRecord(
            handle,
            position,
            (blocksize * operations),
            0x01,
            18);
    ccode = gwrite(handle, &gBufs[0], operations, &gwrites);
    ccode = ClearPhysicalRecord(
            handle,
            position,
            (blocksize * operations));
    }
  end = clock();
  total = end - start;
  printf("\ngwrite() with locks; %li bytes: %li hundredths of \
        a second", (blocksize * operations * 100),
          total);
/****************************************************************
* READ TESTS                                                    *
****************************************************************/
/* to get a baseline, you do tests using the normal read() API */
  /* first with no record locking */
  start = clock();
  for (i = 0; i < 100; i++)
      {
    ccode = lseek(handle, 0L, SEEK_SET);
    for (index = 0; index < operations; index++)
        {
      ccode = read(handle, iobufs[index].buf, blocksize);
      if (switchFlag)
        ThreadSwitch();
        }
      }
  end = clock();
  total = end - start;
  printf("\nread() no locks; %li bytes: %li hundredths of \
       a second", (blocksize * operations * 100),
         total);
/* Again with record locks. This time, you set read-only locks. */
  start = clock();
  for (i = 0; i < 100; i++)
      {
```

```
    ccode = lseek(handle, 0L, SEEK_SET);
    for (index = 0, position = 0;
         index < operations;
         index++, position += blocksize)
       {
      ccode = LogPhysicalRecord(
                  handle,
                  position,
                  blocksize,
                  0x03,
                  18);
      ccode = read(handle, iobufs[index].buf, blocksize);
      ccode = ClearPhysicalRecord(
                  handle,
                  position,
                  blocksize);
      if (switchFlag)
        ThreadSwitch();
      }
    }
end = clock();
total = end - start;
printf("\nread() with locks; %li bytes: %li hundredths of \
     a second", (blocksize * operations * 100),
      total);
/* Now get a time for qread() no locks */
start = clock();
for (i = 0; i < 100; i++)
   {
   for (index = 0, position = 0;
        index < operations;
        index++, position += blocksize)
      {
     ccode = qread(handle, iobufs[index].buf, blocksize,
                 position);
     if (switchFlag)
       ThreadSwitch();
     }
   }
end = clock();
total = end - start;
printf("\nqread() no locks; %li bytes: %li hundredths of \
```

```
            a second", (blocksize * operations * 100),
              total);
    /* time qread() with locks */
    start = clock();
    for (i = 0; i < 100; i++)
        {
        for (index = 0, position = 0;
             index < operations;
             index++, position += blocksize)
            {
          ccode = LogPhysicalRecord(
                      handle,
                      position,
                      blocksize,
                      0x03,
                      18);
          ccode = qread(handle, iobufs[index].buf, blocksize,
                        position);
          ccode = ClearPhysicalRecord(
                      handle,
                      position,
                      blocksize);
          if (switchFlag)
            ThreadSwitch();
            }
        }
    end = clock();
    total = end - start;
    printf("\nqread() with locks; %li bytes: %li hundredths of \
          a second", (blocksize * operations * 100),
            total);
    /* Async read no locks */
    close(handle);
    handle = open(buf, O_RDWR | O_BINARY);
    if (handle == -1)
        {
        printf("\nError re-opening file for async calls: %s",
              strerror(errno));
        goto Exit;
        }
    start = clock();
    for (i = 0; i < 100; i++)
        {
```

```
    for (index = 0, position = 0;
        index < operations;
        index ++, position += blocksize)
        {
      ccode = AsyncRead(
                handle,
                position,
                blocksize,
                &areads,
                semHandle,
                &aBufs,
                &gwrites);
      ccode = WaitOnLocalSemaphore(semHandle);
      AsyncRelease(aBufs);
      if (switchFlag)
         ThreadSwitch();
        }
    }
end = clock();
total = end - start;
printf("\nAsyncRead() no locks; %li bytes: %li hundredths of \
    a second", (blocksize * operations * 100),
     total);
/* AsyncRead with locks */
start = clock();
for (i = 0; i < 100; i++)
    {
    for (index = 0, position = 0;
        index < operations;
        index++, position += blocksize)
        {
      ccode = LogPhysicalRecord(
                handle,
                position,
                blocksize,
                0x03,
                18);
       ccode = AsyncRead(
                handle,
                position,
                blocksize,
                &areads,
                semHandle,
```

```
                    &aBufs,
                    &gwrites);
        ccode = WaitOnLocalSemaphore(semHandle);
        ccode = ClearPhysicalRecord(
                    handle,
                    position,
                    blocksize);
            AsyncRelease(aBufs);
            if (switchFlag)
                ThreadSwitch();
            }
        }
    end = clock();
    total = end - start;
    printf("\nAsyncRead() with locks; %li bytes: %li hundredths \
            of a second", (blocksize * operations * 100),
            total);
Exit:
    close(handle);
    unlink(buf);
    for (index = 0; index < operations; index++)
        if (iobufs[index].buf != NULL)
            free(iobufs[index].buf);
    return(0);
}
```

Building FILEIO.NLM

Listing 14.2 is a make file you can use to build FILEIO.NLM. A
make file provides input to a make utility. The *make utility* issues all
the commands necessary to create the target file (FILEIO.NLM, in
this case). The make file in listing 14.2 is written for POLYMAKE,
which is a popular commercial make utility.

> If you are not familiar with make utilities (and make files),
> you can build FILEIO.NLM the old-fashioned way, as out-
> lined in Chapter 11: run the compiler, create the linker-defi-
> nition file, and run NLMLINK.

Listing 14.2:

A make file for building FILEIO.NLM.

```
#####
##### Simple make file
##### Useful for one source file
#####
##### Usage: make <nlmname> <Enter>
#####
##### For example, to make FILEIO.NLM, type
#####   make fileio.nlm <Enter>
.PROLOG:
      %if %exists(make.sem)
       @>
      @echo Somebody else is currently building $*
      @echo Try again later ...
       %exit 1
       %endif
.EPILOG:
       @>
      @echo Make session completed -
       @systime
       @>
.INIT:
      @systime > make.sem
      @castoff all
      @map p:=bullet\sys:public
      %setenv wcg386=$(BIN)\386wcgl.exe
      %setenv INC386=p:public\nwcnlm\include
.DEINIT:
       @del make.sem
       @caston all
### MACRO DEFINITIONS ###
TARG=$[r, $(FIRSTTARGET)]
BIN=w:\public\wcc90\bin
BINB=w:\public\wcc90\binb
LIB=p:\public\nwcnlm\import       # import list directory
INCLUDE=p:\public\nwcnlm\include  # include files directory
IMP=$(LIB)\CLIB.imp               # import file
EXP=$(TARG).exp                   # export file
OBJS=$(TARG).obj $(LIB)\prelude.obj  # object files
CCOPTS=/ez /od /3s /zq /d1        # compiler options
```

```
CCCMD=wcc386p                    # compiler command
LINKCMD=nlmlinkr                 # linker command
MODS= CLIB                       # auto-loaded NLMs
VER=1,0,0                        # version
### RULES FOR BUILDING THE NLM ###
.c.obj:
        @>
       @echo Compiling $<
        @>
       $(CCCMD) $(CCOPTS) $<
  wdisasm /l /s=$< $(TARG).obj
.obj.nlm:
       .LIS_FILE q:\users\miked\nlm\$(TARG).def
        @>
       @echo Linking $<
        @>
       nlmlinkr < <      ### LINKER DEFINITION FILE ###
COPYRIGHT    "Copyright 1992 Michael Day"
DEBUG
DESCRIPTION "Timing NLM--Advanced File I/O APIs"
IMPORT @$(IMP)
#EXPORT
INPUT $(OBJS)
MAP
MODULE $(MODS)
OUTPUT $(TARG)
SCREENNAME "FILEIO.NLM"
STACK 4096
TYPE 0
THREADNAME "FILEIO"
VERSION $(VER)
<
## END OF FILE
```

The make file shown in listing 14.2 uses several special features, implemented in POLYMAKE, that may not be available in other make utilities. Rather than maintain a separate linker-definition file for FILEIO.NLM, for example, the make file in listing 14.2 uses a *local input script*, which is simply a file created by the make utility and used as input for the link command. You probably recognize some of the linker-definition file key words near the bottom of listing 14.2; they are part of the local input script.

Although not all commercial make utilities have the capability to use a local input script (as POLYMAKE does), virtually all of them enable you to create input files for use with a linker. You should always use your make utility to maintain the linker-definition file.

The Inner Workings of FILEIO.NLM

FILEIO.NLM is relatively simple: after processing its command-line options and allocating its buffers, it executes Netware's advanced file I/O operations the specified number of times; each I/O operation is the specified size. FILEIO.NLM loops on each operation 100 times, which provides more data on which to base timing information.

 FILEIO.NLM performs each type of read or write API both with and without record locking. This capability enables you to perform timing with and without record locking, which may in turn help you to design your DP application.

The command-line option -s enables you to force FILEIO.NLM to relinquish control of the CPU after each file I/O operation. FILEIO.NLM relinquishes control by calling `ThreadSwitch` after each I/O operation returns. If you do not include -s on the command line when you are loading FILEIO.NLM, it does not call `ThreadSwitch`.

Record Locking in FILEIO.NLM

FILEIO.NLM uses two APIs to perform record locking: `ClearPhysicalRecord` and `LogPhysicalRecord`. `LogPhysicalRecord` enables you to attempt to gain a record lock. After you have the record lock, you can write data to the file. After you finish writing data to the file, you should clear the record lock. FILEIO uses `ClearPhysicalRecord` to clear the lock. The following code shows the prototypes for these two APIs:

```
#include <nwsync.h>
int LogPhysicalRecord(int handle,
                      LONG recordStartOffset,
                      LONG recordLength,
                      BYTE lockDirective,
                      WORD timeoutLimit)
int ClearPhysicalRecord(int handle,
                        LONG recordStartOffset,
                        LONG recordLength)
```

The first parameter to both APIs, `handle`, is a standard POSIX file handle you can obtain by calling the `open` API. The second and third parameters, `recordStartOffset` and `recordLength`, together define the locked area of the file.

The fourth parameter to `LogPhysicalRecord`, `lockDirective`, determines whether the NetWare operating system obtains a lock immediately or enables you to log further records for locking at a later time. FILEIO.NLM always passes either 0×01 or 0×03 as the lock directive. These two values indicate an immediate exclusive lock or an immediate shared lock, respectively. (The `read` APIs indicate an immediate shared lock, and the `write` APIs indicate an immediate exclusive lock.)

If your DP application is working with multiple data files and you want to lock a set of records within those files using one call, you specify 0×00 as the `lockDirective`. This action causes NetWare to log the group of records for locking at a later time. When you want to lock the group of records, you can do so by calling the `LockPhysicalRecordSet` API.

The last parameter to `LogPhysicalRecord`, `timeoutLimit`, indicates how long you are willing to wait for NetWare to gain the record lock you are requesting. You always specify the `timeoutLimit` in ticks. (There are approximately 18 ticks per second.)

Using Transaction-Tracking APIs

Chapter 5 described in detail NetWare's Transaction Tracking System (TTS). The following code segment shows you how to build TTS into your DP application. Listing 14.3, extracted from a demonstration program shown in Chapter 15, demonstrates the NetWare transmission control APIs.

Listing 14.3:

Code segment showing NetWare's TTS APIs.

```
/* This is where you write the new, updated, or deleted record to the */
/* database file. You use Transaction Tracking to ensure that failed  */
/* or partial writes do not damage the integrity of the data file.    */
/* Transaction Tracking automatically performs all necessary record   */
/* locks for you.                                                      */
printf("TTSBegin ...");
ccode = TTSBeginTransaction();
if (ccode && ccode != 0xff)
   {
   if(opNode->packet.operation == 0x02)   /* adding a new record */
     addInProgress = 0;
   return;
        }
printf("writing ...");
ccode = fwrite(&opNode->packet.record, sizeof(rec), 1, fp);
if (ccode != 1)
   {
   TTSAbortTransaction();
   if(opNode->packet.operation == 0x02)   /* adding a new record */
     addInProgress = 0;
   return;
   }
else
   {
   printf("TTSEnd\n");
   TTSEndTransaction(&opNode->packet.record.header.transactionNumber);
}
/***** END OF CODE SEGMENT *****/
```

Do not be concerned about the arcane structure references in listing 14.3. Just pay attention to the calls to `TTSBeginTransaction`, `TTSAbortTransaction`, and `TTSEndTransaction`. Adding transaction control to your DP application is as simple as calling these APIs.

Before writing records to one or more data files, you should make a call to `TTSBeginTransaction`. This call alone causes NetWare to log all further writes to data files, and also causes NetWare to gain exclusive record locks on the records to which you attempt to write data.

After calling `TTSBeginTransaction`, you call the appropriate file I/O API. (Listing 14.3 calls the ANSI `fwrite` API.) NetWare procures all necessary record locks and performs all transaction control automatically—your application does not have to do anything else.

If the write operation fails, you should call `TTSAbortTransaction`. This action restores all target data files to their original state. You then can retry the write operation.

Note that your data files must have their transactional attribute set before NetWare will initiate a transaction for them. You can set a file's transactional attribute programmatically (`SetExtendedFileAttributes`) or manually, by using the NetWare FLAG utility.

If the write operation succeeds, you should call `TTSEndTransaction`. This step enables the operating system to perform housekeeping, release record locks, and flush file-cache buffers.

Summary

This chapter discussed working with the NetWare file system. You saw examples of advanced file system APIs and learned ways to use them. You also looked at the FILE10.NLM source code in detail, which is a demonstration program that performs NetWare advanced file I/O APIs.

Finally, the chapter discussed ways to build the TTS into your DP application.

In the next chapter, you will learn ways to create client-server applications.

Topics covered in this chapter:

Looking inside IPX

Using the Client-Server File Manager

Listing the Client-Server Source Code

Chapter 15

IPX Message-Passing Architecture

In a *message-passing architecture*, two or more modules interact by exchanging messages. Technically, message-passing is an advanced form of IPC. It also is the lifeblood of a distributed, client-server application. A client can request a resource from a server, for example, by sending a *request message* to the server. The server, consequently, provides the requested resource by sending a *response message* to the client.

The basic request-response sequence (and other, more sophisticated variations) provides the low-level gears and levers that make distributed, client-server applications possible.

This chapter discusses message-passing using IPX, which is NetWare's native network communications protocol. To demonstrate IPX message-passing, a simple client-server database application is shown in this chapter. Both the client and server modules are written in the C programming language and use APIs and techniques discussed throughout this book.

After reading this chapter, you should understand more fully the benefits of client-server computing. Most important, however, is the knowledge of ways to implement a client-server DP application using NetWare; you will see that doing so is not as difficult as you may have imagined.

You will see also exactly how to use IPX to communicate over a network. For many experienced DP application programmers, programming techniques necessary for network communication remain a mystery—almost a "black art."

NetWare supports communications protocols in addition to IPX: AppleTalk, TCP/IP, and OSI, for example. Moreover, NetWare supports multiple transport protocol programming interfaces. Although the demonstration program in this chapter uses IPX as the foundation for its client-server protocol, your DP application may use any transport protocol supported by IPX. Furthermore, your DP application may use one of the standard transport protocol programming interfaces, such as the Transport Layer Interface (TLI) or Berkeley Sockets.

 Regardless of your DP application's specific transport protocol (or programming interface to the protocol), the basic principles demonstrated in this chapter apply to your DP application. The design of a client-server protocol, for example, which entails the format of request and response packets, is a universal issue for all distributed DP applications.

Looking Inside IPX

At its most basic level, IPX (or any network communications protocol) is a fancy way of copying a portion of a computer's memory to another computer's memory. To copy one memory buffer to another memory buffer in the same computer, for example, you use the C `memcpy` routine. To copy one memory buffer to a memory buffer in a different computer, however, you use IPX. The results of the two operations are the same, with the obvious difference that IPX enables you to copy memory among computers, and `memcpy` enables you to copy memory within a single computer.

All of the programming techniques that make using IPX different from a simple call to `memcpy` solve the problems associated with moving memory among machines. The media on which you move memory contents from one machine to another is the *internetwork*. IPX programming involves controlling the behavior of the media (the internetwork) so that you can transfer data among different physical computers.

Sending and Receiving Packets

Sending and receiving packets using IPX is initially a tricky process, but it is one that becomes familiar quickly. All IPX operations make use of a data structure called an *Event Control Block* (ECB). The purpose of an ECB is to describe fully a packet that an application wants to send or receive. Important information contained in an ECB includes the socket number on which to send or receive the packet and the address and length of buffers that contain the packet header and data. The ECB is defined in the file CLIENT.H, as follows:

```
typedef struct fragment {
  void far *fragAddress;        // DOS version. All pointers
  WORD fragSize;                // are NEAR for an NLM.
}ECBFragment;
typedef struct ecb {            // DOS version. NLM version
  void far *linkAddress;        // is slightly different.
  void far *ESRAddress;
  BYTE inUseFlag;
  BYTE completionCode;
  WORD socket;
  BYTE IPXWorkspace[4];
```

```
   BYTE driverWorkspace[12];
   BYTE immediateAddress[6];
   WORD fragCount;
   ECBFragment fragList[2];
}IPX_ECB;
```

Not all fields in an ECB must be initialized when you send or receive a packet. The `immediateAddress` field, for example, contains the network address of the nearest router that knows the path to the ultimate destination of the packet: you must initialize the `immediateAddress` field only when you are sending a packet.

The most important field in the ECB is the fragment descriptor field: It contains the address and length of the buffers that make up the packet. Buffer zero always must be the IPX header: other buffers can be anything the application defines, and combine to make up the data field of the packet.

When you send a packet, IPX copies the buffers described in the sending ECB's fragment descriptor field and combines them into a packet, which it sends over the network. When you receive a packet, IPX fragments the packet and copies the different components to the buffers described in the receiving ECB's fragment descriptor field.

When you are sending a packet, you also must initialize the packet's IPX header to contain the packet type (4 for IPX packets) and the destination address of the packet.

After you have initialized the ECB and (if necessary) the IPX header, you can post the ECB for sending or receiving by calling either `IPXSendPacket(IPX_ECB *)` or `IPXListenForPacket(IPX_ECB *)`.

The source code for both ENGINE.NLM and CLIENT.EXE contain many examples of the sequence necessary for sending and receiving packets.

Addresses and Sockets

An IPX address is a 12-byte field consisting of a network address (four bytes), a node address (six bytes), and a socket (two bytes). The *network address* is assigned at run time when you load network drivers (for both workstations and servers). The *node address* almost always is a function of the network adapter card installed in the machine. (The node address of a computer using Ethernet, for example, is the serial number of the computer's Ethernet adapter.)

The two-byte *socket* enables a single computer (regardless of whether it is a server or a workstation) to maintain multiple network sessions. If the IPX address did not have sockets, for example, all IPX packets addressed to a server would arrive at the same memory address within the server. By enabling different threads to insert different socket numbers into their 12-bit IPX addresses, an application can maintain multiple network communication sessions. That is, although a computer's network address and node address remain the same for as long as the computer has access to the network, the socket address may differ from application to application, from thread to thread, and even from moment to moment. The use of IPX sockets is demonstrated in detail in the source code later in this chapter.

 An IPX socket is much different from a TCP/IP socket. Remember that Berkeley Sockets is a popular programming interface to TCP/IP. In discussing IPX, do not confuse these different uses of "socket."

Immediate Address

You may have noticed the `ImmediateAddress` field in the ECB structure. The *immediate address* is the address of the nearest IPX router that knows the network route to the destination address of the packet. On a multiserver network, IPX routers act as "traffic cops," ensuring that packets traverse the internetwork and reach their destination. (Each NetWare server is also an IPX router.)

The immediate address provides all the information IPX requires to get the packet on its way. After it is moving, IPX routers take over and route the packet through the internetwork until it arrives at its ultimate destination. You can always obtain the immediate address of a specific packet by calling the `GetImmediateAddress` API. The source code included in this chapter demonstrates (more than once) how to obtain the immediate address.

TIP The use of an immediate address makes it easier to send and receive IPX packets across an internetwork. Specifically, you never have to know the entire route from one node on an internetwork to another node. You have to know only the address of the nearest router (the immediate address). After your packet gets to the nearest router, that router can send your packet across the internetwork to its ultimate destination.

Using the Client-Server File Manager

ENGINE.NLM and its client front end, CLIENT.EXE, together form a distributed-file manager for NetWare v3.11. ENGINE is a demonstration program designed to illustrate several key aspects of NLM development, including the following:

❖ Using IPX for client-server communications

❖ NLM thread control, including use of semaphores

❖ The Service Advertising Protocol (SAP)

❖ Transaction Tracking Services (TTS)

As a side-effect of these specific NLM development topics, EN-GINE also demonstrates multithreaded techniques in the context of nonpreemptive multitasking, and general issues such as NLM exit routines and the NLM development environment.

With the exception of IPX client-server programming, you already have read about the other aspects of NLM development demonstrated by ENGINE.NLM. ENGINE.NLM, however, provides a good way for you to consolidate all the information you have read about by placing it within the framework of a genuine distributed application.

ENGINE.NLM

ENGINE.NLM is the back end of a distributed-record manager. As a record manager, ENGINE is rather simple to be of practical use as a DP application. In all areas other than database management, however, ENGINE.NLM uses advanced NLM programming techniques. Because you are reading this book, you already know about database design and programming. The purpose of ENGINE.NLM, therefore, is to show you how to do what you do not know how to do. As you read about ENGINE.NLM and peruse its source code, think about how you can apply its design to your DP applications. The basic operation of ENGINE proceeds as follows:

1. Initialize.
2. Listen for request packets from clients.
3. When a request packet comes in, spawn a worker thread to perform the client's request.
4. Go to step 3.

The following operations are supported by ENGINE: adding a new record to the database; editing an existing record; reading an existing record; and marking an existing record as deleted. EN-GINE performs all the file I/O itself, on behalf of the client, 32 bits at a time.

A *record* consists of a *record header* and a *data structure*, both of which are defined in the files ENGINE.H and CLIENT.H, as follows:

```
typedef struct recordHeader {
unsigned long status;
unsigned long offset;
unsigned long hashkey;
unsigned long recordNumber;
unsigned long transactionNumber;
unsigned char key[128]; }rHeader;
typedef struct recordData {
time_t creationTime;
time_t lastReferenceTime;
time_t lastUpdateTime;
unsigned char nodeAddress[10];   /* node address of last updater */
unsigned long objectID;          /* object ID of last updater   */
unsigned char data[128]; }rData;
 typedef struct record {
rHeader header;
rData data; }
rec;
```

The status field of the `recordHeader` structure indicates the state of the record: 0 means that the record is deleted or free; 1 means that the record is occupied; and 2 means that the record is the special database header, always located at offset 0 of the data file. The offset field gives the offset of the record within the data file. The `hashkey` field is not used in this version of the record manager, but will be used in a future version that supports hashed keys. The `transactionNumber` field is used in conjunction with Transaction Tracking, a NetWare OS feature that preserves the integrity of data files during I/O errors. The `recordNumber` and key fields of the record header are self-explanatory.

The first three fields of the record's data portion indicate when the record was created, when it was last read or updated, and when it was last updated, respectively. The `nodeAddress` field gives the network address of the last station that requested an update of the record. The `objectID` field gives the NetWare ID of the user who last updated the record. The data field contains the record's data.

Note that an entire record—as much as 576 bytes, including the 30-byte IPX header—fits within a single IPX packet. This capability simplifies things considerably because ENGINE does not have to construct multipacket messages to send an entire record to the client, nor does the client have to defragment them. (Multipacket message support is implemented more easily using NetWare's Sequenced Packet eXchange, or SPX.)

CLIENT.EXE

CLIENT.EXE is the front-end component of the distributed-record manager. Although it provides all data input and display for the user, CLIENT performs absolutely no file I/O. It simply makes requests for the ENGINE.NLM to do so on its behalf and presents the results to the user. This action enables the application to take full advantage of the fast and robust NetWare file system.

The basic operation of CLIENT.EXE is as follows:

1. Initialize.
2. Scan for ENGINE.NLMs located on the internetwork.
3. Enable the user to select a specific ENGINE.
4. Enable the user to select specific operations.
5. Make a request of the ENGINE to perform the operation selected by the user.
6. Display the results of the requested operation.
7. Go to step 4.

CLIENT.EXE communicates with ENGINE.NLM by using a simple client-server protocol. Each packet contains an operation code that tells the ENGINE which operation the client is requesting.

Supported operations are defined in the source files ENGINE.H and CLIENT.H, as follows:

```
#define ADD_RECORD          0x02
#define FIND_RECORD_KEY     0x03
#define READ_RECORD         0xf5
#define EDIT_RECORD         0xf6
#define DELETE_RECORD       0x07
```

Each packet sent or received by either ENGINE or CLIENT consists of an IPX header and either a `shortPacket` or `longPacket` structure:

```
typedef struct ipxheader {
WORD checkSum;
WORD length;
BYTE transportControl;
BYTE packetType;
LONG destNet;
BYTE destNode[6];
WORD destSocket;
LONG sourceNet;
BYTE sourceNode[6];
WORD sourceSocket; }IPX_HEADER;
typedef struct shortPacket {
WORD responseCode;
BYTE operation;
rHeader header; }sPacket;
typedef struct longPacket {
WORD responseCode;
BYTE operation;
rec record; }
lPacket;
```

The only difference between the `shortPacket` and `longPacket` structures is that the `shortPacket` structure contains the record header, and the `longPacket` structure contains the entire record. Both structures have a `responseCode` field and a operation field.

The operation field contains the operation code of a client's request, and the `responseCode` field contains a value that is unique to each request-response sequence. CLIENT uses the `responseCode` field to verify the integrity of response packets it receives from the ENGINE NLM.

Client-Server Protocol

The client-to-server communication follows a simple sequence that is slightly different for each possible operation. The different sequences are as follows:

Add a record:

1. CLIENT enables the user to enter the record key and data fields.
2. CLIENT sends an `AddRecord` request to the ENGINE. The packet includes the entire record to be added.
3. ENGINE attempts to add the record to the data file.
4. ENGINE sends back to the client a response packet containing the record header.
5. CLIENT infers from the status field of the record header (contained in the response packet) whether the record was added successfully.

Read a record:

1. CLIENT enables the user to enter a record key.
2. CLIENT sends a `FindRecordKey` request to the ENGINE. The packet includes only the record header.
3. ENGINE attempts to find the matching record.
4. ENGINE sends back to the client a response packet containing the entire record.

5. CLIENT infers from the status field of the record header (contained in the response packet) whether the record was found.

6. If the record was found, CLIENT displays the record.

Edit a record:

Steps 1 through 5 are the same as in reading a record.

6. If the record was found, CLIENT displays the record and enables the user to edit the record's data field.

7. CLIENT sends an `EditRecord` request to ENGINE. The request packet contains the entire edited record.

8. ENGINE updates the record by writing the edited record to the data file.

9. ENGINE sends back to the client a response packet containing the updated record's header.

10. CLIENT infers from the updated record's status field whether the edit operation was successful.

Delete a record:

Steps 1 through 5 are same as in reading a record.

6. If the record was found, CLIENT changes the record's status field to 0.

Steps 7 through 10 are the same as in editing a record.

Listing the Client-Server Source Code

The source code for the distributed-record manager consists of two header files and two C files. For the NLM (back end) portion, the header file is ENGINE.H and the source file is ENGINE.C. For the DOS front end, the header file is CLIENT.H and the source file is CLIENT.C.

Listing 15.1:

Header file for ENGINE.NLM.

```
/***** FILENAME: ENGINE.H *****/
#include <stdio.h>
#include <stdlib.h>
#include <conio.h>
#include <process.h>
#include <nwsemaph.h>
#include <nwipxspx.h>
#include <nwtypes.h>
#include <nwdir.h>
#include <nwmisc.h>
#include <io.h>
#include <nwtts.h>
#include <advanced.h>
#include <string.h>
#include <direct.h>
#include <errno.h>
#include <signal.h>
#ifndef ENGINE_DEFINES
#define ENGINE_DEFINES
#define ENGINE_SOCKET       0x0099
#define INIT_SOCKET         0x0090
#define ENGINE_TYPE         0x88
#define ADD_RECORD          0x02
#define FIND_RECORD_KEY     0x03
#define FIND_RECORD_NO_KEY 0xf4
#define READ_RECORD         0xf5
#define EDIT_RECORD         0xf6
#define DELETE_RECORD       0x07
typedef struct recordHeader {
  unsigned long status;
  unsigned long offset;
  unsigned long hashkey;
  unsigned long recordNumber;
  unsigned long transactionNumber;
  unsigned char key[128];
}rHeader;             /* hex size of 0x94 */
typedef struct recordData {
  time_t creationTime;
  time_t lastReferenceTime;
  time_t lastUpdateTime;
```

```
    unsigned char nodeAddress[10]; /* node address of last updater */
    unsigned long objectID;        /* object ID of last updater    */
    unsigned char data[128];       /* hex size of 0x9a             */
}rData;
typedef struct record {
  rHeader header;
  rData data;
}rec;
typedef struct shortPacket {
  WORD responseCode;
  BYTE operation;
  rHeader header;
}sPacket;
typedef struct longPacket {
  WORD responseCode;
  BYTE operation;
  rec record;
}lPacket;
typedef struct initPacket {
  char dataFilePath[_MAX_PATH];
}iPacket;
typedef struct opnode {
  IPX_HEADER packetHeader;
  lPacket packet;
}ENGINE_OP_NODE;
#endif
/***** END OF FILE *****/
```

Listing 15.2:

The C source code file for ENGINE.NLM.

```
/**************************************************************************
*                                                                        *
* filename    : engine.c                                                 *
* date        : June 26 1992                                             *
* version     : 1.0                                                      *
* description : back end (NLM) for demonstration client-server record    *
*               manager.                                                 *
* compiler    : Watcom C 386 (see makefile for cc options)              *
*                                                                        *
**************************************************************************/
```

```
#include "engine.h"
/*---- Global Variables ----*/
LONG requestSem, replySem, shutdownSem;          // semaphore handles
char dataFileName[_MAX_PATH + 1];                // database file name
WORD engineSocket = ENGINE_SOCKET;               // primary dispatch socket
WORD initSocket = INIT_SOCKET;                   // initialization socket
int shutdown = 0, shutdownOK = 0;                // for a clean unload
FILE *fp;                                        // database file handle
LONG opNodeSpinCount, opNodeHighSpinCount = 0;   // information variables
LONG recordNumber = 0;                           // how many records in the
file LONG SAPHandle;                             // Service Adver-
tising Protocol
LONG addInProgress = 0;                          // control competing add
threads
ENGINE_OP_NODE opNodes[6];                       // thread-control struc-
tures
#ifndef _NETWARE_311_
WorkToDo workNodes[6];
#endif
/
****************************************************************************
* DoOperation
*
*
*
* This routine is spawned as an asynchronous thread every time
*
* the engine receives a request packet from the client. The
*
* parameter is a pointer to a structure that contains an op code
*
* plus a copy of the request packet.
*
*
*
* Because DoOperation is spawned as a thread, multiple instances
*
* of it can be executing at one moment. This capability enables
*
* the engine to service many clients at once, with no single client
*
```

```
* taking a disproportionate "hit" because of the other clients.
*
*
*
**************************************************************************/
void DoOperation(ENGINE_OP_NODE *callBackNode)
{
  int ccode;
  switch(callBackNode->packet.operation)
    {
    case 0x07: /* mark an existing record as deleted */
    case 0xf6: /* edit an existing record */
    case 0x02: { AddRecord(callBackNode); break; }
    case 0x03: { FindRecordKey(callBackNode); break; }
     default: break;
    }
  callBackNode->packet.operation = 0;
  ExitThread(EXIT_THREAD, 0);
}
/*************************************************************************
*    EngineMain                                                        *
*                                                                      *
*  This routine is the primary dispatcher of work for the engine.      *
*  It is started as a thread by main. EngineMain has two purposes:     *
*                                                                      *
*     1) Listen for request packets                                    *
*     2) Start a worker thread to service each request packet          *
*                                                                      *
*  EngineMain can receive as many as six request packets at the same   *
*  instant without losing a packet. Six packets is usually sufficient  *
*  to service more than 100 clients. If the engine were dropping       *
*  packets, however, it could be altered to receive more packets by    *
*  increasing the number of Event Control Block (ECB) structures.      *
*                                                                      *
*  When EngineMain receives a request packet, it copies that           *
*  packet to an ENGINE_OP_NODE structure and starts a worker thread.   *
*  It then recycles the ECB that received the packet, making it        *
*  available to receive further packets even before the worker thread  *
*  is finished executing the request. Then, large numbers of packets   *
*  can be handled without losing any.                                  *
*                                                                      *
**************************************************************************/
```

```
void EngineMain(void *param)
{
  int ccode, index;
    IPX_ECB listenECBs[6];            // ECBs for receiving packets
    IPX_ECB *thisECB, *tempECB;       // Pointers to unlink ECBs from the
    IPX_ECB *queueHead = NULL;        // list of received packets
    IPX_HEADER listenHeaders[6];      // IPX packet headers
    IPX_HEADER *thisHeader;           // Pointer for copying header to
OpNode
    lPacket listenPackets[6];         // Buffers for received packets
    lPacket *thisPacket;              // Pointer for copying packet to
OpNode
    rec tempRec;                      // Buffer for updating database
file
                                      // upon shutdown

    if (param)
        ;
    printf("\nEngine Main Dispatcher started");
    /* fill out our listen ECBs and post them */
    for (index = 0; index < 6; index++)
      {
      opNodes[index].packet.operation = 0;
      listenECBs[index].queueHead = &queueHead;
      listenECBs[index].semHandle = requestSem;
      listenECBs[index].socket = ENGINE_SOCKET;
      listenECBs[index].fragCount = 2;
      listenECBs[index].fragList[0].fragAddress = &listenHeaders[index];
      listenECBs[index].fragList[0].fragSize = sizeof(IPX_HEADER);
      listenECBs[index].fragList[1].fragAddress = &listenPackets[index];
      listenECBs[index].fragList[1].fragSize = sizeof(lPacket);
      ccode = IpxReceive(0, &listenECBs[index]);
      }
    /* When you get here, all six ECBs are listening for IPX packets */
    /* sent to the engine by clients.                                */
    while(!shutdown)
      {
      /* At this point, the EngineMain thread goes to sleep until    */
      /* a client sends a request packet. When a request packet      */
      /* comes in, the OS links the ECB that describes the packet    */
      /* to a list of 'received ECBs.' Then the OS wakes the         */
      /* EngineMain thread by signaling the requestSem semaphore.    */
      ccode = WaitOnLocalSemaphore(requestSem);
```

```
    if (shutdown)
      break;
    /* IpxGetAndClearQ returns a linked list of all ECBs that     */
    /* describe a received packet. The length of the list depends */
    /* on how many packets the engine has received.               */
    thisECB = IpxGetAndClearQ(&queueHead);
    while(thisECB)
      {
      /* Traverse the list of ECBs that describe received packets */
      /* and dispatch worker threads to perform the operations    */
      /* they request.                                            */
    thisHeader = (IPX_HEADER *)thisECB->fragList[0].fragAddress;
    thisPacket = (lPacket *)thisECB->fragList[1].fragAddress;
    /* Now you need to schedule a worker thread to do your operation.
*/
    /* First, you find a free opNode and fill out the callback struc-
ture. */
    index = opNodeSpinCount = 0;
    while(1)
        {
        if (index == 6)
          {
          ThreadSwitch();
          index = 0;
          }
      if (opNodes[index].packet.operation == 0)
          {
          ThreadSwitch();
          break;
          }
      index++;
      opNodeSpinCount++;
        }
    if (opNodeSpinCount > opNodeHighSpinCount)
      opNodeHighSpinCount = opNodeSpinCount;
    /* Now that you have a free operation node, fill it out so    */
    /* that you can start a worker thread to perform the operation. */
    memcpy(&opNodes[index].packetHeader, thisHeader,
sizeof(IPX_HEADER));
    memcpy(&opNodes[index].packet, thisPacket, sizeof(lPacket));
    /* Dispatch the operation by starting a worker thread */
    ccode = BeginThread(DoOperation,
```

```
                        NULL,
                        0x1000,
                        &opNodes[index]);
        /* Now that you have dispatched the operation, you can repost */
        /* the ECB for further listening. The ECB then is available   */
        /* for receiving packets even before the worker thread has     */
        /* performed the requested operation!                          */
        tempECB = thisECB;
        thisECB = thisECB->next;
        ccode = IpxReceive(0, tempECB);
          }
      }
  printf("\nEngine Main Dispatcher shutting down...");
  /* update the database header and close the data file */
  ccode = fseek(fp, 0L, SEEK_SET);
  ccode = fread(&tempRec, sizeof(rec), 1, fp);
  tempRec.header.recordNumber = recordNumber;
  ccode = fwrite(&tempRec, sizeof(rec), 1, fp);
  fclose(fp);
  shutdownOK = 1;
  printf("Down");
  return;
}
/***********************************************************************
*    InitMain                                                         *
*                                                                     *
*  This thread listens for query packets from clients. Clients send a *
*  query packet when they want to establish a session with the engine. *
*  When InitMain receives a query packet from a client, it sends back  *
*  a response packet to the client. The client then can verify that the *
*  engine is up and running before requesting any operations from it.  *
*                                                                     *
*  Unlike EngineMain, InitMain is capable of receiving only one packet *
*  at any moment. This is not a problem, however, because clients send a *
*  query packet only once to establish a session, after which they send *
*  request packets exclusively. InitMain is started as an asynchronous *
*   thread by main.                                                   *
*                                                                     *
***********************************************************************/
void InitMain(void *param)
{
  IPX_ECB listenECB, sendECB;                 // ECBs for send and receive
```

```
    IPX_HEADER listenHeader, sendHeader;        // IPX headers for send and
receive
    iPacket initPacket;                         // Packet buffer
    int ccode;
    unsigned long transportTime;                // Used for
IpxGetLocalTarget
      if (param)
        ;
    /* Initialize the ECBs. You use the same packet buffer for   */
    /* receiving AND sending. In this case, it's OK to do so      */
    /* because this thread sends a packet only after it has       */
    /* received a packet, and it cannot receive further packets   */
    /* until it has sent a packet. */
    listenECB.queueHead = sendECB.queueHead = NULL;
    listenECB.socket = sendECB.socket = INIT_SOCKET;
    listenECB.semHandle = replySem;
    listenECB.fragCount = 0x02;
    listenECB.fragList[0].fragAddress = &listenHeader;
    listenECB.fragList[0].fragSize = sizeof(IPX_HEADER);
     listenECB.fragList[1].fragAddress = &initPacket;
    listenECB.fragList[1].fragSize = sizeof(iPacket);
    sendECB.fragCount = 0x02;
    sendECB.fragList[0].fragAddress = &sendHeader;
    sendECB.fragList[0].fragSize = sizeof(IPX_HEADER);
    sendECB.fragList[1].fragAddress = &initPacket;
    sendECB.fragList[1].fragSize = sizeof(iPacket);
    sendHeader.packetType = 0x04;           // indicates an IPX packet
    while (!shutdown)
      {
      /* Start listening for query packets. */
      ccode = IpxReceive(0, &listenECB);
      /* Go to sleep until IPX receives a query packet.  */
      /* The OS will wake you up when a packet comes in. */
      ccode = WaitOnLocalSemaphore(replySem);
      /* You received a query packet! */
      printf("\nInit packet received");
      memcpy(&sendHeader.destNet, &listenHeader.sourceNet, 10);
      sendHeader.destSocket = INIT_SOCKET;
      /* Obtain the address of the nearest router that knows    */
      /* the network path to the client that sent this packet. */
      ccode = IpxGetLocalTarget((unsigned char *)&listenHeader.sourceNet,
              &sendECB, &transportTime);
```

```
    if (ccode)
      printf("\nError getting immediate address (InitMain): %#x", ccode);
    /* Put the name of the database file in the response packet. */
    strcpy(initPacket.dataFilePath, dataFileName);
    /* Send a response packet back to the client. */
    ccode = IpxSend(0, &sendECB);
    if (ccode)
      printf("\nError sending init packet (InitMain): %#x", ccode);
    else
      printf("\nInit response packet sent");
    }
  return;
}
/
*************************************************************************
*   AddRecord
*
*
*
*  This function is the workhorse of the entire NLM. AddRecord is called
*
*  by a worker thread (DoOperation) whenever a client makes a request to
*
*  do one of the following:
*
*
*
*      1) Add a new record
*
*      2) Edit (update) an existing record
*
*      3) Read an existing record
*
*      4) Mark a record as deleted
*
*
*
*  AddRecord does not distinguish between ops 2 and 3: The client handles
*
*  the difference. When a client receives a record to edit, for example,
*
```

```
 *   it enables the user to enter a new data field, and then makes an
 *
 *   AddRecord request. When the client receives a record to read, it
 *
 *   just displays the record data and does not allow the client to edit
 it.*
 *
 *
 **************************************************************************/
void AddRecord(ENGINE_OP_NODE *opNode)
{
  int ccode, index, duplicate = 0;
  IPX_ECB sendECB;              // ECB for sending confirmation packet
  IPX_HEADER sendHeader;        // IPX header
  sPacket sendPacket;           // packet buffer for sending conf. packet
  unsigned long transportTime;  // for use with IpxGetLocalTarget
  rec tempRec;                  // buffer for reading database file
  if(opNode->packet.operation == 0x02)  /* client adding a new record */
    {
     printf("\nReceived AddRecord request...");
   /* Check to see whether another worker thread is currently adding a */
   /* record. If one is, wait until it is finished adding the new      */
   /* record. This is the only case in which one worker thread must    */
   /* wait on another. It must do so, however, to retain the integrity */
   /* of the check for duplicate record keys. You do this using a      */
   /* global variable rather than record locks because a global        */
   /* variable is more efficient and serves your purpose just as well  */
   /* in this case. */
   while(addInProgress)
     ThreadSwitch();
   /* Tell other worker threads I am adding a new record. */
   addInProgress = 1;
   /* Try to find a deleted record. This process is a little slow, */
   /* and would be speeded greatly by using an index file or an    */
   /* auxiliary list of deleted records.                           */
   printf("\nSeeking ...");
   ccode = fseek(fp, 0L, SEEK_SET);
   if (ccode)
     {
     printf("\nError seeking to first record (AddRecord)");
     return;
     }
```

```
    printf("\n");
    tempRec.header.status =  1L;
    opNode->packet.record.header.offset = 0L;
    /* Read the file. You are looking for two things: a free record */
     /* and a duplicate record key.                                 */
    while(tempRec.header.status)
       {
      fread(&tempRec, sizeof(rec), 1, fp);
      if (!strcmp(tempRec.header.key, opNode->packet.record.header.key) \
          && tempRec.header.status)
        duplicate = 1;
      if (!tempRec.header.status)
        break;
      opNode->packet.record.header.offset += sizeof(rec);
      if (opNode->packet.record.header.offset >= recordNumber *
sizeof(rec))
        break;
      ThreadSwitch();
       }
    /* If you read the entire file without finding a free record,    */
    /* extend the file. Don't extend the file, however, if the client */
    /* is trying to add a record with a duplicate key.               */

    if (tempRec.header.status != 0 && !duplicate)
       {
      ccode = ExtendDataFile(0x64);
       if (ccode)
         return;
       }
    else
       {
      /* If you found a free record without extending the file, you   */
      /* have to continue reading the record to search for a possible */
       /* duplicate key.                                              */
      while(tempRec.header.offset <=      \
         ((recordNumber + 1) * sizeof(rec)) && \
          !duplicate)
         {
        fread(&tempRec, sizeof(rec), 1, fp);
        if (!strcmp(tempRec.header.key,opNode->packet.record.header.key)
\
          && tempRec.header.status)
```

```
      duplicate = 1;
     break;
      }
    }
  if (duplicate)
    {
    printf("\nDuplicate record key found");
    opNode->packet.record.header.status = 0x03;
    }
   else
    {
    /* You found a free record, and the client is not trying to */
    /* add a record with a duplicate key. Fill out the record.  */
    printf("filling record... ");
    opNode->packet.record.header.status = 0xffffffff;
    opNode->packet.record.header.hashkey = 0;
    opNode->packet.record.header.recordNumber =
tempRec.header.recordNumber;
    opNode->packet.record.data.creationTime = \
      opNode->packet.record.data.lastReferenceTime = \
      opNode->packet.record.data.lastUpdateTime = time(NULL);
    memcpy(opNode->packet.record.data.nodeAddress,
         &opNode->packetHeader.sourceNet, 10);
    /* Prepare for writing the record by seeking to the offset */
     /* of the free record.                                     */
    ccode = fseek(fp, opNode->packet.record.header.offset, SEEK_SET);
     if (ccode)
       {
       printf("\nError seeking to new record offset (AddRecord)");
        return;
        }
      }
    }
  if (opNode->packet.operation == 0xf6)  /* updating an existing record */
    {
    /* The client wants to update an existing record. You don't have */
    /* to search the data file because the client has provided you   */
    /* with the offset of the record.                                */
     printf("\nReceived UpdateRecord request...");
    /* Check for a bad record offset */
    if (opNode->packet.record.header.offset >= recordNumber * sizeof(rec))
       {
```

```
     printf("\nBad record offset received (UpdateRecord)");
      return;
      }
  /* Prepare for writing the updated record by seeking to its offset */
  ccode = fseek(fp, opNode->packet.record.header.offset, SEEK_SET);
  if (ccode)
     {
    printf("\nError seeking to record offset (UpdateRecord)");
      return;
      }
  /* Obtain the current time and node address of the client */
  /* that is updating the record. */
  opNode->packet.record.data.lastUpdateTime = time(NULL);
  memcpy(opNode->packet.record.data.nodeAddress,
       &opNode->packetHeader.sourceNet, 10);
   }
if (opNode->packet.operation == 0x07) /* mark record as deleted */
  {
  /* The client wants to mark an existing record as deleted.   */
  /* You don't have to search the data file because the client */
  /* has provided you with the offset of the record.           */
    printf("\nReceived DeleteRecord request...");
  /* Check for a bad offset */
  if (opNode->packet.record.header.offset >= recordNumber * sizeof(rec))
     {
    printf("\nBad record offset received (DeleteRecord)");
     return;
     }
  /* Prepare for marking the record as deleted */
  /* by seeking to its offset. */
    ccode = fseek(fp, opNode->packet.record.header.offset, SEEK_SET);
  if (ccode)
     {
    printf("\nError seeking to record offset (DeleteRecord)");
     return;
     }
  /* Indicate that this is a deleted record. */
  opNode->packet.record.header.status = 0;
   }
if (!duplicate)
  {
  /* This is where you write the new, updated, or deleted        */
```

```
    /* record to the database file. You use Transaction Tracking to    */
    /* ensure that failed or partial writes do not damage the integrity */
    /* of the data file. Transaction Tracking performs all necessary    */
    /* record locks automatically.                                      */
    printf("TTSBegin ...");
    ccode = TTSBeginTransaction();
    if (ccode && ccode != 0xff)
       {
       if(opNode->packet.operation == 0x02)  /* adding a new record */
         addInProgress = 0;
       return;
       }
    printf("writing ...");
    ccode = fwrite(&opNode->packet.record, sizeof(rec), 1, fp);
    if (ccode != 1)
       {
       TTSAbortTransaction();
       if(opNode->packet.operation == 0x02)  /* adding a new record */
         addInProgress = 0;
       return;
       }
    else
       {
       printf("TTSEnd\n");
       TTSEndTransaction(&opNode->packet.record.header.transactionNumber);
       }
    if(opNode->packet.operation == 0x02)  /* adding a new record */
       addInProgress = 0;
    if (ccode != 1)
       {
       printf("\nNew record not written to database");
       return;
       }
    else
       {
       printf("\nNew record:");
       printf("\n\trecordNumber: %#lx", opNode->packet.record.header.recordNumber);
       printf("\n\toffset: %#lx", opNode->packet.record.header.offset);
       printf("\nKey: %s", opNode->packet.record.header.key);
       printf("\nData: %s", opNode->packet.record.data.data);
       }
```

```
      }
  if (duplicate && opNode->packet.operation == 0x02)
    addInProgress = 0;
  /* Now set up a reply packet and send to the client. When the client  */
  /* receives this packet, it infers that the operation was successful. */
  /* You send a smaller packet containing only the record header.       */
  sendECB.queueHead = NULL;
  sendECB.semHandle = NULL;
  sendECB.socket = ENGINE_SOCKET;
  sendECB.fragCount = 0x02;
  sendECB.fragList[0].fragAddress = &sendHeader;
  sendECB.fragList[0].fragSize = sizeof(IPX_HEADER);
  sendECB.fragList[1].fragAddress = &sendPacket;
  sendECB.fragList[1].fragSize = sizeof(sPacket);
  /* Obtain the network address of the nearest router that knows the */
  /* path to the client.                                             */
  ccode = IpxGetLocalTarget(
          (unsigned char *)&opNode->packetHeader.sourceNet,
           &sendECB,
           &transportTime);
  memcpy(&sendHeader.destNet, &opNode->packetHeader.sourceNet, 12);
  sendHeader.packetType = 4;
  memcpy(&sendPacket.responseCode, &opNode->packet.responseCode, 3);
  memcpy(&sendPacket.header, &opNode->packet.record.header,
sizeof(rHeader));
  ccode = IpxSend(0, &sendECB);
   printf("\nOperation Successful.");
   return;
}
/************************************************************************
 *   FindRecord                                                         *
 *                                                                      *
 *   FindRecord is called by a worker thread whenever a client makes a  *
 *   find record request. The client makes a find record request as a   *
 *   prelude to a read record, edit record, or delete record request.   *
 *                                                                      *
 *   If the engine finds the record requested by the client, it sends back *
 *   to the client a packet containing the entire record.               *
 *   If the engine does NOT find the record requested by the client, it *
 *   sends a null record back to the client.                            *
 *                                                                      *
 ************************************************************************/
```

```
void FindRecordKey(ENGINE_OP_NODE *opNode)
{
  rec searchRec;              // buffer for reading database file
  int ccode;
  IPX_ECB sendECB;            // ECB for sending confirmation packet
  IPX_HEADER sendHeader;
  lPacket sendPacket;
  unsigned long transportTime;
  /* You assume that the packet contains a record header with the key */
  /* filled out. You search on the key. Other possibilities include   */
  /* searching on the record number, transaction number, and          */
  /* going directly to a record offset supplied by the client.        */
  /* A production version of this application would supply some of     */
  /* these more complex searching algorithms.                         */
   printf("\nReceived FindRecordKey request...");
  /* Seek to the beginning of the data file and search for the        */
  /* record key. This method is relatively slow. A production         */
  /* version of the engine would use an indexing method to speed      */
  /* searches for large database files.                               */
  ccode = fseek(fp, 0L, SEEK_SET);
  if (ccode)
    return;
  while(1)
     {
    ccode = fread(&searchRec, sizeof(rec), 1, fp);
    if (ccode != 1)
      break;
    if (searchRec.header.status == 0) /* deleted record */
      continue;
    if (strcmp(opNode->packet.record.header.key, searchRec.header.key))
     continue;
    else
      break;
    }
  if (ccode != 1)    /* you didn't find the record */
    sendPacket.record.header.status = 0L;
  else
   memcpy(&sendPacket.record, &searchRec, sizeof(rec));
  /* Initialize the send ECB, IPX header, and packet buffer. */
  sendECB.queueHead = NULL;
  sendECB.semHandle = NULL;
  /* Obtain the network address of the nearest router that */
```

```
/* knows the path to the client. */
ccode = IpxGetLocalTarget(
        (unsigned char *)&opNode->packetHeader.sourceNet,
        &sendECB,
        &transportTime);
sendECB.socket = ENGINE_SOCKET;
sendECB.fragCount = 2;
sendECB.fragList[0].fragAddress = &sendHeader;
sendECB.fragList[0].fragSize = sizeof(IPX_HEADER);
sendECB.fragList[1].fragAddress = &sendPacket;
if (sendPacket.record.header.status == 0)
  sendECB.fragList[1].fragSize = sizeof(sPacket);
else
  sendECB.fragList[1].fragSize = sizeof(lPacket);
memcpy(&sendHeader.destNet, &opNode->packetHeader.sourceNet, 12);
sendHeader.packetType = 4;
memcpy(&sendPacket.responseCode, &opNode->packet.responseCode, 3);
/* Send the packet to the client. */
ccode = IpxSend(0, &sendECB);
if (sendPacket.record.header.status != 0L)
  {
  /* Now update the lastReferenceTime field for the record.   */
  /* You use Transaction Tracking to ensure that partial or    */
  /* failed writes do not destroy the integrity of the database */
  /* file. Transaction tracking performs all necessary record  */
  /* locking for you.                                          */
  searchRec.data.lastReferenceTime = time(NULL);
  ccode = fseek(fp, searchRec.header.offset, SEEK_SET);
  if (ccode)
    return;
  ccode = TTSBeginTransaction();
  if (ccode && ccode != 0xff)
    return;
  ccode = fwrite(&searchRec, sizeof(rec), 1, fp);
  if (ccode != 1)
    {
    TTSAbortTransaction();
    return;
    }
  else
    TTSEndTransaction(&searchRec.header.transactionNumber);
    printf("Operation Successful");
```

```c
    }
  else
   printf("Record not found");
  return;
}
/****************************************************************************
*   CreateDataFile                                                          *
*                                                                           *
*   This function is called by main when it cannot find the data file.      *
*   When you load the NLM, you can specify an alternative data file         *
*   path using the command line. The main routine uses the data file        *
*   path--if you supply it--to search for the database file.                *
*                                                                           *
****************************************************************************/
int CreateDataFile(char *netWarePath)
{
  int ccode;
  rec temp;
  BYTE extendedAttributes;
  fp = fopen(netWarePath, "w+b");
  if (fp == NULL)
    return(-1);
  printf("\nData file created ...");
  /* Set up a special first record that will serve as an identifier  */
  /* and a special stamp you can use to track certain information.    */
  temp.header.status = 0x02L;        /* status of 2: this is the file header
*/
  temp.header.offset = 0L;
  temp.header.recordNumber = 0x64;
  strcpy(temp.header.key, "NetWare database engine");
  ccode = fwrite(&temp, sizeof(rec), 1, fp);
  if (ccode != 1)
    {
    fclose(fp);
    ccode = unlink(netWarePath);
    return(-1);
    }
  /* Now write 100 empty records to the database file */
  memset(&temp, 0x01, sizeof(rec));
  temp.header.status = 0x0L;
  for(temp.header.recordNumber = 0; \
    temp.header.recordNumber < 0x64; \
```

```
    temp.header.recordNumber++)
    {
   temp.header.offset = ftell(fp);
   ccode = fwrite(&temp, sizeof(rec), 1, fp);
   if (ccode != 1)
      {
      printf("\nError extending database file (CreateDataFile)");
      return(-1);
      }
    }
  fclose(fp);
  printf("file header written.");
  /* Set the transaction bit of the file's extended attribute byte.   */
  /* This enables you to use Transaction Tracking Services (TTS) when */
  /* you are writing records to the file.                             */
  printf("\nSetting Transaction bit");
  ccode = GetExtendedFileAttributes(dataFileName, &extendedAttributes);
  if (ccode)
    printf("\nError getting extended attributes");
  extendedAttributes |= 0x10;    // turn transaction bit ON
  if (!ccode)
    ccode = SetExtendedFileAttributes(dataFileName, extendedAttributes);
  if (ccode)
    printf("\nError setting extended attributes");
  return(0);
}
/
*************************************************************************
*  ExtendDataFile
*
*
*
*  This routine is called by AddRecord whenever it reads the entire
*
*  database file without finding a free record. The parameter,
*
*  newRecords, determines by how many records the data file will be
*
*  extended.
*
*
*
```

```
**********************************************************************/
int ExtendDataFile(int newRecords)
{
  rec tempRec;
  int ccode, index;
  long oldOffset;
  oldOffset = ftell(fp);
  fclose(fp);
  fp = fopen(dataFileName, "ab");
  if (fp == NULL)
    return(-1);
  memset(&tempRec, 0x01, sizeof(rec));
  tempRec.header.status = 0x0L;
  for (index = 1; index <= newRecords; index++)
    {
    tempRec.header.offset = ftell(fp);
    tempRec.header.recordNumber =  (recordNumber + index);
    ccode = fwrite(&tempRec, sizeof(rec), 1, fp);
    if (ccode != 1)
      {
      printf("\nError extending database file (ExtendDataFile)");
      return(-1);
      }
    }
  recordNumber += newRecords;
  ccode = fseek(fp, 0L, SEEK_SET);
  if (ccode)
    {
    printf("\nError reading the database file header (ExtendDataFile)");
    return(-1);
    }
  tempRec.header.recordNumber = recordNumber;
  ccode = fwrite(&tempRec, sizeof(rec), 1, fp);
  if (ccode != 1)
    {
    printf("\nError writing updated header to database file
(ExtendDataFile)");
    return(-1);
    }
  printf("\n%#x New records successfully added to data file", newRecords);
  fclose(fp);
  fp = fopen(dataFileName, "ab+");
```

```
  if (fp == NULL)
    {
    printf("\nError re-opening data file (ExtendDataFile)");
    return(-1);
    }
  fseek(fp, oldOffset, SEEK_SET);
  return(0);
}
/
****************************************************************************
*
*
*  OpenDataFile
*
*
*
*  This routine is called by main every time the engine is loaded.
*
*  It opens the file specified by the command line (if the user
*
*  specified one) or the default (SYS:$ENGINE$.DAT).
*
*
*
*  OpenDataFile reads the first record of the file to verify the
*
*  database file signature and to determine how many records are
*
*  contained in the file.
*
*
*
****************************************************************************/
int OpenDataFile(char *netWarePath)
{
  int ccode;
  rec temp;
  fp = fopen(netWarePath, "r+b");
  if (fp == NULL)
    return(-1);
  printf("\nData file opened...");
  /* read the file header to verify that it is your data file */
```

```
  ccode = fread(&temp, sizeof(rec), 1, fp);
  if (ccode != 1)
    {
   fclose(fp);
   return(-1);
    }
  /* now do checks to verify the file */
  if (temp.header.status != 0x02)
    {
   printf("\nBad status ID on file header");
   return(-1);
    }
  if (strcmp(temp.header.key, "NetWare database engine"))
    {
   printf("Bad signature on file header");
   return(-1);
    }
  /* initialize the global variable recordNumber */
recordNumber = temp.header.recordNumber;
  /* return with the file pointer located just after the file header */
  printf("file signature verified.");
  return(0);
}
/
*****************************************************************************
*
*
*  UnloadCleanUp
*
*
*
*  This routine was registered with the OS in main using the signal API.
*
*  The OS calls this routine whenever a user UNLOADS the engine NLM.
*
*  When UnloadCleanUp is called by the OS, all engine threads are still
*
*  alive. This gives you a chance to kick alive any threads that are
*
*  asleep, letting them clean up before they die.
*
```

```
 *
 *
 ***********************************************************************/
void UnloadCleanUp(int sig)
{
  sig = sig;
  shutdown = 1;
  SignalLocalSemaphore(replySem);
  SignalLocalSemaphore(requestSem);
  SignalLocalSemaphore(shutdownSem);
  return;
}
/
 ***********************************************************************
 *
 *
 *  ShutdownCleanUp
 *
 *
 *
 *  This routine was registered with the OS in main using the atexit API.
 *
 *  The OS calls this routine when the NLM is about to die. When
 *
 *  ShutdownCleanUp is called, all threads are dead. At this point, all
 *
 *  you can do is free OS resources allocated during the life of the NLM.
 *
 *
 *
 ***********************************************************************/
void ShutdownCleanUp(void)
{
  int ccode;
  ccode = CloseLocalSemaphore(replySem);
  ccode = CloseLocalSemaphore(shutdownSem);
  ccode = CloseLocalSemaphore(requestSem);
  ccode = IpxCloseSocket(ENGINE_SOCKET);
  ccode = IpxCloseSocket(INIT_SOCKET);
  ccode = ShutdownAdvertising(SAPHandle);
  return;
}
```

```c
int main(int argc, char **argv)
{
  int ccode;
  DIR *dirStruct, *tempDir;
  char server[_MAX_SERVER + 1];
  char volume[_MAX_VOLUME + 1];
  char directories[_MAX_DIR + 1];
  BYTE extendedAttributes;
  /* Check to see that TTS is enabled on the server. */
  ccode = TTSIsAvailable();
  if (ccode != 0xff)
    {
    printf("\nTTS is currently disabled ...");
    printf("\nPlease enable it and re-load ENGINE.NLM");
    return(ccode);
    }
  if (argc < 2)
    strcpy(dataFileName, "$engine$.dat");
  else
    strncpy(dataFileName, argv[1], _MAX_PATH);
  /* Check to ensure that you have a valid path or, if you have a */
  /* partial path, to obtain the server and volume names.        */
  ccode = ParsePath(dataFileName, server, volume, directories);
  /* if the pathname was invalid, return with a -1 */
  if (ccode)
      {
      printf("\nInvalid path for data file... Exiting");
    return(-1);
      }
  /* now look for the file to see whether it already exists */
  dirStruct = tempDir = opendir(dataFileName);
  readdir(tempDir);
  if (tempDir == NULL)
    ccode = CreateDataFile(dataFileName);
  ccode = OpenDataFile(dataFileName);
  if (ccode == -1)    /* err creating or opening the file */
    {
    closedir(dirStruct);
      printf("\nError opening or creating the data file... Exiting");
    return(ccode);
    }
  closedir(dirStruct); /* close the dir node */
```

```
/* open the Engine's IPX socket and two semaphores for thread control */
IpxOpenSocket(&engineSocket);
IpxOpenSocket(&initSocket);
 printf("\nIPX Sockets opened.");
requestSem = OpenLocalSemaphore(0L);
replySem = OpenLocalSemaphore(0L);
/* open a semaphore that will tell when to shut down */
shutdownSem = OpenLocalSemaphore(0L);
 printf("\nNetWare Semaphores opened.");
/* Now start advertising the ENGINE over the network */
SAPHandle = AdvertiseService(0x88, "Data_Base_Engine");
printf("\nSAP Handle: %#08lx", SAPHandle);
/* Now you have to register functions that will execute  */
/* if somebody unloads ENGINE.NLM at the server console. */
signal(SIGTERM, UnloadCleanUp);
atexit(ShutdownCleanUp);
 printf("\nExit procedures registered with OS.");
/* Now that you have the file open and ready to go, you can */
/* start the main thread group.                             */
ccode = BeginThread(InitMain, NULL, 0x1000, NULL);
ccode = BeginThreadGroup(EngineMain, NULL, 0x2000, NULL);
 if (ccode)
   return(-1);
/* Go to sleep until it's time to shut down. */
WaitOnLocalSemaphore(shutdownSem);
 /* If you are awake at this point, someone has unloaded you. */
while(!shutdownOK)
   ThreadSwitch();  /* give worker threads a chance to clean up */
 return(0);
}
/***** END OF FILE (ENGINE.C) *****/
```

Listing 15.3:
Header file for CLIENT.EXE.

```
/***** FILENAME: CLIENT.H *****/
#include <stdio.h>
#include <stdlib.h>
#include <conio.h>
#include <string.h>
#include <nit.h>
```

```c
#include <time.h>
#ifndef ENGINE_DEFINES
#define ENGINE_DEFINES
#define ENGINE_SOCKET      0x0099
#define INIT_SOCKET        0x0090
#define ENGINE_TYPE        0x88
#define ADD_RECORD         0x02
#define FIND_RECORD_KEY    0x03
#define FIND_RECORD_NO_KEY 0xf4
#define READ_RECORD        0xf5
#define EDIT_RECORD        0xf6
#define DELETE_RECORD      0x07
#define NUMBER_OF_NODES 4
#define win(l, t, r, b, a) window((l), (t), (r), (b)); \
      textattr((a)); clrscr();
typedef struct ipxheader {
  WORD checkSum;
  WORD length;
  BYTE transportControl;
  BYTE packetType;
  LONG destNet;
  BYTE destNode[6];
  WORD destSocket;
  LONG sourceNet;
  BYTE sourceNode[6];
  WORD sourceSocket;
}IPX_HEADER;
typedef struct fragment {
  void far *fragAddress;
  WORD fragSize;
}ECBFragment;
typedef struct ecb {
  void far *linkAddress;
  void far *ESRAddress;
  BYTE inUseFlag;
  BYTE completionCode;
  WORD socket;
  BYTE IPXWorkspace[4];
  BYTE driverWorkspace[12];
  BYTE immediateAddress[6];
  WORD fragCount;
  ECBFragment fragList[2];
```

```
}IPX_ECB;
typedef struct engineInfo {
  int occupied;
  char dataFile[256];
  char serverName[49];
  BYTE engineAddress[12];
  WORD serverType;
}INFO;
typedef struct recordHeader {
  unsigned long status;
  unsigned long offset;
  unsigned long hashkey;
  unsigned long recordNumber;
  unsigned long transactionNumber;
  unsigned char key[128];
}rHeader;
typedef struct recordData {
  time_t creationTime;
  time_t lastReferenceTime;
  time_t lastUpdateTime;
  unsigned char nodeAddress[10];  /* node address of last updater */
  unsigned long objectID;         /* object ID of last updater    */
  unsigned char data[128];
}rData;
typedef struct record {
  rHeader header;
  rData data;
}rec;
typedef struct shortPacket {
  WORD responseCode;
  BYTE operation;
  rHeader header;
}sPacket;
typedef struct longPacket {
  WORD responseCode;
  BYTE operation;
  rec record;
}lPacket;
typedef struct initPacket {
  char dataFilePath[_MAX_PATH];
}iPacket;
#endif
/***** END OF FILE (CLIENT.C) *****/
```

Listing 15.4:

C source code for CLIENT.EXE.

```c
/*****************************************************************
 *                                                               *
 *   filename     :  client.c                                    *
 *   date         :  June 26 1992                                *
 *   version      :  1.0                                         *
 *   description  :  front end (EXE) for demonstration client-server record *
 *                   manager.                                    *
 *   compiler     :  Borland C 3.0 (Large Memory Model)          *
 *   notes        :  WORD alignment must be turned OFF when compiling; *
 *                   otherwise, packets to and from the NLM will be *
 *                   misaligned by one byte.                     *
 *                                                               *
 *****************************************************************/
#include "client.h"
BYTE serverAddress[12];              // network address of ENGINE
INFO info[NUMBER_OF_NODES];          // collect information about
                                     // advertising engines.
extern unsigned _stklen = 0x6000;
/*****************************************************************
 *   GetRecord                                                   *
 *                                                               *
 *   This function makes EditRecord, ReadRecord, and DeleteRecord *
 *   requests. Each of these requests requires that you first issue a *
 *   FindRecordKey request to the engine and verify that the engine *
 *   found the record.                                           *
 *                                                               *
 *   The EditRecord and DeleteRecord requests also require that you *
 *   modify the record returned by the engine and send that record *
 *   back to the engine with the appropriate op code (update or delete). *
 *                                                               *
 *****************************************************************/
int GetRecord(BYTE operation)
{
  /* This function serves three purposes: read a record,        */
  /* delete a record, and update a record. First, however, you  */
  /* must issue a FindRecord request to the server. If the server */
  /* doesn't find the record, you exit with an error code.      */
  /* Otherwise, you perform the requested operation and listen for */
  /* a confirmation packet from the server.                     */
```

```
    IPX_ECB listenECB, sendECB;          // ECBs for sending and receiv-
ing
    IPX_HEADER listenHeader, sendHeader;  // IPX headers
    lPacket listenPacket, sendPacket;     // packet buffers
    int ccode, transportTime, index;
    char c, attr, inputBuf[129], *bufp;
    char *screenBuf;
    struct text_info textInfo;
    clock_t begin, end;                   // use to time-out listening
ECBs
    WORD findResponseCode = 0x00fe;       // verify integrity of received
    WORD opResponseCode = 0x00fd;         // packets

  screenBuf = (BYTE *)malloc(0x1000);
  if (screenBuf == NULL)
    {
    printf("\nOut of memory allocating screen buffer");
    return(-1);
    }
  gettextinfo(&textInfo);
  gettext(5, 7, 75, 18, screenBuf);
  attr = (YELLOW + (BLUE << 4));
  win(5, 7, 75, 18, attr);
  gotoxy(1, 1);
  cputs("_ÄÄÄÄÄÄÄÄÄÄÄÄÄÄÄÄÄÄÄÄÄÄÄÄÄÄÄÄÄÄÄÄÄÄÄÄÄÄÄÄÄÄÄÄÄÄÄÄÄÄ\
      ÄÄÄÄÄÄÄÄÄÄÄÄÄÄÄÄÄÄÄÄÄÄ¿");
  for(index = 2; index <= 10; index++)
    {
    gotoxy(1, index);
      cputs("_
_");
    }
  gotoxy(1, 11);
  cputs("_ÄÄÄÄÄÄÄÄÄÄÄÄÄÄÄÄÄÄÄÄÄÄÄÄÄÄÄÄÄÄÄÄÄÄÄÄÄÄÄÄÄÄÄÄÄÄÄÄÄÄ\
      ÄÄÄÄÄÄÄÄÄÄÄÄÄÄÄÄÄÄÄÄÄÄ_");
  gotoxy(27, 2);
  if (operation == EDIT_RECORD)
    cputs("Record to Edit");
  if (operation == READ_RECORD)
    cputs("Record to Read");
  /* Enable the user to input a record key, and then make a */
  /* FindRecordKey request. */
```

```
gotoxy(10, 12);
cputs("Enter Record Key (press <Enter> when finished)");
gotoxy(3, 4);
cputs("Record Key:  ");
textattr(WHITE + (GREEN << 4));
cputs("                                                    ");
gotoxy(17, 4);
inputBuf[0] = 0x3f;
bufp = cgets(inputBuf);
strncpy(sendPacket.record.header.key, bufp, 0x3f);
strcat(sendPacket.record.header.key, "\0");
/* Now see whether you can find the record. */
/* Initialize ECBs, send header, and send packet for FindRecordKey op.
*/
sendPacket.responseCode = findResponseCode;
sendPacket.operation = FIND_RECORD_KEY;
listenECB.ESRAddress = sendECB.ESRAddress = NULL;
listenECB.socket = sendECB.socket = ENGINE_SOCKET;
listenECB.fragCount = sendECB.fragCount = 0x02;
listenHeader.packetType = sendHeader.packetType = 0x04;
/* Obtain the address of the nearest router that knows the */
/* path to the engine. */
ccode = IPXGetLocalTarget(serverAddress,
                          sendECB.immediateAddress,
                          &transportTime);
/* IPXGetDataAddress constructs a FAR pointer to the first */
/* operand and initializes the second operand with that    */
/* FAR pointer.                                             */
IPXGetDataAddress((BYTE *)&sendHeader,
                  (WORD *)&sendECB.fragList[0].fragAddress);
sendECB.fragList[0].fragSize = sizeof(IPX_HEADER);
IPXGetDataAddress((BYTE *)&sendPacket,
                  (WORD *)&sendECB.fragList[1].fragAddress);
sendECB.fragList[1].fragSize = sizeof(sPacket);
memcpy(&sendHeader.destNet, serverAddress, 10);
sendHeader.destSocket = ENGINE_SOCKET;
IPXGetDataAddress((BYTE *)&listenHeader,
                  (WORD *)&listenECB.fragList[0].fragAddress);
listenECB.fragList[0].fragSize = sizeof(IPX_HEADER);
IPXGetDataAddress((BYTE *)&listenPacket,
                  (WORD *)&listenECB.fragList[1].fragAddress);
listenECB.fragList[1].fragSize = sizeof(lPacket);
```

```
    /* Post ECBs for receiving and sending. */
    IPXListenForPacket(&listenECB);
    IPXSendPacket(&sendECB);
    /* Wait five seconds for a response packet. Enable the user to retry.
*/
    while(listenECB.inUseFlag)
        {
        c = 0;
        gotoxy(10, 12);
        textattr(YELLOW + (BLUE << 4));
        clreol();
        begin = end = clock();
        while(listenECB.inUseFlag)
            {
            end = clock();
            if (end - begin > CLK_TCK * 5)
                {
                gotoxy(10, 12);
                cputs("Confirmation not received -- enter 'Y' to Retry");
                c = getch();
                break;
                }
            }
        if (c != 'y' && c != 'Y')
            break;
        }
    if (listenECB.inUseFlag ||
     listenPacket.responseCode != findResponseCode ||
     !listenPacket.record.header.status)
        {
        /* You didn't get a response packet. You can only assume  */
        /* that the engine did not find the record you requested. */
        /* You cannot read, edit, or delete a packet that the     */
        /* engine did not find, so you return with an error code. */
        if(listenECB.inUseFlag)
            IPXCancelEvent(&listenECB);
        gotoxy(10, 12);
        textattr(YELLOW + (BLUE << 4));
        clreol();
        gotoxy(10, 12);
        cputs("Record NOT found -- press any key to continue");
        c = getch();
```

```
   textattr(textInfo.attribute);
   puttext(5, 7, 75, 18, screenBuf);
 free(screenBuf);
   return(-1);
    }
/* You found the record. If the operation is read record or edit */
/* record, you display the record key and data on the screen.    */
if (operation != DELETE_RECORD)
  {
  textattr(YELLOW + (BLUE << 4));
  gotoxy(3, 6);
  cputs("Record Data: ");
  textattr(WHITE + (GREEN << 4));
  cputs("                                              ");
  gotoxy(17, 6);
  printf("%s", listenPacket.record.data.data);
  }
/* If the operation is read record, you skip the following code */
/* and fall through to the return. Otherwise, you alter the     */
/* received record and send it back to the engine.              */
if (operation == EDIT_RECORD || operation == DELETE_RECORD)
    {
if (operation == EDIT_RECORD)
    {
    /* If the operation is edit record, you enable the user to */
    /* alter the data field.                                   */
    gotoxy(10, 12);
    textattr(YELLOW + (BLUE << 4));
    clreol();
    cputs("Enter new data field for this record and press <Enter>");
  gotoxy(3, 8);
  cputs("New Data: ");
  gotoxy(16, 8);
   textattr(WHITE + (GREEN << 4));
   cputs("                                            ");
   gotoxy(17, 8);
   inputBuf[0] = 0x3f;
   bufp = cgets(inputBuf);
   strncpy(listenPacket.record.data.data, bufp, 0x3f);
   strcat(listenPacket.record.data.data, "\0");
   textattr(YELLOW + (BLUE << 4));
   gotoxy(10, 12);
```

```
    clreol();
      cputs("Enter 'Y' to accept, any other key to cancel");
      c = getch();
      if (c != 'y' && c != 'Y')
        {
        free(screenBuf);
          return(-1);
        }
      }
    /* If the operation is delete record, you mark the record */
    /* as deleted by changing its status to zero.            */
if (operation == DELETE_RECORD)
    listenPacket.record.header.status = 0;
    /* If the operation is edit record or delete record,     */
    /* send the altered record packet back to the engine.    */
    /* Now you can recycle the ECBs. This time, you use the  */
    /* reconstituted listen packet to send back to the server, */
    /* and you use the send packet to receive the confirmation. */
    listenPacket.responseCode = opResponseCode;
    listenPacket.operation = operation;
    IPXGetDataAddress((BYTE *)&listenPacket,
                  (WORD *)&sendECB.fragList[1].fragAddress);
    sendECB.fragList[1].fragSize = sizeof(lPacket);
    IPXGetDataAddress((BYTE *)&sendPacket,
                  (WORD *)&listenECB.fragList[1].fragAddress);
    listenECB.fragList[1].fragSize = sizeof(lPacket);
    IPXListenForPacket(&listenECB);
    IPXSendPacket(&sendECB);
    /* Wait five seconds for a confirmation packet from the engine. */
     /* Enable the user to retry.                              */
    while(listenECB.inUseFlag)
        {
        c = 0;
       gotoxy(10, 12);
      textattr(YELLOW + (BLUE << 4));
        clreol();
       begin = end = clock();
       while(listenECB.inUseFlag)
           {
           end = clock();
           if (end - begin > CLK_TCK * 5)
               {
```

```
            gotoxy(10, 12);
          cputs("Confirmation not received -- enter 'Y' to Retry");
            c = getch();
            break;
             }
        }
    if (c != 'y' && c != 'Y')
       break;
    }
  if (listenECB.inUseFlag || listenPacket.responseCode !=
opResponseCode)
        {
     /* Either you DID NOT receive a confirmation packet, or you
*/
     /* received a confirmation packet with a bad response code.
*/
     /* You can only infer that the record was not updated.
*/
       if(listenECB.inUseFlag)
          IPXCancelEvent(&listenECB);
       gotoxy(10, 12);
     textattr(YELLOW + (BLUE << 4));
      clreol();
      gotoxy(10, 12);
      cputs("Record NOT updated -- press any key to return");
       c = getch();
      textattr(textInfo.attribute);
      puttext(5, 7, 75, 18, screenBuf);
    free(screenBuf);
      return(-1);
        }
    }
  /* You received a good confirmation packet from the engine. */
  /* Indicate success and return.                             */
  gotoxy(10, 12);
  textattr(YELLOW + (BLUE << 4));
  clreol();
  gotoxy(10, 12);
  if (operation == EDIT_RECORD)
     cputs("Record updated -- press any key to continue");
  if (operation == DELETE_RECORD)
   cputs("Record deleted -- press any key to continue");
```

```
  if (operation == READ_RECORD)
    cputs("Press any key to continue");
  c = getch();
  textattr(textInfo.attribute);
  puttext(5, 7, 75, 18, screenBuf);
 free(screenBuf);
  return(0);
}
/************************************************************************
 *  AddRecord                                                          *
 *                                                                     *
 *  This function enables the user to create a new record. It prompts for *
 *  input on the record key and record data fields. It then builds a   *
 *  packet containing a filled-out record and sends that packet to the *
 *  engine.                                                            *
 *                                                                     *
 *  After sending the record packet to the engine, it listens for a    *
 *  response packet from the engine. The response packet contains a    *
 *  record header, from which AddRecord infers that the record was added *
 *  or that the record was not added because of a duplicate key. If no  *
 *  packet comes in from the engine, or if a packet comes in that has a *
 *  bad response code, AddRecord infers that the record was NOT added.  *
 *                                                                     *
 ************************************************************************/
int AddRecord(void)
{
   IPX_ECB sendECB, listenECB;           // ECBs for sending and receiv-
ing
   IPX_HEADER sendHeader, listenHeader;  // IPX headers
   lPacket sendPacket, listenPacket;     // packet buffers
   int ccode, transportTime, index;
   char c, attr, inputBuf[129], *bufp;
   char objectName[49];                  // objectName, objectType, and
   WORD objectType;                      // loginTime are used when
   BYTE loginTime[7];                    // calling
GetConnectionInformation
   char *screenBuf;
   struct text_info textInfo;
   clock_t begin, end;                   // used to time-out response pkt
   WORD responseCode = 0x00ff;           // verifies integrity of
                                         // received packets

  screenBuf = (BYTE *)malloc(0x1000);
```

```c
  if (screenBuf == NULL)
    {
    printf("\nOut of memory allocating screen buffer");
    return(-1);
    }
  gettextinfo(&textInfo);
  gettext(5, 7, 75, 18, screenBuf);
  attr = (YELLOW + (BLUE << 4));
  win(5, 7, 75, 18, attr);
  gotoxy(1, 1);
  cputs("_ÄÄÄÄÄÄÄÄÄÄÄÄÄÄÄÄÄÄÄÄÄÄÄÄÄÄÄÄÄÄÄÄÄÄÄÄÄÄÄÄÄÄÄÄÄÄÄÄ\
     ÄÄÄÄÄÄÄÄÄÄÄÄÄÄÄÄÄÄÄÄÄÄÄ¿");
  for(index = 2; index <= 10; index++)
    {
    gotoxy(1, index);
      cputs("_
_");
    }
  gotoxy(1, 11);
  cputs("_ÄÄÄÄÄÄÄÄÄÄÄÄÄÄÄÄÄÄÄÄÄÄÄÄÄÄÄÄÄÄÄÄÄÄÄÄÄÄÄÄÄÄÄÄÄÄÄÄ\
     ÄÄÄÄÄÄÄÄÄÄÄÄÄÄÄÄÄÄÄÄÄÄÄ_");
  /* Obtain input from the user for this new record. */
  gotoxy(30, 1);
  cputs("Add Record");
  gotoxy(10, 12);
  cputs("Enter Record Key (press <Enter> when finished): ");
  gotoxy(3, 4);
  cputs("Record Key:  ");
  textattr(WHITE + (GREEN << 4));
  cputs("                                            ");
  gotoxy(17, 4);
  inputBuf[0] = 0x3f;
  bufp = cgets(inputBuf);
  strncpy(sendPacket.record.header.key, bufp, 0x3f);
  strcat(sendPacket.record.header.key, "\0");

  textattr(YELLOW + (BLUE << 4));
  gotoxy(10, 12);
  cputs("Enter Record Data (press <Enter> when finished): ");
  gotoxy(3, 6);
  cputs("Record Data: ");
  textattr(WHITE + (GREEN << 4));
```

```
  cputs("                                                      ");
  gotoxy(17, 6);
  inputBuf[0] = 0x3f;
  bufp = cgets(inputBuf);
  strncpy(sendPacket.record.data.data, bufp, 0x3f);
  strcat(sendPacket.record.data.data, "\0");
  textattr(YELLOW + (BLUE << 4));
  gotoxy(10, 12);
  cputs("Enter 'Y' to accept this new record, any other key to cancel");
  c = getch();
  if (c != 'y' && c != 'Y')
    {
    textattr(textInfo.attribute);
    puttext(5, 7, 75, 18, screenBuf);
     return(-1);
    }
  /* Now get the rest of the information you need to supply for the
record. */
  /* GetConnectionInformation gives you your bindery object ID, which */
  /* you place in the objectID field of the new record.            */
  ccode = GetConnectionInformation(GetConnectionNumber(),
                                   objectName,
                                   &objectType,
                                   &sendPacket.record.data.objectID,
                                   loginTime);
  /* IPXGetInternetworkAddress provides you with your node address, */
  /* which you place in the nodeAddress field of the new record.    */
  IPXGetInternetworkAddress(sendPacket.record.data.nodeAddress);
  /* responseCode helps you verify the integrity of the response packet
*/
  sendPacket.responseCode = responseCode;
  /* Insert op code for AddRecord into the send packet */
  sendPacket.operation = ADD_RECORD;
  /* Set up your listen, and send ECBs and post them */
  listenECB.ESRAddress = sendECB.ESRAddress = NULL;
  listenECB.socket = sendECB.socket = ENGINE_SOCKET;
  listenECB.fragCount = sendECB.fragCount = 0x02;
  sendHeader.packetType = 0x04;       // indicates an IPX packet
  /* Obtain the address of the nearest router that knows the */
  /* path to the engine.                                     */
  ccode = IPXGetLocalTarget(serverAddress,
                            sendECB.immediateAddress,
```

```
                              &transportTime);
/* IPXGetDataAddress constructs a FAR pointer to the first */
/* operand and initializes the second operand with that    */
 /* FAR pointer.                                            */
IPXGetDataAddress((BYTE *)&sendHeader,
                (WORD *)&sendECB.fragList[0].fragAddress);
sendECB.fragList[0].fragSize = sizeof(IPX_HEADER);
IPXGetDataAddress((BYTE *)&sendPacket,
                (WORD *)&sendECB.fragList[1].fragAddress);
sendECB.fragList[1].fragSize = sizeof(lPacket);
/* Initialize the destination address fields for the */
/* IPX header used to send the packet. */
memcpy(&sendHeader.destNet, serverAddress, 10);
sendHeader.destSocket = ENGINE_SOCKET;
IPXGetDataAddress((BYTE *)&listenHeader,
                (WORD *)&listenECB.fragList[0].fragAddress);
listenECB.fragList[0].fragSize = sizeof(IPX_HEADER);
IPXGetDataAddress((BYTE *)&listenPacket,
                (WORD *)&listenECB.fragList[1].fragAddress);
listenECB.fragList[1].fragSize = sizeof(lPacket);
/* Post the ECBs for receiving and sending. */
IPXListenForPacket(&listenECB);
IPXSendPacket(&sendECB);
/* Wait five seconds for a response packet from the engine. */
/* Allow the user to retry.                                  */
while(listenECB.inUseFlag)
    {
    c = 0;
    gotoxy(10, 12);
   textattr(YELLOW + (BLUE << 4));
    clreol();
    begin = end = clock();
    while(listenECB.inUseFlag)
        {
        end = clock();
        if (end - begin > CLK_TCK * 5)
            {
            gotoxy(10, 12);
            cputs("Confirmation not received -- enter 'Y' to Retry");
            c = getch();
            break;
            }
```

```
        }
     if (c != 'y' && c != 'Y')
        break;
      }
  if (listenECB.inUseFlag)
      {
     /* If you did not get a response packet from the engine, */
     /* cancel the Receive ECB and return. Record probably    */
      /* wasn't added.                                         */
     IPXCancelEvent(&listenECB);
    textattr(textInfo.attribute);
    puttext(5, 7, 75, 18, screenBuf);
   free(screenBuf);
    return(-1);
      }
  else
   {
     /* If you did get a response packet from the engine, check    */
     /* its integrity and infer whether or not the record was added. */
   gotoxy(10, 10);
    textattr(YELLOW + (BLUE << 4));
     if (listenPacket.responseCode != responseCode)
     cputs("Bad response code in confirmation packet ");
   if (listenPacket.record.header.status == 0x03)
     cputs("Duplicate key -- record NOT added");
    else
     cputs("Record Added!");
    }
  gotoxy(10, 12);
   textattr(YELLOW + (BLUE << 4));
  clreol();
  cputs("Press any key to continue ...");
  c = getch();
   textattr(textInfo.attribute);
   puttext(5, 7, 75, 18, screenBuf);
  free(screenBuf);
   return(0);
}
/
********************************************************************************
*  ScanForService
*
```

```
*
*
*   The ENGINE.NLM advertises itself using the Service Advertising
*
*   Protocol (SAP). You therefore can scan the bindery for advertising
*
*   engines and read their network address. After you obtain the network
*
*   address, you can start a session.
*
*
*
*   This routine finds as many as four advertising engines. When it finds
*
*   an advertising engine, it fills out an info node, which the function
*
*   SelectEngine uses to enable the user to select a specific engine.
*
*
*
*   Note: Just because you discover an advertising engine by scanning
*
*         the bindery does NOT mean that the engine is alive. The engine
*
*         could have gone down very recently. The InitEngine function
*
*         verifies that an engine is alive by sending a query packet to
*
*         it and listening for a response.
*
*
*
*********************************************************************/
int ScanForService()
{
    int ccode, index = 0;
    LONG objectID = -1;
    char objectName[49];
    WORD objectType;
    char objectHasProperties;
    char objectFlag;
    char objectSecurity;
```

```
   BYTE moreSegments;
   BYTE propertyFlags;
   /* Scan for objects of type 0x88. The engine advertises itself */
   /* as an object of type 0x88.                                  */
ccode = ScanBinderyObject("*",
                   0x88,
                   &objectID,
                   objectName,
                   &objectType,
                   &objectHasProperties,
                   &objectFlag,
                   &objectSecurity);
   if (ccode)
      return(-1);
   while (!ccode)
      {
    while(index < NUMBER_OF_NODES)
    if (info[index].occupied)
          index++;
        else
          break;
      if (info[index].occupied)
         return(0);
      info[index].occupied = 1;
      strncpy(info[index].serverName, objectName, 49);
    info[index].serverType = objectType;
      /* Read the engine's network address from the bindery. */
      ccode = ReadPropertyValue(info[index].serverName,
        info[index].serverType,
                           "NET_ADDRESS",
                            1,
                        info[index].engineAddress,
                           &moreSegments,
                           &propertyFlags);
      if (ccode)
         return(0x03);
      /* Continue scanning for more engines, up to four. */
      ccode = ScanBinderyObject("*",
                          0x88,   /* type of server you look for */
                          &objectID,
                          objectName,
                          &objectType,
```

```
                        &objectHasProperties,
                          &objectFlag,
                        &objectSecurity);
        }
   return(0);
}
/
****************************************************************************
*  SelectEngine
*
*
*
*  This routine scans the info nodes for engines discovered by
*
*  ScanForService. It displays the names of discovered engines and
*
*  prompts the user to select one of them.
*
*
*
****************************************************************************/
int SelectEngine(void)
{
  struct text_info textInfo;
  int index, row, found = 0;
  char c;
  BYTE *screenBuf, attr;
  screenBuf = (BYTE *)malloc(0x1000);
  if (screenBuf == NULL)
    {
    printf("\nOut of memory allocating screen buffer");
    return(-1);
    }
  gettextinfo(&textInfo);
  gettext(5, 7, 75, 18, screenBuf);
  attr = (YELLOW + (BLUE << 4));
  win(5, 7, 75, 18, attr);
  gotoxy(1, 1);
  cputs("_ÄÄÄÄÄÄÄÄÄÄÄÄÄÄÄÄÄÄÄÄÄÄÄÄÄÄÄÄÄÄÄÄÄÄÄÄÄÄÄÄÄÄÄÄÄÄÄÄ\
      ÄÄÄÄÄÄÄÄÄÄÄÄÄÄÄÄÄÄÄÄÄÄÄÄ¿");
  for(index = 2; index <= 10; index++)
    {
```

```
   gotoxy(1, index);
      cputs("_
_");
    }
  gotoxy(1, 11);
  cputs("_ÄÄÄÄÄÄÄÄÄÄÄÄÄÄÄÄÄÄÄÄÄÄÄÄÄÄÄÄÄÄÄÄÄÄÄÄÄÄÄÄÄÄÄÄÄÄÄ\
      ÄÄÄÄÄÄÄÄÄÄÄÄÄÄÄÄÄÄÄÄÄ_");
  gotoxy(25, 2);
  cputs("Advertising Engines");
  row = 4;
  for(index = 0; index < NUMBER_OF_NODES; index++)
    {
    if (info[index].occupied)
      {
      found++;
      gotoxy(3, row++);
      printf("%i. Engine Name: %s", index + 1,
          info[index].serverName);
      ++row;
      }
    }
  if (!found)
    {
    free(screenBuf);
    return(0);
    }
  gotoxy(1, 12);
  cputs("Enter Engine Number:");
  c = getch();
  index = (c - 0x30);
  index--;
  textattr(textInfo.attribute);
  puttext(5, 7, 75, 18, screenBuf);
   /* If the user selected a valid engine, copy that engine's network */
   /* address into the global serverAddress variable.                 */
  if (index < NUMBER_OF_NODES && info[index].occupied)
    {
    memcpy(&serverAddress, &info[index].engineAddress, 12);
    free(screenBuf);
    return(index);
    }
  free(screenBuf);
```

```
     return(-1);
}
/
***************************************************************************
*   InitEngine
*
*
*
*   This function sends a query packet to the engine indicated by the
*
*   index parameter. (index is an index into the array of info nodes.)
*
*
*
*   InitEngine then listens for a response packet from the engine.
*
*   This serves to verify that the engine is actually up and running.
*
*
*
***************************************************************************/
int InitEngine(int index)
{
  IPX_ECB sendECB, listenECB;                // send and receive ECBs
  IPX_HEADER sendHeader, listenHeader;       // IPX headers
  iPacket initPacket;                        // packet buffer
  int transportTime, ccode;
  clock_t begin, end;                        // used to time-out receive
ECB
    /* Initialize the send and receive ECBs, and the send header and
packet. */
  listenECB.ESRAddress = sendECB.ESRAddress = NULL;
  listenECB.socket = sendECB.socket = INIT_SOCKET;
  listenECB.fragCount = sendECB.fragCount = 0x02;
  sendHeader.packetType = listenHeader.packetType = 0x04; // IPX type
  sendHeader.destSocket = listenHeader.destSocket = INIT_SOCKET;
    /* Get the address of the nearest router that knows the path */
    /* to the engine.                                          */
  ccode = IPXGetLocalTarget(info[index].engineAddress,
                  sendECB.immediateAddress,
                  &transportTime);
    /* IPXGetDataAddress constructs a FAR pointer to the first */
    /* operand and initializes the second operand with that    */
```

```
    /* FAR pointer.                                        */
IPXGetDataAddress((BYTE *)&sendHeader,
            (WORD  *)&sendECB.fragList[0].fragAddress);
sendECB.fragList[0].fragSize = sizeof(IPX_HEADER);
IPXGetDataAddress((BYTE *)&initPacket,
            (WORD  *)&sendECB.fragList[1].fragAddress);
sendECB.fragList[1].fragSize = sizeof(iPacket);
IPXGetDataAddress((BYTE *)&listenHeader,
            (WORD  *)&listenECB.fragList[0].fragAddress);
listenECB.fragList[0].fragSize = sizeof(IPX_HEADER);
IPXGetDataAddress((BYTE *)&initPacket,
            (WORD  *)&listenECB.fragList[1].fragAddress);
listenECB.fragList[1].fragSize = sizeof(iPacket);
    /* Initialize the destination address of the IPX send header. */
memcpy(&sendHeader.destNet, info[index].engineAddress, 10);
    /* Post for receiving and sending. */
IPXListenForPacket(&listenECB);
IPXSendPacket(&sendECB);
    /* Wait five seconds for a response. */
if(listenECB.inUseFlag)
    {
  begin = end = clock();
  while (listenECB.inUseFlag)
      {
      end = clock();
      if ((end - begin) > (0x5a))
        {
        cputs("\nNo response from ENGINE");
        break;
        }
      }
    }
  if (listenECB.inUseFlag)
    return(-1);
  return(0);
}
/
****************************************************************************
*  menu
*
*
*
*  This function enables the user to add, read, edit, and delete records.
*
```

```
 *
 *
 *************************************************************************/
void menu(void)
{
  int i;
   struct text_info textInfo;
  char c;
  BYTE *screenBuf, attr;
  screenBuf = (BYTE *)malloc(0x1000);
  if (screenBuf == NULL)
     {
     printf("\nOut of memory allocating screen buffer");
     return;
     }
  while(1)
     {
     gettextinfo(&textInfo);
     gettext(25, 5, 55, 15, screenBuf);
     attr = (YELLOW + (BLUE << 4));
     win(25, 5, 55, 15, attr);
     gotoxy(1, 1);
     cputs("_ÄÄÄÄÄÄÄÄÄÄÄÄÄÄÄÄÄÄÄÄÄÄÄÄÄÄÄÄ¿");
     for (i = 2; i <= 9; i++)
        {
        gotoxy(1, i);
          cputs("_                    _");
        }
     gotoxy(1, 10);
     cputs("_ÄÄÄÄÄÄÄÄÄÄÄÄÄÄÄÄÄÄÄÄÄÄÄÄÄÄÄÄ_");
     gotoxy(6, 2);
     cputs("Engine Client Menu");
     gotoxy(3, 4);
     cputs("1. Add new record");
     gotoxy(3, 5);
     cputs("2. Edit existing record");
     gotoxy(3, 6);
     cputs("3. Read existing record");
     gotoxy(3, 7);
     cputs("4. Delete existing record");
     gotoxy(3, 8);
     cputs("5. Quit");
     gotoxy(1, 11);
     cputs(" Select a Menu Item by number");
```

```
  c = getch();
  switch(c)
    {
    case '1': { AddRecord(); break;}
    case '2': { GetRecord(EDIT_RECORD); break; }
    case '3': { GetRecord(READ_RECORD); break; }
    case '4': { GetRecord(DELETE_RECORD); break; }
    case '5':
      {
      textattr(textInfo.attribute);
      puttext(25, 5, 55, 15, screenBuf);
      free(screenBuf);
      return;
      }
    default: break;
    }
  }
}
int main()
{
  struct text_info textInfo;
  char c;
  BYTE *screenBuf, attr;
  WORD engineSocket = ENGINE_SOCKET;
  WORD initSocket = INIT_SOCKET;
  int ccode;
  /* Ensure that IPX is loaded and obtain the address of the IPX    */
  /* entry point. The NetWare C Interface for DOS maintains a global */
  /* variable IPXLocation, that is initialized by this call.   */
  ccode = IPXInitialize();
  if (ccode)
    {
    printf("\nIPX not loaded--load IPX and try again");
    return(ccode);
    }
  /* Open our sockets. */
  ccode = IPXOpenSocket(&engineSocket, 0x00);
  ccode = IPXOpenSocket(&initSocket, 0x00);
  screenBuf = (BYTE *)malloc(0x1000);
  if (screenBuf == NULL)
    {
    printf("\nOut of memory allocating screen buffer");
    return(-1);
    }
```

```
gettextinfo(&textInfo);
gettext(1, 1, 80, 25, screenBuf);
ccode = ScanForService();
 if (ccode)
    {
    printf("\n No Advertising Engines found");
    return(-1);
    }

 while(ccode = SelectEngine() == -1);
ccode = InitEngine(ccode);
if (ccode)
    {
    puttext(1, 1, 80, 25, screenBuf);
    free(screenBuf);
    return(-1);
    }
menu();
puttext(1, 1, 80, 25, screenBuf);
free(screenBuf);
return(0);
}
/***** END OF FILE (CLIENT.C) *****/
```

Polling versus Sleeping

Polling means checking the status of a data structure at regular intervals to determine whether a resource has become available. If an application is listening for an IPX packet to arrive, for example, the application checks (polls) the status of the Event Control Block (ECB) at regular intervals to see whether the packet has arrived.

You probably poll every day. If you check your mailbox, for example, to see whether the mail carrier has arrived, you are polling your mailbox. If you run your electronic-mail program every hour to see whether you have received any messages, you are polling your electronic mail.

Sleeping means waiting on a semaphore until the status of a data structure has changed. In NetWare, the operating system awakens you when a resource becomes available. Sleeping is similar to having an electronic-mail program that pops up when you receive mail. You can go about your business, effectively ignoring your electronic mail until it pops up; then you can run the electronic mail program and read your messages.

What are the implications of polling and sleeping for a DP application? In a nutshell, polling consumes CPU resources. On a single-tasking operating system such as DOS, CPU resources are dedicated entirely to the running program. For a multithreaded operating system such as NetWare, however, CPU resources should be conserved so that all active threads can gain access to the CPU as required. The implications are clear. It is no problem for a DOS program to poll, because it is the sole consumer of CPU resources. It is inefficient, however, for a NetWare thread to poll, because doing so prevents other threads from gaining access to the CPU as often as they would otherwise. The source code for ENGINE.NLM and CLIENT.EXE present perfect examples of times your DP application should poll and times it should sleep. CLIENT.EXE polls ECBs while waiting for an IPX packet to arrive (see listing 15.5).

Listing 15.5:
Polling an ECB to determine when an IPX packet arrives (from CLIENT.C).

```
IPXListenForPacket(&listenECB);
IPXSendPacket(&sendECB);
/* Wait five seconds for a response packet. Enable the user to retry. */
while(listenECB.inUseFlag)
    {
    c = 0;
    gotoxy(10, 12);
    textattr(YELLOW + (BLUE << 4));
    clreol();
    begin = end = clock();
```

```
while(listenECB.inUseFlag)
   {
   end = clock();
   if (end - begin > CLK_TCK * 5)
      {
      gotoxy(10, 12);
      cputs("Confirmation not received -- enter 'Y' to Retry");
      c = getch();
      break;
      }
   }
if (c != 'y' && c != 'Y')
   break;
}
```

In listing 15.5, CLIENT.EXE begins listening for an IPX response packet and immediately sends an IPX request packet. Then it polls the ECB for five seconds, and checks to see whether the response packet has arrived. If the response packet does not arrive within five seconds, CLIENT.EXE prompts the user to listen again for five more seconds. In the case of CLIENT.EXE, polling is not wasteful because no other threads are waiting for the CPU (DOS is a single-tasking operating system). Listing 15.6 shows how ENGINE.NLM performs a similar task by sleeping.

Listing 15.6:

ENGINE.NLM sleeps while listening for IPX packets. The NetWare operating system awakens ENGINE.NLM when a packet arrives.

```
/* fill out your listen ECBs and post them */
for (index = 0; index < 6; index++)
  {
  opNodes[index].packet.operation = 0;
  listenECBs[index].queueHead = &queueHead;
  listenECBs[index].semHandle = requestSem;
  listenECBs[index].socket = ENGINE_SOCKET;
  listenECBs[index].fragCount = 2;
  listenECBs[index].fragList[0].fragAddress = &listenHeaders[index];
  listenECBs[index].fragList[0].fragSize = sizeof(IPX_HEADER);
  listenECBs[index].fragList[1].fragAddress = &listenPackets[index];
  listenECBs[index].fragList[1].fragSize = sizeof(lPacket);
```

```
  ccode = IpxReceive(0, &listenECBs[index]);
  }
/* When you get here, all six ECBs are listening for IPX packets */
/* sent to the engine by clients.                                */
while(!shutdown)
  {
  /* At this point, the EngineMain thread goes to sleep until */
  /* a client sends a request packet. When a request packet   */
  /* comes in, the OS links the ECB that describes the packet */
  /* to a list of 'received ECBs.' Then the OS wakes the      */
  /* EngineMain thread by signaling the requestSem semaphore. */
  ccode = WaitOnLocalSemaphore(requestSem);
  if (shutdown)
    break;
  /* IpxGetAndClearQ returns a linked list of all ECBs that   */
  /* describe a received packet. The length of the list depends */
  /* on how many packets the engine has received.            */
  thisECB = IpxGetAndClearQ(&queueHead);
```

In listing 15.6, ENGINE.NLM begins listening for IPX packets (using six ECBs enables ENGINE.NLM to receive six IPX packets concurrently). As soon as all six ECBs are posted for listening, ENGINE.NLM goes to sleep by calling `WaitOnLocalSemaphore`. The operating system awakens ENGINE.NLM as soon as an IPX packet arrives. ENGINE.NLM then gathers all received packets by calling `IpxGetAndClearQ` and services the requests contained in those packets.

An NLM must sleep rather than poll when it is waiting for the status of data structures to change. This statement is as true when an NLM is waiting for IPX packets to arrive as it is when it is waiting for a file to become available for locking.

NetWare, as a multithreaded operating system, always has a thread that requires access to the CPU. Polling wastes CPU resources because it causes unnecessary thread switches. Sleeping is always more efficient because sleeping threads do not require access to the CPU until they are ready to run (by definition, the data structure they are waiting on has become available.)

Using Worker Threads in ENGINE.NLM

Whenever a DOS client sends a request packet to ENGINE.NLM, the NLM creates a worker thread to execute the client's request. Five client requests, for example, cause the NLM to create five worker threads: each worker thread executes a single request. When the worker threads finish executing their request, they kill themselves by returning to the NLM.

Listing 15.7:
ENGINE.NLM creates a worker thread to handle every individual client request.

```
ccode = BeginThread(DoOperation,
                    NULL,
                    0x1000,
                    &opNodes[index]);
/* Now that you have dispatched the operation, you can repost */
/* the ECB for further listening. This process makes the ECB  */
/* available for receiving packets even before the worker     */
/* thread has performed the requested operation!              */
tempECB = thisECB;
thisECB = thisECB->next;
ccode = IpxReceive(0, tempECB);
```

Why should you create worker threads to handle client requests? The answer is simple. Doing so enables ENGINE.NLM to handle a high volume of requests because dispatching those requests using worker threads means that many outstanding requests can be serviced concurrently by the NetWare operating system. Each client—no matter how many there are—gains a fair share of the operating system's resources and is not penalized by the activity of other clients. The use of worker threads to handle individual client requests enables ENGINE.NLM to scale well when the number of concurrent clients grows.

Retrying IPX Operations

The IPX protocol does not provide the guaranteed delivery of packets. Your DP application, therefore, can send packets that the destination node does not receive. IPX is a "best-effort" protocol—it does not notify you when the packet fails to reach its destination node. IPX is not unique in this sense: UDP (the TCP/IP equivalent of IPX) also does not guarantee delivery of packets.

SPX, a higher-level network communications protocol supported by NetWare, is a guaranteed-delivery protocol (much like TCP). SPX guarantees delivery by forcing the recipient of a packet to acknowledge its reception. If SPX does not receive acknowledgment, it informs the application and retries the operation.

Most applications can handle the best-effort design of IPX by enabling client and server modules to retry requests and responses. ENGINE.NLM uses the retry method. The key to enabling retries is to remember that your DP application may receive duplicate request packets (if the client decides to retry a request). Your DP application should be intelligent enough to receive duplicate requests without causing the database to become corrupted.

Although IPX does not guarantee delivery of packets, dropped (not received) packets are rare. Because dropped packets are possible, however, you should plan for them. If dropped packets are unacceptable, you can use SPX rather than IPX. (The SPX programming interface is the same as the IPX interface.)

Summary

This chapter dealt with IPX message-passing architecture. You learned about IPX in detail and ways to use the distributed-file manager. The source code for the distributed record manager was also discussed in detail.

Topics covered in this chapter:

Understanding abends

Understanding Error Handling and Fault Tolerance

Relinquishing Control of the CPU

Looking at MEMWRAP.OBJ

Chapter 16

NLM Reliability

A data-processing application must be, above all else, reliable. Reliability means that the integrity of the data that is maintained and processed by the DP application be preserved. A DP application must also run error-free at all times. Obviously, certain errors occur over which the DP application has no control, such as a hardware failure in the host computer. It is critical, however, that the DP application be well behaved, and that it does not cause the system to suffer errors.

This chapter discusses the most common NLM programming mistakes that have an adverse effect on NLM DP applications. These mistakes include the following:

❖ Making errors in pointing memory-addressing

❖ Failing to relinquish control of the CPU

❖ Failing to unload cleanly

❖ Inadvertently creating a sparse file by seeking past the end of a file

Before reading the rest of this chapter, remember that NetWare protects your DP application against hardware failures. The fault-tolerant features you read about in Chapter 5, such as disk mirroring and duplexing, transaction tracking, read-after-write verification, and hot-fixes, mean that hardware failures will rarely, if ever, corrupt your application's data.

 Although NetWare prevents hardware failures from corrupting data files, they still cause the server to "go down," or halt.

This chapter concentrates on helping you to avoid introducing errors into the very stable NetWare platform (specifically, to avoid making the errors in your application that can bring down the system.

Understanding abends

An *abend* is programming shorthand for "*ab*normal *end*" (a total system halt). NetWare stops running. An abend happens as the result of a corruption of an internal NetWare memory structure. NetWare continually performs consistency checking of its internal data structures. Whenever it detects an inconsistency, it abends.

The most frequent cause of an abend is memory corruption due to programming errors in an NLM that is running on the system. (Remember, NetWare has no memory protection.) The fact that some memory is corrupted raises the possibility that other memory is corrupted (memory that has not yet been checked for consistent format). Thus, in turn, other data may be corrupt, including file-cache buffers.

The reason that NetWare halts when it detects memory corruption is that NetWare must not allow some corrupt memory to cause further corruption. If a file-cache buffer is corrupt, for example, NetWare would corrupt file data if it flushed that file cache buffer to disk. So, rather than keep running, NetWare halts.

Although it is annoying to experience an abend on your server, you should feel confident that NetWare, as long as it is running, is as solid as a rock. That is, NetWare halts whenever it detects corrupted memory. By inference, then, if NetWare does not halt, memory is not corrupt.

The trick, of course, is to avoid abends in the first place. By definition, a NetWare server that remains running for more than a few minutes after you have loaded all the NLMs is a stable system, including the NLMs loaded on the server. Chances are that if the server remains running for a little while, it will run forever. The exception, of course, is that hardware failures (such as bad memory chips) also can cause an abend to occur. (Of course, you certainly do not want NetWare to run with bad hardware.)

Specific programming errors almost always cause abends. These errors include the following:

- ❖ Writing to operating-system memory
- ❖ Freeing memory you have not allocated
- ❖ Unloading an NLM that has not closed its semaphores
- ❖ Using uninitialized pointers
- ❖ Calling library functions (such as `printf`) with bad pointers

The remainder of this chapter discusses ways to avoid these and other programming errors, including providing a tool you can use to trap memory errors.

Understanding Error Handling and Fault Tolerance

It is always good C programming practice to check for errors after making function calls. Programmers call this practice *error handling*. When you are writing a NetWare-based DP application in C, error handling is especially important. The following sections discuss some specific instances in which error handling is critical to your DP application.

Whenever you open a file, check to ensure that the open call was successful before writing to or reading from that file. If you are using the `fopen` API, the file handle is a NULL pointer in the case of an error. If you use the lower-level POSIX `open` API, the file handle is an integer with the value zero. Whenever you allocate memory, check the pointer returned by the `malloc`, `calloc`, or `realloc` API: if the allocation failed, the pointer is NULL.

 Never use a screen or a semaphore without verifying that your application opened it successfully.

When you are checking for errors within your DP application, remember that different APIs indicate errors differently. Some APIs return zero in case of an error; other APIs return a nonzero value in case of an error. Fault tolerance in your DP application means that you handle errors correctly and, whenever possible, recover from those errors.

If your DP application experiences a failure in allocating memory, for example, perform a thread switch and try again to allocate memory (perhaps some memory became available while your application was trapping the error). The same is true for opening files, semaphores, and screens. Because of NetWare's multithreaded design, resources that were unavailable a millisecond ago might have become available since then.

Fault tolerance in your DP application means also that it can detect bad inputs and trap them. In a client-server application, for example, the server-based component should be capable of handling malformed request packets without crashing. Client applications should detect and trap user input that is out-of-range or incorrect.

Fault tolerance means that your DP application makes use of NetWare's built-in fault-tolerance capability. For example, your DP application should use transaction tracking for all database updates. If you deem it necessary, your DP application should open files in write-through mode when you do not want the file's data to be cached. (The `FEOpen` API enables you to open a file in write-through mode.)

Relinquishing Control of the CPU

If your application does not relinquish control of the CPU frequently, operating-system threads and other NLMs are not capable of performing their work. This limitation can have a range of effects on server operation, from slowing performance to causing the server to drop client connections.

The key to relinquishing control of the server's CPU lies in understanding which NetWare APIs relinquish control and which do not. For example, `printf`, `malloc`, `OpenSemaphore`, `opendir`, and many other APIs relinquish control (or go to sleep) before they return to your application. When you call these APIs (and many others like them), your application implicitly relinquishes control of the CPU. Consequently, your DP application does not have to do anything explicitly to relinquish control of the CPU.

Other NetWare APIs do not relinquish control (`memcpy`, `memset`, `strcpy`, `fseek`, `lseek`, `clock`, and `time`, for example). Still other APIs sometimes relinquish control but frequently do not. For example, most of the file I/O APIs (except those APIs that open files) go to sleep when file data does not reside in the cache, but do not go to sleep when file data is cached.

> Although no documentation states which APIs relinquish control and which do not, a good rule of thumb is that all APIs that allocate resources from the operating system (resources such as memory, file handles, semaphores, and screens) relinquish control of the CPU before returning to your application.

When you find a spot in your DP application at which it is necessary to relinquish control of the CPU explicitly, you can do so by calling one of two simple APIs: `ThreadSwitch` or `delay`. `ThreadSwitch` forces the NetWare scheduler to place the calling thread at the end of the run queue, which causes other threads to gain access to the server's CPU ahead of your thread. When all of the other threads have executed and relinquished control of the CPU (either implicitly or explicitly), your thread again has control of the CPU. The following line shows the prototype for `ThreadSwitch`:

```
void ThreadSwitch(void);
```

The `delay` API goes further than `ThreadSwitch`—it forces the NetWare scheduler to take your thread completely off the run queue for a specified number of milliseconds. After the specified interval has expired, the scheduler places your thread at the end of the run queue. The prototype for delay is as follows:

```
void delay(unsigned milliseconds);
```

Note that there are 1,000 milliseconds in a second. To sleep for one second, therefore, a thread calls `delay`, as follows:

```
delay(1000);
```

If you explicitly relinquish control within the body of tight loops throughout your DP application, chances are that the application will not prevent other threads from gaining control of the CPU in a timely manner. For example:

```
BYTE memArray[50][512];
int i;
BYTE *p = &someDataStructure;
for (i = 0; i < 50; i++)
  {
  memcpy(&memArray[i], p, 512); // no implicit
thread switch
  ThreadSwitch();                      // relinquish con-
trol at the
  }                                    // bottom of tight
loop
```

Looking at MEMWRAP.OBJ: A Memory Allocation Wrapper

Memory errors are the most frequent and most treacherous area of NLM programming, due to the nature of the C programming language (not because of any characteristic of NetWare). NetWare's lack of memory protection, however, makes discovering memory errors more difficult than in an operating system that has memory protection (such as UNIX).

Detecting memory errors during the development process is the key to creating stable server-based DP applications. For this reason, consider MEMWRAP.OBJ. MEMWRAP is a memory-allocation wrapper that tracks your application's allocation of memory, traps errors, and reports memory use. You should link

MEMWRAP.OBJ to all of your server-based applications. During development, you activate MEMWRAP by defining the preprocessor MEMWRAP variable. (You can define this variable on the compiler command line or in your source code.) When you go into production with your application, you undefine the MEMWRAP preprocessor variable to make MEMWRAP inactive.

To use MEMWRAP, you must include the header file MEMWRAP.H in your source code. You must include this special header file in your DP application if you want to use the memory debugging features of MEMWRAP.OBJ. The primary function of MEMWRAP.H is simple: redirect all calls that your DP application makes to the memory APIs `malloc`, `calloc`, `realloc`, and `free` to special debugging-oriented calls contained in the library MEMWRAP.OBJ. To do this, MEMWRAP.H uses the C preprocessor to redefine the calls to memory APIs in your source file to call instead special corresponding APIs in MEMWRAP.OBJ.

When your application calls `malloc`, for example, the C preprocessor redefines the source code to call `MWMalloc` instead. The same step occurs for the other memory APIs: a call to `calloc` becomes a call to `MWCalloc`; a call to `realloc` becomes a call to `MWRealloc`; and a call to `free` becomes a call to `MWFree`. Notice that the redefined calls to memory APIs also produce two extra parameters: the name of the source file making the call and the line in that source file. MEMWRAP.H accomplishes this by using the ANSI C macros __FILE__ and __LINE__.

Listing 16.1 shows the source code for MEMWRAP.H. Later, this chapter discusses the source code for MEMWRAP.OBJ and how it works, and then presents a sample program that demonstrates MEMWRAP.OBJ.

Listing 16.1:
MEMWRAP.H.

```
/**********************************************************************
*  MEMWRAP.OBJ
*
*                                                                     *
*  Memory debug library                                              *
*--------------------------------------------------------------------*
*                                                                     *
* filename         :  memwrap.h                                       *
* date             :  Sept 5 1992                                     *
* version          :  1.0                                             *
* compiler         :  Watcom C 386 (see makefile for cc options)     *
*                                                                     *
**********************************************************************/
#include <nwtypes.h>
#include <stdio.h>
#include <string.h>
#include <malloc.h>
#include <assert.h>
#include <conio.h>
#include <nwtypes.h>
#include <process.h>
#ifdef MEMWRAP
   #define SENTINEL 0xffaaffaa
   #define MODULES 100
   #ifndef MEMWRAP_STRUCTS
   #define MEMWRAP_STRUCTS
   typedef struct{
      char file[13];
      } MOD;
/* The following structure must be aligned on DWORD boundaries */
   #pragma pack(4)            // force DWORD alignment
   typedef struct memNode{
      LONG size;
      LONG line;
      int modIdx;
      struct memNode *next;
      struct memNode *prev;
      LONG begSentinal;
      } MEM_NODE;
   #pragma pack()             // return to default alignment
```

```
    #endif
/**** NEVER CALL THE FOLLOWING SIX FUNCTIONS FROM YOUR PROGRAM ****/
      void *MWMalloc(size_t, char *, unsigned long);
      void *MWCalloc(size_t, size_t, char *, unsigned long);
      void *MWRealloc(void *, size_t, char *, unsigned long);
      void MWFree(void *, char *, unsigned long);
      void AddNodeToList(MEM_NODE *);
      void DelNodeFromList(MEM_NODE *);
/**** YOU MAY CALL THE FOLLOWING FIVE FUNCTIONS FROM YOUR PROGRAM ****/
/*---- These functions are debugging utilities: You can leave ----*/
/*---- them in your source code because the preprocessor      ----*/
/*---- disables them when MEMWRAP is NOT defined.             ----*/
   void DumpList(void);
   void BiteTheWall(char *message, char *file, unsigned long line);
      void FreeList(void);
      void CheckAlloc(void);
      int  CheckPointer(void *);
/**** PREPROCESSOR DEFINITIONS OF MEMORY CALLS ****/
   #define malloc(x) MWMalloc((x), (__FILE__), (__LINE__))
   #define calloc(x, y) MWCalloc((x), (y), (__FILE__), (__LINE__))
   #define realloc(x, y) MWRealloc((x), (y), (__FILE__), (__LINE__))
   #define free(x) MWFree((x), (__FILE__), (__LINE__))
#endif
#ifndef MEMWRAP
   #define DumpList()
   #define CheckAlloc()
   #define BiteTheWall()
   #define FreeList()
   #define CheckPointer(x) 0
#endif
/***** END OF FILE (MEMWRAP.H) *****/
```

Using MEMWRAP.H

Near the beginning of MEMWRAP.H, the MEM_NODE structure
provides control information for every allocation that your application makes. MEMWRAP.OBJ maintains a linked list of allocation-control structures, which is how it tracks your DP
application's use of memory.

The allocation-control structures are hidden from your DP application. MEMWRAP.OBJ returns a pointer to usable memory, just as the standard `malloc`, `calloc`, and `realloc` APIs do. Similarly, MEMWRAP.OBJ frees memory, just as the standard `free` API does.

The differences in your application's behavior are apparent when you make programming mistakes. If you call a memory API using a bad parameter, for example, MEMWRAP.OBJ traps the call and sends an alert message to the server-console screen. This action prevents the application from corrupting server memory. In addition, to enable you to fix the problem immediately, the alert includes the source-code file and the line that generated the bad call, so that you know exactly where it originated.

Some of the errors trapped by MEMWRAP.OBJ include the following:

- ❖ Attempting to allocate zero bytes of memory
- ❖ Calling an allocation API with a negative size parameter
- ❖ Attempting to free unallocated memory
- ❖ Making use of an uninitialized pointer
- ❖ Attempting to free an uninitialized pointer
- ❖ Failure to free allocated memory
- ❖ Failure to check for the success of an allocation

Debugging Utility Routines

In addition to redirecting ANSI C memory APIs, MEMWRAP.H includes the prototypes for five debugging utility routines you can use within the source code of your DP application. The five debugging utility routines are `DumpList`, `BiteTheWall`, `FreeList`, `CheckAlloc`, and `CheckPointer`. Do not be concerned about removing these calls from your source code when it is ready to go into production: MEMWRAP.H disables the calls when you undefine the preprocessor variable MEMWRAP. Even if you leave calls to these utility routines in your production source code, therefore, they resolve to null statements and have no effect on the execution of your production DP application.

DumpList dumps control information for all of your application's active (unfreed) memory allocations. The control information includes the size of the allocation, its address in server memory, and the source code file and line in which your application made the allocation. You can call DumpList anywhere within your application.

BiteTheWall is a simple reporting routine that displays an alert message to the server console, including the source file and line number you pass to it. In addition, BiteTheWall forces the user to acknowledge the alert by blocking on the keyboard (pressing a key before execution of the application continues).

FreeList traverses the linked list of memory-control structures and frees all active allocations your DP application has made. The best place to use FreeList is at the end of your application (or in your application's unload function).

You should use FreeList carefully because it really frees memory. Use it only while you are debugging.

A production DP application should be capable of freeing all of its allocated memory without the help of a debugging tool such as MEMWRAP. CheckAlloc is a simple check routine you can call when you think your application has freed all of its allocated memory. If you are wrong (if your application has not freed all of its memory), CheckAlloc displays an alert and then dumps the control information for all unfreed memory.

CheckPointer enables you to verify the integrity of a pointer before you use it. If the pointer is uninitialized or corrupted, CheckPointer returns –1. Otherwise (if the pointer is valid), CheckPointer returns 0.

 You should use CheckPointer only with pointers containing addresses of memory allocated by calling alloc, calloc, or realloc when MEMWRAP is active.

The MEMWRAP.C Source Code File

The MEMWRAP.C source-code file contains the "smoke and mirrors" that allow memory debugging in an NLM. To see what happens in the background in MEMWRAP.C, look at how MEMWRAP.OBJ works (see listing 16.2).

Listing 16.2:
The source code for MEMWRAP.OBJ.

```
/************************************************************************
* MEMWRAP.OBJ
*
*                                                                      *
* Memory debug library                                                 *
*----------------------------------------------------------------------*
*                                                                      *
* filename        :  memwrap.c                                         *
* date            :  Sept 5 1992                                       *
* version         :  1.0                                               *
* compiler        :  Watcom C 386 (see makefile for cc options)        *
*                                                                      *
************************************************************************/
#include <stdio.h>
#include <string.h>
#include <malloc.h>
```

```
#include <assert.h>
#include <conio.h>
#include <nwtypes.h>
#include <process.h>
#define SENTINAL 0xffaaffaa
#define MODULES 100
typedef struct{
char file[13];
} MOD;
/* The following structure must be aligned on DWORD boundaries */
   #pragma pack(4)              // force DWORD alignment
   typedef struct memNode{
     LONG size;
     LONG line;
     int modIdx;
     struct memNode *next;
     struct memNode *prev;
     LONG begSentinal;
     } MEM_NODE;
   #pragma pack()              // return to default alignment
MEM_NODE *MWhead = NULL;
MOD MWmodules[MODULES];
LONG MWallocations = 0;
/*********************************************************************
* BiteTheWall                                                       *
*-----------------------------------------------------------------*
*                                                                   *
* Prints an error message and forces the user to acknowledge it by  *
* blocking on the keyboard.                                         *
*                                                                   *
* Callable from application                                         *
*                                                                   *
*********************************************************************/
void BiteTheWall(char *message, char *file, unsigned long line)
{
   printf("\n**** MEMORY ERROR\ *****");
   printf("\n\t%s", message);
   printf("\n\tFILE: %s; LINE: %li\n", file, line);
   PressAnyKeyToContinue();
   return;
}
/*********************************************************************
```

```
* AddNodeToList                                                            *
*--------------------------------------------------------------------------*
*                                                                          *
* Adds a new allocation node to the linked list                            *
*                                                                          *
* DO NOT CALL FROM APPLICATION                                             *
*                                                                          *
***************************************************************************/
void AddNodeToList(MEM_NODE *newNode)
{
   MEM_NODE *temp;
   if (MWhead == NULL)
      {
      _disable();
      MWhead = newNode;
      _enable();
       }
   else
       {
      temp = MWhead;
      while(temp->next)
         temp = temp->next;
      assert(temp->next == NULL);
      _disable();
      temp->next = newNode;
      newNode->prev = temp;
      _enable();
      ThreadSwitch();
       }
   return;
}
/*****************************************************************************
*                                                                          *
* DelNodeFromList                                                           *
*--------------------------------------------------------------------------*
*                                                                          *
* Deletes a memory-allocation node from list                               *
*                                                                          *
* DO NOT CALL FROM APPLICATION                                             *
*                                                                          *
***************************************************************************/
void DelNodeFromList(MEM_NODE *oldNode)
{
   MEM_NODE *temp;
```

```
   if (oldNode == MWhead)
      {
      if (oldNode->next == NULL)
         {
         _disable();
         MWhead = NULL;
         _enable();
         return;
         }
      _disable();
      MWhead = oldNode->next;
      MWhead->prev = NULL;
      _enable();
      return;
      }
   assert(oldNode->prev != NULL);
   _disable();
   if (oldNode->next)
      {
      oldNode->next->prev = oldNode->prev;
      oldNode->prev->next = oldNode->next;
      }
   else
      oldNode->prev->next = oldNode->next;
   _enable();
   return;
}
/*************************************************************************
 * DumpList                                                             *
 *---------------------------------------------------------------------*
 *                                                                      *
 * Displays the contents of the linked list of allocation nodes.       *
 * You may call DumpList at any time from your application to view      *
 * unfreed memory allocations, the source file and line that caused     *
 * the allocation, the size of the allocation, and the address of the   *
 * allocation.                                                          *
 *                                                                      *
 * Callable from application                                            *
 *                                                                      *
 *************************************************************************/
void DumpList(void)
{
   MEM_NODE *temp;
   int i = 0;
```

```
   printf("\n\n*** DUMPING MEMORY WRAPPER NODES ***\n");
   if (MWhead == NULL)
      {
      printf("\n\nNo nodes on list");
      assert(!MWallocations);
      }

   temp = MWhead;
   while(temp)
      {
      printf("\nFILE: %s; LINE: %li",
            MWmodules[temp->modIdx].file,
             temp->line);
      printf("\n\tSIZE: %li bytes; ADDRESS: %p",
             temp->size,
             temp + 1);
      if (temp->begSentinal != SENTINAL)
         printf("\n\t*** SENTINAL DAMAGED ***");
      _disable();
      temp = temp->next;
      _enable();
       i++;
      ThreadSwitch();
       }
   printf("\n*** END OF MEMORY WRAPPER NODE DUMP: %i nodes ***\n", i);
   PressAnyKeyToContinue();
}
/***********************************************************************
 *                                                                     *
 * FreeList                                                            *
 *-------------------------------------------------------------------* *
 *                                                                     *
 * Frees all unfreed allocation nodes. Because THIS CALL FREES MEMORY  *
 * don't use it unless you are ready to free all your unfreed allocations*
 *                                                                     *
 * Callable from application                                           *
 *                                                                     *
 ***********************************************************************/
void FreeList(void)
{
   MEM_NODE *temp;
   printf("\n\n*** FREEING MEMORY WRAPPER NODES ***\n");
   assert(MWhead != NULL);
   while (1)
```

```
      {
      _disable();
      temp = MWhead;
      MWhead = MWhead->next;
      _enable();
      free(temp);
      if (MWhead == NULL)
          break;
      ThreadSwitch();
       }
    return;
}
/**********************************************************************
 * CheckAlloc                                                         *
 *------------------------------------------------------------------- *
 *                                                                    *
 * Checks to see whether your application has any unfreed memory. If it *
 * does, it displays all unfreed memory by calling DumpList. This is a *
 * good routine to call at the end of your application, before it is  *
 * unloaded.                                                          *
 *                                                                    *
 *                                                                    *
 * Callable from application                                          *
 *                                                                    *
 **********************************************************************/
void CheckAlloc(void)
{
   if (MWallocations)
      {
      printf("\n*** UNFREED MEMORY NODES ***");
      DumpList();
      }
   return;
}
/**********************************************************************
 * CheckPointer                                                       *
 *------------------------------------------------------------------- *
 *                                                                    *
 * Checks to see whether pointer refers to memory actually allocated by *
 * the application. If so, returns zero. If pointer does not refer to  *
 * memory allocated by the application, returns -1. Good routine to call *
 * before dereferencing a pointer or writing to memory the pointer it  *
 * refers to. If pointer has been corrupted, returns -1.               *
 *                                                                    *
```

```
 * Callable from application                                          *
 *                                                                    *
 *********************************************************************/
int CheckPointer(void *pointer)
{
   MEM_NODE *temp;
   if (MWhead == NULL)
      {
      assert(!MWallocations);
      return(-1);
      }
   temp = MWhead;
   while (temp)
      {
      if ((temp + 1) == pointer)
         return(0);
      _disable();
      temp = temp->next;
      _enable();
      }
   if (!temp)
      return(-1);
}
/*********************************************************************
 * MWMalloc                                                          *
 *------------------------------------------------------------------*
 *                                                                   *
 * Wrapper for CLIB malloc routine. Allocates a MEM_NODE structure plus *
 * any memory requested by the application. Links the MEM_NODE into the *
 * linked list of allocation nodes. Checks for bad parameters passed by *
 * the application and traps them. Increments global MWallocations    *
 * variable. Returns usable memory to the application.               *
 *                                                                   *
 * DO NOT CALL FROM APPLICATION                                      *
 *                                                                   *
 *********************************************************************/
void *MWMalloc(size_t size, char *file, unsigned long line)
{
   MEM_NODE *newNode;
   BYTE *p;
   if (size < 1)
      {
      BiteTheWall("Attempted malloc with invalid size", file, line);
      return(NULL);
```

```
       }
    if (size > 0x100000 )
       {
        BiteTheWall("Attempted malloc over 1MB", file, line);
       return(NULL);
       }
    newNode = (MEM_NODE *)malloc(size + sizeof(MEM_NODE) + sizeof(LONG));
    if (newNode == NULL)
       {
       BiteTheWall("Unable to malloc new node", file, line);
       return(newNode);
       }
    newNode->prev = newNode->next = NULL;
    newNode->begSentinal = SENTINAL;
    newNode->line = line;
    newNode->size = size;
    for(newNode->modIdx = 0; newNode->modIdx < MODULES; newNode->modIdx++)
       {
       if (!strcmp(file, MWmodules[newNode->modIdx].file))
          break;
       if (!strlen(MWmodules[newNode->modIdx].file))
          {
          strncpy(MWmodules[newNode->modIdx].file, file, 12);
          break;
          }
       if (!strlen(MWmodules[newNode->modIdx].file))
          BiteTheWall("Out of module name storage", file, line);
       ThreadSwitch();
       }
    MWallocations++;
    AddNodeToList(newNode);
    return(newNode + 1);
}
/************************************************************************
* MWCalloc                                                             *
*---------------------------------------------------------------------*
*                                                                      *
* Wrapper for CLIB calloc routine. Allocates a MEM_NODE structure plus *
* any memory requested by the application. Links the MEM_NODE into the *
* linked list of allocation nodes. Checks for bad parameters passed by *
* the application and traps them. Increments global MWallocations      *
* variable. Returns usable memory to the application.                  *
*                                                                      *
* DO NOT CALL FROM APPLICATION                                         *
```

```
 *                                                                        *
 ************************************************************************/
void *MWCalloc(size_t num, size_t size, char *file, unsigned long line)
{
   MEM_NODE *newNode;
   BYTE *p;
   if (size < 1)
      {
      BiteTheWall("Attempted calloc with invalid size", file, line);
      return(NULL);
      }
   if (num < 1)
      {
      BiteTheWall("Attempted calloc with invalid number", file, line);
      return(NULL);
      }
   if (size > 0x100000 )
      {
       BiteTheWall("Attempted calloc over 1MB", file, line);
      return(NULL);
      }
   if (num > 0x100000)
      {
       BiteTheWall("Attempted calloc number over 0x100000", file, line);
      return(NULL);
      }
   size *= num;
   newNode = (MEM_NODE *)malloc(size + sizeof(MEM_NODE) + sizeof(LONG));
   if (newNode == NULL)
      {
      BiteTheWall("Unable to malloc new node", file, line);
      return(newNode);
      }
   newNode->prev = newNode->next = NULL;
   newNode->begSentinal = SENTINAL;
   newNode->line = line;
   newNode->size = size;
   memset(newNode + 1, 0, size);
   for(newNode->modIdx = 0; newNode->modIdx < MODULES; newNode->modIdx++)
      {
      if (!strcmp(file, MWmodules[newNode->modIdx].file))
         break;
      if (!strlen(MWmodules[newNode->modIdx].file))
         {
```

```
         strncpy(MWmodules[newNode->modIdx].file, file, 12);
          break;
           }
      if (!strlen(MWmodules[newNode->modIdx].file))
         BiteTheWall("Out of module name storage", file, line);
      ThreadSwitch();
         }
   MWallocations++;
   AddNodeToList(newNode);
   return(newNode + 1);
}
/*************************************************************************
* MWRealloc                                                             *
*----------------------------------------------------------------------*
*                                                                       *
* Wrapper for CLIB realloc routine. Allocates a MEM_NODE structure plus *
* any memory requested by the application. Links the MEM_NODE into the  *
* linked list of allocation nodes. Checks for bad parameters passed by  *
* the application and traps them. Copies contents of old allocation into*
* the new allocation. New allocation may be either larger or smaller    *
* than old allocation. If parameter for old allocation is null, behaves *
* just like MWMalloc. If parameter for old allocation is NOT null,      *
* verifies that application has allocated the old allocation.           *
*                                                                       *
* DO NOT CALL FROM APPLICATION                                          *
*                                                                       *
*************************************************************************/
void *MWRealloc(void *node, size_t size, char *file, unsigned long line)
{
   MEM_NODE *newNode, *oldNode, *temp;
   if (size < 1)
      {
      BiteTheWall("Attempted realloc with invalid size", file, line);
      return(NULL);
      }
   if (size > 0x100000 )
      {
       BiteTheWall("Attempted realloc with size over 1MB", file, line);
      return(NULL);
      }
   if (node && !MWhead)
      {
      BiteTheWall("Realloc called with non-null pointer and no \
previous allocations", file, line);
```

```
      return(NULL);
      }
  if (node && MWhead)
     {
     temp = MWhead;
     while(temp)
        {
        if (temp + 1 == node)
           break;
        _disable();
        temp = temp->next;
        _enable();
        ThreadSwitch();
        }
     if (temp == NULL)
        {
        node = NULL;
        BiteTheWall("Unable to locate node in list", file, line);
        goto NotAllocated;
        }
     oldNode = temp;
     newNode = (MEM_NODE *)malloc(size + sizeof(MEM_NODE) +
sizeof(LONG));
     if (newNode == NULL)
        {
        BiteTheWall("Unable to malloc new node", file, line);
        return(newNode);
        }
     newNode->prev = newNode->next = NULL;
     newNode->begSentinal = SENTINAL;
     newNode->line = line;
     newNode->size = size;
     if (newNode->size > oldNode->size)
        memcpy(newNode + 1, node, oldNode->size);
      else
        memcpy(newNode + 1, node, newNode->size);
     for(newNode->modIdx = 0; newNode->modIdx < MODULES; newNode-
>modIdx++)
        {
        if (!strcmp(file, MWmodules[newNode->modIdx].file))
           break;
        if (!strlen(MWmodules[newNode->modIdx].file))
           {
           strncpy(MWmodules[newNode->modIdx].file, file, 12);
```

```
        break;
         }
      if (!strlen(MWmodules[newNode->modIdx].file))
        BiteTheWall("Out of module name storage", file, line);
      ThreadSwitch();
       }
    AddNodeToList(newNode);
    if (oldNode->begSentinal != SENTINAL)
      BiteTheWall("*** SENTINAL DAMAGED ***", file, line);
    DelNodeFromList(oldNode);
    free(oldNode);
    node = newNode + 1;
    return(newNode + 1);
    } /**** if (node && MWhead) ****/
NotAllocated:
  assert(node == NULL);
  newNode = (MEM_NODE *)malloc(size + sizeof(MEM_NODE) + sizeof(LONG));
  if (newNode == NULL)
    {
    BiteTheWall("Unable to malloc new node", file, line);
    return(newNode);
    }
  newNode->prev = newNode->next = NULL;
  newNode->begSentinal = SENTINAL;
  newNode->line = line;
  newNode->size = size;
  memset(newNode + 1, 0, size);
  AddNodeToList(newNode);
  for(newNode->modIdx = 0; newNode->modIdx < MODULES; newNode->modIdx++)
    {
    if (!strcmp(file, MWmodules[newNode->modIdx].file))
      break;
    if (!strlen(MWmodules[newNode->modIdx].file))
      {
      strncpy(MWmodules[newNode->modIdx].file, file, 12);
      break;
      }
    if (!strlen(MWmodules[newNode->modIdx].file))
      BiteTheWall("Out of module name storage", file, line);
    ThreadSwitch();
    }
  MWallocations++;
  node = newNode + 1;
  return(newNode + 1);
```

```
}
/**************************************************************************
* MWFree                                                                  *
*-------------------------------------------------------------------------*
*                                                                         *
* Wrapper for CLIB free routine. Checks to ensure that application is     *
* not freeing a null pointer and not freeing unallocated memory. Checks   *
* to ensure that SENTINAL is not damaged. Unlinks allocation node from    *
* linked list. Frees allocation node.                                     *
*                                                                         *
* DO NOT CALL FROM APPLICATION                                            *
*                                                                         *
**************************************************************************/
void MWFree(void *node, char *file, unsigned long line)
{
   MEM_NODE *temp;
   if (!node)
      {
      BiteTheWall("Attempt to free NULL pointer", file, line);
      DumpList();
      abort();
      }
   if (!MWallocations || MWhead == NULL)
      {
      BiteTheWall("Attempt to free memory when MEMWRAP list is empty",
                  file, line);
      abort();
      }
   temp = MWhead;
   while(temp)
      {
      if (temp + 1 == node)
         break;
      _disable();
      temp = temp->next;
      _enable();
      ThreadSwitch();
      }
   if (!temp)
      {
      BiteTheWall("Attempt to free unallocated memory ", file, line);
      DumpList();
      abort();
      }
```

```
    if (temp->begSentinal != SENTINAL)
        BiteTheWall("*** SENTINAL DAMAGED ***", file, line);
    DelNodeFromList(temp);
    free(temp);
    MWallocations--;
}
/***** END OF FILE (MEMWRAP.C) *****/
```

Using MEMWRAP.OBJ

To use MEMWRAP.OBJ in your DP application, you should first compile the source file MEMWRAP.C into an object file (MEMWRAP.OBJ). After you have created the object file, you can link it to any other NLM.

To link MEMWRAP.OBJ to your DP application, you should include the header file MEMWRAP.H in all of your applications' source files. Because MEMWRAP.H prevents the redefinition of structures and variables, you do not have to be concerned about including it too many times in your application.

Finally, to make MEMWRAP.OBJ active, you must define MEMWRAP, using either the C preprocessor or the compiler command line. (You can define a preprocessor variable on the WATCOM command line using the /d switch: /dMEMWRAP, for example.)

The MEMTEST.NLM Sample Program

MEMTEST.NLM is a contrived piece of software whose sole purpose is to demonstrate MEMWRAP.OBJ (see listing 16.3). MEMTEST.NLM makes some errors in dealing with memory and pointers, among other things. (Running MEMTEST.NLM without MEMWRAP activated causes the server to abend.)

Listing 16.3:

MEMTEST.NLM, the test harness for MEMWRAP.OBJ.

```
/***************************************************************************
* MEMTEST.NLM                                                              *
*                                                                          *
* Test harness for MEMWRAP library                                         *
*--------------------------------------------------------------------------*
*                                                                          *
* filename     : memtest.c                                                 *
* date         : Sep 5 1992                                                *
* version      : 1.0                                                       *
* compiler     : Watcom C 386 (see makefile for cc options)               *
*                                                                          *
* This program is not copyrighted.                                         *
*                                                                          *
***************************************************************************/
#define MEMWRAP
#include "memwrap.h"
#include <stdio.h>
#include <string.h>
#include <malloc.h>
#include <assert.h>
#include <conio.h>
#include <nwtypes.h>
int main(void)
{
   char *p;
   p = (char *)malloc(-1);   // try allocation of negative in size
   if (p != NULL)
      free(p);
   p = (char *)malloc(0);    // try allocation of zero bytes
   if (p != NULL)
      free(p);
   p = (char *)malloc(25);    // non-error case
   strcpy(p, "MEMORY TEST");
   printf("\n%s", p);         // display memory contents
   PressAnyKeyToContinue();
   if (p != NULL)
      free(p);
   p = (char *)malloc(25);
   strcpy(p, "MEMORY TEST");
   p = realloc(p, 128);           // test MWRealloc
   printf("\n%s", p);             // display memory contents
```

```
PressAnyKeyToContinue();
DumpList();                      // dump node list
p = realloc(p, 10);             // test MWRealloc to a
*(p + 9) = 0;                   // SMALLER size
printf("\n%s", p);              // display memory contents
PressAnyKeyToContinue();
DumpList();                      // dump node list
free(p);
p = (char *)calloc(10, 10);     // allocate a bunch of
                                // memory using the same
p = (char *)malloc(1);          // pointer. Don't free the
p = (char *)malloc(1);          // memory. This normally
p = (char *)malloc(1);          // would cause the memory
p = (char *)malloc(1);          // to be "lost."
p = (char *)malloc(1);
p = (char *)malloc(1);
p = (char *)malloc(1);
p = (char *)malloc(1);
CheckAlloc();                    // trap unfreed memory nodes
FreeList();                      // free unfreed memory nodes
                                // NLM should unload without
return(0);                       // producing any alerts
                                // (Otherwise, you would see
                                // some alerts when the NLM
                                // terminated.)
}
/***** END OF FILE (MEMTEST.C) *****/
```

Listing 16.4 shows the make file for building MEMTEST.NLM.

Listing 16.4:
The make file for building MEMTEST.NLM.

```
#####
##### Simple make file
##### Useful for one source file
#####
.PROLOG:
      %if %exists(make.sem)
       @>
      @echo Somebody else is currently building $*
      @echo Try again later ...
       %exit 1
```

```
        %endif
.EPILOG:
        @>
        @echo Make session completed -
        @systime
        @>
.INIT:
        @systime > make.sem
        @castoff all
        @map p:=atm\code:bld\920813\nlmsdk
        %setenv wcg386=$(BIN)\386wcgl.exe
        %setenv INC386=p:\bld\920813\nlmsdk\include
.DEINIT:
        @del make.sem
        @caston all
TARG=$[r, $(FIRSTTARGET)]
BIN=w:\public\wcc90\bin
BINB=w:\public\wcc90\binb
LIB=p:\bld\920813\oslib\import
INCLUDE=p:\bld\920813\nlmsdk\include
IMP=$(LIB)\CLIB.imp
EXP=$(TARG).exp
## include MEMWRAP.OBJ in the list of object files to link
OBJS=$(TARG).obj memwrap.obj $(LIB)\prelude.obj
CCOPTS=/ez /od /3s /zq /d1
CCCMD=wcc386p
LINKCMD=nlmlinkp
MODS=CLIB
VER=1,0,0
.c.obj:
        @>
        @echo Compiling $<
        @>
        $(CCCMD) $(CCOPTS) $<
  wdisasm /l /s=$< $(TARG).obj
.obj.nlm:
        .LIS_FILE q:\users\miked\nlm\$(TARG).def
        @>
        @echo Linking $<
        @>
        nlmlinkr < <
COPYRIGHT    "This program is not copyrighted"
DEBUG
DESCRIPTION "Memory Wrapper Test Harness"
```

```
IMPORT @$(IMP)
#EXPORT
INPUT $(OBJS)
MAP
MODULE $(MODS)
OUTPUT $(TARG)
SCREENNAME "MEMTEST.NLM"
STACK 8192
TYPE 0
THREADNAME "MEMTEST"
VERSION $(VER)
<
### END OF FILE (MAKEFILE.MAK) ###
```

You can use the make file in listing 16.4 also to build
MEMWRAP.OBJ. Just issue the following command:

```
make memwrap.obj
```

To build MEMTEST.NLM, you issue the following command:

```
make memtest.nlm
```

MEMTEST.NLM does not test every MEMWRAP.OBJ function. It
doesn't try, for example, to use or free a NULL pointer. The current
version of MEMWRAP.OBJ aborts if you try to free a null pointer
(before MEMWRAP.OBJ aborts, it displays an alert.) The abort
provides a safe exit from a situation that would cause the server to
abend.

You should experiment with MEMTEST.NLM and insert a
few of your own memory errors. This practice gives you a
better idea of MEMWRAP.OBJ's debugging capabilities.

Some tasks are beyond the scope of MEMWRAP.OBJ. It does not, for example, trap non-ANSI memory-allocation APIs, such as `alloca`. In NetWare, however, non-ANSI memory-allocation APIs are unnecessary. A number of NetWare APIs allocate memory that you also must free and are not trapped by MEMWRAP.OBJ: `CreateScreen`, `opendir`, and `AsyncRead`, for example. These specialized APIs are easier to debug because they are used less frequently than the ANSI memory-allocation workhorses trapped by MEMWRAP.OBJ.

Summary

A well-written and well-tested NLM can take advantage of NetWare's high-performance architecture within a very stable and robust environment. An errant NLM, however, can quickly corrupt the server environment. The key, of course, is that the developer of the DP application must use all the tools available to ensure the integrity of the application. This chapter has described the most common source of NLM bugs and how to avoid them.

Memory errors are the most common problem associated with NLM development. This chapter also has provided a useful tool for debugging NLM memory problems.

Part Five: Downsizing Tools

NetWare-to-Host Communications

Btrieve: NetWare's Built-in File Manager

Choosing a Commercial DBMS for NetWare v3.11

Application Toolkits

Nondistributed Record Managers

Topics covered in this chapter:

Understanding NetWare-to-3270 Connections

Understanding NetWare-to-TCP/IP Connections

Chapter 17

NetWare-to-Host Communications

Although the ultimate goal of downsizing may be to replace larger, more expensive systems, that replacement cannot happen until there has been a long period of coexistence. During that period, users on the new LANs must communicate with the old installed systems to access old programs and old data.

Even after the old systems are replaced, a need for LAN-to-host communications may still exist: very likely, LAN users will talk to wider and wider circles of networks within and outside of the organization. For example, the TCP/IP-based Internet is growing rapidly in popularity among commercial users as a way to move electronic mail and transfer files. NetWare-to-host connectivity to TCP/IP will be important even after downsizing within an organization is complete.

The goal of NetWare-to-host connections is to let the user access the host system as a "native user" of the environment to which the user is connecting. For most host systems, that means transforming the user's workstation into a terminal on the host's network.

The alternative is to have the host system adapt—to have the host system become part of the LAN network. Although this is easier on the user, it is a hard transformation for most host systems. Because it is not as common, having the host system adapt to the LAN is not discussed further in this chapter. This chapter focuses on the way a LAN workstation becomes a terminal on a host system. Two popular networks are used as bases for explanation: the IBM 3270 network and the TCP/IP-based Internet network.

Understanding NetWare-to-3270 Connections

IBM 3270 communications networks are found world-wide and are used for a wide variety of applications. They are the most common form of mainframe networks, so there are plenty of opportunities for LAN-to-3270 communications.

IBM's 3270 networking system was developed in the 1960s to service the space program. Processing power was centralized and expensive when the 3270 was developed. Batch processing was king before the 3270 emerged, and time sharing was the giant leap forward of the decade. The designers of the 3270 distributed processing power only to make the communications line work more reliably.

Telephone systems of the 1960s handled voice traffic well enough, but dial-up lines were so scratchy that 300 baud was the top speed. Because this wasn't fast enough for average 3270 applications, the 3270 environment was optimized to use leased lines on remote connections and high-speed coax on local connections.

Because aerospace applications are "spare-no-expense" applications and are intolerant of errors, the 3270 is reliable. The tradeoff was flexibility—neither the hardware nor the tasks of the operators can be reorganized quickly on a 3270 network.

Differences between a 3270 Environment and LAN Environments

PC-based LANs were developed in the 1980s; 3270 networks were developed in the 1960s. This 20-year difference gave LAN designers communications tools that performed thousands of times faster than the original 3270 tools and cost much less. LAN designers were also working after personal computers had changed users' expectations of computers.

 Personal computers started life as "toys"—they were not cursed with having to be important from birth. Because PCs were not used for risky tasks, performance was more important than reliability. Because they were not held to a risk-adverse standard, they evolved rapidly. Because they were optimized for single-user use, the operating systems were simplified and applications designers concentrated on perfecting user-friendly features, rather than working on security and accounting features. Personal computers were developed in an environment opposite to that in which the 3270 was developed.

LAN designers realized that their products had to be personal computer-compatible; applications run on the periphery of the network, not at its center. The network center is transformed into the file-server assistant of the workstations. As LAN designers developed ways to network these "toys," personal-computer features such as user-friendliness and the PC-compatible standardized hardware platform became part of the starting parameters.

These parameters were extended by NetWare designers into a file-server technology and a NetWare product that can operate with many different kinds of LAN boards.

The latest transformation of NetWare is the further development of the client-server concept. Throughout the 1980s, the file server was the only kind of server a workstation could call on. As the 1990s progress, many other kinds of servers are appearing: print servers, database servers, and communications servers.

Reasons To Connect LANs and Mainframes

Connecting LANs and mainframes such as the 3270 is a lot of work. Why go to the trouble of connecting these disparate systems? Several reasons make the trouble in connecting them worthwhile.

Users like working with personal computers, but they need to work with data from other systems. Data comes from two kinds of older systems: those to be replaced by downsized systems and those that will survive the downsizing trend. Connecting with soon-to-be-replaced equipment is a transitional phase and is useful primarily for moving historical data.

 Older systems that survive downsizing will do so because they are specialty networks doing jobs that LANs do not service well. For example, it is unlikely that a NetWare LAN will be used to support automatic teller systems; this is a job better suited to the security and hierarchy offered by mainframe 3270 systems. However, it is quite likely that a NetWare LAN will carry the reports generated by activity on the ATM system.

Another reason to move data from LANs to mainframes and back is to take advantage of the facilities offered by existing older systems. Minicomputer and mainframe systems often have high-capacity printers and excellent backup facilities. Making these minicomputer and mainframe facilities available to the LAN is a good reason to communicate with the older system.

To access facilities or to move data between systems, an easy cross-over between the LAN and the older system must exist; this means the differences between the two systems must be overcome.

An Overview of a 3270 Communications Network

IBM's 3270 network is a communications standard. It allows terminals and printers to communicate with a variety of mainframes and minicomputers.

The 3270 is a hierarchical network. The heart of the 3270 network is the host computer, which is the place where applications run. At the periphery of the network are the terminals and printers. In between is a series of devices that connect host applications and terminals. Figure 17.1 shows a typical 3270 network arrangement. The following sections detail each of the components of this layout.

The Host Computer

The *host computer* in a 3270 network runs the applications. The host computer comes in a variety of sizes and runs a variety of operating systems and environments. Although applications and databases run on the host computer, the host computer does not control the communications network. Controlling the network is left up to the next machine in line: the communications controller.

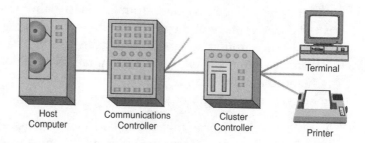

Figure 17.1:
A typical 3270 network layout.

The Communications Controller

The *communications controller* is in charge of the communications network. It sorts out the idiosyncrasies of talking with cluster controllers connected over varieties of communications lines.

Communications lines can range from local coax or token-ring connections to synchronous modems operating over a variety of dedicated lines, such as leased lines, microwave linkages, satellite linkages, and dial-up connections.

The communications controller "knows" the network. It is through the communications controller that network operators control which terminals can attach to the network and which applications each terminal can reach.

The communications controller is programmed separately from the host computer. It is in its own language, and is optimized for reliability and security rather than for flexibility. Traditionally, it is an "over-the-weekend" task to change terminal connections.

The communications controller is always located close to the host; smaller machines locate the communications controller in the same box as the host. Traditionally, the communications controller is a twin to the host, and they sit side-by-side in the computer room. The communications controller connects to cluster controllers, which are the next machines in line.

The Cluster Controller

Cluster controllers are the first line of remote devices. Their job is to make the job of the terminals and printers easier by providing a standard interface to which these devices attach. Cluster controllers are smart devices; they come with lots of RAM and are programmable, but they don't run applications. The programmability of cluster controllers is used to deal with communications idiosyncrasies; the massive RAM is used to build display pages for terminals and print pages for printers.

The Terminals and Printers

In the 3270 world, the cluster controller takes care of communications-line variables, so the link between the cluster controller and the terminal devices (the terminals and printers) is standard: a high-speed coax cable connection. Originally, this cable was strictly point-to-point. Later, multiplexing was introduced so that many terminals could be connected to a multiplexer (MUX) unit with a single cable strung from the MUX to the cluster controller.

Because the coax link is high speed and the cluster controller is so smart, the terminals and printers don't have to be smart at all— they just have to look pretty and take keystrokes. For terminals, the typical sequence of events for entering data is as follows:

1. The cluster controller builds a screen image and sends it to the terminal.

2. The operator fills in the screen; each keystroke is sent by the terminal to the cluster controller. The cluster controller uses the keystrokes to fill in a virtual screen in its RAM. The cluster controller checks as those keystrokes are made to see whether they are appropriate entries for

the current field (numbers into numeric fields, letters into alphabetic fields, and so on).

3. The operator presses the SEND key. The cluster controller strips off the screen image it built and sends only the operator's keystrokes and information about what fields the keystrokes belong into the communications controller.

4. The communications controller acknowledges receipt of the data and tells the cluster controller which screen to display next. If necessary, the communications controller downloads the screen to the cluster controller, and the cycle begins again.

This list synopsizes the hardware cycle. The next section describes the software cycle.

Connections between a Terminal and an Application

In the 3270 world, applications and terminals are firmly tied together. The connection process is aptly called *binding*. It is a connection-oriented process—much like making a phone call from a dedicated phone line found near airline baggage claims to a hotel. Pick up a phone and you find yourself connected to a hotel clerk; turn on a 3270 terminal and you find yourself connected to an application for a session. Figure 17.2 shows the typical relationship of terminal and application in the 3270 mainframe environment.

Figure 17.2:
Binding terminals and applications.

Changing a session can be difficult. For a user who spends the day filling out insurance forms or airline reservations, changing sessions is not a problem. It is a problem, however, for the user who wants the personal computer-like ability to move from application to application during a day's work. The 3270 environment's solution to that demand is to offer devices that can set up multiple sessions with a host, in which each session is a connection to a different application. Figure 17.3 shows a single terminal involved in three sessions, each to a separate application on the host.

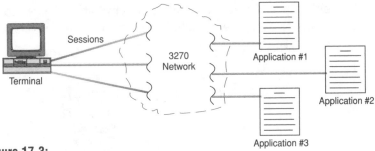

Figure 17.3:
One terminal can have many sessions.

The 3270 network started as a purely hierarchical network: all network activity was between the host-communications controller and terminals of various sorts. When IBM announced Systems Application Architecture (SAA), it also announced support for peer-to-peer network activities, as well as hierarchical ones. The tools that made peer-to-peer activities possible were two new types of connections for the network: the LU6.2-type connection and the PU2.1-type connection.

Peer-to-peer connections are still rarities on 3270 networks. If you need compatibility with peer-to-peer, look for devices that support LU6.2 and PU2.1.

Reaching a 3270 Network from a LAN Workstation

Commonly, devices attach to a 3270 network in one of two places: either as a terminal or printer attaching to a cluster controller or as a cluster controller attaching to the communications controller (see fig. 17.4).

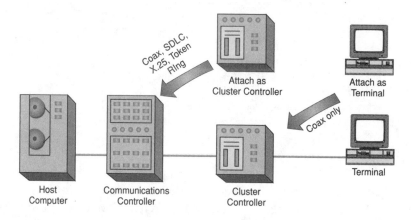

Figure 17.4:
Places for a LAN workstation to attach to a 3270 network.

The cluster controller is a point of standardization; any device that attaches to it does so in a standard way: through a coax connection. A device attached to the cluster controller communicates with the cluster controller in IBM's standard, proprietary fashion. The device becomes a "logical unit" on the network; it counts on the cluster controller to build screens and establish the network connection.

This is the kind of connection that the first DCA's IRMA products made with the IBM 3270 world. The advantage of attaching to the 3270 network in this way is that it is conceptually simple and tightly standardized. The disadvantage is that it requires one device per workstation and that the cluster controller isn't replaced. (The cluster controller can be an expensive piece of equipment.)

The cluster controller is the "smart" device at the remote end of the communications line (by 1960s standards, anyway). The cluster controller "talks" with the communications controller over standard phone lines using the open SNA/SDLC protocol, and is a physical unit on the network, rather than a logical unit the way a terminal is. As a physical unit, the cluster controller is in charge of binding and unbinding sessions with the communications controller.

Replacing the cluster controller with third-party alteratives helps to save money. Once a third party, like a LAN workstation, takes control of the cluster controller, inexpensive ASCII-based equipment can be used in place of IBM-standard EBCDIC-based equipment. Some third-party cluster controllers support ASCII terminals and printers. Some cluster controllers support PC-compatibles; others support Macintosh equipment. Combination cluster controller/terminal products exist. All these alternatives are attractive because equipment costs in the ASCII/PC-compatible marketplace are lower than in the 3270 world.

The newest way of attaching LAN workstations to a 3270 network is through a token-ring connection. In this arrangement, the cluster controller is a device with a token-ring connection, and it "talks" with communications controllers also attached to the token ring. Token ring also supports the new peer-to-peer protocols PU2.1 and LU6.2.

NetWare for SAA

Through the years, Novell has offered several ways into the 3270 environment. The most comprehensive way is NetWare for SAA (Systems Application Architecture).

NetWare for SAA is a suite of products that enable workstations and printers on a NetWare LAN to attach to a 3270 network and to act like terminals and printers on the 3270 network. Table 17.1 summarizes the advantages offered by NetWare for SAA, which is a collection of NLMs that allow a NetWare v3.11 server to establish a host-to-LAN connection.

NetWare 3270 LAN Workstation for DOS, Windows, and Macintosh work with NetWare for SAA. They run on their respective workstations and transform the workstations into terminal emulators. Each can emulate a variety of IBM display units, depending on what display hardware is available on the workstation and what is called for by the host application. NetWare 3270 LAN Workstation reprograms the keyboard of the workstation to be compatible with 3270 terminal use and sets up one of the keys as a hot key to jump back and forth between terminal-emulation and workstation modes. Workstations can send files to or receive files from a host.

The NetWare Communications Services Manager (NCSM) is part of the package. It is a real-time network-management application that uses a Windows-based graphical interface to map and manage network resources. It can talk with IBM's NetView so that LAN and host maintenance can be integrated. When NCSM is in place, a NetView operator can reset workstation nodes on the LAN as well as on the rest of the network and change the operation of a NetWare 3.11 file server. Table 17.2 shows the types of object that NCSM can monitor.

Table 17.1:

What NetWare for SAA Looks Like to a 3270 Network

Features	What NetWare for SAA Supports
Display or printer emulated	3278/79 3178/79 3270PC 3287
Host sessions	506
Workstations	506
Environments supported	MS-DOS Windows Macintosh UNIX
Connection type	
Remote	Modem attachment to 37x5 communications controller or AS/400
Token Ring	Token-ring connection to 3174, 37xx, 937x, or AS/400
Data-link protocol	
Remote	SNA/SDLC
Token Ring	ITRN
Maximum data rate	
Remote	0.064M per second
Token Ring	16M per second
Workstation software	NetWare 3270 LAN Workstation
Hardware required	
Remote	Novell Synchronous adapter, Novell Synchronous/V.35 adapter, NetWare for SAA Synchronous adapter, or IBM Multiprotocol adapter
Token Ring	IBM 16/4 Token Ring Network or PC adapter
Memory required	4M plus 4M for NetWare 3.11

Table 17.2:

Concerns of the Communications Services Manager

Class Monitored	Kinds of objects in the Class
Objects	Interface boards
	Disks
	Ports
	Drivers
	Event logs
	Audit logs
	SAA service profiles
Attributes	Severity thresholds
	Filters
Actions	Manages servers
	Runs diagnostic traces
	Queries log files

NetWare for SAA sets up a server, typically a file server, as a communications link. The server can be connected to a 3270 network in a variety of methods:

❖ It can use an SDLC link to talk with any of the standard 3270 communications controllers or an AS/400

❖ It can make a token-ring connection with a 3174 cluster controller

❖ It can use a QLLC link to an X.25 network that then links to a 3270 network

Figure 17.5 shows a typical arangement for connecting a NetWare LAN and a 3270 network using NetWare for SAA.

The server supports up to 506 sessions spread among as many as 506 workstations. Workstations and printers attached to the server emulate LU type 1, 2, 3, or 6.2 devices. The server itself emulates PU type 2.0 and 2.1 devices and can act as two different PUs. It can connect to two different hosts, or it can have one connection back up the other connection to the same host.

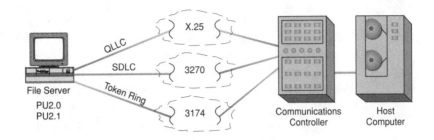

Figure 17.5:

Connection methods using NetWare for SAA.

NetWare for SAA also works with other third-party products. The following list offers a sampling of some what third parties are doing with NetWare for SAA:

❖ IBM and Tangram have software-distribution products that work with NetWare for SAA

❖ DCA, Wall Data, and Cleo have client emulators that let Windows, OS/2, Macintosh, and UNIX client workstations attach to a NetWare for SAA server

❖ Gupta uses NetWare for SAA to link its SQLGateway/ APPC, which runs on NetWare, to the 3270 world so that it can send queries to DB2 databases

These are just a few of the products available; new ones are coming out all the time.

Connecting a LAN workstation to an AS/400 is slightly different than connecting to other 3270 hardware. The AS/400's native language is 5250, not 3270, and it doesn't have a separate communications controller. NetWare for SAA deals with the AS/400 in one of two ways: either by having the AS/400 emulate a 3270 or by using an LU 6.2 connection (the AS/400 remains in 5250 mode).

NOTE To summarize, NetWare for SAA is a comprehensive way of making a connection between a LAN and a 3270 network. It emulates a cluster controller, can be attached in numerous ways, enables workstations on the LAN to access the 3270 hosts as terminals, and enables workstations to transfer files. NetWare for SAA also works with IBM's NetView to provide good network maintenance and provide a platform that other third-party developers can use for their LAN-to-host communications products.

Understanding NetWare-to-TCP/IP Connections

TCP/IP was developed under the sponsorship of Defense Advanced Research Project Agency (DARPA) to provide a connectivity protocol for the diverse minicomputer systems being used in the defense industry and on college campuses of the 1970s. TCP/IP became a standard part of BSC UNIX and is now available for many UNIX-based systems. It is also available for Macintoshes, PC-compatibles, VAXs, and other minicomputers and mainframes.

TCP/IP was a success and several networks emerged quickly: ARPANET, MILNET, NSFnet, CSNET, and Cypress Net, to name a few. These networks were later joined to make one large network, now called the Internet.

The 1970s roots of TCP/IP produced a network with a different emphasis than the 3270 network. 3270 networking, with its aerospace roots, emphasizes reliability and security, TCP/IP networking, with its university roots, emphasizes connectivity.

In the 1990s, many business organizations are joining the Internet. It is growing so rapidly, in fact, that changes in the TCP/IP's addressing system are being actively pursued.

The Nature of the Internet

Although 3270 networks can be very large, they tend to be specialized networks; that is, they are networks designed to accomplish narrowly defined tasks. For example, the 3270-based ATM network is nationwide but is dedicated to the task of handling ATM transactions. TCP/IP networks tend to be broader in scope. The Internet, for example, carries electronic mail, electronic forums, and diverse scientific applications. Internet users are scientists, administrators, and business people whose work centers around the academic community or the defense industry. Reaching out to TCP/IP and the Internet with a LAN workstation accomplishes something quite different than reaching out to a 3270 network.

Table 17.3:
TCP/IP and SNA Layers

OSI Model	SNA Model	TCP/IP Model
Application	Transaction Services	Process
Presentation	Function Management	
Session	Data Flow Control	
Transport	Transmission Control	Host-to-Host
Network	Path Control	Internet
Data Link	Data Link Control	Network Access
Physical	Physical Layer	

The TCP/IP protocol is different from the 3270 protocol. The 3270 protocol splits the communicating task into seven layers. TCP/IP accomplishes the task in only four layers.

TCP/IP is simpler than 3270, in part because TCP/IP was designed 10 years after the 3270 and took advantage of communications and data-processing improvements developed in the interim. (LAN standards, coming 10 years after TCP/IP, take further advantage of the communications and data-processing improvements made possible by PCs-with-LAN-boards technology.)

The TCP/IP environment is not as hierarchical as the 3270 environment. Terminals and hosts are connected together through a bus. The terminals can be connected to this bus through a concentrator of some sort, but this isn't necessary.

Differences between Internet and LAN Environments

Because the TCP/IP environment started as a pre-personal computer environment, the standard relationship between data-processing components is terminal-host rather than client-server. Just as in the 3270 world, when a user attaches a personal computer to a TCP/IP, the link usually is done with a terminal-emulation program and the personal computer becomes a terminal accessing a host somewhere on the network.

TCP/IP has standardized several basic functions. The following functions all work the same way, no matter what kind of hardware they are run on:

- ❖ A standard set of terminal commands (TELNET)
- ❖ Two standard ways of transferring files (File Transfer Protocol—FTP—and Trivial File Transfer Protocol—TFTP)
- ❖ An electronic-mail standard (Simple Mail Transfer Protocol—SMTP)

Internet Naming Conventions

Because the Internet embraces thousands of different systems, naming is an important issue. The largest unit of naming is the *domain*. The following four major domains exist on the Internet:

MIL, used by the military

EDU, used by colleges and universities

COM, used by businesses

ARPA, used by Internet managers

Domains can contain subdomains separated by periods. At the beginning, though, comes the host computer's name itself. For example, a Cray computer used for cryptology by the Crunchy Cookie Co. might have an Internet address like this: CRIP-CRAY.CRUNCH.COM. These names are transformed by Internet routing tables into numeric addresses; packets use these numeric addresses to find their ways to destination systems on the network.

NetWare TCP/IP

NetWare TCP/IP is a suite of programs designed to allow workstations to attach easily to the Internet or other TCP/IP networks. In addition to supporting TCP/IP connections, NetWare TCP/IP supports network management, IP routing, and IP/IPX tunneling.

 IP routing is establishing TCP/IP routes within the LAN for other networks to use. *IP/IPX tunneling* enables native NetWare packets (IPX packets not understood by TCP/IP) to travel from one NetWare server to another using a TCP/IP network.

NetWare TCP/IP supports Simple Network Management Protocol (SNMP). This protocol enables the user to monitor or configure network parameters for many hosts from a single location.

NetWare TCP/IP also supports Network File System (NFS), Line Printer Demon (LPD), mail gateway, and TCP/IP Developer's Tool Kit NLMs. The NFS NLM lets the server support UNIX-style files and directories so that UNIX users on the Internet can access the file server's files. The *mail gateway* is a link between SMTP and NetWare's Message Handling Service (MHS), so that NetWare and TCP/IP users can transfer mail. The *Developer's Tool Kit* enables NetWare users to develop their own TCP/IP applications using either the 4.3 BSD UNIX socket interface or the AT&T Streams Transport Layer (TLI).

NetWare TCP/IP can communicate with Ethernet, token ring, or ARCNET LAN boards. When Ethernet boards are used, however, special consideration is needed. After the Ethernet standard was devised by Xerox, the IEEE defined a nearly identical standard called 802.3, and the Ethernet waters got a little muddy.

Native NetWare uses the 802.3 format without a Logical Link Control (LLC) header. TCP/IP networks use 802.3 format with the LLC, often called Ethernet II. The two kinds of packets can flow over same Ethernet cable without interfering with each other but they are understood only by boards set to the same standard. To allow NetWare to understand TCP/IP Ethernet packets, the Ethernet II driver must be installed on the file-server Ethernet board, along with native NetWare 802.3. Token ring and ARCNET don't have this twin-standard problem.

The Simple Network Management Protocol (SNMP)

The Simple Network Management Protocol (SNMP) enables a network manager to get information from other TCP/IP systems and devices. The manager also can issue commands to the other devices. TCP/IP uses the *manager-agent concept*, in which managers such as SNMP talk to *agents*, or programs in other network devices that are designed specifically to talk with manager programs. Agents are found in TCP/IP hosts, routers, terminal servers, and other SNMP managers. The manager talks to a standardized—but not completely standard—Management Information Base (MIB), found in controllable TCP/IP devices. Managers query agents about interface statistics, routing tables, and addresses.

Agents also can speak out on their own and typically do so to alert the manager when they are about to reset, lose, or restore a communications link; or when an attempt is made to access the MIB without proper authentication.

The LAN Workplace for DOS

Novell's LAN Workplace for DOS is an another way into the TCP/IP world. LAN Workplace for DOS is a connection that doesn't use a file server as a gateway: it loads directly into a workstation and is good for those situations in which a workstation is attached directly to a TCP/IP cable. LAN Workplace for DOS performs TELNET, FTP, and TFTP functions.

Summary

IBM 3270, TCP/IP, and the Internet are two examples of the kinds of hosts that can be reached from NetWare. For the last decade, Novell and NetWare have been working hard to extend the connectivity of LANs, and these are just two fruits of that labor. Other systems to which NetWare can connect are DEC systems running LAT or VMS, and systems that are connected to X.25 networks.

The task of connecting LANs to other networks has three major elements: making hardware that can translate the differing signals and packets used on the various networks; designing software so that once a connection is made, something useful can be accomplished (particularly challenging when the system philosophies rest on the far ends of the reliability and flexibility scales the way personal-computer networks and 3270 networks do); and working out ways to integrate the security and network maintenance features of both systems. Because maintenance and security are hallmarks of older networks, this last element has been perhaps the most challenging part of the LAN connectivity process.

Novell offers many products for making LAN-to-host connections. Novell also actively supports third parties in their efforts to make these connections useful and easy.

One goal of these connections is to enable LAN users to move information quickly and usefully from host systems to their workstations. Another goal is to enable users to move information back to the host systems so that the rest of the organization can be kept up to date.

As downsizing continues, many older systems will be uprooted and displaced, but that will not end the need for LAN-to-host communications. Network applications in which terminal-host architecture makes more sense than client-server architecture will always be needed, and organizations with host-dominated networks will always need to be communicated with. LAN-to-host communications—in all its incarnations—is likely to be around long after "the year of downsizing" has come and gone.

Topics covered in this chapter:

Understanding Btrieve

Using Btrieve's Features

Using Btrieve Utilities

Noting System Requirements for Btrieve Development Kits

Understanding Technical Specifications for Btrieve

Chapter 18

Btrieve: NetWare's Built-in File Manager

In the early days of mainframe computing, businesses used computers for one basic task: processing corporate accounting data. Companies had to keep track of revenue, expenses, cash flow, payroll, taxes, and so on. Mainframe computers used *databases*—collections of related files—to process this accounting data. Eventually, complex software programs called *database management systems* (DBMSs) evolved, enabling sophisticated storing, organizing, sorting, and retrieving of this data.

Although computers now perform many tasks in addition to tracking accounting data, DBMSs are still the most important applications used by most businesses. Databases are vital centers of information; in this information age, their importance is bound to increase.

This chapter concentrates on Novell's first and most fundamental database product: Btrieve.

Understanding Btrieve

Introduced in 1983, Btrieve is a key-indexed record-management system. It runs at the back end and enables various front-end applications to retrieve, insert, erase, or update data by key value, using either random-access or sequential methods. A *key* can be an account number, last name, or social security number, for example.

Btrieve, which is a programming tool rather than an end-user product, is based on the B-tree file-indexing system, a powerful hierarchical data-access method. Btrieve offers interfaces to more than 20 programming languages, including BASIC, COBOL, FORTRAN, Pascal, and C.

When a companion product such as NetWare SQL is added, Btrieve works with many different relational DBMSs; they run on workstations, whereas Btrieve resides on the server.

In one sense then, Btrieve offers the best of both worlds by supporting a high-performance hierarchical database at the back end and flexible relational databases at the front end.

Because Novell includes Btrieve (officially called *NetWare Btrieve*) with every version of NetWare sold, the product is widely available. Well over one million copies of this server-based engine are now in the field.

Programmers can create two kinds of Btrieve applications: *client-based applications* (which run on workstations) and *server-based applications* (which run on the server).

Server-based applications can run as Value-Added Processes (VAPs) or NetWare Loadable Modules (NLMs). Server-based applications have the following advantages over the client-based variety:

❖ Network traffic is reduced because there is less data back and forth between the server and the workstations

❖ Network performance improves because of fewer network requests

❖ Centralized processing enables efficient multiserver controls

Three Btrieve developer's products are available: Btrieve for DOS, Btrieve for OS/2, and Btrieve for Windows. Code written for one version is compatible with code written for either of the others.

 These toolkits enable programmers to develop applications compatible with client-based Btrieve run times or with the server-based engine. Each toolkit includes language interfaces, developer utilities, a programming manual, and the client-based version of Btrieve.

Any client-based version of Btrieve can run on a network or on a stand-alone machine.

Because Btrieve's indexing algorithms use caching and automatic balancing, access speed is not adversely affected as files grow. And a single Btrieve call retrieves and inserts sets of records.

In most programming languages, a simple subroutine call invokes Btrieve. Btrieve uses pre-imaging, transaction control, and a read-after-write verify option to maintain data integrity. Btrieve also uses NetWare's Transaction Tracking System and enables you to recover data in the event of a hardware or software failure.

Btrieve runs in multiserver environments, using record locking to prevent concurrency problems. It also provides file-level password protection, as well as dynamic encryption and decryption of data.

Because Btrieve files expand dynamically as records are added, you do not need to preallocate disk space. And Btrieve automatically recycles disk space after records are deleted.

Btrieve supports the following:

- ❖ Records of different lengths (as many as 65,536 bytes)
- ❖ Data compression
- ❖ Blank truncation

BSERVER

NetWare Btrieve's core program, BSERVER, runs on the server. It must be loaded on every server that stores Btrieve files. BSERVER handles the following tasks:

- ❖ Transfers data from Btrieve files to and from the disk
- ❖ Locks and unlocks files and records at the server
- ❖ Packages all Btrieve requests and sends them to another server or to a workstation

BREQUEST

BREQUEST, which enables client-based applications to communicate with BSERVER, must be loaded at any workstation that makes Btrieve requests. BREQUEST handles the following tasks:

- ❖ Accepts Btrieve requests from the workstation-based application and forwards them to BSERVER
- ❖ Sends results of Btrieve requests to the application

BROUTER

BROUTER, which enables server-based applications to communicate with BSERVER, handles the following tasks:

- ❖ Offers other server-based applications (on the same server) memory-to-memory access to BSERVER

❖ Offers other server-based applications (on other servers) SPX-based access to BSERVER

❖ Maintains unique ID codes for all applications (thus enabling locks and other access-control functions to operate without conflict across the entire network)

❖ Serializes Btrieve requests (thus enabling multiple server-based applications to use BROUTER without conflict)

Using Btrieve's Features

The following sections describe the key features of Btrieve.

Security

Btrieve assigns owner names to files and encrypts and decrypts data.

File Integrity

To maintain data integrity, Btrieve locks records and files, defines logical transactions, detects deadlock conditions, stores images of files before changing them, and automatically recovers data corrupted by hardware failure.

Index Support

Btrieve supports indexes in the following ways:

❖ Each file can have as many as 24 indexes

❖ Supplemental indexes can be added or dropped after a file is created

❖ Key values can be any of 14 data types

❖ Key values can be unique, modifiable, segmented, null, ascending, and descending

Memory Management

Btrieve enables you to configure memory according to your resources and the demands on your server. Generally, the more memory you can reserve for the cache buffers, the better Btrieve performs. When an application requests a record, BSERVER first checks whether the page containing the record is already in cache. If the record is in cache, BSERVER sends it from cache to the application's data buffer. If the record is not in cache, BSERVER retrieves the file from the hard disk, copies it into cache, and then sends it to the application.

File Control

Btrieve provides the following features for file specification:

❖ Consistency among file structures

❖ Consistency among file-definition and file-management routines

❖ Files as large as 4 billion bytes

❖ An unlimited number of records

Using Btrieve Utilities

Btrieve offers two key utilities: BUTIL, for creating and managing Btrieve data files; and B, for testing and debugging application programs.

BUTIL

BUTIL includes a variety of commands to help you create, maintain, and recover Btrieve files. You must start BREQUEST before running BUTIL. Use the following syntax for BUTIL commands:

```
<drive:> BUTIL -COMMAND[parameters][-O<owner>]
```

Replace `<drive:>` with the name of the logical drive that contains the Btrieve program files. Using the default disk drive enables you to omit the logical drive.

Replace `-COMMAND` with the appropriate BUTIL command (such as CREATE or DROP).

Replace `[parameters]` with the parameters you want to invoke.

Replace `<owner>` with the Btrieve file owner name or with an asterisk (in which case you are prompted for an owner name).

BUTIL includes the following commands:

Command	Action
CLONE	Creates new file with same specs as an existing file
COPY	Copies contents of one file to a second file
CREATE	Creates an empty file, according to your specs
DROP	Removes a supplemental index from a file
EXTEND	Extends existing file across two logical drives
INDEX	Builds external index file
LOAD	Inserts sequential file records into Btrieve file
RECOVER	Retrieves data from a corrupted Btrieve file
RESET	Releases workstation resources used by BREQUEST
SAVE	Retrieves records from a Btrieve file

Command	Action
SINDEX	Produces supplemental index for a Btrieve file
STAT	Retrieves file statistics for a Btrieve file
STOP	Removes BREQUEST from workstation memory
VER	Tells which BREQUEST version is loaded at workstation

The B Utility

The B utility (Btrieve Function Executor) provides an interactive interface for performing Btrieve operations. This utility is valuable for learning about Btrieve and for testing and debugging programs.

You run B by using the following syntax:

```
B <Enter>
```

A menu appears, listing the following prompts for parameters required by Btrieve calls:

Prompt	Meaning
Function	Code for the operation you want to perform
Key Path	Key number for the operation
Position Block	Number identifying the given file
Status Code	Enables you to see status code changes
Data Buffer Length	Enables you to choose data buffer length
Data Buffer	To enter data for Insert or Update operations
Key Buffer	To enter file name or key value

For complete details on using BUTIL and B, see Novell's *Btrieve Library Reference*.

Noting System Requirements for Btrieve Developers' Kits

The three versions of Btrieve have different system requirements. With Btrieve for DOS, you need an IBM PC or compatible machine, 128K of RAM, PC DOS or MS-DOS 3.0 or higher, or DOS-compatible OS, and 38K of RAM for Btrieve's removable TSR run-time program. Btrieve for OS/2 requires an IBM PC AT or compatible (or an IBM PS/2) and an OS/2 operating system. To use Btrieve for Windows, you need an IBM-compatible 286/386, at least 640K of RAM, PC DOS or MS-DOS 3.0 or higher, and Windows 3.0 or higher.

 The following lists the maximum specifications for Btrieve:
File size: 4G

    Record size: 64K
    Records per file: no limit
    Key length: 255 bytes
    Keys per file: 24
    Open files: no limit (15 with BASIC interpreter)

Key attributes are duplicate, unique, modifiable, nonmodifiable, segmented, ascending, descending, null, manual, autoincrement, and noncontiguous.

Understanding Btrieve Language Interfaces

Table 18.1 lists the languages that each version supports.

Table 18.1
Btrieve Language Interfaces

Version	Supports
Btrieve for DOS	Most C, BASIC, Pascal, and COBOL compilers
Btrieve for OS/2	IBM C/2 Family Application Programming Interface (FAPI) or Protected Mode
	IBM C/2 OS/2 Interface
	Microsoft BASIC
	Microsoft Quick BASIC
	IBM BASIC for OS/2
	Micro Focus COBOL 2
Btrieve for Windows	Microsoft C

Enhancing with Btrieve Companion Products

Novell offers three products that enhance and supplement Btrieve's record-managing capabilities: XQL, NetWare SQL, and Xtrieve.

XQL

XQL is a multilevel database development system that facilitates development of SQL database applications based on Btrieve. Like Btrieve, XQL is a programming tool, not an end-user product.

Using a programming language such as BASIC, COBOL, or C and a run-time version of XQL, programmers can develop applications that enable end users to access databases by using SQL commands or relational primitives. (*Relational primitives* are lower-level functions that operate more efficiently than complete SQL statements.)

XQL's two application programming interfaces (APIs) are the SQL Manager and the relational primitives. The SQL Manager uses highly efficient SQL statements to manipulate relational-database files. Relational primitives handle a variety of tasks, including defining and modifying tables, retrieving data, and specifying directory paths.

An XQL database consists of Btrieve data files and a data dictionary—from three to seven Btrieve files containing complete descriptions of the files, views, and fields that make up your database.

The Data Dictionary

The data dictionary is a series of files that describe the structure, relationships, indexes, and data files of the database. The dictionary is neither an index nor a data file but rather a map of the database as a whole.

The data dictionary—which stores such information as file names, field names, data types, and display attributes—is itself stored in the following seven files:

File Name	Includes
FILE.DDF	The file name, file ID number, and the path
FIELD.DDF	Information about all field names and supplemental indexes
INDEX.DDF	Information about index fields for all dictionary-defined files
ATTRIB.DDF	Field-attribute information
VIEW.DDF	View definitions (information relating to joined files, fields, and other attributes)
USER.DDF	Name and password information for XQL users
RIGHTS.DDF	Information about the privileges of XQL users

XQL Features and Requirements

XQL's key features include the SQL editor, data manipulation, and distributed data-management processing.

XQLI, an interactive query application that accepts SQL statements and responds with the appropriate function calls, enables programmers to query data files with SQL statements and display the results on-screen. XQLI is useful for testing SQL statements, looking through files, and writing programs.

With XQL's data-manipulation capability, programmers can move backward and forward through a database, access data by field name, and manipulate composite records.

NetWare SQL makes distributed data-management processing possible. All applications produced with XQL can use NetWare SQL (described next) without having to recompile and relink.

Requirements for XQL are as follows:

❖ DOS 3.1 or higher (or OS/2)

❖ Btrieve 4.11 or higher

❖ An IBM PC, XT, AT, PS/2, or true compatible

❖ 97K to 187K of RAM (for relational primitives)

❖ 80K to 118K of RAM (for SQL Manager)

❖ 32K to 75K of RAM (for NetWare SQL Requester)

NetWare SQL and its Requirements

NetWare SQL provides a back-end database engine that resides on the server (sitting above Btrieve) and supports a variety of front-end applications. NetWare SQL is an *open-interface product* (any vendor can write programs to it). Tightly integrated with NetWare v3.x, NetWare SQL runs as an NLM. This tight integration offers users the benefits of disk mirroring, fault tolerance, and enhanced security.

Together with workstation programs, NetWare SQL provides NetWare users with a flexible way to manage data created by internally developed or commercial Btrieve-based applications.

NetWare SQL also supports Macintosh computers through Apple's Data Access Language (DAL). By supporting the Mac platform, NetWare SQL enables users to share common Btrieve databases with DAL-compatible applications, including spreadsheets, query tools, and application development tools.

A wide variety of third-party products support NetWare SQL. Contact Novell for a list of those products.

NetWare SQL offers the following tools:

❖ Client requesters for DOS, OS/2, and Windows

❖ An interface to Gupta Technologies' SQL Windows

❖ An interface to Lotus 1-2-3

❖ Utilities, including SQL Scope, a Windows tool that simplifies data interaction

❖ NetWare Runtime (available with NetWare SQL 20-user or above)

❖ Xtrieve PLUS, an interactive data-query system and report writer (described next)

NetWare SQL requires the following:

❖ NetWare v3.11 or higher

❖ 4M of RAM per NetWare SQL server (in addition to NetWare's memory requirements)

❖ DOS 3.1 or higher

❖ 80K of RAM (DOS Requester)

❖ 90K of RAM (OS/2 or Windows Requester)

❖ OS/2 Standard or Extended Editions (OS/2 Requester)

❖ Windows 3.0 or higher (Windows Requester)

❖ 100K of RAM at the server for each Macintosh login

Xtrieve PLUS

With Xtrieve PLUS, which is a menu-based report generator and report writer for Btrieve files, programmers can define and modify databases created by Btrieve and NetWare SQL. Xtrieve PLUS can be used also to create and modify NetWare SQL data dictionaries.

A key feature of Xtrieve PLUS is that it enables users to manipulate data and write reports without having to use SQL or any other programming language. A series of menus and windows help users to enter data, create queries, and write reports.

With the report writer, users can create and print form letters, mailing labels, statistical summaries, and other types of reports.

Xtrieve PLUS is available for DOS or OS/2 and supports any of the following:

❖ NetWare Btrieve

❖ Client-only versions of Btrieve

❖ Any version of NetWare SQL

Xtrieve PLUS checks user input against user-defined criteria to ensure accuracy and consistency. Users can assign default values or ranges for each database field. They can also customize Xtrieve PLUS to display command menus, help files, and error messages.

Many vertical applications—such as accounting packages—are based on Btrieve. (Many vertical-application developers use Btrieve, which essentially has become the de facto standard among LAN record-management solutions.)

Xtrieve PLUS can help users customize queries and manipulate data to meet specific needs. Someone using a Btrieve-based accounting package may need to use database information in another format, such as a spreadsheet, for example. By executing the Xtrieve PLUS TRANSLATE command, such users can easily save data in an ASCII file and then incorporate that file into a spreadsheet.

The widespread acceptance of Btrieve makes using Xtrieve PLUS to exchange database information among a wide variety of software packages possible.

Summary

Distributed processing is more powerful than multiprogramming because it takes full advantage of all resources offered by multiple computers. In addition, distributed processing supports many different front ends while maintaining database integrity at the back end. Even people using different hardware, operating systems, and applications can access the same database.

Btrieve is a high-performance record-management system that draws on the strength of hierarchical databases and the flexibility of relational databases. Btrieve and its companion products work with many different front-end applications and give users great freedom in manipulating and exchanging data.

Through such features as record locking, data encryption, file indexing, and memory management, Btrieve can safely handle mainframe-style databases. NetWare v.311 is a 32-bit operating system designed to handle multiple servers, heavy transaction processing, terabytes of disk storage, and large numbers of users. Btrieve takes full advantage of these capabilities in organizing records, thus offering an excellent downsizing alternative for users of mainframe and minicomputer databases.

Topics covered in this chapter:

Commercial DBMSs

Creating Guidelines

Surveying Commercial DBMSs for NetWare

Making the Ultimate Decision

Chapter 19

Choosing a Commercial DBMS for NetWare v3.11

O ver the years, the burgeoning use of computers in business has created a large market for commercial third-party database management system (DBMS) products. This chapter explains exactly what a commercial DBMS product is, giving you some important questions to ask when you consider a commercial DBMS for NetWare v3.11, as well as some criteria to use as you make a decision. The chapter also includes an overview of the three leading commercial database management systems on the market today.

Before proceeding, you should realize that the most important criterion for choosing a commercial database management system frequently is your existing DP application. Specifically, if you are already using a commercial DBMS, your first question should be whether a version of that specific product is available for NetWare v3.11. If not, this chapter tells you about some of the options for easing the switch from one database management system platform to another.

Understanding the Commercial DBMS

A *commercial DBMS* is a heavy-duty, general-purpose database management engine, plus tools. A commercial database management system is not a DP application; rather, it is the unfinished core of a DP application, as well as a series of tools with which you build on the core to create a DP application.

When you buy a commercial database management system, you are really starting the process of developing your own custom DP application. The "core" of the application—represented by the database engine component of the commercial DBMS—provides all of the data-management routines, security routines, transaction control primitives, concurrence control primitives, and other routines you otherwise would have to implement yourself. The tools provide a development environment and utilities you can use to finish the job of creating a fully customized DP application.

Most commercial DBMS products have many characteristics in common. The products described in this chapter, for example, are all fully distributed products, designed specifically to help you create distributed DP applications. Secondly, most commercial DBMS products feature support for the Sequenced Query Language (SQL) and adhere to the relational data model.

 The relational data molel is discussed in Chapter 3.

Finally, most commercial DBMS products originated in the host world, either on mini- or mainframe computers, or on UNIX hosts. With the increased importance of microcomputers, these DBMS products have been ported to microcomputer operating systems (usually to OS/2, with mixed results). The specific commercial database management system products described at the end of this chapter are products that have been developed as NLMs, or server-based NetWare applications. Without exception, commercial DBMS products running as NLMs offer a stunning performance, frequently rivaling the performance offered by vastly larger host systems.

Speeding the Development Process

Why would you purchase a product in an unfinished state? Specifically, you would do so because the purchase represents the quickest way to create a custom DP application. Because of the unfinished state of commercial database management systems, you can finish the job any way you want, tailoring the finished DP application to your specific requirements.

Commercial database management systems have other advantages, however. When you use a commercial DBMS to create many different DP applications, you implicitly build a degree of integration among those applications. The key is that every DP application you build using a commercial database management system shares the same internal machinery as all other applications created using that DBMS.

Furthermore, the integration among DP applications translates equally well to interoperability among host computer platforms. The major commercial database management systems all come in versions that support the major computing platforms in the field, including NetWare, IBM mainframes, VAX minicomputers, and UNIX systems. By using a single commercial DBMS to create DP applications for different computing platforms, you build into your DP applications cross-platform and cross-application interoperability.

Dealing with Downsizing of Commercial DBMSs

The unfinished nature of commercial database management systems and their cross-platform compatibility also lead to their disadvantages. First, as you already have learned, after purchasing a commercial DBMS you must do development work before you have an application. Although an existing core means that you give up some of the flexibility you normally have when designing an application from scratch, the maturity of most commercial DBMS packages makes the problem less than it once was. The vendors of these products have been in business long enough to know exactly what most customers need in a DP application. This experience is built into the major commercial database management systems in the form of extra features and programming interfaces.

Second, in order to achieve cross-platform interoperability, commercial database management systems are written with portability as a major concern. This concern affects even the lowest-level internal routines used by the core DBMS engine. Most commercial database management systems achieve cross-platform interoperability by compiling their products from common source files, whenever possible, regardless of the target platform. Because of these development practices, a commercial DBMS rarely takes advantage of special-purpose operating-system features.

This portibility means that commercial database management systems do not take advantage of the very features that make NetWare such a great platform for downsizing, including the NetWare file system cache, transaction tracking, and advanced file system APIs. Rather, commercial database management systems (some to a greater degree than others) implement these types of features themselves, at a higher level and in a more portable fashion. As a result, these products perform well, but not as well as they might if they really took advantage of the host operating system.

Creating Guidelines

The following sections present specific guidelines to consider when you evaluate a commercial database management system. Together, these guidelines form the criteria for selecting a commercial DBMS. Feel free, however, to alter these criteria to meet your own requirements.

Architectural Criteria

For this discussion, *architectural criteria* include the basic design elements of the back-end database engine. Although architectural criteria lay the foundation for the features most commercial DBMS vendors like to talk about, "architecture" and "features" are not equivalent. You can evaluate *features* by reading a marketing specification sheet. *Architecture*, however, gives you clues to the quality of the product, clues you may or may not be able to discover by reading a list of the product's features.

A commercial database management system engine, or back-end, should feature at least the following architectural characteristics:

❖ Multithreaded execution (which implies multitasking capabilities)

❖ Distributed database

❖ Transaction control

❖ Concurrence control

❖ Tight user security

❖ Support for multiple network transport protocols

An explanation of each item on the preceding list follows. When you evaluate commercial DBMS products, you must determine not only *whether* a specific product meets these criteria but also (if possible) *how* the product meets those criteria.

Supporting Multithreaded Execution

In a nutshell, multithreaded execution dramatically increases a DP application's efficiency, causing excellent gains in performance.

 The advantages of multithreaded execution for a DP application are explained thoroughly in Chapter 12.

 Because you cannot reap the benefits of NetWare's multithreaded execution unless you base your DP application on a multithreaded commercial DBMS engine, you should consider purchasing only commercial database management system engines that have a multithreaded architecture.

Distributing the Database

A *distributed database* is one that spans NetWare volumes and (even better) NetWare servers. Although NetWare is quite capable of supporting volumes of many gigabytes, reasons other than the size of the database exist for distributing databases. Doing so may give your application a level of redundancy and fault tolerance, for example. Also, you may want to store data files on servers that are physically adjacent to groups of clients that generate the highest access rates to those specific files.

Distributing the database among servers also enables an intelligent DBMS engine to divide the heavy processing work among copies of the same product running on other servers. Mostly, however, being able to distribute a single database among NetWare volumes and servers gives flexibility and expandability to your DP application. Most IS organizations expect to use a given DP application for many years, during which time the underlying computer technology may change dramatically. You may not need to be able to distribute a database today, but how can you be certain that you will not need that capability in the years to come?

Controlling Transactions

Any industrial-strength DP application must include transaction control. NetWare's built-in transaction tracking provides an operating-system level, robust, high-performance implementation of basic transaction control. Most commercial database management systems offer richer (if not more robust) options for controlling transactions, however. The option to transactions forward as well as back is an example. With NetWare's transaction tracking, you can only roll back, or undo, transactions.

Furthermore, the capability to distribute a database across servers raises the DP application's requirements for transaction control above what NetWare's transaction tracking offers.

 Specifically, the commercial DBMS must be able to accomplish a two-phased commit. A *two-phased commit* is a two-level implementation of transaction control in which the first level involves specific file-based transaction control, whereas the second level integrates all first-level transactions into a "second-phase" transaction.

The capability to roll back a second-phase transaction, then, means that all specific file-level transactions (regardless of the server upon which their files reside) may be undone and redone as a logical group.

Note that no exclusivity is necessary regarding a commercial DBMS's implementation of transaction control and that of the NetWare operating system. A commercial DBMS may build on

NetWare's operating-system-level transaction control to provide richness at a higher level. In fact, this is the preferred approach, although not the universal one.

Frequently, implementation of transaction control in a commercial DBMS is linked closely to the engine's data-buffering architecture. Despite the NetWare file system's massive file data cache, most commercial database management systems implement their own record-level data cache (primarily for portability, because most platforms do not implement massive file caching, as NetWare does).

Controlling Concurrence

The concurrence-control story among commercial DBMS engines is similar to the transaction-control story. That is, these products usually implement a richer set of options for locking files than the level implemented by the NetWare operating system. Doing so is usually fine, provided that the commercial DBMS engine uses NetWare's concurrence-control APIs as the underlying, low-level locking routines.

Securing Data

Security is an extremely critical factor in selecting a commercial database management system. Security is one area in which you must insist on tight integration with the NetWare operating system. Do not make any exceptions on this point. Your DP application's security architecture must be tied directly to NetWare's security architecture. This implies that all users of your DP application are also defined as users with the NetWare server.

The only exception to this rule may occur when you want to grant access to a NetWare-based DP application to users of non-NetWare platforms (granting access to DP data hosted by a NetWare server, for example, to users of a VAX session).

Supporting Multiple Network Transport Layers

By definition, downsizing a DP application means that it will be running over a network. By inference, that network has different types of operating systems and (probably) different network-transport protocols. (This assumes that you downsize gradually, maintaining old systems while introducing new systems.) Consequently, your commercial DBMS, should you decide to implement one, must support multiple transport protocols.

Note that the support (or lack of support) a particular commercial DBMS provides for multiple network transport protocols is independent of such support provided by the underlying operating system. That is, the fact that NetWare supports multiple transport protocols does not imply equivalent support in a commercial DBMS running on NetWare.

A commercial DBMS must explicitly provide support for multiple transport protocols because, like all client-server software, a commercial DBMS must implement some type of client-server protocol. If the vendor decides to base the DBMS's client-server protocol solely on one transport protocol (such as TCP/IP), you are locked into using the supported transport protocol, regardless of NetWare's capability to support other transport protocols.

Evaluating Client Tools and Support

The architectural criteria mentioned earlier are primarily back-end issues, being the domain of the core DBMS engine. Other criteria you must evaluate concern the front-end tools that provide NetWare clients with access to the back-end database engine. These criteria include the following:

❖ Full-scale API

❖ Client language support

❖ 4GL support

❖ Administrative tools

❖ Interactive tools

Full-Scale API

With a full-scale API, the commercial DBMS has no feature to which you may not gain access programatically. *Full-scale API* is another way of saying *fully programmable*. You can automate every aspect of any DP application you base on a commercial DBMS that has a full-scale API. Having this capability is important, even if you do not plan to take advantage of it immediately. Many commercial DBMS products that are touted as being fully programmable, nevertheless require you to perform some operations (such as database maintenance) manually.

Client Language Support

Client language support refers to the number of languages from which client programs may gain access to the commercial database management system's API. Can you call DBMS routines from assembly language, from C, or from BASIC, for example?

Evaluating this area is tricky, especially because a commercial DBMS may provide uneven client language support, supporting some languages better than others. For the full story on a product's client language support, you must do some research.

4GL Support

Fourth-generation languages (4GLs) are newer, higher-level languages than traditional languages such as C and Pascal. Frequently, however, a good 4GL can be just as powerful as a lower-level language, provided that you apply it to the types of programming tasks for which it was designed.

Most 4GLs are optimized for developing data management applications. By doing much of the "grunt work" involved in writing DP applications (writing user interfaces, writing, reports, indexing and sorting packages, and so on), 4GLs make programmers more productive. By using a 4GL, a programmer can concentrate more on the overall design and logic of a DP application and worry less about the repetitive areas of application programming.

Administrative Tools

Administrative tools enable you to create databases, manage user security, start and stop the database engine, and so on. A commercial DBMS usually includes good administrative tools because these tools must perform a static core of functions that all of the product's customers need.

Because all customers need administrative capabilities, the DBMS vendors should not leave it to you to write administrative utilities. You can write other, more specialized utilities that perform jobs specific to your needs.

Interactive Tools

Interactive tools are "bare-bones" client programs that enable you to perform basic data-management functions without having to create a full-blown client application, such as a command-line utility that enables you to log in to a database server, issue a query, and read the results.

Interactive tools are not the basis for a DP application, but they give you access to the back-end engine without requiring you to do any programming. You can use interactive tools to perform special one-time (or few-time) operations.

In summary, a good commercial DBMS should provide all the aforementioned types of client support (API, language support, a 4GL, and both administrative and interactive tools). After all, an especially good DBMS engine is of little use unless you can access its features—and you need client tools to do so.

Surveying Commercial DBMSs for NetWare

The major commercial DBMS platforms on the market today are Oracle, Informix, and SyBase. Each of these products originated on centralized host computers; all have evolved so that they now feature excellent client-server architectures. Most important, each of these products is now available in NLM form, tailored specifically to NetWare v3.11.

Oracle

Not only is Oracle's commercial DBMS, the Oracle Server, the most popular commercial DBMS today, but it also supports the most host platforms. The Oracle Server originated as a VAX VMS relational database engine. Most people who have been around for a few years know that Digital Equipment Corporation has been very enthusiastic about network technology.

DEC computers have supported key networking technologies (such as Ethernet) and a limited form of distributed processing since before the local area network industry existed. Some of this networking savvy has rubbed off on the Oracle Server, originally developed for DEC computers. (Note, however, that DEC's enthusiasm for networking has, until recently, dropped off dramatically in terms of non-VAX computers.)

 As a company, Oracle prides itself on ensuring that the Oracle Server has more features than any comparable product, and that the Oracle Server runs on more platforms that any comparable product.

The Oracle Server consistently has been on the leading edge of DBMS technology when it comes to supporting new platforms. Oracle was the first commercial DBMS vendor to release a version of its product for OS/2, for Banyan VINES, and for NetWare. The Oracle Server for OS/2, released in 1988, was the first major commercial DBMS to run on a microcomputer operating system. Since the release of the Oracle Server for NetWare in the spring of 1992, the NetWare version has outsold the OS/2 version by more than four-to-one, and the installed base of the Oracle Server for NetWare has overtaken the installed base of the Oracle Server for OS/2.

The Oracle Server also excels in client language support. Oracle consistently provides support for more client operating systems and more programming languages than any other vendor. Additionally, Oracle excels at providing *hooks*, whereby users of productivity applications can gain access to Oracle Servers. Oracle was the first company to provide Macintosh users of HyperCard access to Oracle databases, for example. (HyperCard support, although not critical to your downsizing efforts, gives you an idea of the breadth of support Oracle provides for different client platforms.)

Informix

As a company, Informix has concentrated on the UNIX market, declaring early on that its product would run on all UNIX operating systems on the market. (The name "Informix" derives from the combination of "Information" and "UNIX.") The current Informix commercial DBMS offering is called Informix On-Line.

Although Informix is the leader in the UNIX market, its product is not as widely used as Oracle's, nor does it sport as many advanced features. Informix On-Line is a very good product, however, and the company enjoys a solid reputation.

 Informix made an ill-fated attempt at an NLM-based product in 1988 (the product was never released). The attempt failed for two reasons. First, Informix tried to do a straight port of its DBMS to NetWare, not taking advantage of NetWare's built-in features. Because NetWare's environment is so different from that of UNIX, the Informix port did not perform up to expectations.

The second reason for the Informix port failure is that Novell was late in adding TCP/IP support to its operating system. Because Informix declined to support IPX/SPX, its aborted NetWare offering could not run in a NetWare environment.

Informix now has a totally new NetWare offering: Informix On-Line for NetWare. As of this writing, Informix On-Line for NetWare is in beta and close to shipment. A look at the product shows that Informix used the experience of its first attempt at NLM development to do a great job on its second attempt.

Informix On-Line for NetWare contains all the features users have come to expect from Informix, yet it is also tailored to the NetWare NLM environment. Informix On-Line also supports multiple network transport protocols, including IPX/SPX and TCP/IP.

Database administrators generally are positive about Informix On-Line, whereas programmers are extremely enthusiastic about Informix 4GL, which is a full-featured fourth-generation programming language designed specifically for Informix DBMS products.

Although rating programming languages is always difficult because different programmers prefer different characteristics in a programming language, the consensus among programmers who work with commercial database management systems is that Informix 4GL is the finest fourth-generation language for DBMS programming. Informix 4GL is a mature and robust programming language; many of its capabilities are the result of feedback from programmers.

Programmer enthusiasm for a particular system should be a strong factor in influencing your choice of a commercial DBMS. As mentioned earlier, the best database engine in the world is of little value if clients cannot access the engine. If you plan more than minimal client development, you should consider seriously your programming staff's wishes regarding the tools they will use to build your DP application.

Sybase

The Sybase commercial DBMS offering is called the Sybase SQL Server relational database manager. Of all the major DBMS vendors, Sybase (which picked up where IBM's research in relational DBMS technology left off in the 1970s) has always offered the most purely relational product. Sybase has garnered less publicity and fewer sales than Oracle or Informix, but it has always had a reputation for producing the most technically excellent—if not the most popular—product.

Sybase came to the forefront in the late 1980s, when Microsoft agreed to be the OEM of an OS/2 version of the Sybase SQL server called the LAN Manager OS/2 SQL Server. Although the Oracle Server for OS/2 was the first commercial DBMS available for OS/2, the Sybase-Microsoft SQL Server generally is viewed as the better of the two products.

Sybase now offers SQL Server for NetWare, which is a pure NLM version of the Sybase SQL server. Of the three vendors discussed in this chapter, Sybase clearly has done the best job of tailoring its product to NetWare. Working closely with Novell OS engineers throughout the development process, Sybase made an extra effort to leverage the NetWare operating system as much as possible.

The effort has clearly paid off. The Sybase SQL Server for NetWare performs better than all other commercial DBMS products that run on microcomputers—regardless of the underlying operating system. The traditional Sybase technical excellence really shows through.

Sybase also offers excellent client language support, and has worked with other software vendors to enable access to the Sybase SQL server from productivity software such as Microsoft Excel.

Making the Ultimate Decision

As you make the decision about which commercial DBMS product to use as the foundation of your downsizing effort, remember that you should not choose the best commercial DBMS for NetWare. Rather, you should choose the best commercial DBMS for your site. You must consider other factors, the most important of which is your current installation.

If you are a UNIX shop running Informix On-Line, for example, you should have a good reason for choosing any NetWare-based product other than Informix On-Line for NetWare. The same holds true for all commercial DBMS products. You simply cannot switch overnight (nor over a week-end) from product "A" running on a VAX to product "B" running on NetWare. You can switch with relative ease (and according to your own schedule), however, from product "A" running on a VAX to product "A" running on NetWare.

Remember also to consider all the criteria discussed in this chapter. Back- and front-end issues are equally important; you must research both. Consider also specific client operating systems running at your site, making certain that the commercial DBMS you buy is capable of supporting all your clients.

Summary

All three of the vendors discussed in this chapter, Oracle, Informix, and Sybase, offer excellent products for NetWare. Although these products differ in performance and in other areas, all are capable of running world-class DP applications. The commercial DBMS industry has truly embraced microcomputer networking technology. It is only a matter of time until microcomputer-based commercial DBMS products outsell those products that are created for larger computers.

Topics covered in this chapter:

Defining DP Application Toolkits

Working with Toolkit Data Models

Integrating Toolkits with Other Code Libraries

Building Downsized DP Applications

Working with your Programming Staff

Enhancing with DP Toolkits

Using Other Programming Tools

Chapter 20

Application Toolkits

C hapter 19 discussed commercial DBMS engines and how they provide the core of an unfinished application to enable you to finish producing a highly customized DP application. This chapter presents even lower-level tools: programming libraries and utilities you can use to produce world-class DP applications for NetWare. Although commercial DBMS engines provide a programmable back-end database engine, programming libraries enable you to build your own back-end engine and front-end clients. Programming libraries, therefore, are even more raw than commercial DBMS engines, but they provide even greater flexibility and freedom.

Defining DP Application Toolkits

A DP *application toolkit* is a programming library that provides precoded and portable functions you can use to build a DP application from scratch. An application toolkit, therefore, can save programmers hundreds of hours and still enable them to build an application precisely the way they want.

A good DP application toolkit should provide easy-to-use functions and routines for implementing the logical database and the conceptual schema, and should give you a measure of control over the physical database.

A good DP application toolkit provides support for all the theoretical aspects of a DBMS, described in Chapter 3.

A toolkit also enables you to alter its source code to take advantage of specific operating-system features, such as NetWare's transaction tracking or security architecture. By necessity, most application toolkits are coded in a generic and portable manner; they can support different development environments and host operating systems. This capability is both a benefit and a drawback of application toolkits: you can use the same toolkit to generate DP applications for many different machines and operating systems, but support for NetWare's most outstanding features is not built into the toolkit.

The best part of an application toolkit is that you can modify its source code to do the things you want it to do, including making use of NetWare's more powerful features.

In an ideal world, every IS staff involved in a downsizing project uses a good DP application toolkit. In the real world, however, application toolkits require more resources to implement than do commercial DBMS engines. You must consider whether the extra freedom gained by altering a toolkit's source code is worth the programming resources it consumes.

Working with Toolkit Data Models

One unalterable quality of a DP application toolkit is the data model it uses (hierarchical, relational, or network). You purchase, in effect, a collection of precoded routines for managing data. The routines supplied with an application toolkit for storing, indexing, and retrieving data must (and do) assume a specific data model. The specific data model used by an application toolkit, therefore, is "hard coded" into routines throughout the toolkit. Supporting a data model that is different from the one coded into an application toolkit requires rewriting all the routines affected by the data model (a process that is tantamount to coding the entire toolkit from scratch).

Another concern in hard-coding data models into DP application toolkits is the existence of certain static limits. How many indexes, for example, does a particular toolkit enable you to have open at one time? How many data files? It may seem strange at first that a product consisting almost entirely of programming source code has such static limits, but all application toolkits do.

 Static limits within an application toolkit usually exist because of the definitions of global data structures referenced throughout the toolkit's code. You can change the definitions of such data structures, of course, to raise these limits. Changing them, however, is often an extremely difficult and error-prone process. Adding functions to a toolkit is easier than changing the basic framework of the toolkit, which is what you do when you alter global data structures.

Integrating Toolkits with Other Code Libraries

Programmers typically integrate an application toolkit with other toolkits (such as user interface libraries) to produce a final application. Invariably, building a DP application using a toolkit produces conflicts with other programming tools. Most DOS user-interface toolkits, for example, maintain a large area of global memory (for tracking windows, forms, or key mappings). Likewise, DP application toolkits maintain large areas of global memory (for a data dictionary, scratch storage, or for searches in progress). Most DOS programs, however, can have only 64K of global memory (because of the segmented DOS memory architecture). If the combination of global data maintained by the user interface library and the DP application library is greater than 64K, the application *never* works correctly.

Altering the code to use different segments for interface and database global memory is tricky because you must change the linking process of the application and the start-up code (which defines the application's data segments) and the library code. (These concerns do not apply to NLM development using toolkits.)

Building Downsized DP Applications

Despite the problems mentioned in the preceding section, DP application toolkits have an excellent downsizing track record. A relatively large number of companies that are downsizing, in fact, use one of the two toolkits discussed later in this chapter. These toolkits can do any type of downsizing project. DP applications must be tailored to a specific business function or functions. Other than writing every line of code yourself, there is no substitute for the flexibility of building your own application using precoded routines.

 The flexibility offered by application toolkits extends to the area of distributed processing. Specifically, when you use these products to construct a DP application, you can decide how you want to distribute the application. You decide, on a routine-by-routine basis, which components of the application belong on the NetWare server and which ones belong on client components. This decision can be critical, especially for performance. Nothing works better than a finely distributed application for high-performance data processing.

Working with Your Programming Staff

An essential step in choosing a DP application toolkit is to let your programming staff help you choose the product. Your programmers have to make the toolkit work, and they must live with your decision for many years. The calling conventions of the toolkit's routines, the way its routines are named and organized, and the way they are documented can have impacts on the productivity of programmers who use the product to create a finished DP application.

 You should allow your programming staff to evaluate, if possible, each candidate toolkit by writing an application using the toolkit. As in most areas of the computer business, the only certain way to evaluate a product—especially tools for programmers—is by hands-on experience.

Never buy a DP application toolkit unless you also receive the product's source code. Most vendors include the source code with their product. Some vendors, however, charge extra for the source code. Remember that if you do not have a toolkit's source code, you do not have the flexibility that buying the product is supposed to provide. Some vendors still do not ship source code, and you should not even consider buying their products.

Enhancing with DP Toolkits

The Raima Data Manager and the c-tree Plus toolkits, discussed in the following sections, are for professional programmers. Both products are capable of creating true enterprise DP applications. Some of the users of these products, in fact, are commercial software vendors who use the toolkits to produce commercial production software. Your primary challenge with either product lies in distributing your application to NLM and client components. You also must add support for specific NetWare features by modifying the source code. (You would have to do these things anyway, however, if you coded your DP application from scratch.) These products give you a jump start by offering data-management routines that already are coded and tested.

Using c-tree Plus

The c-tree Plus toolkit, available from Faircom Corporation, is an industrial-strength DP application toolkit that is considered highly portable C source code. c-tree Plus uses a hierarchical data model (based on a B-tree indexing system, such as Novell's Btrieve), and provides higher-level access to data records. You can implement a relational-style indexing scheme if, for example, you invest a little time.

One c-tree Plus drawback is that it is not distributed. In other words, if you develop an application using c-tree Plus, that application runs entirely on the client computer.

 You can overcome this major shortcoming by doing some of your own programming work on the c-tree source code. An experienced NetWare programmer can readily distribute a c-tree application.

Faircom offers a back-end server that works with c-tree Plus applications. Faircom's server, however, does not run on NetWare as an NLM, nor does it support IPX/SPX (it supports TCP/IP and NetBIOS.) For all practical purposes, the Faircom server does not support NetWare. (You should code NetWare support into the c-tree Plus application.)

 Faircom appears to assume that if you want full transaction-processing capabilities in your application, you will purchase the Faircom server. This is unfortunate because Faircom does not market a version of its server for NetWare. You can use NetWare's built-in transaction tracking, however, to add transaction-processing capabilities to a c-tree application.

Faircom's excellent documentation enables your programming staff to get up to speed quickly with this toolkit. c-tree Plus has good multiuser support, including record and file locking. It does not use NetWare's concurrency-control routines, however, for providing this support—you must code these features yourself.

The c-tree Plus toolkit is definitely a programmer's tool. A programmer must do a large amount of work before calling any c-tree routines. This workload is appropriate, however, because if c-tree did everything itself, it would lose its vital flexibility.

This toolkit offers excellent performance, especially in using very large databases (those having more than 20,000 records). This performance, in addition to your total access to all areas of this product, make it a suitable choice for a downsizing effort. Remember that you must implement NetWare support yourself. You can contact Faircom at this address:

Faircom Corporation
4006 West Broadway
Columbia, MO 65203
314-445-6833

Raima Data Manager

The Raima Data Manager, available from Raima Corporation (formerly db_Vista), is probably the best DP application toolkit on the market. Unlike Faircom, Raima does not also market back-end engines (such as Faircom servers). Because of this focus, traditional back-end functionality is a standard component of the Raima Data Manager, which is a big plus for NetWare.

Raima develops and markets its toolkit with an approach that is opposite of Faircom's approach. Faircom seems to assume that you are developing a client-based data manager (and offers a different product for database servers); Raima seems to assume that you are developing a database server, or back end, and offers different toolkits for creating client components.

You can use the Raima toolkit to readily develop NLM back ends. Raima also sells front-end querying and reporting toolkits, which you can use to generate your application's client components.

Raima uses a *hierarchical* indexing model (B-tree), to which you can gain access at many different levels. Raima client toolkits enable you to gain access to Raima databases using SQL. In this sense, Raima is similar to Btrieve, which—by using NetWare SQL—emulates a relational data model.

The best features of the Raima Data Manager are in its multiuser area, including transaction tracking (not NetWare's), file and record locking, and database server functionality. A back-end application based on Raima can hold open many different database files and indexes, which is a critical capability for any database server.

Like the NetWare operating system, the Raima Data Manager's data-processing routines perform many internal consistency checks on records and file structures. Combined with NetWare's fault-tolerant features, this excellent capability helps make a robust DP platform.

Most programmers find Raima more difficult to learn than c-tree Plus. This difficulty should be expected, however, because Raima includes more back-end style routines, which tend to be more complex than routines designed to run on a client. For NLM development, you may find that your programmers are more productive, despite the steeper learning curve, because most of the tasks that they need their back-end engine to do is included already in the Raima source code. As always, however, you must build specific NetWare features into your Raima application. You can contact Raima Corporation at the following address:

Raima Corporation
3245 146th Place SE
Bellevue, WA 98007
206-747-5570

Using Other Programming Tools

You may find a number of additional programming tools useful in your effort to implement DP applications for NetWare. The remainder of this chapter offers an (incomplete) information survey of these products, without recommendations.

ExtendBase for NetWare 386

ExtendBase for NetWare 386 converts Clipper and dBASE applications into partially distributed client-server DP applications. The client portion runs on DOS, and the server portion runs on NetWare as an NLM. ExtendBase converts indexing and reporting functions into client-server requests and responses. You can contact Extend Systems at the following address:

Extend Systems
6123 N. Meeker Avenue
Boise, ID 83704

Lattice RPG II Development System

If you use the IBM System/36, you can use the Lattice RPG II Development System available from Lattice, Inc., to port your RPG applications to DOS PCs. Although the applications are not distributed (they were not distributed on the System/36 either), they run on a NetWare system, which might be all you need. You can contact Lattice, Inc., at the following address:

Lattice, Inc.
3010 Woodcreek Drive
Suite A
Downers Grove, IL 60515

Forest and Trees

Forest and Trees, available from Channel Computing, is a Windows-based data-extraction tool that enables you to construct *executive information systems*. These applications extract data from a variety of sources and build graphically oriented reports from that data.

Forest and Trees is designed specifically for businesses that have too much data or spend lots of resources consolidating data into executive reports. This potentially valuable tool can extract data from virtually any type of database system, including all systems supported by NetWare. You can contact Channel Computing at the following address:

Channel Computing
53 Main Street
Newmarket, NH 03857

Data Junction

The Data Junction program, available from Tools & Techniques, Inc., can convert almost any type of database file from its current format to virtually any other format. If you are moving to a different DBMS as part of your downsizing effort, or if you want to consolidate your data into a single format, you can use Data Junction to convert your data. Naming a data-file format is difficult on any type of computer, or in any type of operating system or product that Data Junction cannot read and convert.

In addition to strict data-file conversion, Data Junction enables you to filter and "massage" data files in a number of ways. This popular product has gathered many accolades. You can contact Tools & Techniques, Inc. at the following address:

Tools & Techniques, Inc.
1620 W. 12th
Austin, TX 78703

CICS

CICS, available from Realia, is a CICS-to-COBOL preprocessor for DOS. If your installation uses CICS, a popular database programming language for IBM shops, you can port your applications to DOS with CICS.

COBOL

COBOL is a COBOL compiler for DOS. This product also is available from Realia.

Professional COBOL

Professional COBOL, available from Micro Focus, is a full-featured DOS COBOL development system that has extensions for hooking into OS/2, Windows, and SQL products. Professional COBOL also has a screen designer and code generator, in addition to several other programming tools.

COBOL Optimizing Compiler

COBOL Optimizing Compiler, Microsoft Corporation's COBOL development package, includes many DOS extensions and support for OS/2 and Windows. This package has also a good COBOL debugger.

Norcomm Programmer Tools

Norcomm produces a suite of PC COBOL development tools that work with most available COBOL development systems for the PC. On DOS machines, you can gain access to the NetWare client API from COBOL programs if your development system enables you to generate DOS interrupts (most of them do). Using Norcomm's tools, you can port existing COBOL applications to DOS and NetWare. You can contact Norcomm at 907-780-6464.

Btrieve Starter Kit

Norcomm's Btrieve Starter Kit provides access to Btrieve, Novell's server-based file manager, from COBOL programs.

Btrv++

Btrv++ is a C++ class library that provides object-oriented access to Btrieve, the Novell data manager (see Chapter 18). The somewhat cryptic Btrieve `programming` API can make coding Btrieve applications easier if you know C++. You can contact Class Software, which makes Btrv++, at 313-677-0732.

C Library for Btrieve

The C Library for Btrieve, available from Mobius, Inc., is a C programming library for Btrieve that has routines for many NetWare function calls. Using this library shortens the learning curve for Btrieve programming. Most set-up, calling, and cleanup tasks in Btrieve are tedious; this library does the "pick and shovel" work for you.

REXX

REXX, which is a popular batch-oriented programming language, which is available from Kilowatt Software, was developed by IBM and is supplied on most IBM systems. Some users develop full-fledged DP applications with this remarkably capable language. REXX is used primarily to automate maintenance tasks; and you can use it for many other procedures. Because most REXX users eventually depend on having REXX available on potential new platforms, it is comforting to know that you can get REXX for PCs.

Summary

Although the application toolkits and products discussed in this chapter are primarily designed for experienced programmers, you can use them to develop excellent NetWare-based applications.

In the next chapter, you will read about DOS-based products that require less programming expertise to use.

Topics covered in this chapter:

Ensuring Data Integrity

Maximizing Memory Use at the
Workstation

Chapter 21

Nondistributed Record Managers

T his chapter discusses ways to ensure data integrity and to use the features of the NetWare operating system with several popular relational databases packages: Clipper, dBASE IV, FoxPro/LAN, and Paradox.

Ensuring Data Integrity

To integrate a multiuser relational database successfully on a NetWare server, you first must ensure data integrity and consistency by implementing file and record locks. Before reading about the specific file- and record-locking features of each database, you should have a general understanding of these commonly used techniques. (Keep in mind that each of the techniques may or may not meet the criteria of the individual database application.)

File and Record Locking

The DOS-based database packages (Clipper, dBASE, FoxPro, and Paradox) create their own file and record locks; do not use NetWare's locking routines. Typically, these packages open a database file, which causes NetWare to generate an exclusive lock for the entire file. By gaining access to the file by way of the database package, however, users can read from or write to records in the file, even though NetWare technically locks the file. The database package controls all the file activity, and enables users to read and write records. The reading and writing activities appear to NetWare as if only the database package is working with the file, even though users of the package are causing the reads and writes to occur.

 The database package is controlling concurrency, independently of NetWare, by implementing its own record and file locks. These locks are invisible to NetWare. Sometimes this invisibility causes problems with NetWare. You should build NetWare file- and record-locking routines into these database packages by using the package's external programming interfaces.

File locking works as a type of arbitration, in which the locking system determines who can use a file at a particular time. *Record locking* enables a user to lock a specific record in the data file and prevent other users from accessing it. For each unique database application, file- and record-locking requirements are determined by the type functionality of the application and the user's needs.

Two distinct levels of locking—exclusive and nonexclusive (shared)—commonly are used by the database programs discussed in this chapter. These two levels define the way a developed application works in a multiuser environment, in respect to the operations to be performed on the data files and the operations other users are allowed to perform. In Paradox, exclusive and shared locking are slightly different, but have the same concept.

Nonexclusive locking means that a user can lock the complete file (file locking) or part of the file (record locking), and enable users to read from that file—even from the locked portion. The function of nonexclusive locking is to prevent users from writing to locked portions of a file until the user holding the lock has removed the lock. In this way, nonexclusive locking in a multiuser environment enables users to use the database without waiting for a lock to be released by another user.

Exclusive locking means that only one user at a time can lock the database file. Other users are not allowed to access the file during the exclusive lock—not even to read it.

 Because using exclusive locking on data files in a multiuser environment does not offer the best performance, it should rarely be used. If you have a 200-user network database, for example, each user uses the database information during an eight-hour period. Usually, one user has the file or record locked for a while when another user needs to use the file. Because file locking works as a type of arbitration, when the current file-locking user releases the file, the next user requesting the lock gets the file. In this scenario, performance is severely downgraded, even with a high-performance network.

Another problem with using exclusive file locking is the possibility of *hanging the database*. Hanging the database usually occurs when a user reboots the machine or switches a task (if he or she is using a nonmultitasking client operating system), or when a workstation locks up while the file is locked (reading or writing). If this happens, each person after the initial hang waits for the file to unlock or for the database administrator to resolve the problem. Remember that the locks discussed here are "invisible" to NetWare. If these packages generated true NetWare locks, NetWare would release the locks if the user's station crashed or if something similar happened. But because NetWare doesn't know what is happening with these application-specific locks, problems occur.

Not every file used in a multiuser database environment should be used non-exclusively or shared: explicit exclusive locks have their place. Database development packages, for example, require that the data file be locked exclusively in building index files. You should have exclusive locks only when they are needed—not for regular routines in the application.

NetWare's Transactional Tracking (TTS)

In addition to correct file and record locking, transactional tracking is a technique that is used with multiuser databases to ensure database integrity. This technique can be used in three different ways: application transactional tracking, NetWare's transactional tracking (Transactional Tracking System), or explicit NetWare TTS system calls integrated into the database application.

Some database-development packages implement their own transaction-tracking capabilities. Although these features work well, with the Transaction Tracking System (TTS), they are not necessary. TTS prevents multiuser-network database corruption by backing out incomplete transactions during network failure. When transactions are *backed out*, the data and index files are rolled back to the state they were in before the transaction.

NetWare's TTS system calls offer better performance than implementing application-based transaction tracking. TTS system calls take advantage of the network operating system and server cache.

In all cases, consider NetWare's TTS before you begin the task of controlling transaction in your application.

TTS is divided into two categories: implicit transaction tracking and explicit transaction tracking. *Implicit transaction tracking* is built into the network operating system and requires no transactional tracking coding in the database application. This feature can be enabled or disabled.

Explicit transaction tracking requires database applications to have NetWare TTS system calls coded into the application. This requirement enables applications to provide logical and physical locks in using the TTS system calls. By using explicit transactions, database applications can get added performance by enabling the NetWare operating system to track transactions. To use the NetWare TTS system calls, you must purchase the NetWare C Interface kit or a third-party development package that has these system calls in it. (Not all database packages have third-party development packages.)

These third-party NetWare libraries can make the user interface between the database and the server transparent. All access rights, mappings, and printing functions can be made available without your having to know anything about networking. The transaction functions usually that are included enable you to start and stop transactions, obtain the status of transactions, and roll back failed transactions.

Clipper

Clipper, available from Computer Associates., provides a database development environment that is similar to the dBASE environment. Open architecture is the primary reason that Clipper became popular; programmers can use high-level languages such as C and Pascal to enhance their applications. With the combination of Clipper's open architecture and built-in file-locking features, it can be easily integrated into a NetWare environment.

Data integrity for Clipper is supported on two levels: exclusive and shared. In earlier versions of Clipper, using *exclusive* locking required using the SET EXCLUSIVE ON command. This command no longer is needed, but it can be used for compatibility purposes.

To use a Clipper data file in exclusive mode, you use this command:

```
USE <xcDatabase> EXCLUSIVE
```

Rebuilding indexes is the most common use of the EXCLUSIVE option. The syntax is as follows:

```
USE <xcDatabase> EXCLUSIVE
INDEX ON <expKey> to <xcIndex>
```

or

```
REINDEX
```

The following four commands require exclusive data-file locking:

```
SET INDEX TO
REINDEX
ZAP
PACK
```

To use a Clipper data file in shared mode, you use the following command:

```
USE <xcDatabase> SHARED
```

 Shared mode is used when you want users to place locks freely on the file or record and still enable other users to read from that file.

The NetErr() function should be used to test whether a database file was opened successfully in exclusive mode before the index file is created. NetErr() returns a logical true (.T.) if an error occurs during the attempted network operation, or a logical false (.F.) if no error occurs. The following code is an example of the way NetErr() can be used:

```
USE <xcDatabase> EXCLUSIVE
IF NetErr()
```

```
    ...  // Error recovery statements are placed here.
ENDIF
INDEX ON <expKey> to <xcIndex>
```

The `NetErr()` function is useful in a multiuser database environment in which other users can use the database file exclusively.

As mentioned, Clipper became popular by enabling programmers to integrate high-level languages such as C and assembly into their applications. The functionality of Clipper's Extend System makes it possible for a programmer to use NetWare system calls to take advantage of NetWare's explicit TTS system calls.

To use the Clipper Extend System, the C and assembly source code should contain the appropriate `include` file to declare macros, function prototypes, and constants. To implement the C language, you must include the header file EXTEND.H in your function. The following line shows the syntax:

```
#include "extend.h"
```

The functionality of using both C and assembly routines in your database can open up new opportunities for integrating explicit TTS commands and other network functions.

Third-Party Programming Libraries

Because of Clipper's open architecture, third-party programming libraries for Clipper and NetWare are available to make integrating NetWare system calls into applications even easier. The NetLib library, by Pinnacle, has specific NetWare-related functions that can make an application "network aware." The following list shows a few NetWare-specific libraries for Clipper:

❖ dMILL Network Kit Clipper, avaliable from Database Software

❖ NetLib, available from Pinnacle

❖ Segue, available from HRF Associates

❖ dBASE IV, available from Borland International

dBASE IV

dBASE IV, which was developed at Borland International before
MS-DOS became available, provided solutions for CP/M computer users for several years. Shortly after the introduction of MS-
DOS and personal computers, dBASE IV was made available for
the personal computer. The dBASE IV concept and language have
become somewhat of an industry standard for most other relational database packages. Other packages may provide a different
language and functionality, but they have adapted to become
somewhat "dBASE IV compatible." Because of this compatibility,
other databases use the same concepts of file and record locking
that dBASE IV uses.

Database Integrity

dBASE IV provides several other data-integrity features in addition to exclusive or nonexclusive use of files (or parts of files). One
feature protects the number and correctness of database records. In
a database environment, you should have only one copy of a database record. With relational functions (procedures in which two or
more database files are combined), second copies of some records
are made. To keep the database correct and avoid confusion with
other copies of the records, dBASE IV builds a *virtual result data set*,
which is a temporary database that resides in memory only during
the time it is being used. During a modification to the record, the
original database is updated or the change is discarded. After the
procedure, none of the other records is kept, which avoids later
confusion.

The second data-integrity feature is built-in transaction processing
in the database. In dBASE IV multiuser databases, the update
transactions are controlled by using the following commands:

```
BEGIN TRANSACTION...END TRANSACTION
```

and

```
ROLLBACK
```

 These features can be used to get better performance by using NetWare's Transaction Tracking System or NetWare's explicit TTS system commands.

To help implement explicit TTS system commands in a dBASE IV application, a programmer can use the LOAD and CALL commands to load and execute binary program files. The LOAD command loads the binary file into memory, and dBASE IV recognizes it as a subroutine or memory module, not as an external file. After the file is loaded, the CALL() function can be invoked to execute the binary file.

To prepare an assembly program for dBASE execution, you first must use an assembler program to assemble the source file (.asm) into an object file (.obj). The object file then is linked into an executable file (.exe), and a binary file can be created from the executable file. If you use Borland's Turbo Assembler, you use the following commands:

```
TASM    <source>
TLINK   <target>
EXE2BIN <target>
```

Note: EXE2BIN is supplied with MS-DOS and DR DOS.

The following sample assembly program can be used with dBASE IV:

```
; Strsubst.asm (Source for Strsubst.bin)
;
; Substitute characters in a character string.
;
CODE    SEGMENT BYTE PUBLIC 'CODE'
STRSUB  PROC  FAR
```

```
    ASSUME    CS:CODE
              PARAM1 EQU ES:[DI+0]
              PARAM2 EQU ES:[DI+4]
              PARAM3 EQU ES:[DI+8]
              PARAM4 EQU ES:[DI+12]
              PARAM5 EQU ES:[DI+16]
              PARAM6 EQU ES:[DI+20]
              PARAM7 EQU ES:[DI+24]
START:
     PUSH BP           ;SAV
     MOV  BP, SP
;Quit if there are not at least three parameters
     CMP  CX, 3
     JL   DONE
;Load first byte of second parameter in CL
     LDS  BX, PARAM2       ;DS:BX points to second
parameter
     MOV  CL, [BX]         ;Store first byte
;Load first byte of third parameter in CH
     LDS  BX, PARAM3       ;DS:BX points to third
parameter
     MOV  CH, [BX]         ;Store first byte in CH
;Point DS:BX to first parameter
     LDS  BX, PARAM1
;Loop for each character in first parameter
AGAIN:   MOV  AL, [BX]     ;Get next character in AL
         CMP  AL, 0        ;Is it end of string?
         JE   DONE         ;Yes--exit
         CMP  AL, CL       ;Is it character you are
searching for?
         JNE  NEXT         ;No--do not replace
         MOV  [BX], CH     ;Yes--replace
NEXT:    INC  BX           ;Point to next
JMP  AGAIN
; DONE: POP  BP            ;Restore stack frame
     RET
STRSUB   ENDP
CODE     ENDS
         END
```

Database Protection

On a NetWare server, the network administrator can establish system security to protect data from accidental loss or unauthorized access. dBASE IV data security also provides another layer of protection. The PROTECT utility enables the system administrator to establish database passwords, which are independent from the network.

PROTECT security can be broken down into three levels: logon security, file and field access security, and data encryption.

Logon security enables the system administrator to establish a database logon name and password (user account) for each user. Each user uses the logon name and password to obtain access to the database.

File and field access security can protect certain file and field information from being read or modified. This feature is useful in databases that contain highly confidential information that is combined with information that is not highly confidential. It protects fields from being viewed by restricted users.

Data encryption enables certain data to be encrypted until a correct password is given to unencypt the data. This feature works for both data fields and files.

dBASE SQL Features

Using SQL with dBASE IV as the programming language provides an easier transfer from the mainframe or minicomputer environment. The SQL commands embedded in the dBASE applications provide similar functions as dBASE programs. SQL and dBASE have the same structure; have virtually the same commands and functions; have the same use of memory variables, error handling, and transaction processing; and have the same operation in a network environment.

Despite their similarities, dBASE and SQL access data differently. Because of this difference, dBASE IV was designed to have applications switch automatically between dBASE and SQL modes, therefore making the task of using SQL much easier.

FOXPRO/LAN 2.0

Although FoxPro/LAN, available from Microsoft Corporation, is not the most NetWare-aware relational database, its speed, ease of development, and possible network capabilities make it a popular database package. FoxPro's speed has been one of its most highly recognized features. Despite this somewhat subjective recognition, FoxPro 2.0 uses a new data-access technique to increase performance. This technology, called Rushmore technology, enables personal computers to handle data-access routines at speeds comparable to mainframe database systems.

Data Integrity

Like other multiuser relational databases, FoxPro/LAN supports both exclusive and shared use. To define whether the database will be used in exclusive mode, the following commands can be used in the following code:

```
SET EXCLUSIVE ON
USE <filename>
```

or

```
USE <filename> EXCLUSIVE
```

To help implement explicit TTS system commands in a FoxPro 2.0 application, a programmer can use the LOAD and CALL commands to load and execute binary program files. The LOAD command loads the binary file into memory, and FoxPro 2.0 recognizes it as a subroutine or memory module, not as a external file. After the file is loaded, the `CALL()` function can be invoked to execute the binary file.

To prepare an assembly program for FoxPro execution, you first must use an assembly program to assemble the source file (.asm) into an object file (.obj). The object file then is linked into an executable file (.exe), and a binary file can be created from the executable file. If you use Borland's Turbo Assembler, you use the following commands:

```
TASM    <source>
TLINK   <target>
EXE2BIN <target>
```

Note: EXE2BIN is supplied with MS-DOS and DR DOS.

SQL Support

As part of FoxPro 2.0, the SQL commands SELECT, CREATE TABLE, and INSERT are supported. These SQL commands can provide optimal performance by relieving some of the database's housekeeping duties.

The SELECT command enables FoxPro to perform complex single- or multidatabase queries expressed in the nonprocedural SQL language.

The Rushmore technology and the SELECT command can be used together to optimize performance for multiple database queries.

The CREATE TABLE command is used to create a database, and the INSERT command appends a record to the end of an existing database file.

Maximizing Memory Use at the Workstation

Like Paradox, FoxPro/LAN does not limit the use of conventional memory. FoxPro/LAN can use LIM 4.0-compatible expanded memory. This feature (which is not available with all relational databases) is important when you are working with PC workstations—it makes more conventional memory available for network drivers and TSRs.

FoxPro 2.0's External Routine API provides programmers with the capability to integrate C and assembly routines into FoxPro applications. With this type of open architecture, NetWare function calls can be made to tightly integrate the database application and NetWare network. This capability is especially important for integrating explicit NetWare TTS calls into a FoxPro application. (The External Routine API is available in FoxPro's Library Construction Kit.)

Paradox

Paradox, available from Borland International, uses a method of developing and using a database application that is different from the other relational database packages discussed in this chapter. The data organization is broken down into data tables. Within the data tables, data is organized into horizontal *records* (rows) and vertical *fields* (columns). Paradox's data-integrity mechanism in a multiuser database environment, therefore, is based on locks of tables, forms, reports, and other objects.

Paradox's data integrity and consistency features ensure that all users using the database view a correct version of each table. Explicit and automatic locks of tables, forms, reports, and other objects are provided; and the use of temporary objects on the network is controlled.

Paradox offers five different types of locks: dir lock, full lock, write lock, prevent write lock, and prevent full lock.

Placing the *dir lock* (directory lock) on a shared data directory is equivalent to placing write locks on all the tables in the directory. All users, therefore, including the user that placed the dir lock, can have only read-only access to the directory's files. A dir lock can be explicitly locked and removed only by a user using the application. Using this Paradox feature can improve performance when users access objects in a directory.

The *full lock* places a complete lock on objects. This lock is the most restrictive lock that a user or Paradox can place on objects. With this lock, no other user can access the object, not even to view it, until the lock is released. This feature is used frequently during an update of tables.

The *write lock* prevents other users from changing information by granting them read-only access. You use this feature during an update or when you do not want other users to change information.

The *prevent write lock* prevents other users from invoking a lock on an object. This feature is important in a multiuser environment, in which users simultaneously make changes to tables. When changes are being made simultaneously, you do not want one user to issue a write lock while others are making changes.

The *prevent full lock* prevents other users from starting operations that require full locks. This feature enables other users to print reports, query tables, enter data in a table, or perform any other operation that does not require exclusive use. Applying the prevent full locks feature to tables can increase performance on a network.

If an attempt to access an object in the database fails, Paradox informs the user who currently has it locked. It does this by default, using the NetWare operating system to associate the database user and NetWare username.

When you use Paradox on a network, a *working directory* is established for the use of shared tables and other objects. Each Paradox user must have a *private directory* in which temporary tables, temporary objects, and nontemporary objects that you do not want to share with others are stored. All temporary files created by Paradox are stored in the user's private directory, to ensure that the query result is pulled from the correct table. Storing the temporary files there prevents temporary files from being overwritten by other users on the network.

Using Paradox SQL Link To Connect to NetWare SQL

The Paradox SQL Link enables Paradox-developed applications to utilize NetWare's SQL. By using Paradox's SQL Link, a database can take advantage of NetWare's SQL performance and security.

The client file, NOVSQL.PRP, can use the file from a local hard disk or network. The primary purpose of NOVSQL.PRP is to provide a communications link between the Paradox database and the NetWare SQL requesters (NSREQ and NSREQS). The NetWare workstation's shell and LAN card then communicate the request with the NetWare server LAN cards and communications components. The request is handed to the NetWare operating system, the Btrieve engine, and then to NetWare SQL.

SQL Link supports server security in both the network and the database server. To access NetWare SQL, you must have security privileges on the network and on the database server. Network privileges include a valid username and password, with rights to the location where the database is stored. Database privileges include a valid username and password, with specific rights to information inside the database.

Summary

This chapter on nondistributed record managers showed you ways to ensure data integrity and to use the features of the NetWare operating system with several relational database packages. You also learned how to maximize memory use at the workstation.

Index

B

C

D

J & K

L

Q

U

V